Macmillan Books for Teachers

Learning Teaching

A guidebook for English language teachers

Second Edition

Jim Scrivener

MACMILLAN

Contents

Help index

Basics

I need to ...	Chapter	Section
survive my first lessons	2	2
learn students' names	16	5
plan 'getting to know you' activities	16	5
run a 'Find someone who ...' activity	16	5
find general instructions for running an activity	3	1
run a pairwork information-gap activity	3	3
run a small-group discussion	3	4
run a pairwork grammar activity	3	5
use classroom management techniques	5	2–9

Classroom management skills

How can I ...?		
use varied interaction patterns in class	5	2
arrange the seating in class	5	3
use the board	5	7
give clear instructions	5	4
monitor activities	5	5
use gestures to help instructions	5	6
elicit language and ideas from learners	5	9
get feedback from students	4	4
avoid talking unnecessarily	5	4, 12

Planning

How can I ...?		
use Needs analysis to find what learners want and need	4	3
plan a lesson	6	1–7
write a lesson plan	6	4
write aims	6	5
plan informally	6	7
plan a course	6	8

Speaking
How can I ...?

	Chapter	Section
plan and run a discussion/conversation lesson	7	1
plan and run a communicative activity	7	2
encourage students to use English	5	10
run a pyramid discussion	7	2
plan and run a role-play	7	3
plan and run a real-play	7	3
use scaffolding techniques to help learner speaking	7	4
correct after a fluency activity	7	4
	14	1

Listening, reading, writing
How can I ...?

	Chapter	Section
set listening tasks	8	1, 2
use the task–feedback circle with skills work	8	2
use jigsaw listening/reading tasks	8	4
set skimming and scanning tasks	8	5
plan top-down listening and reading lessons	8	3
integrate lexis and skills work	11	3
	12	4
plan a writing lesson	9	1, 2
use fast-writing techniques for collecting ideas	9	2
use brainstorming techniques for collecting ideas	9	2
use a computer for writing work	9	2
	16	9
correct (or not correct) writing work	9	3

Language systems
How can I ...?

	Chapter	Section
analyse grammatical form	10	2
get an overview of English grammar	10	3
analyse concept (with lexis)	10	4
make and use concept questions (with grammar)	10	5
understand how lexis is different from grammar	11	1
analyse communicative function	10	6

Different classes
How can I teach ...?

	Chapter	Section
ESP or Business English	15	1
exam classes	15	2
large classes	15	4
teenagers	15	3

Further questions
I want to find out about ...

accuracy compared with fluency	7	4
Carl Rogers	1	4
Communicative Language Teaching (CLT)	2	3
Community Language Learning (CLL)	2	3
different methods	2	3
English as an international language	6	10
extensive reading	8	6
genre	7	5
gist	8	3
Grammar–Translation Method	2	3
individual differences	4	1
language systems compared with language skills	2	1
learning from observing teachers and being observed	17	2
skimming and scanning	8	5
Task-Based Learning (TBL)	2	3
the Common European Framework	6	8
the experiential learning cycle	1	3
the transmission view of teaching	1	2
top-down compared with bottom-up	8	3
Total Physical Response (TPR)	2	3
world Englishes	6	10
writing hot and cold feedback	17	3

About the author

Jim became an English teacher as a temporary measure until he could decide what career to choose. His first post was with Voluntary Service Overseas in a rural school in Kenya, and since then he has worked as a Lecturer with the British Council in the USSR, as Director of Education at International House Hungary and as Director of Studies of Teacher Training at International House, Hastings (the town he seems to keep coming back to). He has run numerous short courses around the world and is a regular conference speaker.

Jim was leader of the team that designed the EURO language exams. He has written *Teaching Grammar* (Oxford) and is author of teacher's books and resource materials for the *Straightforward* coursebook series. He writes a monthly 'teaching tips' column for the *Guardian Weekly* and *onestopenglish.com*. He has an MA in Creative Writing, but hasn't yet worked out what he can do with it.

About the series

Welcome to the Macmillan Books for Teachers series. These books are for you if you are a trainee teacher, practising teacher or teacher trainer. They help you to:
* develop your skills and confidence;
* reflect on what you do and why you do it;
* improve your practice and inform it with theory;
* become the best teacher you can be.

The books, written from a humanistic and student-centred perspective, offer:
* practical techniques and ideas for classroom activities;
* key insights into relevant background theory;
* ways to apply techniques and insights in your work.

The authors are teachers and trainers. We take a 'learning as you go' approach in sharing our experience with you. We help you reflect on ways you can facilitate learning, and bring your personal strengths to your work. We offer you insights from research into language and language learning and suggest ways of using these insights in your classroom.

Adrian Underhill

Titles in the series

An A-Z of ELT	Scott Thornbury
Beyond the Sentence	Scott Thornbury
Blended Learning	Pete Sharma and Barney Barrett
Children Learning English	Jayne Moon
Discover English	Rod Bolitho and Brian Tomlinson
Learning Teaching	Jim Scrivener
Sound Foundations	Adrian Underhill
Teaching Practice	Roger Gower, Diane Phillips and Steve Walters
Teaching Reading Skills	Christine Nuttall
Uncovering Grammar	Scott Thornbury
700 Classroom Activities	David Seymour and Maria Popova
500 Activities for the Primary Classroom	Carol Read

Introduction

Teacher: One who carries on his education in public. **Theodore Roethke**

This is a book for language teachers. Mostly it's a guide to methodology – to what might work in the classroom.

Learning Teaching can help you learn to teach in more effective ways. It is about a kind of teaching where you are also learning. However, it is not a book about the right way to teach. Indeed, there is no scientific basis yet for writing such a description of an ideal teaching methodology. Instead, we can observe teachers and learners at work and take note of strategies and approaches that seem to be more beneficial than others, not necessarily in order to copy them, but to become more aware of what is possible.

The act of teaching is essentially a constant processing of options. At every point in each lesson, a teacher has a number of options available; he or she can decide to do something, or to do something else, or not to do anything at all. In order to become a better teacher, it seems important to be aware of as many options as possible. This may enable you to generate your own rules and guidelines as to what works and what doesn't.

Language teaching happens in a wide variety of locations and contexts, with a wide variety of colleagues and learners. Whatever I describe in this book, your own experiences will be different. For that reason, no book like this can definitively tell you **how** to do it. You can get ideas and step-by-step guidelines and a little inspiration, but bear in mind that everything you read also needs to go through the filter of your own understanding and be checked out in terms of the local context you work in.

Thus, rather than saying 'This is how to do it,' I've tried to say 'Here are some ways that seem to work.' I aim to give you a 'toolkit' of possibilities from which you can take those ideas and options that you find most useful.

Situations and examples are mainly drawn from the world of English teaching, but the ideas and techniques may also be useful to teachers of other languages. The book is primarily aimed at teachers starting out on a training course or in their first year or two of work, but I hope that you will find something interesting in it wherever you are in your career.

The order of chapters in this book may partly reflect the order a new teacher finds topics of interest and importance when learning to teach. I aim to give you some essential background information and core survival techniques early on. I also suggest that you use the Help index at the front of the book to find whatever sections are of live interest to you.

To encourage you to engage with the material in the book, there are many tasks. Sometimes these are questions to answer or think about; sometimes they are bigger problems or things to try out. If you prefer, you can simply read the tasks and go straight on to the commentaries.

In this book, I use *he* and *she*, *him* and *her* largely at random.

Jim Scrivener

Chapter 1 Classrooms at work

This chapter offers a general introduction to ways of working in a language classroom and using a range of teacher and learner roles. It also asks how people learn.

1 Looking round some classroom doors

Task 1: Classroom snapshots

A friend who knows nothing about language teaching has asked you to describe a 'snapshot' of a typical moment in a language classroom – a picture that captures the look, the atmosphere, the learners' mood, the teacher's attitude, etc. What would your instant snapshot show?

Commentary ■ ■ ■

Your image probably captures some assumptions you hold – about what a teacher's job is, what learners can do and how they should work, etc. If you are on a training course and haven't started teaching yet, your snapshot might be very different from, say, a teacher who has been working for twenty years. In this book, we will look in detail at lots of lesson ideas, activities, methods and techniques; but before that, it may be useful just to get a more general picture of what goes on in language teaching – to look round a few classroom doors and glimpse what's going on inside. ■

Watching different classes

In my own teaching career, I have found that one of the most useful things is simply to watch other people teach. I often take away tangible things from this observation, such as ideas for specific activities, the pace they work at or a particular 'something' that the teacher said or did. Over the years, I find that I have incorporated a lot from this into my own teaching.

Some aspects of lessons can be difficult to interpret. Sometimes I feel that the 'atmosphere' in a room is excellent or that the class is particularly engaged or working in a distinctively autonomous manner. But it isn't always easy to work out how these apparently 'natural' things have been achieved.

One thing I have concluded over the years is that much of the 'magic' that makes a good lesson (often attributed purely to 'natural' skill or 'personality') is something that is almost always achieved by very specific actions, comments and attitudes – even when the teacher isn't aware of what he or she has done. And because of this, we can study these things and learn from them.

Task 2: Different lessons

Read the following brief 'snapshot' descriptions of moments from different lessons in different locations.

Which one (if any) is most like how you see yourself as a teacher? Are there any characteristics or approaches you find interesting and would like to use yourself – or would reject?

Classroom 1: Andrea

Andrea is working with 34 fourteen-year-old learners. Although the large desks are fixed in their places, she has asked the students to move so that they are sitting around both sides in ways that they can work in groups of six or seven. Each group has just finished discussing and designing a youth club on a sheet of A3 paper and is now working on agreeing a list of ten good arguments to persuade the other groups to choose its youth club design (rather than one of the others). Each group will have to make a presentation of its arguments in front of the class in about ten minutes' time.

There is a lot of noise in the classroom. Andrea is walking around listening in unobtrusively to what is going on in the groups. She smiles when she hears good ideas, but she isn't intervening or taking any active part in the conversations. She answers basic questions when a learner asks (e.g. if someone wants to know the word for something), but she avoids getting involved in working closely with a group, even with one group that is getting stuck – in this case, she makes a quick suggestion for moving forward and then walks away to another group.

Classroom 2: Maia

At a first glance, nothing much seems to be happening here. Maia is sitting down in a circle with her eight students, and they are chatting, fairly naturally, about some events from the previous day's news. Although Maia isn't doing much overt correction, after watching the lesson for a while it's possible to notice that she is doing some very discreet 'teaching', i.e. she is managing the conversation a little, bringing in quieter students by asking what they think and helping all learners to speak by encouraging, asking helpful questions, echoing what they have said, repeating one or two hard-to-understand sentences in corrected English, etc.

Classroom 3: Lee

Lee is standing at the front of a class of eleven young adult students. He is introducing *going to* as a way of talking about predicted events in the future. He has put up a large wallchart picture on the board showing a policeman watching a number of things in the town centre. The picture seems to immediately suggest a number of *going to* sentences such as *They're going to rob the bank*, *He isn't going to stop* and *It's going to fall down*. Lee is pointing at parts of the picture and encouraging learners to risk trying to say a *going to* sentence. When they do, he gently corrects them and gets them to say it again better. Sometimes he gets the whole class to repeat an interesting sentence. It's interesting that he's actually saying very little himself; most of his interventions are nods, gestures, facial expressions and one- or two-word instructions or short corrections. Generally, the learners are talking rather more than the teacher.

Classroom 4: Paoli

Paoli's lesson is teaching some new vocabulary to an adult evening class of older learners; the current lesson stage is focused on learner practice of the new items. Everyone in class is sitting in a pair, face to face. They are using a handout designed by Paoli which gives the learners in each pair (known as A and B) slightly different information. The task requires them to use some of the new vocabulary in relatively natural ways to try and discover information from their partner. There is a lot of talking in the room, though it's clear that not everyone is participating to an equal degree. One or two pairs are almost silent, and one pair seems to be whispering in their own language rather than in English. Paoli is moving round the room trying to notice any such problems and encouraging students to complete the task in the intended way.

Commentary ■ ■ ■

We have glimpsed four different lessons. The descriptions below summarise some distinctive features of each. ■

Some typical language-teaching classes

The first class described above involved groups working co-operatively on a task. The teacher saw her role as primarily 'managerial', making sure that the activity was set up properly and being done properly. She took care that she allowed enough space (i.e. time to think and plan without interference or 'unhelpful help') so that learners could get on and achieve the result.

In the second class, we saw a teacher apparently doing fairly little that might be traditionally viewed as 'teaching'. However, even at this glimpse, we have noticed that something was going on and the teacher was 'managing' the conversation and the language more than might have been apparent at first glance. Is this a valid lesson? We'll look at possible aims for lessons like the first and second snapshots when we get to Chapter 7.

The third class involves a lesson type known as a 'presentation', i.e. the teacher is drawing everyone's attention to his focus on language. Interestingly, although the teacher is introducing new language, he is doing this without a great deal of overt explanation or a high quantity of teacher talk. We look at grammar presentations in Chapter 12.

In the fourth lesson, the learners are doing a pairwork vocabulary task. The teacher's role was initially to set up the activity, and at the end it will be to manage feedback and checking. At the moment, he can relax a little more, as nothing much requires to be done beyond monitoring if it is being done correctly.

Out of these four lessons (which I think may be fairly typical snapshots of modern language classroom life), we have seen relatively little overt 'teaching' in the traditional manner, although we have seen a number of instances of the teacher 'managing' the seating and groupings, 'managing' the activities (starting, monitoring, closing them), 'managing' the learners and their participation levels, and 'managing' the flow of the conversation and work.

I think it's reasonable to argue that much of modern language teaching involves this 'classroom management' as much or more than it involves the upfront explanations and testing that many people imagine as the core of a teacher's job. This is partly to do with the peculiar subject matter we work with, i.e. the language we are using to teach with is also the thing we are teaching.

Although there is a body of 'content' in language teaching, the main thing we want our students to do is use the language themselves – and therefore there are many reasons why we mainly want our students to do more and therefore for us to do (and talk) less.

You could now use:

- Observation Task 1 (in Appendix 1 at the back of the book) to make 'snapshot' observations of teachers at work in your school;
- Observation Task 2 to get a more detailed picture of classroom management in their lessons.

2 What is a teacher for?

Language learners don't always need teachers. They can set about learning in a variety of ways. Some learn by studying on their own at home with books, CDs, cassettes, multimedia computer programs, video tapes and so on; others seem to 'pick up' a language just by living and communicating in a place where the language is used (this is known as **immersion**).

Of course, many students do learn in classes with other students and a teacher – whether that's a class they chose to come to (for example, at a language school) or maybe a class they were required to attend (such as in a high school). And much language learning will involve elements of all three ways: self-study, 'picking it up' and classroom work.

But, if it's possible to learn successfully **without** a teacher, then what difference does having a teacher make to the learning process? Why do some people pay to have a teacher? What do students expect from them? To put it bluntly, what on earth are teachers for? If you are (or are planning to be) a teacher, it's important to consider such basic questions.

To start answering, let's look at some widespread popular images of what a teacher is and does.

Task 3: Picturing 'a teacher'

When you picture 'a teacher' in your head, what images first come to mind?

Commentary ■ ■ ■

Some images you might have thought of:

- a favourite (or hated teacher) from your own schooldays;
- yourself in class;
- an entertaining, performing 'Hollywood' teacher, someone being very jolly and witty, talking a lot in spellbinding ways, using their voice and gestures to be entertaining, maybe even jumping on tables and whisking their astonished charges on a journey of intellectual discovery;
- a sort of generic, 'traditional' teacher, standing at the front of the class, talking, explaining, while the class listen attentively (or snooze) in polite rows. ■

Teachers from your schooldays

Many teachers have been very influenced by the teaching that they were exposed to in their own schooldays. If you think about it, you have watched and experienced an awful lot of teaching being done to you – and this can often remain a subtle and deep-seated influence. Whether we acknowledge it or not, much of our view of what a teacher is and what a teacher should do can often be traced back to these many years of lesson observation from the pupil's seat. Sadly, a lot of the teaching that has left a deep impression on us was not necessarily very good teaching. As well as some excellent teachers, most of us have probably seen examples of teachers who were boring, unkind, incompetent, sarcastic or inept.

'Entertainer' teaching

Learners come to class to learn a language rather than to be amused by a great show. Certainly no one would wish their lessons to be boring, but it's important to check out if the classes of an 'entertainer' style of teacher are genuinely leading to any real learning. It's easy to get swept up in the sheer panache of one's own performance; the teacher who constantly talks a lot, telling stories and jokes, amusing the class with their antics, etc. can provide a diverting hour, but it may simply cover up the fact that very little has been taken in and used by the students. The monologue may provide useful exposure to one way of using language, but this isn't sufficient to justify regular lessons of this kind. I've found that quite a number of teachers suspect that this 'performer' style is a goal they should aim for. I hope that I can persuade you otherwise.

Traditional teaching

For many of us, school teaching was in a style we could characterise as 'traditional'. While the details may vary considerably from school to school and between different countries and cultures, there will still be many aspects of 'traditional' teaching that are familiar to many.

Task 4: Traditional teaching

List some of these characteristic features of traditional teaching (e.g. Where does the teacher stand/sit? How are students seated? How is the class managed?). What do you think are the disadvantages of a traditional teaching approach for language teaching and learning?

Commentary ■ ■ ■

The next section considers some common characteristics of traditional teaching. ■

Characteristics of traditional teaching

'Traditional' teaching comes in many varieties, but is often characterised by an emphasis on 'chalk and talk' – in other words, the teacher spends quite a lot of class time using the board and explaining things – as if 'transmitting' knowledge to the class – with occasional questions to or from the learners. After these explanations, the students will often do some practice exercises to test whether they have understood what they have been told. Throughout the lesson, the teacher keeps control of the subject matter, makes decisions about what work is needed and orchestrates what the students do. In this classroom, the teacher probably does most of the talking and is by far the most active person. The students' role is primarily to listen and concentrate and, perhaps, take notes with a view to taking in the information. Often the teacher takes as if by right (usually, but not always, benignly) permission to direct, give orders, tell off, rebuke, criticise, etc., possibly with limited or no consultation.

This 'transmission' view of the role of a teacher is relatively widespread, and in many cultures represents the predominant mode of education. Students will expect that a teacher will teach in this way, and fellow teachers may be critical or suspicious of teachers who do not. In such cases, it's important to remember that your choice of methodology is not simply a matter of what you believe to be best, imposed at any cost, but it is also about what is appropriate in a particular place with particular people. What you do in any school or with any learner will often represent your best compromise between what you believe and what seems right in the local context. You then have the interesting possibility of starting to persuade your colleagues and students to your ideas … or maybe learning from them about why their approaches work better.

The process by which traditional teaching is imagined as working is sometimes characterised as 'jug and mug' – the knowledge being poured from one receptacle into an empty one. It is often based on an assumption that the teacher is the 'knower' and has the task of passing over knowledge to the students, and that having something explained or demonstrated to you will lead to learning – and if it doesn't, it is because the teacher has done this job badly or the student is lazy or incompetent.

In many circumstances, lecture or explanation by a teacher may be an efficient method of informing a large number of people about a topic. However, if our own educational experience has mainly been of this approach, then it is worth pausing for a minute and questioning whether this is indeed the most effective or efficient teaching method. Whereas most teachers will need to be good 'explainers' at various points in their lessons, a teaching approach based solely or mainly on this technique can be problematic.

Teaching and learning

We never know how much 'learning' is taking place. It is tempting to imagine that if teaching is going on, then the learning must be happening; but in fact, 'teaching' and 'learning' need to be clearly distinguished.

Here is the great and essential formula (one that all teachers should probably remind themselves of at least once a day!):

$$T \neq L$$

'Teaching' does not equal 'learning'. Teaching does not necessarily lead to learning. The fact that the first is happening doesn't automatically mean the other must occur. Learning – of anything, anywhere – demands energy and attention from the learner. One person cannot learn anything for anyone else. It has to be done by your own personal effort. Nobody else can transmit understanding or skills into your head.

It is quite possible for a teacher to be putting great effort into his or her teaching and for no learning to be taking place; similarly, a teacher could apparently be doing nothing, but the students be learning a great deal.

As you'll find when you talk to some students (and parents), there is a surprisingly widespread expectation that simply being in a class in the presence of a teacher and 'listening attentively' is somehow enough to ensure that learning will take place. This suggests a very active role for the teacher, who is somehow responsible for 'radiating' knowledge to the class. Conversely, in this viewpoint, there is an assumption of a more passive role for the student, whose job is mainly to absorb and store the received learning. But this isn't an accurate view of how people learn.

In a traditional class of, say, 25 students, one lesson is being 'taught'. But we could equally think of it as a range of different lessons being received:

Perhaps some students are listening and trying to follow the explanations (but only one of them is able to relate it to her own experiences); some other students are making detailed notes, but not really thinking about the subject; one person is listening and not really understanding anything; one (having missed the previous lesson) thinks that the teacher is talking about something completely different; three students are daydreaming; one is writing a letter; etc.

Here, the teaching is only one factor in what is learned. Indeed, teaching is actually rather less important than one might suppose. As a teacher, I cannot learn for my students. Only they can do that. What I can do is help create the conditions in which they might be able to learn. This could be by responding to some of the student complaints above – perhaps by involving them, by enabling them to work at their own speed, by not giving long explanations, by encouraging them to participate, talk, interact, do things, etc.

How useful are explanations?

Language learning, especially, seems not to benefit very much from long explanations. If the explanation is done in the language being learned, then there is an immediate problem; learners have – by definition – limited understanding of this new language, and therefore any lengthy or difficult explanation in the 'target language' will be likely to be more difficult for them than the thing being explained. And even if the explanation is done in their native tongue, explanations about how language works, while of some value, seem to be most useful in fairly brief hints, guidelines and corrections; language learners do not generally seem to be able to make use of complex or detailed information from lengthy 'lectures', not in the same way that, say, a scientist might make active use of understanding gained from a theoretical talk. Ability to use a language seems to be more of a skill you learn by trying to do it (akin to playing football or riding a bicycle) than an amount of data that you learn and then try to apply.

Language learners seem to need a number of things beyond simply listening to explanations. Amongst other things, they need to gain exposure to comprehensible samples of language (not just the teacher's monologues) and they need chances to play with and communicate with the language themselves in relatively safe ways. If any of these things are to happen, it seems likely that classroom working styles will involve a number of different modes and not just an upfront lecture by the teacher. Of course, a lot of teaching work will involve standing and talking to (or with) students, but a teaching style that predominantly uses this technique is likely to be inappropriate.

Students need to talk themselves; they need to communicate with a variety of people; they need to do a variety of different language-related tasks; they need feedback on how successful or not their attempts at communication have been.

So what's a teacher for? Short answer: to help learning to happen. Methodology, such as we discuss in this book, is what a teacher uses to try and reach that challenging goal.

Task 5: Learners' expectations of teachers

Imagine that you are about to start studying a new language in a class with other beginners. Consider your expectations of the teacher's role. What are some of the general things she can do to assist your learning?

3   Teaching and learning

Let's look outside the classroom for a moment. How do people learn things in everyday life? By trial and error? By reading a manual and following the instructions? By sitting next to someone who can tell you what to do and give feedback on whether you're doing OK?

The experiential learning cycle

The process of learning often involves five steps (see Figure 1.1):

1 doing something;
2 recalling what happened;
3 reflecting on that;
4 drawing conclusions from the reflection;
5 using those conclusions to inform and prepare for future practical experience.

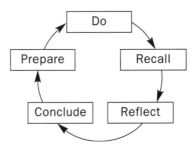

Figure 1.1   An experiential learning cycle

Again, it is important to distinguish between learning and teaching. Information, feedback, guidance and support from other people may come in at any of the five steps of the cycle, as shown in Figure 1.2, but the essential learning experience is in doing the thing yourself.

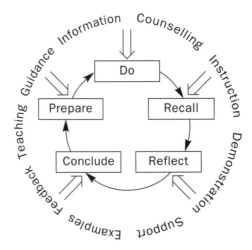

Figure 1.2   Teaching and the experiential learning cycle

This cycle, known as an **experiential learning cycle**, suggests a number of conclusions for language teaching in the classroom. For example:

- If this cycle does represent how people learn, then the 'jug-and-mug' explanation-based approach may be largely inappropriate if it dominates classroom time. Giving people opportunities to do things themselves may be much more important.
- I may become a better teacher if I worry less about teaching techniques and try to make the enabling of learning my main concern, i.e. the inner circle of the diagram rather than the outer one.
- I need to ensure that I allow my students practical experience in doing things (e.g. in **using** language rather than simply listening to lectures **about** language).
- It may be that being 'over-helpful' as a teacher could get in the way of learning. I cannot learn for my students. The more I do myself, the less space there will be for the learners to do things.
- It may be useful to help students become more aware about **how** they are learning, to reflect on this and to explore what procedures, materials, techniques or approaches would help them learn more effectively.
- It's OK for students to make mistakes, to try things out and get things wrong and learn from that … and that's true for me as a 'learning teacher' as well.

One fundamental assumption behind this book and the teaching approaches suggested in it is that people learn more by doing things themselves rather than by being told about them. This is true both for the students in your classes and for you, as you learn to be a better teacher. This suggests, for example, that it may be more useful for a learner to work with others and role-play ordering a meal in a restaurant (with feedback and suggestions of useful language) than it would be to listen to a fifteen-minute explanation from the teacher of how to do it correctly.

A second assumption is that learners are intelligent, fully functioning humans, not simply receptacles for passed-on knowledge. Learning is not simply a one-dimensional intellectual activity, but involves the whole person (as opposed to only their mental processes such as thinking, remembering, analysing, etc.). We can no longer be content with the image of the student as a blank slate. Students may bring pen and paper to the lesson, but they also bring a whole range of other, less visible things to class: their needs, their wishes, their life experience, their home background, their memories, their worries, their day so far, their dreams, their anger, their toothache, their fears, their moods, etc. Given the opportunities, they will be able to make important decisions for themselves, to take responsibility for their learning and to move forward (although their previous educational experience may initially predispose them to expecting that you, the teacher, need to do all that for them).

New learning is constructed over the foundations of our own earlier learning. We make use of whatever knowledge and experience we already have in order to help us learn and understand new things. Thus the message taken away from any one lesson is quite different for different people. The new learning has been planted in quite different seed beds. This is true both for your learners meeting a new tense in class and for you reading this paragraph and reviewing it in the light of your own previous experience and knowledge. You can check this out for yourself. Is the information you are finding in this book being written in your head on a sort of 'blank slate' or is it connecting in some manner with your previous knowledge, ideas, thoughts, prejudices, etc.?

The two assumptions listed above inform my teaching. They remind me that my 'performance' as a teacher is only one, possibly minor, factor in the learning that might occur. They remind me that some of the teaching I do might actually prevent learning. They remind me that teaching is, fundamentally, about working with people – and about remaining alive to the many different things that go on when people hack their own path through the jungle towards new learning.

Although this book concentrates mainly on teaching techniques, it is important to bear in mind that knowledge of subject matter and methodology are, on their own, insufficient. A great deal of teaching can be done with those two, but I would suspect that the total learning would not be as great as it could be. However, an aware and sensitive teacher who respects and listens to her students, and who concentrates on finding ways of enabling learning rather than on performing as a teacher, goes a long way to creating conditions in which a great deal of learning is likely to take place.

Methodology and knowledge of subject matter are important, but may not necessarily be the most important things.

4   Different kinds of teacher

Task 6: Remembering teachers you have known

- Think back to some teachers (of any subject) you have had in your life. What do you remember about them and their lessons? The teacher's manner? How you felt in their presence? Can you recall any specific lessons? Specific teaching techniques? What it was like to be a student in that room?

- To what extent do you think your personal style as a teacher is based to some degree on these role models?

- Find some words or phrases that characterise the atmosphere of the classes (e.g. positive, encouraging, boring, friendly, like an interrogation, sarcastic, humorous, respectful, scary, quiet, etc.).

Commentary ■ ■ ■

When I started teaching, I found that my basic image of what a teacher's job was and how a teacher should behave were drawn largely from what I had seen my own teachers doing. These internal images were quite deeply held and quite hard to challenge. Any teacher starting out needs to check if they have in-built assumptions about teaching from this exposure to hours and hours of observing your own teachers at work. ■

The importance of rapport

Interestingly, when I recall my own teachers at school, I find it quite hard to recall details of any specific individual lessons, but I can recall – quite strongly – the way that the teacher related to the class and how I felt in this teacher's presence. I think of some whose lessons were bright and enjoyable, some whose lessons were frightening and tense, some who seemed to bring out the best in me and some who closed me up. The way the teacher related to the learners – and consequently how learners related to each other – was significantly different in different classrooms.

What creates this distinctive atmosphere of each teacher's class? What makes the difference between a room where people are defensive and anxious, and a room where people feel able to be honest and take risks? Teachers and trainers often comment on the importance of 'rapport' between teachers and students. The problem is that, whereas rapport is clearly important, it is also notoriously difficult to define or quantify. Sometimes people equate it with 'being generally friendly to your students'. While this is a reasonable starting point, I think we need to find a wider definition, involving many more aspects to do with the quality of how teacher and learners relate.

This does raise a problem, though. If a significant part of a class's success is down to how well the teacher and students relate, does that suggest that successful teachers are born, and if they don't naturally relate well to people, then they are a write-off? Is your 'rapport' 100% natural or is it something that can be worked on and improved?

Task 7: Creating a positive learning atmosphere

Figure 1.3 lists some features that may be important in creating a positive relationship and a positive learning atmosphere. Decide which items are 'inborn' and which could be worked on and improved.

In a positive learning atmosphere the teacher ...

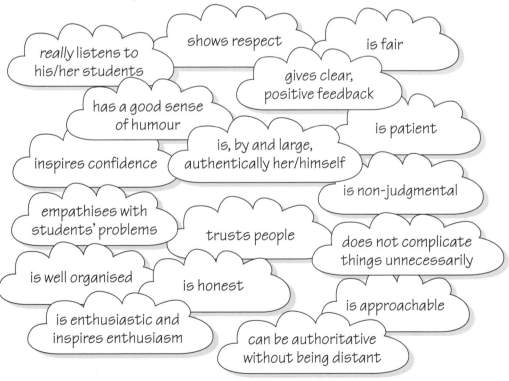

Figure 1.3   Features which create a positive relationship and atmosphere

Commentary ■ ■ ■

Arguable maybe, but I would say that all of these are things that can be studied and improved on. Some are more difficult than others.

Of course, although it's a good start, a positive learning atmosphere isn't everything. Being jokey, chatty and easy-going doesn't necessarily lead to good teaching – one of my teachers was very friendly and funny, but his lessons ended up in confusion. Contrastingly, lessons from one of the quieter, more serious teachers were often very memorable. This is simply the first building block of teaching, but it's an important one. ■

Respect, empathy and authenticity

Carl Rogers, an American psychologist, suggested that there are three core teacher characteristics that help to create an effective learning environment. These are **respect** (a positive and non-judgmental regard for another person), **empathy** (being able to see things from the other person's perspective, as if looking through their eyes) and **authenticity** (being oneself without hiding behind job titles, roles or masks).

When a teacher has these three qualities, the relationships within the classroom are likely to be stronger and deeper, and communication between people much more open and honest. The educational climate becomes positive, forward looking and supportive. The learners are able to work with less fear of taking risks or facing challenges. In doing this, they increase their own self-esteem and self-understanding, gradually taking more and more of the responsibility for their own learning themselves rather than assuming that it is someone else's job.

Rogers and Frelberg (1994) considered that, out of these three teacher characteristics, authenticity was the most important. To be yourself. Not to play the role of a teacher, but to take the risk of being vulnerable and human and honest. Gaie Houston (1990) has written that 'The foundation of rapport is to learn yourself enough that you know what style you have and when you are being truthful to yourself.'

Although there are some practical techniques you can learn to improve your communication with others, real rapport is something more substantial than a technique that you can mimic. It is not something you do to other people. It is you and your moment-by-moment relationship with other human beings. Similarly, 'respect' or 'empathy' or 'authenticity' are not clothes to put on as you walk into the classroom, not temporary characteristics that you take on for the duration of your lesson. You cannot role-play 'respect' – or any of the other qualities. On the contrary, they are rooted at the level of your genuine intentions.

In order to improve the quality of our own relationship in the classroom, we do not need to learn new techniques; we need to look closely at what we **really** want for our students, how we really feel about them. It is our attitude and intentions rather than our methodology that we may need to work on.

Having said all that, it also suggests that I can't teach you how to do this in a book. For this reason, the main subject matter of the book concerns the more technical aspects of creating a successful class.

Three kinds of teacher

There are obviously many ways of teaching, and part of the enjoyment of being a student in a good classroom is in sharing the unique personal identity, style, skills and techniques that a teacher brings to a lesson.

Having said that, it sometimes gives things a clearer perspective if we simplify rather than complicate. Adrian Underhill has suggested that there may be three broad categories of teaching styles (summarised in Figure 1.4).

The explainer

Many teachers know their subject matter very well, but have limited knowledge of teaching methodology. This kind of teacher relies mainly on 'explaining' or 'lecturing' as a way of conveying information to the students. Done with style or enthusiasm or wit or imagination, this teacher's lessons can be very entertaining, interesting and informative. The students are listening, perhaps occasionally answering questions and perhaps making notes, but are mostly not being personally involved or challenged. The learners often get practice by doing individual exercises after one phase of the lecture has finished.

The involver

This teacher also knows the subject matter that is being dealt with. (In our case, this is essentially the English language and how it works.) However, she is also familiar with teaching methodology; she is able to use appropriate teaching and organisational procedures and techniques to help her students learn about the subject matter. 'Teacher explanations' may be one of these techniques, but in her case, it is only one option among many that she has at her disposal. This teacher is trying to involve the students actively and puts a great deal of effort into finding appropriate and interesting activities that will do this, while still retaining clear control over the classroom and what happens in it.

The enabler

The third kind of teacher is confident enough to share control with the learners, or perhaps to hand it over to them entirely. Decisions made in her classroom may often be shared or negotiated. In many cases, she takes her lead from the students, seeing herself as someone whose job is to create the conditions that enable the students to learn for themselves. Sometimes this will involve her in less traditional 'teaching'; she may become a 'guide' or a 'counsellor' or a 'resource of information when needed'. Sometimes, when the class is working well under its own steam, when a lot of autonomous learning is going on, she may be hardly visible.

This teacher knows about the subject matter and about methodology, but also has an awareness of how individuals and groups are thinking and feeling within her class. She actively responds to this in her planning and methods and in building effective working relationships and a good classroom atmosphere. Her own personality and attitude are an active encouragement to this learning.

	Subject matter	Methodology	People
Explainer	✓		
Involver	✓	✓	
Enabler	✓	✓	✓

Figure 1.4   Three kinds of teacher

These three descriptions of teachers are, of course, very broadly painted. There is no way to categorise all teaching under three headings; many teachers will find elements of each category that are true for them, or that they move between categories depending on the day, the class and the aims of a lesson. However, this simple categorisation may help you to reflect on what kind of teaching you have mostly experienced in your life so far and may also help you to clarify what kind of teacher you see yourself as being now or in the future.

On teacher-training courses, I have come across many participants whose initial internal image of a teacher is based on the 'explainer', but who are keen to move to becoming an 'involver' in their own teaching. Such a move may be your aim in reading this book – and the book is mainly geared towards giving you information, ideas, options and starting points that may help you reach that goal. Essentially, therefore, this is a book about methodology. Throughout the book, I have also tried to keep in mind the important skills, qualities, values and techniques associated with the 'enabling' teacher and to give guidance and information that may influence your role and relationships in the classroom.

When I think back on my own experiences of being taught, it is the teaching techniques that I remember least. I certainly remember teachers who made subject matter come alive, through their great knowledge and enthusiasm. But the teacher I recall with most pleasure and respect was the one who listened to me, who encouraged me, who respected my own views and decisions. Curiously, this teacher who helped me most was the one who actually did least 'teaching' of the subject matter and was, seemingly, technique-free, being basically 'himself' in class. My memories of his lessons are of what I did, rather than what he did, of my learning rather than his teaching.

Task 8: Explainer, involver, enabler

Think of some people you have been taught by in the past. Which of the three descriptions above (explainer, involver, enabler) best suits each one? This may give you some idea about which images of teaching you have been exposed to and influenced by.

Chapter 2 **Starting out**

This chapter is an introductory overview of:

- the subject matter of language teaching;
- some first lesson hints and suggestions;
- what we mean by method.

1 The subject matter of language teaching

What exactly are we teaching? What is the subject matter of language teaching?

An outsider might imagine that the content would comprise two major elements, namely knowledge of the language's grammar and knowledge of lots of vocabulary. Of course, these do form an important part of what is taught/learned, but it is important to realise that someone learning a language needs far more than 'in-the-head' knowledge of grammar and vocabulary in order to be able to be use language successfully.

In staff rooms, you'll find that teachers typically classify the key subject matter of language teaching under two main headings: 'Language systems' and 'Language skills'. There are other important subject areas as well (including 'Learning better ways of learning', 'Exam techniques', 'Working with and learning about other people').

Language systems

We can analyse a sentence such as *Pass me the book* in different ways.
We could consider:

- the sounds (phonology);
- the meaning of the individual words or groups of words (lexis or vocabulary);
- how the words interact with each other within the sentence (grammar);
- the use to which the words are put in particular situations (function).

If we extend our language sample into a complete (short) conversation, e.g.
A: Pass me the book.
B: Mary's gone home.
then we have an additional area for analysis, namely the way that communication makes sense beyond the individual phrase or sentence, analysing how the sentences relate (or don't relate) to each other (known as **discourse**).

Figure 2.1 shows a brief analysis of the language sample from each of these viewpoints.

Phonological	/pɑːs miː ðə ˈbʊk/ or /pæs miː ðə ˈbʊk/ The stress is probably on *book*, but also possible (with different meanings) on *Pass* or *me*. The words *me* and *the* probably have a weak vowel sound.
Lexical	*Pass* = *give*; *hand over*; *present* *me* = reference to speaker *the book* = object made of paper, containing words and/or pictures and conveying information
Grammatical	Verb (imperative) + first person object pronoun + definite article + noun
Functional	A request or order
Discoursal	Assuming that the reply *Mary's gone home* is intended as a genuine reply to the request, it may suggest a reason why the book cannot be passed (e.g. I can't because Mary took the book with her). In order to fully understand the meaning, we would need to know more about the situational context (i.e. who is talking, where, etc.) and more about the surrounding conversation (i.e. what knowledge is assumed to be known or shared between the speakers).

Figure 2.1   Analysis of a language sample

So we have five language systems, though all are simply different ways of looking at the same thing. If we are considering teaching an item of language, one thing we need to decide is which system(s) we are going to offer our learners information about.

We might plan a lesson focused on only one area, e.g. grammar, or we might deal with two, three or more. An example of a commonly combined systems focus in many language lessons would be:

grammar + pronunciation + function

(i.e. how the language is structured, how to say it and how it's used).

Task 9: Recognising language systems

Imagine that you intend to do some teaching using this piece of language:
Can you play the guitar? Match some points you might focus on with the correct system name:

1 the construction *can* + pronoun
2 the meaning of *play* and *guitar*
3 variations, e.g. strong /kæn juː/ vs. weak /kən jə/, stress on *guitar*, etc.
4 asking about ability
5 typical question-and-reply sequences containing this language

a function
b discourse
c lexis
d grammar
e pronunciation

Answers
1 d   2 c   3 e   4 a   5 b

Task 10: Distinguishing language systems

You want to teach a lesson contrasting two potentially confusing areas of language. Classify each of the following teaching points as 'G' for grammatical, 'L' for lexical, 'P' for phonological, 'F' for functional.

Example: *house* compared to *flat* = L (lexical)

1 *I went to Paris* compared to *I've been to Paris*
2 *Lend us a fiver* compared to *Could you possibly lend me £5?*
3 *library* compared to *bookshop*
4 *woman* compared to *women*
5 *Sorry* compared to *Excuse me*
6 *hut* compared to *hat*
7 *impotent* compared to *important*
8 *some* compared to *any*

Answers
1 G   2 F   3 L   4 G/P   5 F   6 P (changing vowel sound)
7 P (changing word stress)/L   8 G

Language skills

As well as working with the language systems (which we can think of as what we know, i.e. 'up-in-the-head' knowledge), we also need to pay attention to what we **do** with language. These are the language skills. Teachers normally think of there being four important macro language skills: listening, speaking, reading, writing. Listening and reading are called 'receptive skills' (the reader or listener receives information but does not produce it); speaking and writing, on the other hand, are the 'productive skills'. Skills are commonly used interactively and in combination rather than in isolation, especially speaking and listening. It's arguable that other things (e.g. 'thinking', 'using memory' and 'mediating') are also language skills.

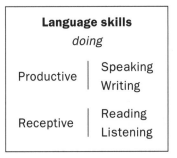

Figure 2.2   Language systems and skills

The main four skills are referred to as 'macro' because any one of them could be analysed down to smaller micro skills by defining more precisely what exactly is being done, how it is being done, the genre of material, etc. For example:

Macro skill   Listening

Some micro skills
- Understanding the gist of what is heard, e.g. Who is talking? Where are they? What are they doing? What is their relationship? How do they feel?
- Understanding precise information re. quantity, reference numbers, prices, etc. when listening to a business telephone call where a client wants to place an order.
- Compensating for words and phrases not heard clearly in an informal pub conversation by hypothesising what they are, based on understanding of the content of the rest of a conversation and predictions of likely content.

Task 11: Listening to a radio weather forecast

Consider briefly how you listen to the radio weather forecast in your own language. What would be different if you listened to one in a foreign language that you have been studying for a year or so?

Commentary ■ ■ ■

Many of the skills that we have in our own native language are directly transferable to a foreign language. But we do need practice in a number of areas. For example, I know how I listen to a weather forecast in my own language: I only half-listen until I hear the forecaster mention my part of the country, then I 'switch on' and concentrate to catch the key phrases about it, then switch off again. But when I listen to a weather forecast in a foreign country in a different language, I will have problems, even if I know all the words and all the grammar the forecaster uses. Trying to decipher words in the seemingly fast flow of speech, trying to pick out what is important and what is not, is a skill that needs to be practised; it is work that needs attention in its own right, quite apart from the study of the grammar and vocabulary involved. ■

The importance of skills work

Don't underestimate the importance of skills work. Not every lesson needs to teach new words, new grammar, etc. Lessons also need to be planned to give students opportunities to practise and improve their language skills. Skills work is not something to add in at the end of a five-year course in English. There is no need to wait for extensive knowledge before daring to embark on listening and speaking work. On the contrary, it is something so essential that it needs to be at the heart of a course from the start. Even a beginner with one day's English will be able to practise speaking and listening usefully.

A purpose-based view of course content

Another way of looking at possible course content is to consider the communicative purposes that students need language for. The Common European Framework (see page 134) focuses on what learners can do with language. For example, can an individual learner successfully attend company planning meetings? Or take notes in physics lectures at university? Or give unambiguous instructions to junior doctors on a ward? An analysis of such *can do* requirements suggests a different kind of course content, one based around students planning, undertaking and reflecting on tasks that reflect these real-life purposes. This course content would clearly include systems and skills work, but would be organised around this key idea of real-world uses.

Changes of emphasis

Traditionally, language teaching in many countries concentrated on grammar and vocabulary reinforced by reading and writing. The reading and writing was primarily to help teach the grammar and vocabulary rather than to help improve the students' skills in reading or writing. In the twentieth century, teaching approaches based mainly around oral language practice through repetition and drilling were also widely used. Until the 1960s, a lot of courses were based on mainly grammatical syllabuses, but in the late 1970s and 1980s, a number of courses and coursebooks used a functional syllabus, grouping language by the purpose for which it could be used (e.g. the language of greeting or requesting or apologising).

Nowadays, most interest is expressed in work on all language systems and skills, particularly emphasising listening and speaking (because in everyday life we often do far more speaking and listening than we do reading and writing). Grammar is typically still the language system that features most prominently on courses and in coursebooks – and, at lower levels, is also the area that many students say they want or expect to study in most detail. Often coursebooks teach grammar with an emphasis on **communication of meaning** rather than purely mechanical practice.

Despite the continuing predominance of grammar, the implications of a more lexically oriented view of language (see page 226) are increasingly having an impact on material and task design. The growing influence of the Common European Framework (see page 134) has encouraged course designers, teachers and examiners to increasingly see successful communication in real-world tasks as a more important goal than that of accurate language use.

Task 12: Balancing systems and skills

Here are two teaching situations. What balance of systems and skills would make a useful course for these learners?

1 A 24-year-old Japanese learner has studied grammar at school for nine years; she can read and understand even complex texts well. She has arrived in England to take a two-week intensive course. In her placement test (which was mainly multiple-choice grammar questions), she scored very well, but at the initial interview, she had trouble answering even simple questions about herself and often haltingly asked the interviewer to repeat the question.

2 A group of three undergraduate science students have enrolled for an English course at a language school in the Czech Republic. They know no English at all.

Commentary ■ ■ ■

1 The Japanese learner clearly needs a lot of work on the skills of listening and speaking. As she knows a lot of grammar, the course could concentrate on helping her activate this passive knowledge; the main thrust of the work could be on realistic listening and speaking activities to promote fluency and improve communicative abilities.

2 Most beginners need a balanced course that introduces them to the five systems and four skills. In their future careers, these science learners may well need to read and write English quite a lot, but may also need to visit other countries, listen to conference speeches (and give them), greet visiting scientists, etc. If they are likely to meet English-speaking people soon, it might be sensible to focus on speaking and listening, alongside work to help them read and write more effectively. ■

The communicative purpose of language learning

It is important to remember that no one area of skills or language systems exists in isolation: there can be no speaking if you don't have the vocabulary to speak with; there's no point learning words unless you can do something useful with them.

The purpose of learning a language is usually to enable you to take part in exchanges of information: talking with friends, reading instructions on a packet of food, understanding directions, writing a note to a colleague, etc. Sometimes traditional teaching methods have seemed to emphasise the learning of language systems as a goal in its own right and failed to give learners an opportunity to gain realistic experience in actually using the language knowledge gained; how many students have left school after studying a language for years, unable to speak an intelligible sentence?

Task 13: Recognising skills or systems aims

Every activity is likely to involve some work on both language systems and skills, though, usually, the aim is directed more to one area than the other. In the following list, classify each activity as 'mainly skills' or 'mainly systems' by ticking the appropriate box. Then decide which skills or which language systems are being worked on.

	Mainly systems	Mainly skills
1 You write a grammar exercise on the board which learners copy and then do.		
2 Learners read a newspaper article and then discuss the story with each other.		
3 Learners underline all past simple verb forms in a newspaper article.		
4 Learners chat with you about the weekend.		
5 Learners write an imaginary postcard to a friend, which you then correct.		
6 Learners write a postcard to a friend, which is posted uncorrected.		

	Mainly systems	Mainly skills
7 You use pictures to teach ten words connected with TV.		
8 You say 'What tenses do these people use?' Learners then listen to a recorded conversation.		
9 You say 'Where are these people?' Learners then listen to a recorded conversation.		

Commentary ■ ■ ■

In Activity 1, the students do read and write, but use few of the skills that we need when we read and write in our normal life. Certainly, comprehending the teacher's handwriting and forming one's own letters on the page may be quite demanding for some students (especially for those whose native language does not use roman script), but beyond this, the activity's main demand is on use of grammar correctly.

Activity 2 involves the skills of reading and speaking in ways very similar to those in the outside world. Vocabulary and grammar will be encountered in the reading, but the main aim is for understanding rather than analysis and study. Compare this with Activity 3, where the same material is used, but now with a specific grammar aim. Compare then with Activities 5 and 6, and 8 and 9. The aim in Activity 4 is to encourage fluent speaking. The aim in Activity 7 is to teach some vocabulary, and the speaking and listening and writing involved are of less importance. ■

Other areas that are part of language learning

The map of language systems and language skills is useful to keep in mind as an overview of the subject matter of English language teaching. However, it may well be an over-simplification. Elsewhere in this book, you'll come across some doubts about it (for example, when we ask if grammar is more fruitfully viewed as a 'skill' students need practice in using rather than as a 'system' to learn). And, of course, there is more to English language teaching than simply the language itself:

• Students may be learning new ways of learning: for example, specific study skills and techniques.
• They will also be learning about the other people in their class, and exploring ways of interacting and working with them.
• They may be learning about themselves and how they work, learn, get on with other people, cope with stress, etc.
• They may be learning a lot about the culture of the countries whose language they are studying.
• They may be learning how to achieve some specific goal, for example passing an exam, making a business presentation at an upcoming conference, etc.
• They may also be learning about almost anything else. The subject matter of ELT can encompass all topics and purposes that we use language to deal with.

Many teachers seem to become quite knowledgeable on the environment, business protocol, the British education system, desert survival techniques, etc. This is probably what keeps the job interesting! Some coursebook texts seem to achieve nearly legendary status amongst teachers! (Ask a teacher who's been in the business a few years if they know anything about a nun called Sister Wendy!)

If we start using English in class to do more than simple mechanical drills, then the subject matter becomes anything that we might do with language, any topic that might be discussed with English, any feelings that might be expressed in English, any communication that we might give or receive using English. The people who use the language in class, and their feelings, are, therefore, also part of the subject matter. This might be a little daunting and may lead you to keep the uses of language in class at a more mechanical, impersonal level, without allowing too much 'dangerous' personal investment in what is said or heard. This seems sad to me; I believe that we need to give our students chances to feel and think and express themselves in their new language.

2   First lessons – hints and strategies

In your early lessons as an English teacher, you may find that 'survival' is your main priority. You would like to teach well and for your students to learn and enjoy what happens, but more than that you want something that you can prepare easily, something that is guaranteed (or nearly guaranteed) to work, something that will let you go into the classroom, do some useful work with the learners and get out alive. This section offers a number of hints and strategies that might help you do this.

Key hints when planning your first lessons

*   **Use the coursebook (if there is one)**
    Don't feel that you have to come up with stunning original lesson ideas and creative new activities. If you have a coursebook, then you have an instant source of material. It's fine to rely on the longer experience of the coursebook writer and do the lesson exactly as it was written. Take your time before the lesson to read carefully through the unit (and give the same attention to the Teacher's Book, if you have access to one). There's a reasonable chance you'll end up with a workable lesson. Many teachers also use ideas books, known as 'recipe books', which do exactly what that nickname suggests – give you everything you need to know to be able to walk into class with the right ingredients to 'cook up' a good activity.

*   **A lesson is a sequence of activities**
    Think of the lesson as a series of separate but linked activities. Your first planning job is to select some appropriate activities. Read Chapter 3 and be clear what an activity is and how you can organise it in class.

*   **Learn something about your students**
    If possible, talk to other teachers and find out something about the class and the people in it.

*   **Plan student-focused activities**
    Don't plan first lessons that will put you upfront in the spotlight feeling the

need to burble. That leads to panic and muddle. Plan activities that are based on the following route map:

1 Lead-in (a brief introduction to the topic, e.g. you show a picture to the class and invite comments).
2 Set up the activity (i.e. you give instructions, arrange the seating, etc.).
3 Students do the activity in pairs or small groups while you monitor and help.
4 Close the activity and invite feedback from the students.

Steps 1, 2 and 4 should take relatively little time. The heart of this sequence is Step 3. This route-map lesson plan is looked at in more detail in the Chapter 3.

- **Make a written plan of the running order of your activities**
  Write out a simple list showing the activities in order. You don't need to include a lot of detail, but make sure you have a clear idea of your intended sequence of stages, perhaps with estimated timings.

- **Consider aims**
  Think about what students will get from your lesson, i.e. what is the point of them spending their time in this lesson?

- **Fluency or accuracy?**
  Decide, for each stage in the lesson, if you are mainly working on fluency or accuracy – this a key choice for many activities (see Chapter 7, Section 4).

- **Get the room ready; get yourself ready**
  If the timetabling and organisation of your school allows it, take time before any students arrive to make sure everything is ready before the class starts. Make sure the room is set up as you wish (e.g. how will you arrange the seating?). Make sure you have everything you need (e.g. chalk or board pens) – don't expect them just to magically be there! And most importantly, just feel what it's like to be in that room. Start to settle into it, to exercise ownership over it. For the length of the lesson, it's your space.

- **Have at least one emergency activity!**
  Prepare your own personal emergency 'Help I've run out of things to do and still have five minutes left' activity (e.g. a word game, an extra photocopied game, etc.). Keep this and add more emergency ideas day by day.

Key hints when teaching your first lessons

- **Talk to the students as they come into the room**
  Don't hide or do not-really-necessary 'business' while you wait for all students to arrive. This quickly builds up a tension and distance between you and the students and makes the start of the lesson much more demanding. Instead, think of the lesson as starting from the first moment a student arrives in the room. You can calm your own nerves and break the ice with students very quickly by chatting with each of them as they come into the room. Try sitting with them (even just for a minute or two) rather than standing in front of them. Welcome them. Ask them their names. You'll immediately start to learn something about them as real people rather than as generic 'students', and you'll find that you can start to relax a little.

- **Learn names as soon as possible**

  There is a huge difference in comfort levels if you know people's names. They stop being scary anonymous entities and start to become humans. In everyday life, if we meet a number of people in one go, say at a party, we are often a little careless about learning names. But in class, it is a very important teacher skill, and you should aim to internalise names as soon as possible. It is a bit embarrassing if you have to ask people their names over and over again. Don't say 'I'm bad at remembering names.' Make learning names quickly and accurately your first priority. If for any reason the pronunciation of names is a problem, take time to get the sounds right; if you are teaching in another country, maybe get a local speaker to help you.

  Practical Ideas

  1 As you ask each student for their name, write it down on a mini-sketch-map of the classroom. When you have all the names, test yourself by covering up the map, looking at the class and saying the names to yourself. Check and repeat any names you don't yet know.

  2 Ask students to make a small place card for themselves by folding an A5 piece of paper in half. They should write their names on this so that every name is visible to you at the front. As the lesson proceeds, turn individual cards around when you think you know the student's name. (Some teachers use cards like these through whole courses; that seems rather lazy to me! This strategy is to help you learn names, not a substitute for that learning!)

  3 Use name games from Chapter 16, Section 5. If it's not just you, the teacher, who is new, but your students are also new to each other, then using some of these name-game activities will definitely be a good idea.

- **Be yourself**

  Don't feel that being a teacher means you have to behave like a 'teacher'. As far as possible, speak in ways you normally speak, respond as yourself rather than as you think a 'teacher' should respond. Students, whether children, teens or adults, very quickly see through someone who is role-playing what they think a teacher should be. Authenticity in you tends to draw the best out of those you are working with.

- **Teaching doesn't mean 'talking all the time'**
  Don't feel that when you are 'in the spotlight', you have to keep filling all the silences. When you are teaching a language, the priority is for the learners to talk, rather than the teacher. Start to notice the quantity of your own talk as soon as possible – and check out how much is really useful. High levels of teacher talk is a typical problem for new teachers. Read more about this in Chapter 5.

- **Teaching doesn't mean 'teaching' all the time**
  Don't feel that being a teacher means that you have to be doing things all the time. It may feel a little odd, but it really is quite OK to sit down and do nothing when students are working on a pair or group task. There are times when your 'help' will actually be interference. Take the chance to recover from your exertions, check your notes, enjoy watching your class at work, etc.

- **Slow down**
  A large number of new teachers tend to do things much too fast. They often seriously underestimate how difficult things are for students, or are responding to a fear that students will find things boring. Learning to really slow down takes time – but it's worth bearing in mind from your first lesson onwards. For example, don't ask a question and then jump straight in again because you think they can't answer it. Instead, allow three times the length of time you feel students need (this is sometimes called **wait time**).

Key hints for starting to teach better (once you've got past the first few classes)

- **Turn your radar on**
  You are likely to be a little self-focused during your early lessons, but as soon as you can, start to tune in more to the students. Start to ask for comments and brief feedback on things you do. Watch the students at work and learn to notice what is difficult, what is easy, what seems to engage, what seems boring. Study your students.

- **Don't teach and teach … teach then check**
  Practice is more important than input. Checking what students have understood and testing if they can use items themselves is usually more important than telling them more about the new items. Don't do endless inputs. Teach a very little amount … then check what students have taken in. Give students the opportunity to try using the items, e.g. a little oral practice, a written question or two, or even simply 'repeat'. (Here's a rule-of-thumb ratio to experiment with: Input 5%, Checking and practice 95%.)

- **Are you teaching the class … or one person?**
  When you ask questions/check answers, etc., are you really finding out if they all know the items … or is it just the first person to call out? If one person says an answer, does that mean they all know? What about the others? How can you find out?

3   Method? What method?

Task 14: Your own teaching method

- What teaching method do you use? Can you name it?
- Can you describe key features of it?
- Can you describe any of its underlying principles?

Commentary ■ ■ ■

A **method** is a way of teaching. Your choice of method is dependent on your **approach,** i.e. what you believe about:

- what language is;
- how people learn;
- how teaching helps people learn.

Based on such beliefs, you will then make methodological decisions about:

- the aims of a course;
- what to teach;
- teaching techniques;
- activity types;
- ways of relating with students;
- ways of assessing.

Having said that, some methods exist without any apparent sound theoretical basis! ■

Some well-known methods and approaches

Well-known methods and approaches include:

The Grammar-Translation Method
Much traditional language teaching in schools worldwide used to be done in this way, and it is still the predominant classroom method in some cultures. The teacher rarely uses the target language. Students spend a lot of time reading texts, translating them, doing exercises and tests, writing essays. There is relatively little focus on speaking and listening skills.

The Audio-Lingual Method
Although based on largely discredited theory, the techniques and activities continue to have a strong influence over many classrooms. It aims to form good habits through students listening to model dialogues with repetition and drilling but with little or no teacher explanation.

Communicative Language Teaching (CLT) or *Communicative Approach (CA)*
This is perhaps the method or approach that most contemporary teachers would subscribe to, despite that fact that it is widely misunderstood and misapplied. CLT is based on beliefs that learners will learn best if they participate in meaningful communication. It may help if we distinguish between a stronger and a weaker version of CLT:

Strong CLT: students learn by communicating, i.e. doing communication tasks with a limited role for explicit teaching and traditional practice exercises.

Weak CLT: students learn through a wide variety of teaching, exercises, activities and study, with a bias towards speaking and listening work.

Most current coursebooks reflect a version of weak CLT.

Total Physical Response (TPR)
A method devised by Dr J. Asher, mainly useful with beginner and lower-level students. Learners listen to instructions from the teacher, understand and do things in response, without being required to speak until they are ready (see page 281).

Community Language Learning (CLL)
A method based around use of the learners' first language and with teacher help in mediating. It aims to lower anxiety and allow students to communicate in a more genuine way than is typically possible in classrooms (see page 309).

The Natural Approach
Devised by Stephen Krashen, this is a collection of methods and techniques from many sources, all intended to provide the learner with natural comprehensible language so that the learner can pick up language in ways similar to a child learning their first language.

Task-Based Learning (TBL)
A variant of CLT (see above) which bases work cycles around the preparation for, doing of, and reflective analysis of tasks that reflect real-life needs and skills.

The Silent Way
Devised by Caleb Gattegno, this method requires the learner to take active ownership of their language learning and to pay great attention to what they say. Distinctive features include the relative restraint of the teacher (who is not completely silent!) and the use of specially designed wallcharts. The use of Cuisenaire rods in mainstream ELT arose from this method.

Person-Centred Approaches
Any approach that places learners and their needs at the heart of what is done. Syllabus and working methods will not be decided by the teacher in advance of the course, but agreed between learner and teacher.

Lexical Approaches
Proposed by Michael Lewis and Jimmie Hill. On the back of new discoveries about how language is really used, especially the importance of lexical chunks in communication, proponents suggest that traditional present-then-practise methods are of little use and propose a methodology based around exposure and experiment.

Dogme
Scott Thornbury's proposed back-to-basics approach. Teachers aim to strip their craft of unnecessary technology, materials and aids and get back to the fundamental relationship and interaction of teacher and student in class.

Some schools (or individual teachers) follow one of these named methods or approaches. In naming a method, a school suggests that all (or most) work will fit a clearly stated, recognisable and principled way of working. Other schools sometimes advertise a unique named method of their own, e.g. the Cambridge Method. These are usually variations on some of the methods listed above, or not a method at all but something else, e.g. simply the name of the coursebook series being used (e.g. the Headway Method), a way of dividing levels according to a familiar exam system, or an eclectic contemporary lucky dip.

Personal methodology

Despite the grand list of methods above, the reality is that very few teachers have ever followed a single method in its entirety (unless they work in a school that demands that they do and carefully monitors adherence).

I remember watching many language teachers at work in the (then) Soviet Union, which was well known as a bastion of traditional Grammar-Translation teaching. Yet I was struck by how every teacher had their own personal way of working in the classroom. There were some similar factors between different teachers, and if I listed all the most frequently observable features and added them together I could have found a core of things that were recognisably Grammar-Translation. But the truth was that there was no monolithic method at work.

Many teachers nowadays would say that they do not follow a single method. Teachers do not generally want to take someone else's prescriptions into class and apply them. Rather they work out for themselves what is effective in their own classrooms. They may do this in a random manner or in a principled way, but what they slowly build over the years is a **personal methodology** of their own, constructed from their selection of what they consider to be the best and most appropriate of what they have learned about. The process of choosing items from a range of methods and constructing a collage methodology is sometimes known as **principled eclecticism**.

I offer some suggestions for a way to construct your own principled personal methodology in Chapter 6 on planning.

Chapter 3 **Classroom activities**

A key teaching skill is to successfully prepare, set up and run a single classroom activity or task. This chapter looks at some typical classroom activities, and there is also guidance on planning similar activities.

1 Running an activity

The basic building block of a lesson is the **activity** or **task**. We'll define this fairly broadly as 'something that learners do that involves them using or working with language to achieve some specific outcome'. The outcome may reflect a 'real-world' outcome (e.g. learners role-play buying train tickets at the station) or it may be a purely 'for-the-purposes-of-learning' outcome (e.g. learners fill in the gaps in twelve sentences with present perfect verbs). By this definition, the following are all activities or tasks:

- Learners do a grammar exercise individually then compare answers with each other in order to better understand how a particular item of language is formed.
- Learners listen to a recorded conversation in order to answer some questions (in order to become better listeners).
- Learners write a formal letter requesting information about a product.
- Learners discuss and write some questions in order to make a questionnaire about people's eating habits.
- Learners read a newspaper article to prepare for a discussion.
- Learners play a vocabulary game in order to help learn words connected with cars and transport.
- Learners repeat sentences you say in order to improve their pronunciation of them.
- Learners role-play a shop scene where a customer has a complaint.

Some things that happen in the classroom are **not** tasks. For example, picture a room where the teacher has started spontaneously discussing in a lengthy or convoluted manner the formation of passive sentences. What are students doing that has an outcome? Arguably, there is an implied task, namely that students should 'listen and understand', but, by not being explicit, there is a real danger that learners are not genuinely engaged in anything much at all.

This is a basic, important and often overlooked consideration when planning a lesson. As far as possible, make sure that your learners have some specific thing to do, whatever the stage of the lesson. Traditional lesson planning has tended to see the lesson as a series of things that the teacher does. By turning it round and focusing much more on what the students do, we are likely to think more about the actual learning that might arise and create a lesson that is more genuinely useful. (And if you plan everything in terms of what the students will do, you might find you worry less about what the teacher has to do!) Even for stages when you are 'presenting' language, be clear to yourself what it is that students are supposed to be doing and what outcome it is leading to. Think of a complete lesson as being a coherent sequence of such learner-targeted tasks.

Task 15: Using coursebook material

Here is some material from a student coursebook. In using it as the basis for a class activity, which of the following working arrangements would be possible?

1 Students think and then write answers on their own.
2 Students prepare a short monologue statement of their own views which they then present to the whole class.
3 A whole-class discussion of ideas and answers.
4 Pairwork discussion.
5 Small-group work.
6 Students walk around and mingle with other students.
7 Written homework.

2 a) If you were the prime minister or president of your country, what would you do? Look at the ideas below.

build better hospitals/schools
pay teachers/politicians more
open more universities/cinemas
make the weekend four days long/the working day shorter
make the army bigger/smaller
build more roads/shopping malls
clean up cities/rivers
give more money to old people/the unemployed

Commentary ■ ■ ■

Even a simple task like this can be used in a variety of ways – and all the suggested uses are possible. Combinations of ideas are also possible; for example, students could first think on their own for a few minutes and then compare in pairs. Whatever you choose, there are then further options as to how you do the task; for example, you could ask students to compare, discuss and question each other's views or, alternatively, to reach a consensus compromise solution. These variations lead to two very different types of speaking activity. More variations are possible when considering the stages that immediately precede or follow the activity. Your choices as to how the task will be done depend partly on the aim of the activity, i.e. what you want students to get out of it. ■

Teacher options

Bear in mind that, even where coursebook tasks include explicit instructions such as 'Compare answers with a partner' or 'Work in pairs', you always have the option as a teacher to give a different organisational instruction. For example, you may feel that a 'work with a partner' exercise might be more interesting done in small groups. And even if you follow the book's instruction, you still have the possibility of manipulating the organisation a little, for example:

• you could tell each student who he or she must work with (e.g. 'Petra, work with Christina');
• the students can choose partners for themselves;
• the pairings can be the result of some random game or humorous instruction (e.g. 'Find someone whose shoes are a different colour from your own').

The coursebook provides the raw material which only comes alive in class. You have important choices as to how to do this. Figure 3.1 summarises some basic options you could consider for many basic short coursebook activities (e.g. for short discussion tasks such as the 'Prime Minster' task above).

What arrangements can you use?	A few variations on the arrangements
Individual work	Students talk together and write nothing; they are permitted to write.
Pairwork	You choose pairs; students choose pairs; pairs are randomly selected (e.g. from a game); face to face; back to back; across the room (shouting); communicating in writing only
Small groups (three to six people)	Groups have a secretary (note-taking duty); groups have an appointed leader; membership of groups is occasionally rearranged; groups are allowed to send 'ambassadors'/'pirates' to other groups (to compare/gain/steal ideas)
Large groups	(as above)
Whole class: mingle (all stand up, walk around, meet and talk)	Students may only talk to one other person at a time; groups may meet up to maximum of three/four/five people, etc.; time limits on meetings; you ring bell/stop background music, etc. to force rearrangements
Whole class: plenary	The conversation/activity is managed by you/by a student/by a number of students; whole-class work with brief 'buzz' intervals of pairwork/small-group discussion.

A few more variations for running an activity
- Do it at speed, with a very tight time limit.
- When a group finishes, they disperse and join other groups.
- Each person makes a quick answer which is noted but not discussed; then, when all have spoken, the discussion begins, using the notes as a starting point.
- Require compromise/consensus single answers.
- Introduce task by dictating instructions/problem, etc.; individuals dictate answers back to the whole class.
- Students prepare a report-back presentation summarising their solutions.
- Students prepare a role-play dialogue incorporating their answers.
- Students do the exercise as homework.

Figure 3.1   Activity options

Activity route map

Here is a basic route-map plan for running a simple EFL activity. In some bigger activities, there may be a number of clearly separate 'sections' within the task, in which case you would go through Steps 3, 4 and 5 a few times.

---

1 Before the lesson: familiarise yourself with the material and activity; prepare any materials or texts you need.
2 In class: lead-in/prepare for the activity.
3 Set up the activity (or section of activity), i.e. give instructions, make groupings, etc.
4 Run the activity (or section): students do the activity, maybe in pairs or small groups while you monitor and help.
5 Close the activity (or section) and invite feedback from the students.
6 Post activity: do any appropriate follow-on work.

Looking at each step in more detail:

1 Before the lesson
- Familiarise yourself with the material and the activity.
- Read through the material and any teacher's notes.
- Try the activity yourself.
- Imagine how it will look in class.
- Decide how many organisational steps are involved.
- What seating arrangements/rearrangements are needed?
- How long will it probably take?
- Do the learners know enough language to be able to make a useful attempt at the activity?
- What help might they need?
- What questions might they have?
- What errors (using the language) are they likely to make?
- What errors (misunderstanding the task) are they likely to make?
- What will your role be at each stage?
- What instructions are needed?
- How will they be given? (Explained? Read? Demonstrated?)
- Prepare any aids or additional material.
- Arrange seating, visual aids, etc.
- Most importantly, you need to think through any potential problems or hiccups in the procedures. For example, what will happen if you plan student work in pairs, but there is an uneven number of students? Will this student work alone, or will you join in, or will you make one of the pairs into a group of three?

2 Lead-in/Preparation
This may be to help raise motivation or interest (e.g. discussion of a picture related to the topic), or perhaps to focus on language items (e.g. items of vocabulary) that might be useful in the activity. Typical lead-ins are:
- Show/draw a picture connected to the topic. Ask questions.
- Write up/read out a sentence stating a viewpoint. Elicit reactions.
- Tell a short personal anecdote related to the subject.
- Ask students if they have ever been/seen/done/etc.

- Hand out a short text related to the topic. Students read the text and comment.
- Play 'devil's advocate' and make a strong/controversial statement (e.g. 'I think smoking is very good for people') that students will be motivated to challenge/argue about.
- Write a key word (maybe the topic name) in the centre of a word-cloud on the board and elicit vocabulary from students which is added to board.

3 Setting up the activity

- Organise the students so that they can do the activity or section. (This may involve making pairs or groups, moving the seating, etc.).
- Give clear instructions for the activity. A demonstration or example is usually much more effective than a long explanation.
- You may wish to check back that the instructions have been understood (e.g. 'So, Georgi, what are you going to do first?').
- In some activities, it may be useful to allow some individual work (e.g. thinking through a problem, listing answers, etc.) before the students get together with others.

4 Running the activity

- Monitor at the start of the activity or section to check that the task has been understood and that students are doing what you intended them to do.
- If the material was well prepared and the instructions clear, then the activity can now largely run itself. Allow the students to work on the task without too much further interference. Your role now is often much more low-key, taking a back seat and monitoring what is happening without getting in the way.
- Beware of encumbering the students with unnecessary help. This is their chance to work. If the task is difficult, give them the chance to rise to that challenge, without leaning on you. Don't rush in to 'save' them too quickly or too eagerly. (Though, having said that, remain alert to any task that genuinely proves too hard – and be prepared to help or stop it early if necessary!)

5 Closing the activity

- Allow the activity or section to close properly. Rather than suddenly stopping the activity at a random point, try to sense when the students are ready to move on.
- If different groups are finishing at different times, make a judgement about when coming together as a whole class would be useful to most people.
- If you want to close the activity while many students are still working, give a time warning (e.g. 'Finish the item you are working on' or 'Two minutes').

6 Post-activity

It is usually important to have some kind of feedback session on the activity. This stage is vital and is typically under-planned by teachers! The students have worked hard on the task, and it has probably raised a number of ideas, comments and questions about the topic and about language. Many teachers rely on an 'ask the class if there were any problems and field the answers on the spot' approach. While this will often get you through, it can also lead you down dark alleys of confusing explanations and long-winded spontaneous teaching. It can also be rather dull simply to go over things that have already been done thoroughly in small groups. So, for a number of reasons, it is worth careful planning of this stage in advance – especially to think up alternatives to putting yourself in the spotlight answering a long list of questions.

- Groups meet up with other groups and compare answers/opinions.
- Students check answers with the printed answers in the Teacher's Book (which you pass around/leave at the front of the room/photocopy and hand out, etc.).
- Before class, you anticipate what the main language problems will be and prepare a mini-presentation on these areas.
- During the last few minutes of a long task, go round the groups and warn them that each group will be asked to 'report back' to the whole class. Ask them to appoint a spokesperson and to agree on the main message they want to say. You could ask them to choose just one point from their discussion that they think is worth sharing.
- When checking answers, ask for groups to exchange and compare their answers across the room themselves …
- … or get a student to come up front and manage the answer-checking, rather than doing it all yourself (you could give this student the answer sheet!).
- Collect in all answer sheets then redistribute them for 'correcting' by other students. When everything has been checked, students pair up with those who marked their paper and listen/explain/justify/argue, etc.
- Correct one student's answers; that student then goes on to correct other answers, etc.
- Divide the board up into spaces for answers and throw pens to different students who fill the board up with their answers (each answer written by different student). The whole group looks at the finished board and comments/corrects.

Task 16: Planning a procedure for a coursebook activity

Plan a basic procedure for using the following material in class, using the steps described above.

Starting up	**A** In your opinion, which factors below are important for getting a job? Choose the seven most important. Is there anything missing from the list?

> age/sex   appearance   astrological sign   contacts and connections
> experience   family background   handwriting   hobbies   intelligence
> marital status   personality   qualifications   references
> sickness record   blood group

2   Exploiting an activity

In this section, we look at one simple activity in detail. This may help you to similarly analyse your own teaching material in future.

Task 17: Analysing a coursebook activity

Read this activity from a student coursebook and answer the following questions on content and classroom procedures.

Anecdote   **4**   Think about your life at the age of eight. You are going to tell your partner about it. Choose from the list the things you want to talk about. Think about what you will say and the language you will need.

'My son, Eric, won't be coming to school today; he's in dreadful pain.'

- ☐ Did your life use to be very different to how it is now?
- ☐ Where did you use to go to school? How did you get there?
- ☐ Do you remember any of your teachers?
- ☐ Were there any you particularly liked or disliked? Why?
- ☐ Who were your friends?
- ☐ What did you use to do before/after school or during the breaks?
- ☐ Did you ever do anything naughty? Were you caught and punished?
- ☐ What was your favourite game?
- ☐ What were your favourite sweets?
- ☐ Was there one of the older children you particularly admired?
- ☐ What was your greatest wish?

Analysis of	Questions
1 Language content	What language systems and skills will the students probably be practising when they do this activity?
2 Other content	What other purposes (apart from getting students to practise language) might this activity serve?
3 Preparation	What preparation needs to be made? Are any special materials or visual aids needed?
4 Steps	As with many activities, it's important to note that there are actually quite a number of separate steps bundled within the single printed instruction. What are the steps in this task?
5 Instructions	You could simply tell the class to read the coursebook instructions and do the activity, without further guidance. But if you wanted to give instructions orally, what are some important considerations?
6 Organisation	What organisational arrangements could you use in class?

Commentary ■ ■ ■

1 The main language areas are:
   - preparing and giving a 'long turn' monologue describing their memories of school life;
   - using *would* and *used to* to talk about things that were regular habits in the past but are not true now;
   - using other past tense forms (past simple and past progressive), especially asking and answering questions about the past.

2 As well as working on language, the activity involves students in:
   - talking and listening to one another on a personal level. This may help to build good relationships within the class and help create a good working atmosphere;
   - recalling and reconsidering some quite specific personal memories; students may find that they are thinking about things forgotten till now. This degree of personal investment and self-discovery tends to be a frequent element in many contemporary coursebook units and may lead students to find that they are also learning about themselves, others and the world as much as about the language. (Some teachers feel uncomfortable with this kind of work and try to keep the focus on language work rather than what they see as more intrusive general and personal education. But of course language is intertwined with our lives and our understanding of the world, and any teaching approach which seeks to disentangle the two may be hard to implement and may miss out on some essential elements.)

3 No special preparation is necessary and no special materials or visual aids are needed.

4 This is one possible analysis:
   1 Students think about their life at the age of eight.
   2 Students read list in book and select some or all topics to deal with in detail.
   3 Students consider their own answers for questions and maybe make notes.
   4 Students plan language to express these ideas.
   5 Students tell partner about their thoughts.
   6 Students listen to their partner's ideas.
   Other interpretations of stages and sequence are possible. The fact that there are possibly six sub-steps within a single task reminds us that a teacher does need to take care in (a) checking activities before offering them to students, and (b) preparing clear uncomplicated instructions.

5 - Instructions need to be simple, short and clear.
   - If a task has a number of separate steps or stages within it, it is sometimes a good idea to give instructions for these stages one at a time, and wait till that stage is completed before giving the next instruction. With this task, you could first ask the class to 'Think about your life when you were eight years old', then allow thinking time or maybe even elicit a response or two from students before going on to the second part of the task and the second instruction. Separating activities and instructions into different steps is an important technique. At each point, the learners know what they need to know without possible confusion from instructions for later parts of the activity.

- Demonstrations are often a better way of introducing a task than a wordy explanation. In this example, there may not seem to be very much to demonstrate, but you could still work through an example sentence or two (maybe saying your own answers aloud), rather than simply explaining the instructions. By doing this, the learners may become clearer about what the activity involves.

6 This task would work in many arrangements. It is likely to start with individual thinking and note-taking, which may then be followed by comparing in pairs, small groups or whole class. ■

Task 18: Interpreting a lesson description

Below is a brief description of a teacher, Ricardo, using the above activity in his class of seventeen young adults. Before you read it, visualise for yourself what might happen. What are the learners doing? What is the atmosphere in the classroom like? As you read the text, notice points where he adds to – or alters in some way – the printed task.

Lesson description

Ricardo says, 'I've been thinking about when I was young — about eight years old. I wonder if you can remember back so far?'

Some of the students say 'Yes', some 'No'.

'Ask me some questions,' continues Ricardo. 'Can you find out some information about me when I was eight years old?'

Students are often curious to find out about their teacher, and the tactic works here. They now begin to ask questions such as 'Did you live in this town?' 'Which school did you go to?' etc. When it gets too noisy, Ricardo uses gestures to indicate which student should speak next. He also encourages students to rephrase or correct each other when their questions contain errors related to the language aim of the activity. Sometimes he corrects an error himself. At one point, two students get interested in some of the pop groups Ricardo mentioned from his childhood and they tell the class about some CDs they bought recently. Ricardo visibly enjoys the chat, but after a minute or so brings the focus back to the main task.

When a number of useful questions have been asked, Ricardo asks the students to think back to the questions they had asked him. As they recall questions (e.g. 'Did you like school?'), Ricardo writes them up on the board.

When a number of questions are up, Ricardo says, 'OK — now it's your turn to think about when you were eight years old. I'm going to give you one minute to remember that time.'

The class falls silent. Ricardo deliberately refuses to take questions at this point and he says 'Ssssh' to a group in the corner who are giggling and not being serious about being quiet.

'OK,' says Ricardo, 'open your books at page 49 and read the list of questions in Exercise 4. Decide which are the three most interesting questions for you.' Again, he allows a silent period while students do the reading.

When he feels students are ready, he asks a few students, 'Do you have three questions?' When he is confident that the students have done this successfully, he says, 'Now, you have five minutes to make notes about your answers to the three questions you chose. Don't write whole sentences, just ideas.'

He waits while the students do this, keeping an eye out for the moment when the majority of them have finished (rather than strictly keeping the arbitrary time limit he set). Then he says, 'In two minutes, you're going to work in pairs and tell your partner about your life when you were eight. Look back at your notes and think about the language you'll need to describe this.'

When the preparation time is over Ricardo says, 'Find someone to work with.' Chaos follows for a minute or so while students reorganise themselves. Some walk across the room to find a partner, some just turn to the person next to them.

When they are sitting down again, he says, 'Turn your notes over so you can't see them. Tell your partner about your life when you were eight. You can quickly check your notes if you want to, but don't just read them aloud. Your partner can ask questions to find out more information.' The students start talking in pairs. There is a lot of noise from the conversations. Ricardo wanders around the room at the start of the activity to check that the students have understood the instructions and are doing what was asked. He then sits quietly in a corner of the room apparently taking little notice of what the students are doing. At one point, a student asks Ricardo for help (the right way to say something); Ricardo says a short phrase quietly, but offers no further help. The conversations continue for about seven minutes.

When most have finished talking, Ricardo calls attention back to himself by standing up and saying 'OK' and waiting (patiently) for silence. Then he asks, 'Did you find out about any stories?' A short feedback discussion starts. One student says, 'When Julio was eight, he naughty…'

Commentary ■ ■ ■

Two key additions/alterations: Ricardo asks students to make written notes; he asks them to choose only three questions to answer. ■

Task 19: Analysing a lesson description

Look back at the description of the lesson in Task 18. Which of the following sentences are true?

1 The teacher had a lead-in to the activity rather than simply giving the instructions straight away.
2 The teacher demonstrated how to do the activity rather than simply giving instructions.
3 Instructions were clear and simple.
4 The teacher clearly separated the various steps of the planned activity.
5 The teacher corrected the students in some parts of the activity but not in others.
6 The teacher spent some time presenting and practising the main target language for the activity.

7 The teacher had thought of at least one possible problem with the activity and tried to prevent this by giving an additional instruction.

Commentary ■ ■ ■

1 True. Ricardo started by getting students to ask questions about his own childhood.
2 Not really, though you might consider the lead-in as a sort of demo of the later task. Beyond this, all instructions are given as normal spoken instructions.
3 True. Instructions were concise and to the point. This may look simple enough, but it's a really hard-earned skill. If you are just starting out teaching, you're quite likely to find that your instructions last for ages and twine around themselves!
4 True. The steps were separated into quite distinct stages. Note that even the getting into pairs is treated as a stand-alone instruction with its own time to be completed. This kind of careful step-by-step thinking is the mark of a really competent organised teacher.
5 True. He corrected (and encouraged student correction) at the beginning when the class was working with him, but when the pairwork started, he did no correction at all.
6 False. You may find this a bit odd, but Ricardo didn't even mention that the activity gave them the chance to use *used to*. There was certainly no explicit presentation of the target language. (Don't take this as a 'rule'; you might well decide to do some language work before a task!) Ricardo's decision here may have been because he was using the activity as a 'test' to see how much they knew and used naturally; having found this out, he could decide what he needed to focus on when he taught *used to* later in this lesson or in a future lesson. Another reason might be that his aim was to focus on the speaking and communication in the task rather than the grammar.
7 True. Ricardo had thought that the activity would probably work less well if students simply read their notes aloud, so he specifically asked them to put their notes away. He also predicted a possible problem if students hadn't selected three questions from the list and so took care to check that this had been done successfully before moving on to give the next instruction. ■

Task 20: Opinions about a lesson description

What is your opinion about the following things that happened during the activity? Do you think they were appropriate or useful? Would you do the same or not?

1 There were a number of very noisy stages in the activity, e.g. when the students were changing places, and when they were all talking to each other.
2 Ricardo allowed a brief diversion from his plan while the students talked about music.
3 The teacher told off some students (saying 'Ssssh!') at one point.
4 Ricardo only offered minimal help to a student who asked.

Commentary ■ ■ ■

My own opinions:

1 Learning is often quite a noisy business. If people speak or move or do things, then there is very likely to be noise, especially if lots of people are doing things

at the same time. Obviously sometimes noise serves no useful purpose, but it is often evidence that a lot of important work is going on.

2 This diversion allowed students to talk about something of interest to them without deviating from the original lesson plan for too long. I usually feel that such moments are not wasted time but are actually important (as long as they don't take over the whole lesson). For once, the students are using English to do something they want to do, rather than something I have asked them to do!

3 Most teachers nowadays don't feel very comfortable with telling off of this kind (especially in an adult class!). However, it surely is a teacher's responsibility to make sure that as many students as possible get as much as possible out of an activity. At times, it may be necessary to use one's authority appropriately – not unkindly or disrespectfully, but clearly and unambiguously – to keep the class on track and make sure that the activity stands a chance of working.

4 At first glance, this seems rather cruel. Is it possible that it is sometimes more useful for a teacher not to help than to help? ■

3   Pairwork information gaps

Introduction to common activity types

This section and the next two introduce three very common activity types:

- pairwork information gaps;
- small-group discussions;
- pairwork grammar activities.

In the Resources section at the back of the book (Appendix 2), you'll find materials for all three types of activity. All are potentially suitable for early lessons in your teaching; all should be relatively straightforward to set up in class, yet they all stand a reasonable chance of not flopping! From the students' perspective, the activities should be engaging and useful. Even if you don't use the specific material, you may feel that you can draw something from the general ideas and devise similar activities yourself.

The tasks are all based around getting the students to speak and exchange information and ideas, i.e. using language to communicate. There is some possibility for you to input some language, but speaking rather than learning new items is the primary aim.

This section offers detailed instructions for using Resource 1 from Appendix 2 at the back of the book – a pairwork information exchange (beach scene pictures) suitable for a range of learners from Elementary to Intermediate levels.

Task 21: Defining 'information gap'

What is an 'information gap'? If you don't already know, work it out by studying Resources 1–3 in Appendix 2.

Commentary ■ ■ ■

When one person knows something that another person doesn't, we can say that there is a 'gap' of information between them. Most real-life communication comes about because of such gaps of information (or of opinions or ideas, etc.).

When someone knows something we don't, there is a reason for talking (or writing/reading). By creating classroom activities that include such information gaps, we can provide activities that mimic this reason for communication, and this may be more motivating and useful to language learners than speaking without any real reason for doing so. ■

If you're interested in the reasons for doing speaking work in pairs (as opposed to, say, with the whole class), read Chapter 5.

Task 22: Predicting uses for material: pairwork information gap

Have a look at the pictures for Resource 1 in Appendix 2. Before you read the commentary below, work out your own way to use the activity route-map (see page 44 and summarised below) with this material.

Activity route map

1 Pre-class: familiarise yourself with the material and activity; prepare any materials or texts you need.
2 In class: Lead-in/prepare for the activity.
3 Set up the activity.
4 Run the activity: students do the activity (maybe in pairs or small groups while you monitor and help).
5 Close the activity and invite feedback from the students.
6 Post-activity: do any appropriate follow-on work.

Commentary ■ ■ ■

Here are my own instructions and guidelines, using the activities route map.

Route map	Instructions
1 Pre-class: Familiarise yourself with the material and activity. Prepare any materials or texts you need.	The material consists of two similar but not identical pictures; there are fifteen differences between the pictures. The task is 'Spot the difference', but each student will only see one of the pictures. Students will work in pairs. Without looking at each other's pictures, they should describe their pictures and compare details, trying to discover as many differences as they can. Photocopy enough pictures so that you have one 'A' and one 'B' for every pair of students.
2 In class: Lead-in / prepare for the activity	Draw a simple picture of a beach on the board.

	Ask students where it is. Ask what people do there. If students are in a country where people take beach holidays, you could ask for their own opinions. e.g. whether they like beaches. Ask students to tell you some things you find at the beach. Write the words on the board as they come up. If necessary, add new things to the picture (e.g. ice cream). Make sure that a number of useful words from the task picture are mentioned. (NB You don't have to exhaustively 'pre-teach' everything.) You could ask students to copy the picture and labels.
3 Set up the activity	Rearrange students into pairs, facing each other. Hand out the pictures, making sure that in each pair there is one 'A' and one 'B' picture. Students must understand that they cannot look at each other's pictures. (Saying the word *secret* with a 'hiding-the-picture' mime may help make this clear.) Explain the task simply and clearly, i.e. the students must find what is different between the two pictures by talking and describing, not by looking.
4 Run the activity: students do the activity (maybe in pairs or small groups while you monitor and help.)	As students start doing the activity, walk around unobtrusively, just to check that they are following the instructions correctly (i.e. they understand the task and are doing it in English). After that, you could continue with discreet monitoring or maybe sit down and wait for students to finish the task. If you monitor, you could collect overheard examples of good or problematic sentences. Don't feel the need to join in or take an active part in the work; this stage is for students to work together.
5 Close the activity and invite feedback from the students.	Keep an eye on students as they finish (the task will take different pairs different lengths of time). When about half of the pairs have finished, announce that everyone has one minute to finish. After you stop the activity, ask students what was easy or difficult; help them with expressions or vocabulary they ask for – or use other feedback ideas.

6 Post activity: do any appropriate follow-on work	If you collected any sentences while you were monitoring, write them up on the board. Ask students to work in pairs again and decide which sentences from your list are good English and which not. They should also work out corrections for any errors. Alternatively, use any other follow-on activity, e.g. 'You are one of the people in the picture. Work in pairs and write a paragraph describing your day at the beach.'

■

Task 23: Deciding on the aims of an activity

When the activity has finished, what might the students have learned or be better able to do, i.e. what was the aim of the activity?

Commentary ■ ■ ■

Amongst other things, students may be better able to:

- speak more fluently;
- describe objects, their location, decoration, shape, etc. in precise detail;
- listen carefully and decide which information is important;
- ask for further clarification of information;
- name some typical objects and activities associated with the sea, holidays, beaches, etc.;
- interact effectively and use time efficiently to solve a specific, challenging puzzle.

It's worth noting that the students are practising fluent speaking under some degree of pressure. They have limited time to prepare what they are going to say and cannot worry about getting their grammar 100 per cent accurate. Students will become more focused on the message they wish to communicate and on getting that across successfully. This shift of values from 'getting the grammar' right to 'achieving successful communication' is an important one for many students to come to terms with. While a fair degree of good grammar is necessary to succeed in the task, successful communication is a more important real-world goal than simply being perfect. For more on fluency and accuracy, see Chapter 7, Section 4. ■

Task 24: Planning further lessons using the route map

Resources 2 and 3 in Appendix 2 are similar to Resource 1 and are designed around the same idea of pairs exchanging information. In Resource 4, the learners are two people who witnessed the same incident. They must share information and decide exactly what happened. In Resource 5, the learners have information about some events on in town. They should discuss the various possibilities and agree their favourite event to recommend to other people in class as a good day out.

Refer to the detailed instructions for Resource 1 and use the route map to plan your own exploitation of the material in the other resources.

4   Small-group discussions

This section offers detailed instructions for using Resource 6 in Appendix 2 at the back of the book – a small-group discussion task (board game) suitable for a range of learners from Intermediate to Upper Intermediate levels.

Task 25: Predicting uses for material: board game

Look at the board game handout. Before you read the full instructions, think how you might use such material in class.

Commentary ■ ■ ■

The activity uses a board game to get students discussing in small groups. The game element helps focus attention, and students may find that it adds something exciting and humorous to a more serious discussion topic. The activity is adaptable for a wide range of topics. One example set of cards on general discussion topics for Intermediate level and above is given in Appendix 2 (Resource 7).

Route map	Instructions
1 Pre-class: Familiarise yourself with the material and activity. Prepare any materials or texts you need.	Photocopy one game board for every four students in your class. You will need a die for all groups and a counter for each player (these could be coins). Cut some paper into a lot of small blank 'cards'. Decide what topic you want the students to discuss and prepare a list of interesting discussion questions (or use the set of sample discussion cards from the Resources section). Photocopy and cut up one set for each group.
2 In class: Lead-in / prepare for the activity	Obviously, your lead-in will depend on which topic you have chosen. If you have chosen a single topic (e.g. 'globalisation'), it might be an idea to first clarify exactly what the term means. You could do this by writing the word on the blackboard and eliciting definitions and examples of one or two arguments for and against. Or you could choose one of the more extreme viewpoints from the cards and say it to the class, hoping to get a reaction. This initial mini discussion may prepare them for the conversation in the game itself.
3 Set up the activity	Form small groups of four to five students and hand out a pack of cards to each group. Students keep the cards face down. Explain that students should take it in turns to throw the die and move their counter around the board.

	If they land on a square with a '?', they should take a card, read it out and ask the group to discuss it for at least 30 seconds. If they land on a 'Talk' square, they should express their own opinion about it for at least 30 seconds. Everyone else in the group can then join in a short discussion about the question. Every time a learner passes 'Bonus' (i.e. having circled the board once), they get a point. The winner at the end is the one with most points.
4 Run the activity: students do the activity(maybe in pairs or small groups while you monitor and help.)	Monitor as usual.
5 Close the activity and invite feedback from the students.	It may be tricky to decide when it's appropriate to stop the activity. Some teams might really get into the discussion; others may race through it faster. The best thing to do is watch and judge when most groups have had the most value from it. If any groups finish very quickly, go over and tell them to play another round. It seems natural to extend the group work into a whole-class comparison of views (if students aren't sick of the subject already).
6 Post activity: do any appropriate follow-on work	Writing follow-ups might include writing a summary of each individual's own opinions, preparing a poster or newspaper article, writing a letter to a politician, etc. You could link the discussion into reading a relevant magazine article. The topic may provide a useful context for working on some grammar points, e.g. globalisation could help introduce *We should ... The government ought to ... If we don't ...*, etc.

5 Pairwork grammar activities

This section offers detailed instructions for using Resource 8 in Appendix 2 at the back of the book – a grammar lesson that involves quite a lot of pairwork suitable for learners around Elementary or Pre-Intermediate levels.

Task 26: How students learn to use grammar

If you don't 'explain' grammar points to students, what other ways are there that they could become better at using grammar?

Commentary ■ ■ ■

One answer is that learners can try using language that they already know – or half-know – and experimenting with it, as in a chemistry laboratory, mixing components together and seeing what kinds of outcomes arise. As we will see in the later chapter on grammar (page 252), studying grammar only partially involves a need for teacher explanation; the essential heart of learning grammar seems to be that students have lots of opportunities to try things out themselves. This is a 'trying things out themselves' kind of lesson. ■

Task 27: Predicting uses for material: grammar

Have a look at the pictures in Resource 8 and think of a way to use them for working on grammar.

Commentary ■ ■ ■

The heart of this task is based around learners making sentences and questions in a range of tenses (which you can specify in the task instructions). To some extent, the activity's level is self-grading. If the students don't know some language items, they simply won't use them.

The basic activity involves pairs looking at a picture and making sentences, passing on the sentences to another pair and receiving another pair's sentences (about a different picture) themselves. Each pair must now try to recreate the other pair's original picture from the information they have received.

Instructions

Here are my own instructions and guidelines, using the activities route map. By the way, this activity has two sections and therefore goes through Steps 3, 4 and 5 twice.

Route map	Instructions
1 Pre-class: Familiarise yourself with the material and activity. Prepare any materials or texts you need. happened yesterday).	The material consists of various pictures showing events happening. Decide whether you want students to mainly work on present progressive (to describe what is happening now) or past simple. Students will be able to use more than these tenses, but it's important that you establish whether the events are now or in the past.

	Prepare a large copy of Picture A and copies of the other pictures – one for each pair. If you have more pairs than pictures, reuse them, but be careful not to hand out the same picture to two pairs sitting next to each other.
2 In class: Lead-in / prepare for the activity	Put Picture A on the board. Tell them that it is shows what is happening now (or yesterday afternoon if you want learners to work using past tenses). Invite learners to think up good sentences about the picture. When a student suggests one, write it up without acknowledging whether it is good or bad English. Invite students to check and suggest amendments or improvements. Collect ten sentences. If students produce over-simple ones, upgrade the challenge by asking, for example, for 'sentences at least seven words long' or 'exactly thirteen words long' or 'you must include the word *although*,' etc. This has effectively been a demonstration of the task students will now do in pairs.
3A Set up the section 1 of the activity	Put students in pairs. Hand out the other pictures, one to each pair. Emphasise that pictures are secret. Pairs should take care that other pairs do not see their picture. Give task instructions.
4A Run section 1 of the activity: students do the activity(maybe in pairs or small groups while you monitor and help.)	Students work in their pairs and make ten sentences (as in the demo). You may set minimum sentence lengths or other requirements. Go round and point out any obvious errors or problems. Try not to 'over-help'. Make sure students are writing clearly on a separate piece of paper.
5A Close section 1 of the activity	When students have all finished ask them to turn over their pictures.
3B Set up section 2 of the activity	Ask pairs to pass on their sentences (but not pictures) to another pair. Each pair receives sentences from the pair they gave theirs to. Give instructions for the next section. (This has not been demonstrated!)

4B Run section 2 of the activity: students do the activity(maybe in pairs or small groups while you monitor and help.)	Pairs read the sentences they have received. They have a new blank piece of paper. Students interpret the ten sentences and work out what the original picture must have been, drawing it as best they can on the paper.
5B Close section 2 of the activity	Stop the activity when most pairs seem to have a reasonable picture. Get pairs to meet up. They compare pictures and sentences. There may be some amusement at misunderstandings and alternative interpretations.
6 Post activity: do any appropriate follow-on work	You could now extend the activity by collecting a range of sentences (from different pairs) down the left-hand side of the board and inviting different students to draw on the right-hand side, slowly building up a composite picture with features from different originals. Alternatively, redistribute the pictures and repeat the original activity 'live', i.e. basically the same, but have pairs work with other pairs from the start and say the sentences to them as they think of them (rather than write them down).

■

Task 28: Exploiting material differently

Can you think of any completely different way to exploit these pictures?

Chapter 4   Who are the learners?

This chapter looks at ways that learners (and classes) differ, and asks what you can do to work with such differences.

1   Individuals and groups

Task 29: First meeting with a class

You walk into the room, and there in front of you is your new class.

1 What can you learn about a class at first glance?
2 How can you learn more about them and what they might be thinking about you?
3 What kind of relationship do you hope to achieve with them?

Commentary ■ ■ ■

At first glance, we can discover some basic facts, such as:

What is the apparent age of learners? How many are there? What is the male/female ratio? Do they have books, materials, pens, etc.? How they are seated? Are they silent? Talking? Actively doing something? Restless? What do they do in reaction to your presence? etc.

Beyond this, we can gain a number of more intangible, intuitive impressions based on our interpretation of eye contact, body posture, comments overheard, etc.

Do they know each other? How do they relate to each other? Are they happy and positive? Do they seem to be ready for a language lesson? Is the atmosphere welcoming to me? Do they seem to like me? Does their reaction feel challenging to me in a positive way or threatening in a negative way? Are the learners waiting for me to say or do something? Is there a 'good buzz' about the room?

Of all these, teachers are often initially most concerned with their perception of what the learners think of them. 'Do they like me?' and 'What do they expect from me?' seem to be fundamental issues for many teachers – and until they have been positively resolved, teachers often feel unable to work successfully. Meeting a class is an important moment. It involves meeting a number of people at once, and many initial impressions may be formed in those first few seconds. ■

Task 30: 'I wanted them to love me'

Here is Yvette – an experienced teacher – talking about what she used to worry about when she first met a class. Do you relate to her feelings at all?

'When I started teaching, I seemed to spend a lot of my time worrying about whether the class liked me or not – well, I could almost say I was desperate that they should love me. I felt as if I couldn't do anything unless they were on my side, as it were. I think this got me spending too much time trying to entertain the class – which led to some funny lessons and we all had a good laugh – but I'm not sure they got what they really needed from me. I think nowadays I still want to have a good relationship with my students, but somehow I've come to terms with the fact that whatever I do, some people probably won't adore me or what I do. That sort of

sets me free to worry about the lessons and the students and what they are learning – more than worrying too much about my own feelings.'

Task 31: The character of groups

Do groups have a character distinct from that of the individuals in it?

Commentary ■ ■ ■

Groups do have characters and moods. I'm sure you've heard fellow teachers in a staff room saying things like 'Oh, they're a lovely group' or 'The group seems to have gelled' or 'They are so open – happy to do anything'. Of course, you might also hear negative interpretations of group character as well: 'It's like stirring mud in there today' or 'They're very negative'.

It is interesting to notice how different teachers may evoke a markedly different response from the same group. Such variation can be particularly noticeable on training courses when maybe two or three teachers teach the same class, one after the other. You can sometimes watch the class that has just been active and engaged 'close down' when a new teacher starts – speaking less and looking down all the time as if some switch had been turned off inside them. ■

Task 32: Changes in class mood

List some possible factors that might explain a change in class mood from one teacher to the next.

Commentary ■ ■ ■

This is clearly a basic, essential question – and is probably more to do with teacher attitude than with the tasks, games, methodology, etc. used. Students respond to the way you respond to them. If they find you unhelpful or not listening to them, then no amount of jolly games will put back the sparkle.

Whatever you find when you enter class, remember that part of what you see and understand is related to what you yourself bring into the room, i.e. you often find what you expect to find. Teachers who go in thinking that a group of students will be 'keen' or 'motivated' or 'dull' or 'unhelpful' may tend to find exactly what they look for. ■

Task 33: Similarities of people in a group

1 In what ways are people in a language class similar to each other?
2 How might a teacher's description of a 'homogenous group' be a simplification?

Commentary ■ ■ ■

It's tempting for a teacher (or a school) to view a class as a fairly homogenous group with a single 'level' and similar behaviour, preferences, interests and ways of working.

The individuals in a class may have a number of things in common with each other. Some may be friends with others; they may come from the same geographical district or work in the same place. The one thing that everyone has in common is that they are in a language-learning class (though of course they

may not have chosen to be there). Often these people are in the same room at the same time with strangers only because they have been placed there by the school.
■

Beyond any common features, there will be significant differences between people; it's not only age or level that differs in learners – they may also have:

Individual differences

Learners may have different …

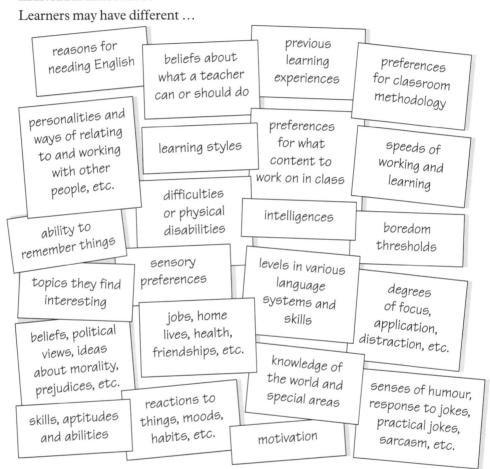

reasons for needing English

beliefs about what a teacher can or should do

previous learning experiences

preferences for classroom methodology

personalities and ways of relating to and working with other people, etc.

learning styles

preferences for what content to work on in class

speeds of working and learning

ability to remember things

difficulties or physical disabilities

intelligences

boredom thresholds

topics they find interesting

sensory preferences

levels in various language systems and skills

degrees of focus, application, distraction, etc.

beliefs, political views, ideas about morality, prejudices, etc.

jobs, home lives, health, friendships, etc.

knowledge of the world and special areas

senses of humour, response to jokes, practical jokes, sarcasm, etc.

skills, aptitudes and abilities

reactions to things, moods, habits, etc.

motivation

Motivation

Many learners have strong external reasons why they want to study (to get an exam pass, to enter university, to get promotion, to please their parents, etc). Others may be studying just for rewards within the work itself (the fun of learning, setting oneself a personal challenge, etc). In either case, the strength of their motivation will be a factor in determining how seriously they approach the work, how much time they set aside for it, how hard they push themselves, etc. You may see this reflected in things such as how often homework is done, how thoroughly new items are revised between classes, how 'tuned in' students are during lesson times. A frequent cause of difficulties within classes is when there is a significant mismatch of motivation levels amongst the course participants, e.g. some students who desperately need to pass an exam next month alongside others who want a relaxed chance to chat and play games in their new language.

Multiple intelligences

The traditional idea of humans having a single, unified 'intelligence' may be rather limiting. Howard Gardener has suggested that people could have seven 'intelligences' (maybe more!):

1 linguistic
2 visual
3 musical
4 logical/mathematical
5 bodily/feeling,
6 interpersonal (contact with other people)
7 intrapersonal (understanding oneself)

Gardener suggests that we probably all have these seven intelligences but in different proportions. So one person might be strong in musical and bodily intelligence, while another may be stronger in language and understanding other people. Traditional education systems may have tended to focus on some intelligences over others, especially on language and logical intelligences.

Sensory preferences

Writers in the field of NLP (Neuro-Linguistic Programing) have noted that humans tend to have different sensory preferences, i.e. some people respond best to hearing things (auditory), others to seeing them (visual), while others learn best when they can touch and feel tangible, physical objects (kinaesthetic). When planning classes, you may naturally bias lesson ideas towards your own sensory preferences, so it's worth remembering to ensure that, over time, there is a range of working modes appealing to visual, auditory and kinaesthetic learners.

Task 34: Working with individual differences

What implications does the list of individual differences above have for the teacher? Here are three different teachers' views. As a generalisation, do you feel more in common with György, Tibor or Edit?

György

You can't really take all these individual differences into account. The important thing is to 'teach the class'.

Tibor

I teach very little to the class as a whole – but my class has lots of individual tasks and small-group work. I think the classroom is always a set of private lessons – as many as there are individuals.

Edit

You can adapt class lessons to respond to many individual needs and differences within the group.

Commentary ■ ■ ■

There is no right answer. The section below compares the views of the three teachers. ■

Teach the class or teach the individuals?

Classes certainly seem to have their own character – one often surprisingly different from the sum total of individuals in it. Many teachers (like György) pitch their lessons at the perceived character, level, needs and likes of a generalised feeling of this group identity. They may not be concerned with any individual differences and feel their primary task is to work with the class 'as a whole', maybe using a supplied syllabus or coursebook and interpreting their job as aiming 'to cover' the required material in a certain period of time. Such teachers may be responsive to some kinds of feedback from the class as a whole, mainly tending to pick up on whether the majority of students are keeping up or not. They expect and accept that some of what is done will be unsuitable or uninteresting or impossible to follow for some members of the class, but they feel that that is 'the price to pay'. Especially with large classes, the priority seems to be to maintain the sense of progress and to hope that as many people can keep up as possible. Such an approach may be problematic, as there is a danger in 'teaching' without close reference to the individuals that are doing (or not doing) the learning.

Tibor takes the opposite position – that whole-class lessons generally won't work because of the variety of people in a class. If he can pull it off, such an 'individualised' approach would probably be a very valuable class to be a part of. Many other teachers might find that his goal of trying to respond to the range of different individuals in a room quite demanding for a teacher, requiring a greater quantity of planning beforehand and, in class, perhaps a constant moving around, with some careful listening and focused individual help.

Edit's solution is a compromise position that involves working with the class as a whole while attempting to also take individuals into account.

Teachers such as Edit may aim to teach the class by pitching the lessons to what they perceive as the majority of the group, but 'keeping in touch' with the others – by asking questions, adding extra comments and explanations, offering special tasks for some students, dividing the class to work on different things at some points, choosing topics that appeal to different groups of learners, designing tasks that appeal to different learning styles and preferences, etc.

Edit's position is one of the classic balancing acts of teaching – to maximise working at every individual's level, fulfilling as many wishes and needs as possible while also keeping the entire group engaged.

György   Edit   Tibor

| Teaching the whole class | Balancing whole-class work with attention to individual differences | Working primarily with individuals' needs – privately and in small groups |

How can we pull off this balancing act? There are no easy answers, but it probably involves a combination of gathering useful feedback from learners (see Chapter 4, Section 4) and using your intuition (see Chapter 17, Section 4).

It is hard to know how best to work with individuals if you know nothing at all about them. However, even to find out a little basic information (say even about one tenth of the items in the 'individual differences' list above) for each person in our class may seem an overwhelming, unrealistic, unachievable task. It might still take the whole school year to just do that! And even if we did know the answers for the entire list, there might seem to be no way we could effectively apply this knowledge.

However, many impossible things turn out to be all right when I try them! Despite the apparently daunting nature of the task, it's still worth a go – as even learning one new thing about a learner can dramatically affect future classes. And the more I manage to find out, the better tuned my lessons become.

If you would like to quiz your students about their differences, try using the questionnaire in Resource 9 (Appendix 2).

2 What level are my students?

Task 35: Organising students into levels

What is your school's structure of class levels?
Do you know of any other ways of organising students into classes?

Commentary ■ ■ ■

The section below describes some typical ways of organising levels. ■

Common level structues in schools

Many schools divide learners into classes at named language levels, often using coursebooks labelled for those levels. A common structure is:

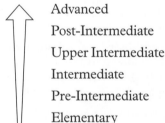

Advanced

Post-Intermediate

Upper Intermediate

Intermediate

Pre-Intermediate

Elementary

Beginner

Each of these levels may be subdivided, e.g. into Intermediate 1, Intermediate 2, etc. Schools often plan progress on an assumption that it will take the average learner a certain period of time to move from one level to the next, e.g. 45–60 hours of classroom time (plus homework) to move through a third of one of the named levels. (Just to add to the confusion, an 'hour' may mean different things in different places: for example, a 'period' of 45–50 minutes is referred to as an 'hour' in many countries.)

There are other level systems you may come across. An influential one from the Council of Europe categorises learners as follows (with approximate indications of their correlation with the earlier level scheme):

C2	Mastery	(= Nearly native-speaker level)
C1	Operational proficiency	(= Advanced)
B2	Vantage	(= Upper Intermediate/Post-Intermediate)
B1	Threshold	(= Intermediate)
A2	Waystage	(= Pre-Intermediate)
A1	Breakthrough	(= Beginner/Elementary)

Other educational institutions may structure class levels around exams that students take, naming classes after the exam they are preparing for, e.g. using the Cambridge ESOL exam suite of KET, PET, FCE, CAE, CPE, etc.

Whereas, with adults, class make-up is typically organised on the basis of their perceived language level, in children's courses classes are more often based on students' ages.

Of course, all of these concepts of level are quite broadly painted. We now need to look more closely at the idea of 'level'.

Task 36: Mixed-level classes

1 Have you ever said 'This class is very mixed level'? What are some cause of mixed-level classes?

2 Do students in your school automatically move up from level to level at the end of a period of time?

Commentary ■ ■ ■

Keep thinking about the questions while you read the following sections. ■

What is a learner's level?

It is tempting to see all learners in one class as at a certain named level, e.g. Pre-Intermediate. Yet teachers often come out of class complaining that the students seem to be very mixed in level, and they may blame teachers who designed the placement tests or the school policy of class creation. The most common reasons are:

- **Grouping by age:** In secondary schools, students are often grouped by age, and this seems very likely to lead to problems if some learners are significantly stronger or weaker than others.
- **Keeping groups together:** A typical problem in many schools is caused by the fact that it is often less troublesome for school administration to keep learners together as a class, course after course, rather than to keep separating them and mixing them up. Because learners will progress at different speeds, this means that, even if a group was similar in level at the start of a course, there may be very different 'exit levels' at the end. If that class now continues en masse to the next course level, the differences between participants will become more and more pronounced.
- **Placement testing:** Placement procedures are another cause of 'mixed-level' problems. Placement by language level sounds sensible, but even this can be

problematic, because an overall 'level' only gives a very general idea as to how good someone will be at, say, listening to a university lecture or how much vocabulary they can use. Placement testers sometimes give priority to friendship or personal requirements rather than level when creating classes.

- **Insufficient levels:** Learners may be together in the same class because the school doesn't have sufficient levels to fine-tune the classes more.

'What level is the class?'

When I hear a teacher asking about the level of a class, I am reminded of the question 'How long is the coastline of Britain?', to which the answer is 'It depends how long your ruler is'. The more closely and carefully you measure, the more complex the answer becomes.

So, concerning level, how close are you looking? If you look from a kilometre away, maybe seeing the class as a group of people when we can't make out any of the individuals, then calling a class 'Pre-Intermediate' can make sense – it's a useful general classification that gives a reasonable overall picture of what they might know and what they might be able to do. It suggests material we can use and activities we can plan, and will probably allow us to teach (and survive) at least until we have a more accurate picture to guide us.

However, as soon as we move in a bit closer, say, to stand a few metres away from them, we notice that this group of people is made up of some very different-looking individuals. If we check the overall abilities of each person, we find that some are 'weak Pre-Intermediate', some 'mid-Pre-Intermediate' and some 'strong Pre-Intermediate'. Maybe there are even some people who seem to belong to another level classification, say 'Elementary' or 'Intermediate'.

If we move in even closer and stand next to one of these people (and talk to her), we might find out even more. We might discover that this person's general 'level' masks the fact that she has a range of levels over the different language systems and skills, e.g. perhaps her knowledge of grammar is very good, her vocabulary is a little weaker and her speaking and listening are very much poorer.

We could look even closer than this, of course, and find the specific kinds of tasks that she is competent in or weak in, e.g. she can fill in an application form, but uses an inappropriate style for writing a formal letter requesting information.

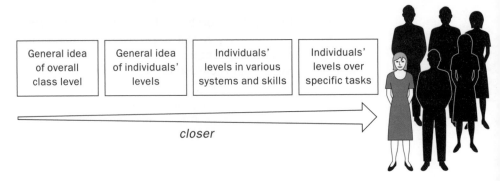

Figure 4.1   Level: how close are you standing?

Conclusions about level

What conclusions can we draw?

- Every learner has an individual range of levels.
- Every class is a mixed-level class.

When we plan lessons, we need to remember that we are planning something that may not be appropriate for some and may be easy or difficult for others, etc. Which is why the planning is only one part of structuring a lesson. In the act of teaching, we need to constantly notice and respond to feedback in order to adjust and redirect work moment by moment to make it as effective for each individual as possible.

3   Learners and their needs

Learners have distinct, individual reasons for being in a class and learning English – even when these are not consciously known or recognised. We can teach better if we know more about these.

Task 37: Ways to find out about learners' needs

What are some practical ways that we could find out useful data about learners' needs for learning a language?

Commentary ■ ■ ■

The various tools, procedures and materials used for finding out about learner needs usually come under the heading of 'Needs analysis'. Often a Needs analysis includes not only information about why learners might need language in the future, but also information about:

- where learners are starting from: their present language level, current problems, etc.;
- what learners would like to learn (which may be different from what they need);
- how they want to study it (people have very different preferences about how they learn things).

We might use formal gathering procedures (e.g. setting questionnaires, tests, etc.) or approach it more informally (e.g. gleaning information from chats and activities over a period of time).

Some key tools would be:

- writing: the learner writes comments, information, answers to questions, etc.;
- speaking: the learner speaks with you or with other students;
- observing: you observe the learner at work (in class or at the workplace).

If we expand on those general headings, we can generate ideas for creating a variety of Needs analyses (NB you're likely to want to combine a few ideas, rather than use one exclusively). ■

Needs analysis

Writing

The learners are asked to:

- fill in a questionnaire (e.g. about their work, interests, previous study, etc.);
- choose the best answer from a selection (e.g. 'I like doing written work for homework,' 'I like to do reading for homework,' 'I like to go over classwork for homework,' 'I don't like homework');
- gap-fill (or complete) sentences (e.g. 'In class, I particularly enjoy working on …');
- delete the things that are not true for you (e.g. I *never / sometimes / often* have to write in English);
- take a language test;
- tick the picture/diagrams that represent their use of English (e.g. pictures of office telephoning, greeting customers, etc.);
- write a paragraph about topics set by teacher (e.g. 'Your successes and difficulties with speaking English');
- write a letter/an e-mail/a note to your teacher (e.g. 'Your hopes for this course');
- write a homework essay about what you want to learn and why.

Speaking

You can:

- interview learners individually or in pairs;
- plan activities to focus learners on specific issues, leading to discussion;
- ask learners to select (and reject) items from a menu or a set of cards, discussing their reasons with each other;
- ask informally for advice about what would be useful to work on next lesson;
- collect oral (or written) feedback comments (e.g. about the usefulness of work you are doing) at the end of lessons;
- show the intended coursebook for the course and discuss it together with the class (e.g. 'Shall we use it?' 'How?' 'How much?' 'Pace?' etc.);
- get learners to help plan the course, the week or the next lesson;
- organise a social event at which informal discussions on needs arise;
- ask learners to describe/draw/make a model of their workplace or a diagram of their company structure, etc.

Observation

- Set the students tasks to do in class that will allow you to observe them working, speaking and using language. This will give you a chance to diagnose their language/skills problems and discover more about what they need.
- If you have a one-to-one student, it may be possible to observe him at his workplace and get a realistic idea of what he needs to do with English.
- Ask each learner to bring in samples of material they work with (or expect to work with in the future): leaflets, letters, tasks, professional magazines, etc.

NB If the learners' language level is low, many of the Needs analysis ideas could be used in their mother tongue.

Or here's a quick answer! Copy the Needs analysis cards or the questionnaires in Appendix 2 (Resources 10–12) to help you find out more about your learners.

Task 38: Using data from a Needs analysis

You've done a Needs analysis with your learners, using a few of the ideas from the list above. You're hoping that the data will be useful to you, but you are also aware that Needs analyses can be problematic.

1 Think of some reasons why the information you have obtained might be unhelpful or even untrue.
2 If the information is useful, what could you do with it now you've got it?

Commentary ■ ■ ■

Needs analyses are not always as useful as teachers hope they might be. This may be because learners (for some reason) have not taken their task seriously enough and have produced little information, or information they have not thought very carefully about, or even untrue information. This suggests that it is essential to carefully introduce a Needs-analysis task so that learners understand the importance and value of what they are doing and take an appropriate amount of time to complete it.

One useful purpose in doing a Needs analysis (even if you entirely ignore the resulting data!) is to allow learners to discover that other people in the room have different views, expectations and needs than themselves. It's natural that a student might imagine that everyone in class has approximately similar ideas to his own; to discover the breadth of different views can be an important 'light-bulb' moment, and thus a Needs analysis can be a vital awareness-raising activity, quite apart from any data that comes out of it. ■

'But, teacher – you know best'

Students may find the concept and practice of Needs analysis difficult. They may greet a Needs analysis with comments such as 'You are the teacher – you know best,' 'You decide. I trust you.' This may be because the learner genuinely doesn't know what he wants or needs, or it may be because he can't be bothered or doesn't think that it is a student's job to think about things like this.

Many students may have spent their whole educational career being told what to do all the time, constantly presented with work that has included minimal elements of choice. They may never have stopped to realise that what they learn and how they do it involves their own personal choice, and that it is their own time and energy they are investing. It may be a real surprise to be asked what they want or need, and not surprisingly they might need a clear explanation as to the purpose of it – and guidance as to how to start thinking about and conveying their ideas.

Humans don't necessarily think first and then write down their ideas. Often I don't know what I think about something until I start writing my ideas down; then I find during the process of writing that my thoughts are becoming clearer and more structured. Maybe then I have to cross out the first two paragraphs, but I needed to write them to get me to paragraph 3 (which is a cracker!). Your students may find that the same thing happens to them when they start to wonder what their needs are. The process of writing (or talking) about things helps to give some form to thoughts that maybe didn't exist in any clarity until then. (I often find myself saying something like the content of this paragraph to suspicious learners; it sometimes helps!)

You may still come across the 100% 'abdicating' student – one who gives up a right to make any decision about his own future. It's worth pointing out to such a student that he is crediting me, the teacher, with magical, wizard-like 'mind-reading' abilities. My response will probably be to state that, yes, I do know something about language and teaching, but I am not an expert on him and have no insight into the inside of his head, his past life and learning, his preferences or his future plans.

I hope – by means of explaining why it is important – to encourage this learner to realise that 'learning' is not another product that one buys ready-made off the shelf, but is something that has to be adjusted and remade every time. It is a 'living' thing, not a piece of dead meat. I don't always manage to persuade every learner, but it's worth trying! Curiously, the hard-line abdicator is often the very same student who complains at the end of courses, saying how unsuitable and useless the course was, and how the teacher knows nothing about what students need.

Other problems with Needs analyses

Other problems with Needs analyses may arise when the learners have not themselves chosen to do the course (e.g. because the students have to attend secondary school or because a course has been chosen and paid for by an employee's company). Of course, in these circumstances, a Needs analysis may serve an additional purpose: encouraging the course participants to start taking ownership of their course, making choices about what they want or need (rather than assuming that everything has already been decided and is cut and dried). When people feel they have some power or responsibility over what happens to them, it can really change their attitude to it.

Of course, with any Needs analysis, there might be a danger that, in asking people what they want or hope for, you might lead them to expect that everything they ask for will happen. Having said that, I guess it's much better to find out rather than to pretend that the differences don't exist.

What can you do with the data?

Anyway, let's assume the information you get is true and useful. There are still potential problems. What can you do with it? Maybe you consider the learners' wishes are inappropriate or not realistic or not possible, or that the range of needs stated are too wide-ranging within the group. What are the options for making use of this data?

Task 39: Balancing course plans and needs

Imagine a situation where you're a class teacher and you've already devised (or been presented with) a course plan before the course starts. How could you let the data obtained from a Needs analysis influence or change that plan?

Commentary ■ ■ ■

This largely depends on your own attitude as a teacher: how much do you want the course plan to be changed? There are a range of possibilities, some of which are listed below in an approximate order from 'taking least account of the data' to 'taking most account'.

Least ↓ Most	
Least	Take no account of the Needs analysis data. Continue with the course as if the data hadn't been collected.
	Review the data, but decide that your original course plan is likely to achieve something very close to the desired outcomes, so continue using the original plan.
	Continue with the course as before, but allow the data to influence small aspects of how you help or deal with individuals in class.
	Continue with the course as before but add in a limited number of extra activities, lessons or variations to satisfy some stated needs or for certain individuals to do for homework (or in class).
	Replan the course, much as before, but aiming to cover the material in faster time (or drop elements) in order to add in a larger number of extra activities or lessons to satisfy some stated needs.
	Replan the course to incorporate substantial elements of the needs alongside relevant elements from the original plan.
Most	Put the original course plan to one side and base a new course plan entirely on the stated needs.

Of course, your original Needs analysis may itself have incorporated an element in which learners themselves helped replan the course, in which case, your best option is probably to try using that!

The options towards the top of the list will probably seem to be (initially, at least) less 'troublesome' to you. In many cases, you will consider it simpler and more straightforward to teach directly from a 'ready-made' course plan or a coursebook with only minimal (or no) reference to learner needs. And it is quite possible that a satisfactory course will ensue, achieving the intended aims for a number of learners.

But, although there is this chance of success, this type of course is also likely to produce learner feedback at the end along the lines of 'It was OK, but it wasn't really what I wanted'. You will only be able to offer learners what they really want or need if you find out what this is (even if they don't think they know what that is themselves) and by doing coursework that directly addresses this.

That's not to say that addressing needs won't be tricky – it may mean seeking out new materials, varying cherished routines and activities, finding ways to satisfy apparently conflicting wishes of different people, etc. – but, in the long run, learners will probably notice and appreciate the way that the course is addressing what they need, rather than simply offering up some 'off-the-peg' solution. ■

4   Getting feedback from learners

Teaching is primarily an act of alert 'tuning in'. By that, I mean that the more you are able to understand the group, the more successful the lesson is likely to be.

The classroom you create

Many teachers operate their lessons as if the class were a machine into which raw materials can be fed and which, when used with certain techniques, will produce predictable outputs. This can lead to classes that move forward through a coursebook or syllabus, but may not lead to much learning that is significant or useful for many of the individuals in the class. It is at this level that many teachers operate on a day-by-day basis. Materials and techniques on their own are sufficient to run a course in a superficially successful way, but although authorities may be satisfied at recordable data (pages turned, books finished, syllabus covered, exams passed, etc.), the learning that has been achieved may be largely illusory. It is all too easy to spend one's entire teaching carreer in this kind of teaching and never to risk the breakthrough through the invisible ceiling into another kind of class, where you approach the class as a living being rather than as a machine. It is this second kind of class that this book encourages you towards.

In observing lessons, it often seems to me that the least successful teachers are those who:

- work 'at right angles' to the class (i.e. they do not notice and take into account the needs and wishes of the learners, but work to their own priorities and in their own choice of ways);
- create a physical and psychological distance between learners and teacher;
- do not pick up (sometimes subtle) signals from learners about what they think, what they want;
- do not elicit feedback about opinions on course, content, methods, working styles, etc.;
- do not deviate from their own plan/agenda;
- keep up their own 'radio babble' (i.e. a constant stream of space-filling, though often low-quality, talk) to block out the incoming signals from the class;
- find time-filling activities (such as writing at length on the board) to save them from having to communicate more with learners.

Ineffective, unhelpful teaching is teaching that proceeds forward (perhaps according to a plan, according to what you wanted to do, according to what the book says, according to a syllabus, according to whatever) without reference to what impact this is having on the learners in class.

The essential engine of a richer, more productive learning environment is communication, two-way feedback from learners to teachers and vice versa.

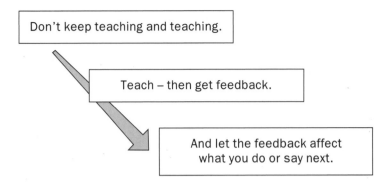

Don't keep teaching and teaching.

Teach – then get feedback.

And let the feedback affect
what you do or say next.

Why is it hard to tune in?

When you start teaching, it's hard to think very much about anyone other than
yourself. If you're anything like I was, you might have a tape recorder of worries
echoing in your head, even more so if you are being observed. When I watch new
trainee teachers in the classroom, I often notice how they have so many concerns
about their own actions and words as a teacher that they find it very hard to tune
in to the other people in the room.

These are a few of the worries you may feel:

- I hope I don't say anything silly.
- What on earth can I do next?
- Do they like me?
- That activity only lasted three minutes, and I thought it'd last 45.
- This is lasting forever, and I thought it would take three minutes.
- I feel so confused.
- I don't really understand this thing I'm teaching.
- Is the observer going to catch me out? What's she writing?
- This is so boring.

Finding a way to turn off this internal noise and start listening to the genuine
voice of feedback from outside is often a difficult, slowly acquired but important
teaching skill. In gaining feedback information from learners, we learn to adjust
and fine-tune our intuitive responses.

Avoiding feedback

Many teachers never ask for feedback from learners. Some teachers ask for
feedback occasionally, often in a way that elicits what they want to hear. Some
teachers get feedback that they allow to affect and alter what they are doing.

Teachers may avoid feedback because they fear hearing comments about their
work. The more they avoid it, the more dangerous it becomes, because ungiven
feedback piles up like floodwater behind a dam. When they do request feedback,
it can be mostly 'token', to feel as if they have 'done some feedback' and found
out what they wanted to hear.

Of course, there may be many reasons why learners don't give useful, honest feedback.

Feedback is probably only really useful when the channels are open all the time, which suggests a different way of working from many traditional teaching situations – and a different relationship. Can you imagine a course in which the students genuinely direct or influence or affect the programme on a consistent basis and with positive outcomes? How could this come about?

Getting useful feedback – some starting points

- Don't think of feedback as a once-a-term thing or just as a formal requirement from your school. Visualise it as moment-by-moment need to find out whether you and the class are on track.
- Clearly, you can overdo it – you don't want the class to groan at being asked 'How useful was that activity?' again and again – but don't let this worry prevent you from even starting to explore their reactions and responses.
- Whether you go for oral or written feedback, vary it. Don't turn it into a ritual.
- Some common feedback opportunities: feedback at the start of a lesson, at the end of a lesson, at the end of a week, at the start of a new coursebook unit, at the end of a unit, before the class does an activity, after an activity, as the core topic of an activity, written at home.
- Ask small questions (e.g. 'Which activity today was most difficult for you?') as well as big ones (e.g. 'How useful is the course for you?'). They are easier to answer.
- Ask simple, factual questions as well as evaluative questions, e.g. 'How many words today were new for you?' as well as 'Which activity did you enjoy most?'
- Design a simple feedback form. Photocopy and hand it out it (or dictate it to students). You could allow them class time to discuss the questions before they write, or ask them to fill it out at home.
- Ask students to write you a letter about the course. Specify exactly what you'd like them to discuss, or leave it open for students to raise any issues that they want to.
- Set aside some time, ask open questions that enable them to say what they want to say, and gear yourself simply to listen and learn (rather than to defend yourself, argue or contradict). Ask them what they really think. If your intention is only to hear 'nice things', then that is probably all you will get.

Doing feedback of any sort may be difficult for you the first time, but the end result of increased honesty, openness and mutual respect will almost certainly have a great long-term benefit, the more so if you implement changes in yourself, the class or the course that are responses to the feedback.

5 Learner training

For me, learner training means 'Raise student awareness about how they are learning and, as a result, help them to find more effective ways of working, so that they can continue working efficiently and usefully, even when away from their teacher and the classroom'. More simply, it means 'Work on teaching learning as well as teaching English'.

Learner training, therefore, includes:

- work on study skills, e.g. use of dictionaries, reference material, workbooks, notebooks, filed material;
- student examination of the process of learning and reflection on what is happening, e.g. of teaching strategies you use (and the reasons why you use them).

In both cases, it seems important to include these as strands throughout a course.

Three ideas

1 Integrate study-skills work

Include study-skills work as an integrated feature of your lessons, e.g. when working on vocabulary, include a short exercise that involves efficiently looking up information in a dictionary. Similarly, when the students have found some new words to learn, you could make them aware of the variety of ways of recording vocabulary in their notebooks. (See Chapter 11, Section 6.)

2 Let them into the secret

Teachers sometimes prefer the 'surprise' approach to teaching methodology; often students don't really know why they followed a particular procedure or did a particular activity. Teachers often assume that their own reasoning will be transparently obvious to their students, but it rarely is. So it can be very useful to tell students before a lesson what's going to happen and why. At the end of the lesson, you can review not only the content, but also the way that it was studied. For example, after a listening skills lesson, talk through the procedure with the students: 'Why did I set a task first? Was it necessary to understand every word? What did we do next? What helped you learn? What didn't help?'

In this way, they will also be learning a methodology that they can repeat for their own use when they listen to a cassette at home or in a language laboratory.

3 Discuss process as well as content and procedure

The content of your lessons is the English language. The 'procedures' are your methodology (which, as I suggested above, is worth talking about with students). The third area is 'process'. By this, I mean the lesson as viewed from the learner's point of view. You're doing certain things as a teacher, but what is going on for each individual student?

It can be very valuable to set aside time in class simply to discuss the subject of 'learning on this course' in order to recall what's happening and reflect on it. This 'process review' will allow you and the learners to clarify what is happening. Simply talking about what is going on seems to have a very beneficial effect, quite apart from any new ideas or solutions that arise from it.

Chapter 5 Toolkit 1: classroom management

1 What is classroom management?

Your most important job is perhaps to 'create the conditions in which learning can take place'. The skills of creating and managing a successful class may be the key to the whole success of a course. An important part of this is to do with your attitude, intentions and personality and your relationships with the learners. However, you also need certain organisational skills and techniques. Such items are often grouped together under the heading of 'classroom management'. Common classroom management areas include:

Grouping and seating
- Forming groupings (singles, pairs, groups, mingle, plenary)
- Arranging and rearranging seating
- Deciding where you will stand or sit
- Reforming class as a whole group after activities

Activities
- Sequencing activities
- Setting up activities
- Giving instructions
- Monitoring activities
- Timing activities (and the lesson as a whole)
- Bringing activities to an end

Authority
- Gathering and holding attention
- Deciding who does what (i.e. answer a question, make a decision, etc.)
- Establishing or relinquishing authority as appropriate
- Getting someone to do something

Critical moments
- Starting the lesson
- Dealing with unexpected problems
- Maintaining appropriate discipline
- Finishing the lesson

Tools and techniques
- Using the board and other classroom equipment or aids
- Using gestures to help clarity of instructions and explanations
- Speaking clearly at an appropriate volume and speed
- Use of silence
- Grading complexity of language
- Grading quantity of language

Working with people

- Spreading your attention evenly and appropriately
- Using intuition to gauge what students are feeling
- Eliciting honest feedback from students
- Really listening to students

Classroom management involves both **decisions** and **actions**. The actions are what is done in the classroom, e.g. rearranging the chairs. The decisions are about whether to do these actions, when to do them, how to do them, who will do them, etc.

At any classroom moment, there will be a range of options as to possible actions. To say one thing or to say something different. To stop an activity or to let it continue for a few more minutes. To take three minutes to deal with a difficult question or to move on with what you had previously planned. To tell off a latecomer or to welcome him. To do something or to do nothing. These options continue throughout the lesson; at every step, your decision will take you forward on your particular route. No one can tell you the 'right' way to do something. There is no single correct answer, no single route through a lesson, though some routes may in the end prove to be much more effective than others. Different people or different situations create different solutions. Your total lesson is created by your choices.

The essential basic skill for classroom management is therefore to be able to look at and read classroom events as they occur and think of possible options available to you, to make appropriate decisions between these options, and to turn them into effective and efficient actions. As you grow in experience, your awareness of possible options will grow.

Thus the basic skills of classroom management can be summarised as follows:

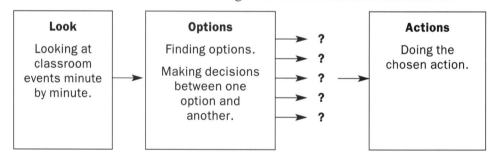

Task 40: Choosing classroom management options

Write two or more options for each of the following situations:

1 A student says 'I don't want to do this exercise'.
2 You expected an activity to take five minutes. It has taken twenty so far, and the students still seem to be very involved. There is something else you would like to do before the lesson ends in ten minutes.
3 The next activity involves students working in groups of five. At the moment, all the desks (which take two people) are facing forward in rows. They are movable, but it takes a few minutes of chaos to do it.

4 The students are working in groups of three. Two groups have finished the task you set them and are now sitting looking bored. The other groups still seem to have a long way to go before they finish.

Commentary ■ ■ ■

Here are a few possible options:

1 You could say 'Fine.'
You could say loudly 'Do it!'
You could ask why the student doesn't want to do it.
You could offer an alternative exercise or activity.
You could say 'Choose something you'd like to do.'
You could explain the point of the exercise.
You could ask other students for their opinion.

Note that in all the above options, you also have further options regarding your attitude and behaviour: you could be patient or impatient, defensive or open, sound as if you mean it or sound as if you don't, etc.

2 You could stop the activity.
You could let it continue (postponing the next activity).
You could announce a time for finishing (e.g. 'Two more minutes').
You could ask the students how much longer they need.
You could offer the students the option of stopping and doing something else.

3 All the students could move the desks.
A small number of students could move the desks while you give instructions to the others.
You could do the activity without moving the desks.
You could ask the students whether it is a good idea to move the desks.

4 You could tell the groups which have finished that they can chat or do something else while the other groups finish.
You could give the groups which have finished a short extra task to keep them busy until the rest finish.
You could set a time limit (say two minutes) for the others to finish.
You could bring the groups which have finished together to compare their answers with each other.
You could invite the finishers to join other groups and help them or listen to them. ■

Increasing your options

Some options come at key moments – the beginning of the lesson, the start of an activity, the end of an activity, when a discipline problem occurs in the lesson, etc. – and your decision at such critical moments has a greater knock-on effect. After a lesson, it may be useful to recall what happened and reflect on (or talk through with a colleague) why certain critical options were taken and to hypothesise about what the outcomes might have been if other things had been done.

Becoming a more effective teacher is partly a matter of increasing your awareness of what options are available. It is also about the skilful selection of the most appropriate option at each point and the ability to efficiently, effectively turn these into actions. Reading books like this, talking to other teachers, observing other teachers at work, getting feedback from observers of your lesson – these are all ways of increasing your range of options and your skill at deciding and acting on decisions appropriately.

Task 41: Selecting alternative options

Read this description of a classroom situation and consider any alternative options available to you at points (a) and (b).

You come into the classroom at the start of the lesson. There are 25 teenage students in the room. About half of them seem very involved in a loud discussion (in their own language, not English) about a current political situation. (a) You shout out 'OK, OK, let's start the lesson; you can continue that later.' The room quietens down a bit; some people continue whispering animatedly to each other. 'Now, today we are going to look at ways of talking about the future,' you continue. One student asks, 'But this subject is very interesting. Could we continue the conversation if we use English?' (b) You say, 'I'm sorry, but we have to get through Unit 9 of the book today. Perhaps we can have a discussion next week. Open your books at page 47.'

Commentary ■ ■ ■

The following are a few of the many possible options for (a):

- You sit down and wait for the class to conclude the discussion in its own time, waiting until they indicate that they are ready for you to start.
- You join in the conversation, but using English.
- You join in the conversation using English and subtly manipulate the discussion so that the students are involved in using the language items you were planning to work on in the first place.
- You stand in front of the class in a way that indicates that you want their attention (making eye contact with as many people as possible, looking authoritative, etc.) and wait for silence. Having established silence, you put to the class the decision about what to do: 'We can either continue the discussion or do what I have planned to do. Which would you prefer?'

Here are some options for (b):

- You say 'OK'.
- As in the fourth option above, you ask the class to make the decision about what to do.
- You explain your aim for the lesson and then offer the possibility of continuing the discussion after some other work. You suggest allowing ten minutes at the end of the lesson and ask the students for their opinion. ■

How can you decide what's best to do?

What influences and informs your decisions between different options? The following are some factors to bear in mind:

- What is the aim of this activity?
- What is the aim of the whole lesson?
- Is what learners are doing useful?

- What is hindering the effectiveness of what we are doing?
- What have I planned to do?
- What would be the best thing to do now?
- Is it time for a change of mood or pace?
- Are we using time efficiently?
- How do the students feel?
- How do I feel?
- What are the possible outcomes of my doing something?

I could add two further factors that are frequently involved in teacher decisions and actions:

- I don't know any other options;
- I know some other options, but I'm avoiding them because they are difficult or troublesome or nerve-wracking.

Classroom decisions and actions are also greatly determined by your own attitudes, intentions, beliefs and values. What do you believe about learning? What is important for you in learning? What is your genuine feeling towards your students? For example, you may ask a student to write on the board (rather than doing it himself). This decision may have grown from your intention to involve students more in the routine duties of the class. This may itself have grown from your belief that trusting your students more and sharing some responsibility with them is a useful way of increasing their involvement in the learning process.

Task 42: Teacher beliefs and attitudes

What teacher beliefs or attitudes might underlie the following classroom actions?

1 The teacher includes a lot of student-to-student communication activities in her lessons.
2 The teacher uses recordings of authentic, natural conversations.
3 In every lesson, the teacher includes at least one activity that involves students moving around the classroom.

Commentary ■ ■ ■

She might believe that ...

1 it is useful to give students opportunities to speak to one another;
 people learn by trying to do things themselves;
 activities like this promote more fluent use of English;
 the students will get to know one another better;
 it will give more students time to speak than if the whole class did something together;
 it gives them a chance to listen to someone other than the teacher.
2 listening work is important;
 students need practice in listening to real, conversational English;
 they need to hear a variety of voices and accents.
3 a lesson needs changes of pace and mood;
 a game is a good way of adding variety to a lesson;
 sitting still in one place for a long time can be difficult;
 getting people to do physical things can be a good way of waking up their mental powers. ■

2 Classroom interaction

In Chapter 3, Section 1, I listed some common types of student grouping in the classroom:

- whole class working together with you;
- whole class moving around and mixing together as individuals (a 'mingle');
- small groups (three to eight people);
- pairs;
- individual work.

In any one lesson, you may include work that involves a number of these different arrangements. Varying groupings is one way of enabling a variety of experiences for the learners.

In this section, we examine the rationale for making use of pairs and small groups as well as whole-class work. There are some suggestions and guidelines for maximising useful interaction in class.

Task 43: Classroom interaction

In the list of statements below about classroom interaction, tick any that you feel you can agree with.

1 a It is more important for learners to listen and speak to you than for learners to listen and speak to each other.
   b Students should get most conversation practice in interacting with other learners rather than with you.

2 a People usually learn best by listening to people explaining things.
   b People usually learn best by trying things out and finding out what works.

3 a The teacher should speak as much as possible in classroom time.
   b The teacher should speak as little as possible in classroom time.

Commentary ■ ■ ■

The following section addresses these questions. ■

Teacher talk and student talk

The language classroom is rich in language for learners, quite apart from the language that learners and teacher may suppose they are focusing on in the subject matter of the lesson. Students learn a lot of their language from what they hear you say: the instructions, the discussions, the asides, the jokes, the chit-chat, the comments, etc. Having said that, it would be unsatisfactory if your talk dominated the lesson to the exclusion of participation from as many learners as possible.

The arguments for statement 1a usually grow from the idea that you know more of the target language and that by listening to you, the learner is somehow absorbing a correct picture of the language; that by interacting with you, the learner is learning to interact with a competent user of the language; that this is far more useful than talking to a poor user. Thus, by this argument, time spent talking to another learner is not particularly useful time. This is OK as far as it goes, but there are a number of challenges to the statements. Some are to do with available time: if you talk most of the time, how much time will learners get to speak? If the only conversation practice learners get is one-to-one with you, they will get very little time to speak at all. In a class of 25 learners, how much time will you have available to speak to individuals? Divide a one-hour lesson by 25 and you get just over two minutes each. That doesn't sound very much.

Statement 1b suggests that we could maximise learner speaking time at certain points of the lesson by putting them into pairs or small groups and getting them to talk to each other. Thus, instead of two minutes' speaking time in a whole lesson, they all get a lot of speaking practice within a short space of time. You could use this time effectively by discreetly monitoring what the students are saying and using the information collected as a source of material for future feedback or other work. (I am, of course, making other assumptions; I'm assuming that it is important to give learners opportunities to have useful interaction with others.)

Statements 2a and 2b are about different ways of learning. I believe, from my own learning experiences and from observing teachers at work, that the most efficient way of learning is for a student to be really involved in a lesson. Explanations, especially long ones, tend to leave me cold; I get bored; I switch off. (A learner might also have real problems in following what is being said.) But challenge me, give me a problem to do or a task I want to complete, and I will learn far more – by experimenting, by practising, by taking risks.

I think you can guess my views on statements 3a and 3b by now. (Neither the extremes of a nor b, but closer to b than a.) Observers who watch new teachers at work often comment that they talk too much. An essential lesson that every new teacher needs to learn is that 'talking at' the learners does not necessarily mean that learning is taking place; in many cases, TTT (Teacher Talking Time) is actually time when the learners are not doing very much and are not very involved. Working on ways to become aware of unnecessary TTT is something to add to your list of priorities (see Observation Task 4 in Appendix 1).

Task 44: Increasing student–student interaction

When working in a whole-class stage, a large amount of interaction tends to go from teacher to student and student to teacher, as shown in Figure 5.1. How could you get more student–student interaction?

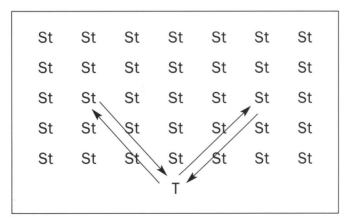

Figure 5.1   Interaction between teacher and students

Commentary ■ ■ ■

Maximising student interaction in class: some ideas

- Encourage a friendly, relaxed learning environment. If there is a trusting, positive, supportive rapport amongst the learners and between learners and you, then there is a much better chance of useful interaction happening.
- Ask questions rather than giving explanations.
- Allow time for students to listen, think, process their answer and speak.
- Really listen to what they say. Let what they say really affect what you do next. Work on listening to the person and the meaning, as well as to the language and the mistakes.
- Allow thinking time without talking over it. Allow silence.
- Increase opportunities for STT (Student Talking Time).
- Use gestures to replace unnecessary teacher talk.
- Allow students to finish their own sentences.
- Make use of pairs and small groups to maximise opportunities for students to speak. Do this even in the middle of longer whole-class stages, e.g. ask students to break off for 30 seconds and talk in pairs about their reactions to what you've just been discussing.
- If possible, arrange seating so that students can all see each other and talk to each other (i.e. circles, squares and horseshoes rather than parallel rows). (See Section 3 on seating.)
- Remember that you don't always need to be at the front of the class. Try out seating arrangements that allow the whole class to be the focus (e.g. you take one seat in a circle).
- If a student is speaking too quietly for you to hear, walk further away, rather than closer to them! (This sounds illogical, but if you can't hear them, then it's likely that the other students can't either. Encourage the quiet speaker to speak louder so that the others can hear.)
- Encourage interaction between students rather than only between student and you, and you and student. Get students to ask questions, give explanations, etc. to each other, rather than always to you. Use gestures and facial expressions to encourage them to speak and listen to each other.
- Keep a diagram like the one in Figure 5.2 in your head as a possible alternative to the one in Figure 5.1. Think 'How can I get students speaking and listening to each other as well as to me?' ■

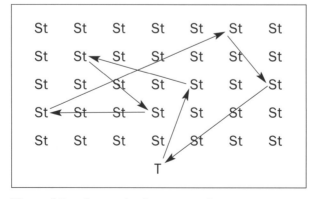

Figure 5.2   Interaction between students

Task 45: Your skills in enabling interaction

Carry out a self-assessment, comparing yourself against some of the guidelines on these pages. What skills do you have in enabling effective classroom interaction? What do you intend to work on?

3   Seating

However your classroom is laid out and whatever kind of fixed or moveable seating you have, it is worth taking time to consider the best ways to make use of it.

- What different seating positions are possible without moving anything?
- Are any rearrangements of seats possible?
- Which areas of the room are suitable for learners to stand and interact in?
- Is there any possibility that the room could be completely rearranged on a semi-permanent basis to make a better language classroom space?

Important considerations are:

- Can learners comfortably work in pairs with a range of different partners?
- Can learners comfortably work in small groups with a range of other learners?

For each activity you do in class, consider what grouping, seating, standing arrangements are most appropriate. Changing seating arrangements can help students interact with different people, change the focus from you when appropriate and allow a range of different situations to be recreated within the classroom, as well as simply adding variety to the predictability of sitting in the same place every time. It's difficult to sit still for a long time; it's worth including activities that involve some movement, even if only to give people the chance to stretch their legs. Students might not like it if there is a constant movement every five minutes, but some variety of working arrangements is often helpful.

In some cultures, students may have clear expectations as to what is acceptable. For example, asking students to sit on their desks may be taboo; a teacher who sits on the corner of his desk may be considered unprofessional. Respect cultural constraints, but don't let them put you off experimenting a little. Be clear about what is genuinely unacceptable and what is merely unknown or unexpected.

Remain aware of the possibilities of using the space you are in; sometimes a complete change in the room can make all the difference. Even with the most immovable of fixed seating, it is often possible to be creative in some way.

Fixed, semi-fixed and large seating

You could ask students to:

- turn around and sit backwards, working with the people behind them;
- sit on the ends of their row and work with people in the next row;
- sit on their desks and talk with people nearby;
- stand up, move around and return to a different seat;
- stand in the aisle space between rows;
- all come to the front (or another open space) to talk.

In the long term, if you have exclusive use of a classroom, or share it with other language teachers, it's worth considering whether a longer-term rearrangement might be useful.

Figure 5.3 shows a school I worked in that had large, one-piece seats/desks for three people fixed in every classroom. They were always used in rows because, although only lightly fixed, there seemed to be no other way to arrange them.

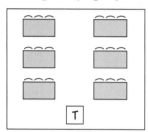

Figure 5.3   Original seating plan

However, when we started thinking about it, we found a number of other arrangements were possible (see Figure 5.4). The horseshoe arrangement, particularly, proved very suitable for the English classes.

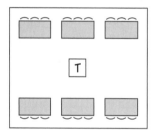 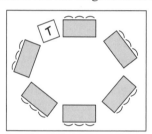 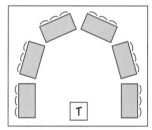

Figure 5.4   Alternative seating arrangements

Task 46: Standing and sitting

1 Why might a circle or horseshoe shape be more effective for language teaching than straight rows?
2 What difference does it make if you sit in a circle with the students rather than standing in front of them?

Commentary ■ ■ ■

1 In a circle or horseshoe, learners can make eye contact with everyone else in the group and thus interact much more naturally. There is also a much greater sense of equality. Weaker students tend to hide away less and stronger students to dominate less.
2 Having you in the circle helps to clarify your role as an equal rather than as someone separate and different. ■

Moveable seating

Some ideas for investigating and exploring the possibilities of moveable seating:

• Ask students to move seats when you create pairs or small groups. Don't let students get stuck in unsuitable seating arrangements when a move is preferable.

- If it's really too noisy, make the discussion of that (and the finding of a solution) part of the lesson as well.
- Figure 5.5 shows some patterns to think about.
- If the students normally sit in rows try forming a circle.
- Turn the classroom around so that the focus is on a different wall from normal.
- Make seating arrangements that reflect specific contexts, e.g. a train carriage, an aeroplane, a town centre or whatever.
- Push all seats up against the wall and make a large, open forum space in the middle of the room.
- Deliberately place your seat off-centre (i.e. not at the front). This is an interesting subversion of expectations and immediately challenges expectations about who a teacher is and what a teacher should do.
- Divide the class into separate groups at far corners of the room.
- Ask 'How can we reorganise this classroom to make it a nicer place to be?' Let the class discuss it, and agree then do it.
- Push the seats or desks up against the wall. Sit on the floor (only if it's a clean classroom!)

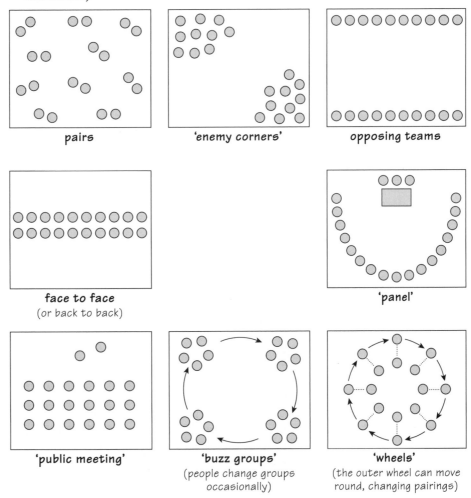

Figure 5.5 Seating possibilities in a standard classroom

Task 47: Seating options in the classroom

What ideas for arranging seating have you not tried? Which would be worth trying? Draw a simple sketch of your classroom. Mark in seats for one new arrangement. When might you use such an arrangement? How can you organise it in class? What might be the benefits? The problems?

4   Giving instructions

I have met a number of teachers who say that they would like to give instructions for activities in English (rather than their students' own language), but find that there are often so many problems with comprehension that it seems impossible. I think it is possible to use only English (and it's often really helpful in creating an 'English' atmosphere in the classroom), but it's often problematic because of the quantity and over-complexity of language used.

Task 48: Complex instructions

Why did the class have problems with the following instruction?

'OK, everybody, would you, Maria, sit down. Now what you have to do is, when you, you take this sheet of paper that I'm handing out now and keep it secret, and some of you are 'A', it's written at the top, and some are labelled 'B'. OK, can you see that? Don't show your paper to anyone and then you have to describe to your partner; sit face to face. Could you move your chairs around and describe what's on your paper so that your partner can find out what's different, and you must agree; when you find something, draw it on your paper? OK. Do you understand?'

Commentary ■ ■ ■

This may sound like a joke, but in fact it's quite typical of an unplanned instruction. Teachers are often unaware that they are talking in this way until they stop and try to listen to what they are saying. A video (or audio) recording of them in action can be very helpful here.

It is clear that this type of instruction is very hard for students to follow. The essential information about what to do is embedded in confusing and unnecessary babble. An essentially simple activity can become impossible, not because the students couldn't do it, but because they didn't understand what to do. Often students are judged to have failed when it is actually the teacher who failed to clarify what was required. ■

How can I give clearer instructions?

I propose five steps towards better instructions:

1 Become aware of your own instruction-giving (listen to yourself; record yourself; ask others to watch you and give feedback).
2 For a while, preplan essential instructions. Analyse the instructions beforehand so as to include only the essential information in simple, clear language, and sequence it in a sensible order. Use short sentences – one sentence for each key piece of information. Don't say things that are visible or obvious (e.g. 'I'm giving you a piece of paper'). Don't give instructions that they don't need to know at this point (e.g. what they'll do after this activity is finished).

3 In class, separate instructions clearly from the other chit-chat, telling off, joking, etc. that goes on. Create a silence beforehand, make eye contact with as many students as possible, find an authoritative tone, make sure they are listening before you start. Use silence and gestures to pace the instructions and clarify their meaning.

4 Demonstrate rather than explain wherever possible.

5 Check that students have understood what to do. Don't assume that everyone will automatically understand what you have said. Get concrete evidence from the students that they know what is required. Getting one or two students to tell you what they are going to do is one very simple way of achieving this.

Task 49: Planning simpler instructions

Look back at the example instruction given in Task 48.

1 Identify the essential instructions the teacher wanted to give.
2 Delete unnecessary language.
3 Write out the instructions in the right order.

Commentary, ■ ■ ■

Here is a preplanned version of the instruction in Task 48.

- Say 'Sit opposite your partner'.
- Wait while they move.
- 'Some of you are "A"' (gesture to letter A on the handouts).
- 'Some are "B"' (gesture).
- 'Don't show your paper to anyone' (mime hiding).
- Distribute the handout.
- 'Some things in picture A are different from picture B.'
- 'Describe your picture.'
- 'When you find something different draw it.' (mime)
- Check understanding of instruction: 'What are you going to do?' Students answer with brief explanation.

Here is another version of the same instruction. This time, it involves demonstration rather than instruction:

- Ask one student to come out in front of the class and sit opposite you.
- Give the handout to the student and take one yourself, making a big show of keeping the handouts secret from each other.
- Pretend to be student A and do one complete example with student B so that the whole class can hear (e.g. A: 'Have you got a tree in your picture?' B: 'Yes.' A: 'Is there a bird on top of the tree?' B: 'No.' A: 'Oh, so that's one difference in my picture: there is a bird on the tree.')
- Distribute handouts to the class: 'Now you do the same. A and B. Find ten differences.' ■

Task 50: Improving instructions

Simplify the following instructions using less confusing language or a gesture.

1 Now, actually, I would really like you, if you could, now stand up, yes everyone, please.

2 It's the unit on, er, travel, somewhere – it's near the middle, pages 35 and 36, can you find that? Have you got it? No, not that one, the next unit, and take a look at the introduction, read it through quickly and jot down your answers to the questions at the top of the page over there, above the illustration.

3 If I were to ask you for your opinion on smoking, what do you think you might say to me in your reply?

4 Would you like to tell everyone the answer you were thinking of again because I don't think they heard it when you spoke so quietly, and I'm sure we'd all be interested in hearing it if you could, please?

5 Well, that wasn't really what I was hoping you'd say when I asked that question. I was actually looking for the name of the verb tense not an example sentence, but what you gave me was fine, only does anyone I wonder have the answer I'm looking for?

Commentary ■ ■ ■

1 Gesture (or 'Stand up').
2 'Page 35.' (Wait quietly till they have found page.)
   'Read these questions.' (Show questions.)
   'Read this.' (Show text.)
   'Write your answers.'
3 'What do you think about smoking?'
4 'Louder.'
5 'What's the name of the tense?' ■

How to get the learners' attention

One important reason why learners may not successfully follow activity instructions (or understand your explanations of something) is that they didn't actually hear them, perhaps because they weren't fully paying attention when they were given. Whereas teachers often invest energy into finding better ways to word their instructions, they may overlook the need to win attention before the instruction is given. It's a vital step. An instruction given over student chatter, or when students are looking the other way, stands little chance of working.

If this has been a problem for you, here is one strategy for getting learners' attention that you might wish to experiment with.

Getting attention before giving an instruction, giving an explanation, etc.

• Start making eye contact with as many people as possible.
• Establish a gesture that means you want to speak (e.g. cupped hand to your ear or holding your hand up).
• Just wait.
• Don't look impatient or anxious. Keep moving your eyes around the room from person to person, patiently.
• Think of this as 'gathering attention'. Enjoy it.
• Wait as long as necessary until there is silence and people are looking your way.
• If this doesn't work, don't alter it dramatically. Just add in a clear attention-drawing word such as 'OK'. Say it once and then go back to the waiting.

In general, you need to establish your authority and use it appropriately. Project your voice clearly, but speak rather than shout. Control the quantity and complexity of what you say. Say what you need to as simply and clearly as possible.

5   Participate, monitor or vanish?

Task 51: Your role in pair and group activities

What is your role once you have set up an activity in which students will mainly work on their own in pairs or groups?

- Sit down and read a book?
- Go out of the room and have a coffee?
- Wander round and look at what students are doing?
- Sit down and work with separate groups one by one, joining in the tasks as a participant?
- Listen carefully to as many students as possible, going over and correcting mistake when you catch them, offering ideas when students get stuck, etc.?

Commentary ■ ■ ■

Well, I think all of these answers are possible, even the first two (which you may have dismissed as unlikely). It all depends, of course, on the nature of the specific activity and on its aims. The next section suggests a general strategy for making decisions about what to do. ■

Deciding on your role while students do an activity

Let's distinguish two steps.

Step 1: The first 30 seconds: are they doing the task set?

Immediately after you have given the instructions for a task and students start doing it, there is often an immediate need to check to make sure that students are doing the activity that you asked them to do and have understood the basic instructions and the mechanics of the activity.

You could do this by quietly and relatively inconspicuously wandering around the room, listening in briefly to snatches from many groups and assuring yourself that students are doing what they are supposed to. We could call this monitoring to check the mechanics.

Step 2: The task itself

In many activities, the prime aim is for learners to get a chance to work on their own, speaking fluently and trying out things without too much interference and correction. If they are doing the task correctly, then possibly they don't need you any more once the task is under way. Your presence might actually be an interference. If you are around and very visible, they might look to you for language items and help whenever they hit a problem, whereas it might be more useful for them to struggle a little and learn to make use of their own resources. So once an activity is safely under way, your options often boil down to the following choices: **monitor discreetly** or **vanish**.

In some tasks – especially those in which students might not move forward quickly, but need ongoing advice, support, input and encouragement – you may find that some kind of more active role is called for. In these cases, your best options are probably **monitor actively** or **participate**.

A Monitor discreetly

Discreet monitoring is when you maintain a presence in the room, but do not overtly offer help, interfere, correct, etc. Your aim is that the students know you are there, but your watching and listening does not in any way disturb them. They will not feel tempted to call on you unless there is a significant problem – and when they do ask for help, do this swiftly and effectively, then return to the discreet monitoring role. You are sending a message that you are interested, but that the main task is for them to do using their own resources as much as possible.

B Vanish

There are cases when any teacher presence can actually interfere with and diminish the usefulness of work being done. Sometimes the best option for you is to vanish, i.e. get out of immediate eyeshot. You could go into a corner of the room and sit quietly.

It is often an idea to have something concrete to do (e.g. read something) in order to prevent yourself from constantly worrying about how students are doing and getting drawn back into it. You need to keep a small percentage of attention on the room, in order to know when the activity is reaching an end or a crisis point, but otherwise restrain yourself from doing too much. Relax and stop being a teacher for a while.

In a few specific cases, you might want to emphasise the point that students need to work without your help, and in such cases even leaving the room for a few minutes may be an option. (Whenever I have done this, I have been interested to learn that most students do not even notice that I have been out of the room!)

C Monitor actively

You can monitor as described above, but be more visible and allow students to be more aware of your presence and of the possibility of calling on you for help and advice. A teacher who is actively monitoring will be walking around, viewing and listening in to many different groups and frequently offering spontaneous advice and corrections, as well as responding to requests and questions from students.

D Participate

You may sit down and join a group (temporarily or for the whole task) and take part as if you were one of the group, offering ideas, helping with questions, joining in discussions. You could quietly move on to another group. By the end of the task, you might have worked with a number of groups.

Task 52: Your choice of role in pair and group activities

Do you recognise one of these four strategies as your own most common choice? Which one?

Is there a choice that you don't use? Would it be interesting to experiment with it in a future lesson?

6 Gestures

Try to develop a range of gestures (and facial expressions) to save yourself repeating basic instructions and increase opportunities for learner talk. For example, I have seen many teachers using a set of gestures to indicate 'time'. This helps them quickly correct learners who use tenses inaccurately. Pointing to the ground indicates the present; pointing ahead is the future; pointing behind, over the shoulder, indicates the past.

Remember that learners will need to learn the meanings of your gestures; they will not magically know that your pointing means 'Use the past tense', but if you give the oral instruction a few times while also gesturing, they will soon associate the gesture alone with that instruction.

Bear in mind that gestures can mean different things in different countries. If you are teaching away from your own culture, learn which gestures to avoid! And always keep alert to the possibility that you might be giving offence!

Task 53: Gestures

Think of gestures you could use for the following instructions:

1 Work in pairs.
2 What do you think?
3 Stand up.
4 Give a longer answer.
5 Five minutes left.
6 Don't show your information sheet to your partner.

Commentary ■ ■ ■

Here are some possible ideas.

■

Task 54: Creating new gestures

Now decide on some personal gestures for each of the following:

- Ask the other learners.
- Repeat.
- The intonation was very dull.
- Please stop talking now.
- Listen to me.
- Come here! (polite)
- Listen to each other.

A lot of teachers also develop and use gestures quite spontaneously, even without noticing. Do you? If so, which?

7   Using the board well

One resource that almost every teacher has is a board, whether it is a small board on an easel, a wide chalk board, a pen board or even an interactive computer board. Although it is possible to write randomly on the board as things occur in class, you'll often find that it's worth paying a little attention to organising items. I'm not naturally a very tidy board user, but I've found that the following idea does make a difference.

At the start of the lesson, draw a few dividing lines on the board, e.g. to form two columns and three larger working areas, like this:

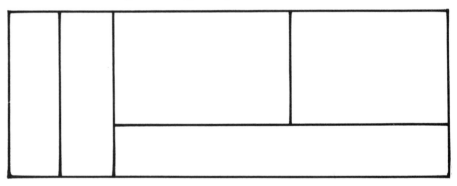

Use these areas to help you organise different content as you write it up, keeping different kinds of things to separate sections of the board, for example:

- a vocabulary column for new words, with a second column for example sentences and notes;
- a substitution table for a new grammar item;
- a space to stick up sketch pictures to help when telling a story;
- questions for students to think about when listening to a recording.

Here are a few more board thoughts:

- Try to avoid long teacher-writing times while students are just watching and waiting.
- Whenever possible, find opportunities to write things up on the board while students are working on other things, so that you are ready when they finish.

- It seems natural enough to write standing in front of the board. Unfortunately, this blocks the view of what you're writing for the class and they can't read it till you've finished (Figure 5.6a). You also can't talk to them easily. When you get a chance in an empty classroom, practise writing on the board in a way that your body doesn't block the view for everyone and you can make eye contact with the class (Figure 5.6b). This requires a slightly sideways position, which will feel odd at first, but it allows you to talk to students, ask questions and look around, all of which can be very helpful in maintaining a good working atmosphere.

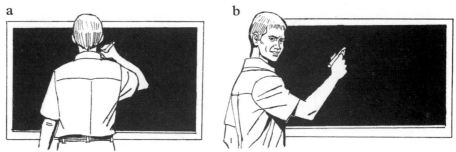

Figure 5.6   Alternative positions when writing on the board

Remember that it's not only teachers who can write on boards – where appropriate, get learners to write up answers and ideas, draw pictures and timelines, etc. The division of the board into sections can also help them to write more tidily.

Watch out that you don't use your own writing on the board as a lengthy time-wasting way to avoid real teaching.

8   Board drawing

Don't say you can't draw! No matter how un-Monet-like your artistry, one picture is often worth many unnecessary words. For the quick explanation of vocabulary items, for setting up a discussion, a dialogue or role-play, for story-building, you need pictures.

Clearly the basic skill is to draw people in some form, and stick people are in many ways better than detailed figures because they're so quick to do.

Add character by giving different shapes of head, fattening up the bodies a little, drawing in simple clothes, adding expression in the mouth and eyes.

Add locations by a few simple props for example, a railway line and a platform makes a station; a table, knife and fork and a vase of flowers makes a restaurant.

Remember that the pictures alone are usually only a starting point. They don't need to do all the work – build from them with questions and discussion. And even if they end up looking like nothing on earth, badly drawn pictures can actually be a rich source of language and humour in the classroom. If they don't understand what on earth you've drawn, whisper the word to a student and get them to draw it.

Task 55: Practice in quick board sketches

Draw quick pictures (single images or a sequence) to illustrate some of the following:
swimming pool, London, happy, escalator, mouse, exhausted, robbery, whale, planet, overtake

What questions could you ask your learners about the sketches to establish that they actually see what you intend them to?

9 Eliciting

'Eliciting' means drawing out information, language, ideas, etc. from the students. It is a technique based on the principles that:

- students probably know a lot more than we may give them credit for;
- starting with what they know is a productive way to begin new work;
- involving people in a question-and-answer movement towards new discoveries is often more effective than simply giving 'lectures'.

Eliciting enables me to start from where the learners are and then to work forward from there. The learners have a real effect on the outcomes of the lesson in terms of ideas, language and pace. With constant learner involvement, I can work more at their speed rather than my own. I can find out where the real difficulties and problems are.

There are three steps to eliciting:

1 I convey a clear idea to the students, perhaps by using pictures, gestures or questions, etc.
2 They then supply the appropriate language, information, ideas, etc.
3 I give them feedback.

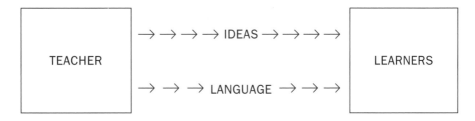

I *can* elicit: language, ideas, feelings, meanings, contexts, memories, etc.
I *can't* elicit: things they don't know.

Here is an example from a lesson:

The teacher is working on the present simple tense for daily routines. On the board, she has written the words *Every day* and drawn a house. She adds a bed to one room.

She looks at the students and gestures that she wants the word. One says 'Bed'. The teacher does not repeat it, but gets other students to repeat the word. Students who didn't hear ask the first student to repeat it.

The teacher does the same procedure with a clock and with the time (seven o'clock). She then draws a stick man and mimes yawning and climbing out of bed. She looks to the students and gestures to encourage them to say a sentence. 'He get up seven o'clock,' says one student. The teacher thanks him for the sentence, but doesn't repeat it. Instead, she uses finger correction (see Chapter 14, Section 7) to establish a corrected version from him (with the help of other class members). When it is correct, she gets the class to repeat the sentence a number of times.

In that sample lesson, the teacher did not model the vocabulary or grammar herself; in fact, she didn't even say the vocabulary or sentence being worked on. The vocabulary was known by at least one student. The grammar, though not accurate, was close enough to be useful to work on. If no student had known *bed* or *clock* or *get up*, then the teacher would have said these herself, having found out that they were really new and needed. As it was, she was able to elicit most of the language from the students and hardly needed to speak at all herself.

With this technique, there is a reduction in unnecessary teacher talk and a maximisation of student talk. The students take an active part in the learning, being involved even in the part of the lesson that might otherwise be only teacher explanation. The teacher is able to pinpoint precisely what students know and what they still need to work on. The language is learned through a process of guided discovery, and it seems likely that it will be more memorable because of the degree of student involvement in the learning. Confidence is built because their use of the language is continuous and does not have to wait for the end of teacher exposition.

Task 56: Advice when eliciting

Here is some advice for elicitors. Two pieces in the list are spurious: cross them out.

1 Give sufficient information. Eliciting doesn't mean 'Guess what's in my head'. Don't try to elicit your grandmother's maiden name.
2 Use hand gestures to indicate who is being asked to speak, either a gesture for 'anyone' or to a specific individual. If everyone speaks at once, it can be hard for students to know which answer was OK and which not.
3 Give very clear feedback on each student utterance. They want to know if what they said was acceptable. You could use simple gestures or facial expressions to register 'OK' or 'Not OK' to students.
4 If someone gives an incorrect answer, get them to repeat it two or three times and then say the correct answer yourself.
5 If they can't provide an answer, don't stretch the eliciting out too long. Silence or wrong answers are evidence that they need your input.
6 When you have an appropriate answer, make sure it is clearly established as a good answer, perhaps by getting it repeated by a variety of individuals.
7 Don't use eliciting with monolingual classes.
8 Use eliciting regularly as a basic technique in most lessons for keeping your class active and involved.

Answers
Points 4 and 7 are the foxes in the henhouse!

Task 57: 'Lead-in' questions

You're planning a lesson on language used when meeting people at parties. What questions could you ask at the start of your lesson in order to interest the learners and to elicit some of their personal feelings and reactions?

Task 58: Planning questions to elicit specific things

Consider the next lesson you need to teach. Write down one specific item of factual information that the students will need to know: maybe a grammar rule, a fact about the topic, what a picture on the board represents, etc. Write a sequence of questions that you could use to lead the students step by step towards finding out that same information for themselves.

If possible, work with someone else to try out your sequence of questions. Practise drawing out the information rather than explaining yourself.

10 Students using their own language

The learners' first language can be a very useful resource in the classroom (which we'll look at in Chapter 14, Section 3), but at other times – when you really want them to use English – it can also get in the way.

'They always talk in their own language. I can't get them to use English.'

This is a common problem in monolingual classes, especially with children and young adults. What might the reasons be?

• Because it's easier to speak my own language.
• Because the teacher always corrects me if I speak English.

- Because I don't want to get it wrong in front of others.
- Because it's not 'in' to speak in English.
- Because the teacher is only pretending not to understand my own language.
- I need to use my own language because I can't say what I want in English.
- Because the teacher can't hear me – so why should I bother?
- Because it's silly to speak English. It's much easier to communicate in the language we all understand.
- Just because …

Task 59: Student attitudes to using English in class

Imagine yourself as a specific individual student in your class. What change in the teacher, students, atmosphere, activities, lessons, etc. would make you comfortable, or even keen, to use English in class?

Commentary ■ ■ ■

Many factors may play a role. Some important ones are discussed in the next section. ■

Using English in class

Some teachers have found that competition and bribery are techniques that get results (e.g. 'Every time you speak Spanish, I'll give a red mark to your team. The team with the fewest red marks at the end gets a bar of chocolate.'). I have some problems with this, as it seems to be building a motivation quite separate from the genuine interest in the subject matter that I am hoping to arouse; it seems to be a case of 'Do this to please the teacher'.

I am sure that inducements, threats, prizes, etc. can all have a limited success in creating an 'English-only' classroom, but I believe that a more complete solution involves looking at the whole atmosphere of the class.

As an ideal, I would like a classroom where learners were free to use their own tongue whenever they wanted, but in fact mostly chose to use English. How would this be possible? Perhaps by creating a climate where it was OK to use English, where using English was normal and natural and not special or frightening. There is no easy way to get to this, but here are some ideas that might help:

- Use lots of listening material to surround them in the sound of English.
- Put English-language posters on the walls.
- Have short, clearly demarcated sections of the lesson when English is the first language; at other times, other languages are possible.
- Negotiate the ground rules with the students or – better – let them set rules completely by themselves.
- Discuss (as opposed to 'Tell') the point of the activity, lesson, course. Agree how it will be done, why using English is important.
- Respond positively to every effort at using English.
- Don't tell learners off for not using English, but keep operating in English yourself.
- Only 'hear' English.
- Spend a lot of time on fluency work without correction.

- Establish that you are delighted for them to speak anything at all; communication is your priority, rather than accuracy.
- Create lots of pair and small-group activities that require them to do something with English without the loss of face of getting it wrong in a bigger group.
- When it becomes a big problem, stop the activity and negotiate again: 'I notice that many of you are using (Portuguese). Is this OK?'
- Be prepared for English use to grow gradually, rather than be established for a whole lesson at the start of the course.

11   Intuition

Use of intuition is fundamental to teaching. It is the skill of spontaneously understanding something, bypassing the supposed conventional route of thinking carefully and reaching a considered decision. Although it sounds somewhat 'magical', it is a quite down-to-earth, if rather unexplored, part of our teaching work. It is something that all teachers exercise to a greater or lesser degree, and it is learnable and improvable.

Intuitive responses are important in teaching because things happen so fast in lesson time and there is so much to notice, flying at us all at once: how the activity is proceeding, how each student is reacting, etc. On-the-spot in class, you don't have much thinking space. Fluent teaching depends on being able to quickly read the classroom situation moment by moment and respond (or choose not to respond) appropriately.

Task 60: Intuition

Do you recognise yourself in any of the following examples?

- You are teaching (or planning teaching) and know suddenly or instinctively what to do or how to do it.
- In class, you decide to do/not to do something without having explicitly thought through 'why'; something just comes to mind.
- You have an understanding of what the learners need that doesn't seem the result of logical reasoning.
- You make a connection between two aspects of the lesson that had not seemed connected before.
- You suddenly realise a sense that there is an overall system, structure or pattern to some things that you previously thought unrelated.
- Pieces of a solution reveal themselves as metaphors, images, puns, etc.
- You know something that you had no apparent way of knowing.
- You get a sudden understanding or insight into a student's character.
- You look at a student (or students) and get a sense of what they are thinking.
- You feel some embarrassment, because your way of working seems to run counter to training and to messages you get from respected peers.

Origins of intuition

Where does intuition come from? How can it be improved? I think intuition is your ability to smoothly access the quantity of experience you have stored inside you to help you interpret what is happening in the present moment. We can get better at it by gaining more (and a wider range of) experience and storing it away.

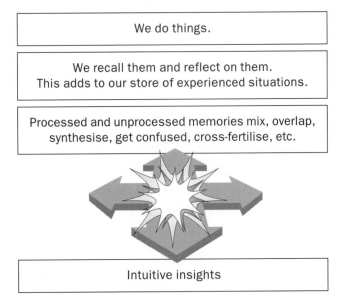

We do things.

We recall them and reflect on them.
This adds to our store of experienced situations.

Processed and unprocessed memories mix, overlap,
synthesise, get confused, cross-fertilise, etc.

Intuitive insights

Figure 5.7   How we use intuition

Task 61: How you learned to teach

Recall how you learned to be a teacher on your teacher-training course. I don't mean how you learned the theory, but what your first lessons were like, how much you could apply what your trainers had taught you to do in class.

Intuition and teaching

If your initial experience of teaching was anything like my own, you had a whole pile of things weighing on your shoulders when you went into class: books you'd read (like this one!), seminars you'd attended, helpful advice you'd been given.

Yet on stepping into the live, real-time situation in class, you probably found that you couldn't just apply all these things, like assembly instructions for putting together some bookshelves. It didn't work like that, because teaching isn't like do-it-yourself or cookery. If I'm learning to cook, I can read some TV chef's book and find out precise step-by-step instructions for making a new dish. If I follow those instructions precisely, I am quite likely to get something similar to the original target dish. There will be some call on my intelligence and some degree of luck and some local variation in terms of what my cooker is like, what ingredients are like, etc., but it is by and large a relatively predictable task.

Teaching isn't like that. The instruction book doesn't work, because every teaching event is significantly different. And it happens too fast before your eyes. You very quickly find that you have to use something else, from Lesson 1 onwards, when the handed-down guidelines break down in the face of real people with real unpredicted responses. You are already working on intuition: taking risks, trying things out, learning not to be frightened, realising that this is the way to move forward, that the things that go wrong contribute to you being better able to do it next time. And recalling and reflecting on what you do after you do it seems to add to the pool from which this intuition draws. You don't have to process the learning very deeply to draw specific conclusions – it may often be enough just to recall it, sift through it.

So, new teachers starting out make a lot of use of intuitive decisions – deciding to do something on the spur of the moment. What happens as a result then itself feeds into the stock of data available to them for future decisions.

New teachers also make intuitive readings of how people are reacting. Interestingly, their intuitive readings are often incorrect; for example, trainees often tend to misread whether students are bored with an exercise or how difficult a listening task is. New teachers often transfer their own nerves, doubts, worries and expectations about how students will respond and then find what they expected to find in the learners' faces, body language, voices, etc.

There is a danger that such incorrect readings may get set in concrete. One needs to constantly challenge and consciously upgrade one's intuition – and I suspect that much of the process of learning to be a better teacher is a process of collecting concrete feedback and information (about learners, language, teaching ideas, etc.) in order to become more spontaneously and accurately intuitive in class, i.e. becoming a 'learning teacher'.

Training courses tend to expect trainees to put into practice certain ways of working propounded by the course. Teachers often try to do what they are asked to do and come badly unstuck – tripping up on the sheer difficulty of following prescribed steps through a dance that in reality has no fixed pattern. The 'painting by numbers' approach to teaching is possible, but with very limited outcomes.

Yet, some trainees dare to put the training requirements to one side – muffling the trainer's voices in their head – and manage to reach back to their own natural intuitive skills. They start to feel that buzz that teaching brings; the shiver of excitement when an activity starts working, the thrill that pushes them on to experiment more and to enjoy it more. This isn't an argument against training or against academic input, but it is a reminder that, just as teachers can't do the learning for their students, trainers can never directly hand over their own teaching skills to their trainees.

We need to study things, but we also need to put them to one side; we need to forget things, we need to lose things inside us, we need to worry less about the exact instructions. If we hold other people's guidance in front of us as infallible route maps to follow, we are likely to get lost. And that's probably true of cooking as well – maybe we won't be a real cook till we can leave the book closed. This same process, I think, is how we then go on to become the teachers we are.

Most people will discover that they didn't learn to be teachers from seminars or books or conferences or observation feedback, though all of these have a very definite impact. You learn to teach by teaching. You learn to teach by doing it.

Task 62: Your use of intuition

As a teacher, how much do you make use of intuition to know what your students are thinking, to read their reactions to things, to decide if they like a task or not, to determine if they are bored, etc.? What informs your intuition?

12 How to prevent learning – some popular techniques

Here are some ways that teachers unintentionally hinder or prevent learning.

TTT (Teacher Talking Time)

TEACHER: When nothing else is happening in the classroom, I open my mouth. I've no idea what I say most of the time. But it stops those horrible silences. It's probably useful for them to listen to me speaking English. After all, I ...

The more you talk, the less opportunity there is for the learners. They need time to think, to prepare what they are going to say and how they are going to say it. Allow them the time and the quiet they need. Don't feel the need to fill every gap in a lesson. Explore the possibilities of silence.

Echo

STUDENT: I went to the cinema.
TEACHER: You went to the cinema. Good. You went to the cinema.

Who gets more language practice here – the student or the teacher? If you become aware of your echoing and then start to control it, you will find that learners get more talking time and that they start to listen to each other more. When you echo, they soon learn that they don't need to listen to anyone except you, because they know that you'll repeat everything! That has a dramatically negative effect on interaction patterns within the classroom.

Helpful sentence completion

STUDENT: I think that smoking is ...
TEACHER: ... a bad thing. Yes, I agree. When I went into the pub ...

You can be so desperate for a student to say what you want them to say (so that the lesson can move on to the next stage) that you are already predicting the words the student will produce and eagerly wishing for them to be said – so much so that you often find yourself adding 'tails' to sentence after sentence. But this kind of 'doing the hard work for them' is often counter-productive. People need to finish their own sentences. If students can't complete the sentence themselves, they need help – but help to produce their own sentence, using their own words and their own ideas. By letting students finish what they are saying, you also allow yourself more time to really listen to the student and what he is saying.

Complicated and unclear instructions

TEACHER: Well, what I'm gonna do is I'm gonna ask you to get into pairs, but before that there are some things we've gotta work out. So just jot down if you've got a pen, could you write this, then when we've finished that we're going to do the next thing which involves more ...

Unplanned, unstructured instructions are extremely confusing to students. They probably understand only a small percentage of what you say – and guess what you want them to do from one or two key words they did catch. Work out what is essential for them to know and tell them that, without wrapping it up in babble.

Not checking understanding of instructions

TEACHER: My instructions were so clear – but all the students did different
             things, and none of them did what I asked them to do.

Even the clearest instructions can be hard to grasp so, after you've given them, it's
worth checking that they have been understood. A simple way is to ask a student
or two to repeat them back to you: 'So, José, what are you going to do?' In this way,
you satisfy yourself that the task has been understood. Having done that, make
sure you monitor the start of the activity to see if they really do what you wanted!

Asking 'Do you understand?'

TEACHER: Do you understand?
STUDENT: … er … yes …

When you want to check learners' understanding, questions such as 'Do you
understand?' are often useless. If you get a 'Yes' reply, it could mean 'I'm nervous
about seeming stupid' or 'I don't want to waste the class's time any more' or 'I
think I understand, but ...'. You often need to get clear information about what
students have taken in. The best way to do this is to get students to demonstrate
their understanding, for example by using a language item in a sentence, or by
repeating an instruction, or by explaining their interpretation of an idea. This
provides real evidence, rather than vague, possibly untrue information.

Fear of genuine feedback

TEACHER: Did you like my lesson?
STUDENT: … er … yes …

In an active, forward-moving class, the learners will constantly be giving you
feedback on what they have understood, what they think, what they need, how
they feel, etc. Many teachers believe in the importance of open, honest feedback,
but find that, in practice, it can be hard to get. This is partly to do with the
classroom atmosphere, partly to do with the questions asked, and mainly to do
with the attitude and response to feedback received. The more you see feedback
as a threat to you and to your position and your confidence, the more you will
attempt to avoid feedback, or to defend yourself against perceived attack when
you do get feedback. If you can open yourself up to the possibilities of really
listening to what students have to say with a view to simply hearing them –
without self-defence, justifications or arguments – then you may find that you can
start to find out what they are really thinking, and that you can work on
responding appropriately to that.

Insufficient authority/over-politeness

TEACHER: So if you don't mind, it would be very nice if you could just stop
             the activity if you feel that's OK.

This kind of pussyfooting is a common way in which teachers undermine
themselves. Be clear. Say what you need to say without hiding it. If you want to
stop an activity, say 'Stop now, please'. Feel your own natural authority and let it
speak clearly.

The running commentary

TEACHERS: So now what I'm gonna do is I'm gonna move my chair over here and sit down and just get comfortable and now I'm gonna tear up these pieces of paper, and I had to use these because I couldn't get any card, so I found these at the back of the teacher's room, and I'm gonna tear them up now and when I've done that what I'm gonna ask you to do is if you don't mind …

Don't give a running commentary about the mechanics of past, present and future activities. Boring, hard to follow, unnecessary. Tell students what they need to know – and stop.

Lack of confidence in self, learners, material, activity/making it too easy

TEACHER: I wonder why they look so bored?

A common cause of boredom in classrooms is when the material used is too difficult or too easy. The former isn't hard to recognise – the learners can't do the work. A more difficult problem is when work is simply not challenging enough. Teachers often have rather limited expectations about what people can do, and keep their classes on a rather predictable straight line through activities that are safe and routine. Try to keep the level of challenge high. Be demanding. Believe that they can do more than they are aware of being able to do – and then help them to do it.

Over-helping/over-organising

TEACHER: Yes, now you can ask her your question. Mmm, that's a good question. What do you think? What's your answer going to be, Silvia? Yes. Go on – tell her what it is …

When you give students a task to do in a group, it's often best to let them get on with it. A lot of 'teacher help', although well intentioned, is actually 'teacher interference' and gets in the way of students working on their own. As long as you are around, they will look to you for guidance, control and help. If you go away, they are forced to do the work themselves. That is when learning might happen. It can be a difficult lesson to learn, but sometimes our students will do much better without us, if only we have the courage to trust them.

Flying with the fastest

TEACHER: So – what's the answer?
STUDENT A: Only on Tuesdays unless it's raining.
TEACHER: Yes, very good – so, everyone got that? And why did he buy the elastic band?
STUDENT A: So he wouldn't lose his letters.
TEACHER: Good. Everyone understands then!

If you only listen to the first people who speak, it's very easy to get a false impression of how difficult or easy something is. You may find that the strongest and fastest students dominate, and you get little idea of how the majority of the class finds the work. This can lead you to fly at the speed of the top two or three students and to lose the rest completely. Make sure you get answers and feedback from many students. Try directing questions at individuals (e.g. 'What do you think, Dominic?') and sometimes actively 'shh!' the loud ones – or simply 'not hear' them.

Not really listening (hearing language problems but not the message)

STUDENT: I am feeling bad. My grandfather he die last week and I am …
TEACHER: No, not 'die' – say 'died' because it's in the past.
STUDENT: … he died last week …
TEACHER: Excellent. Now, did anyone else's grandfather die last week?

Because we are dealing in language as the subject matter of our courses, it's very easy to become over-concerned about the accuracy of what is said and to fail to hear the person behind the words. The example above is an extreme one, but on a minute-by-minute basis in class, teachers frequently fail to hear what learners say. The only point in learning language is to be able to communicate or receive communication – it is vital that work on the mechanical production of correct English does not blind us to the messages conveyed. Check yourself occasionally – are you really listening to your students, or only to their words?

Weak rapport: creation of a poor working environment

TEACHER: I try to be nice – but my classes always seem so dull.

If rapport seems to be a problem, then plan work specifically designed to focus on improving the relationships and interaction within the class (rather than activities with a mainly language aim). Until the relationships are good within a class, the learning is likely to be of a lower quality, so it's worth spending time on this. Bear in mind the three teacher qualities that help to enable a good working environment: authenticity, respect and empathy

Don't be too worried by this terrible list! These are the kinds of problems we all have. You'll find yourself doing these things, so notice yourself doing them and note the ways in which they do or don't seem to 'prevent' learning. But also accept that this is a part of the natural process of your own learning and development. As your awareness and confidence grow, you'll find that you not only become more able to recognise such problems in your own teaching, but that you can also start to find effective alternative options that enable rather than hinder learning.

Chapter 6 Planning lessons and courses

1 Planning is a thinking skill

Before you go into a lesson, it helps to be clear about what you want to do. A lot is going to happen on the spot in the class – you can't ever completely predict how learners will respond to anything – but the better prepared you are, the more likely it is that you will be ready to cope with whatever happens. It is possible to teach (very good lessons sometimes) without any pre-planning, but planning increases the number of your options – and in doing so, increases your chances of a successful lesson.

Although training courses tend to ask you to prepare detailed written plans, it's important to realise that planning is essentially a thinking skill. Planning is imagining the lesson before it happens. It involves prediction, anticipation, sequencing, organising and simplifying. I sometimes wonder if the key planning skill is an ability to visualise before class how things might look, feel and sound when they are done in class.

A written plan is evidence that you have done that thinking. It can also serve as a useful in-lesson reminder to you of your pre-lesson thoughts. Beyond that, however, it is not holy writ. It is not set in concrete. As a general rule: **Prepare thoroughly. But in class, teach the learners, not the plan.** What this means is that you should be prepared to respond to the learners and adapt what you have planned as you go, even to the extent of throwing the plan away if appropriate. A carefully worked-out plan is the end result of thinking logically through the content of the lesson before the lesson. It then informs your teaching in class, whether you actually follow it completely or not. Thinking through possible content and problems before class provides you with informed choices that set you free in class. But a teacher who is mainly concerned with following a lesson plan to the letter is unlikely to be responding to what is actually happening in class.

There are a number of general areas to think about:

- **Atmosphere**
  Can you visualise the characteristic atmosphere and look of the lesson? Can you imagine what the experience of the lesson will feel like for any one specific student?
- **The learners**
  How will the lesson engage the learners? Will they enjoy doing the lesson? Will they benefit from it?
- **The aims**
  What will the learners achieve? What are you hoping to achieve yourself?
- **The teaching point**
  What is the subject matter of the lesson – the skills or language areas that will be studied and the topics you will deal with?
- **The tasks and teaching procedures**
  What are the things that the learners will do? What activities will you use? What sequence will they come in?

- **The challenge**
  What in the lesson will challenge the learners?
- **Materials**
  What texts, recordings, pictures, exercises, role cards, etc. will you use?
- **Classroom management**
  What will you say? How will the seating be arranged? How much time will each stage take? etc. Can you picture the working groups/the movement/the changing pace of the class?

Task 63: Considerations when planning a lesson

The list below shows some more things you might consider when planning a lesson. Decide which items go with which of the above headings.

- How many separate activities will there be?
- Where will I stand or sit?
- What do learners need?
- What skills will learners be working on?
- How will I control timing?
- What are some of the things that could cause difficulties or go wrong?
- How am I going to deal with mistakes?
- Is there going to be variety of activity in the lesson?
- How do the lesson aims fit in with longer-term goals?
- What do they know already?

Commentary ■ ■ ■

I'll leave you to work out your own answers here! ■

Important considerations for a lesson plan

The two key questions are often considered to be:

- What is my procedure? (i.e. What sequence of tasks, activities, etc. will I use?)
- What are the aims of the lesson?

However, if you can answer the latter question, i.e. if you can be clear about what you hope your learners will have achieved by the end of the lesson, then perhaps the other questions will become easier to answer. If your aim is, for example, 'By the end of this lesson, my learners will have improved their ability to hear and pronounce the vowel sounds /ɪ/ and /iː/', then you are already clear about where the lesson is going and you can begin to think more clearly about how you can go about achieving this end, what materials you need, how you will arrange the chairs, etc. and you can start to select or invent some interesting activities to help reach this aim. (There's more on aims in Section 5 of this chapter.)

My own experience of planning is that it only becomes a linear, logical thing in its later stages. Earlier on, it's a process of trying to think how certain material might work with my students or what material is needed to allow them to do something specific. Initially, at least, a lot of this thinking tends to be unfocused, following vague lines of thought or jumping from idea to idea. The semi-chaos may not last long, but allows my personality and creativity to start owning the material. It usually coalesces fairly soon into something more concrete and usable.

If you're having trouble planning, here's a possible starting point:

Look at the next unit of your coursebook (or whatever material you intend to teach with). Think about your students. Don't start writing yet! Let your mind wander and explore a number of ways that the two (material and learners) can meet. Don't dismiss the impossible or ludicrous ideas if they come; just enjoy them and keep wandering. Imagine having a conversation with one (or some) of your students about anything that appears on the coursebook page. What do they find interesting or problematic in terms of topic, activity, language?

After a while (one minute? ten minutes?), start organising your thoughts more systematically. Can you get a sense of the whole lesson? You'll probably need to start writing around this point!

Planning becomes a lot easier if you have a clear idea as to how you think that people learn. We will look at this in the following sections.

2 How do people learn language?

If we want to plan lessons that are more than simply random entertainment, we need a clear idea of how we think people learn language. The activities we plan can then closely reflect those things that we believe are an important part of the learning process.

Task 64: A student's progress when learning a new item

The following list charts one possible explanation of a student's progress when learning a new item of language (e.g. a new piece of grammar). Match the labels to the numbered stages listed below.

Active use   Noticing   Ignorance   Practice   Exposure   Understanding

1 The learner doesn't know anything about the item.

2 The learner hears or reads examples of the item (maybe a number of times), but doesn't particularly notice it.

3 The learner begins to realise that there is a feature he/she doesn't fully understand.

4 The learner starts to look more closely at the item and tries to work out the formation rules and the meaning, possibly with the help of reference information, explanations or other help.

5 The learner tries to use the item in his/her own speech or writing (maybe hesitantly, probably with many errors).

6 The learner integrates the item fully into his/her own language and uses it (without thinking) relatively easily with minor errors.

Commentary ■ ■ ■

From top to bottom, the labels are:

1 Ignorance; 2 Exposure; 3 Noticing; 4 Understanding; 5 Practice; 6 Active use ■

Ignoring 'Ignorance', we could put the other items together in a slightly expanded diagram showing how they might all fit together (see Figure 6.1).

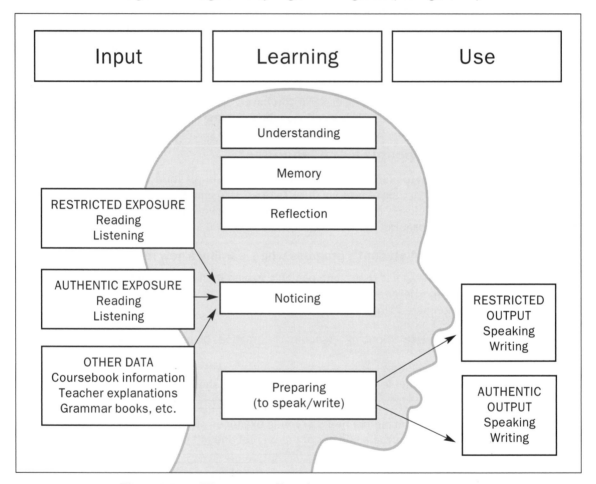

Figure 6.1   The process of learning

Task 65: 'Restricted' and 'Authentic' exposure

The diagram is a little more complex than the shorter explanation given earlier.

Exposure is separated into 'Restricted' and 'Authentic' exposure – what might this mean?

Commentary ■ ■ ■

Exposure to language may come through texts that are specially prepared and simplified for students (restricted) or are unadapted, authentic texts from non-specialist sources (authentic). The following section looks at these distinctions in detail. ■

Exposure

The distinction between authentic and restricted is whether the exposure comes from a text that is realistic – or reasonably like a normal natural text (= authentic exposure) – or if it is from a text that is recognisably simplified or perhaps including an unnaturally high number of examples of a specific target item (= restricted exposure). From a teaching perspective, the distinction is important, as we may need to adopt different approaches to a text that is not specifically learner-friendly than towards material written to achieve specific teaching purposes.

Authentic exposure

This is exposure to language when it is being used fairly naturally. For example:

- Reading magazines, books, articles, product labels, etc.
- Listening to small talk and listening to recordings, radio, etc.
- Watching English films or television channels (e.g. Cartoon Network)
- Living in a place where the language is used
- Hearing incidental language used in class
- Reading pieces of language on notices, posters, etc. around the classroom

Restricted exposure

Exposure to texts specifically designed to be accessible to learners – and probably to draw attention to specific language points.

The texts will often:

- be specially designed for learners, providing clear examples of target language items being used in context;
- be simplified through use of graded language;
- have unusually high quantities of specific target language items.

Learners may:

- listen to you say sentences that exemplify the language point you are aiming to work on;
- read or listen to coursebook texts designed to present features of certain language items;
- read examples of particular features of language in a grammar book.

A passion for 'authentic materials' (e.g. newspapers, advertisements, letters, etc.) has dominated language teaching for some years. This was a natural reaction to the previously very unnatural texts of many earlier teaching materials. However, it's probably less important to strive for authenticity in classroom materials in favour of selecting material that is intrinsically interesting, engaging and relevant for your specific group of learners.

Stephen Krashen has hypothesised a distinction between **acquisition** (i.e. language that we pick up subconsciously when we are engaged in communicating and understanding messages) and **learning** (i.e. language we consciously study and learn about, for example in a classroom).

Krashen suggests that acquisition is the significant process here, and that language we learn is only of any use to us in monitoring and checking our communication. In order to acquire language, we need to be exposed to **comprehensible input**, i.e. real messages communicated to us that are comprehensible but just a little above our current level. If i stands for a learner's current level, then ideal comprehensible input would be $i + 1$ (i.e. just above the current level). This suggests an important role in the classroom for exposure that is **restricted** (i.e. graded) in order for it to be at an appropriate level, i.e. not too simple, but just above the level of the learner.

Output

We can make a similar distinction between output that is deliberately simplified or controlled – maybe because of a teacher instruction or by the nature of a particular task that makes the load on the learner less demanding (= restricted output) – and freer or more natural interaction which might have many stresses and pressures (= authentic output). The focus on restricted output tends to be on getting language right, whereas the emphasis on authentic output is more often the quality of communication of messages.

Authentic output

Speaking or writing using the full range of language learners have at their disposal. For example:

- Discussions
- Meetings
- Small talk in the café
- Writing a postcard
- Negotiations
- Chatting in class

Restricted output

Speaking or writing that requires learners to use less than the full quantity of language they know. Learners get a chance to practise using language in ways that are controlled or deliberately simplified (maybe by a teacher instruction or by the nature of a particular task) in a way that makes the load on the learner less demanding. For example:

- Drills
- Written gap-fill exercises
- Grammar practice activities
- 'Repeat what I say'
- Simple games based on saying very similar sentences (e.g. 'Simon says')

This analysis only defines some broadly different types of learning stages. In reality, it's not always clear-cut as to which category things falls into – and for both exposure and output, 'authentic' and 'restricted' are really end points on a continuum, rather than two all-excluding categories!

Figure 6.1 also added other elements – showing things that go on inside the learner's head, such as noticing, understanding, memory and preparing. For the moment, we'll just address one of these: noticing.

Task 66: Noticing

Recall a specific example – from 'real life' or from a class you have taught/observed – that shows someone 'noticing' or having their attention drawn to an item of language.

Commentary ■ ■ ■

Noticing is seeing or having one's attention drawn to the meaning, form or use of language items. For example:

- When a learner is reading a text, she stops and thinks 'I've seen that structure before – I wonder why it has that ending?'
- In class, a teacher says 'Look at line 3 – is that verb in the past or present?' ■

What is *your* theory of learning?

It's important to remember that Figure 6.1 represents one generalised (and possibly incorrect) theory of how a language item is learned. It's important that you check out whether this theory fits with your own personal idea of how people learn – and then, when you read any other book on this subject, check the theory out again. Quite a few teachers laugh at or reject the idea that 'theory' should play any part in what they do in class. I'd say that, at the very least, you do need to tackle one basic question: how do **you** think people learn language? Without some personal answer to this, the work you do in class is hit-and-miss. You need to sort out why you are doing the things you do. (And make sure you keep doubting and questioning!)

Figure 6.1 only shows the process of learning. It doesn't describe how that might be brought about, e.g. in a classroom lesson. It isn't a lesson plan! So, the next problem is to decide what we can do as teachers to help such a learning process happen. And obviously we will want to devise classroom work that fits in with our personal description of how we think learning comes about.

3 Sequencing lesson components

How can you decide what to plan and what order to put the stages in? For lessons where there will be a substantial focus on language study (e.g. grammar, lexis, function), one straightforward way is to think of parts (or 'stages') of a lesson as 'building brick' components (using features from the learning diagram we looked at in the previous section). We can build different lessons by putting the bricks together in various sequences.

Figure 6.2 shows a lesson procedure based on three bricks.

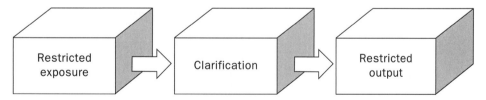

Figure 6.2   'Building bricks' lesson procedure

This is a popular lesson shape for many teachers. Let's look at it more closely.

- In the first stage, the learners get to see or hear examples of language being used (maybe in a reading text or by listening to a recording).
- **Clarification** refers to a lesson stage in which the learners focus in on a piece of language, to see it, think about it and understand it, to become much clearer on its form, meaning and use. It can be done in a variety of different ways

(e.g. students look it up for themselves in a grammar book). For the moment, in this lesson example, let's assume it means 'teacher explains the language point'.

- After this, the learners try using the language for themselves in relatively unthreatening ways.

This type of lesson is often called 'present – practise', i.e. first the learners meet (or are 'given') new language items, then they practise using them.

Of course, the building-brick metaphor is something of a simplification. In practice, aspects of the bricks are likely to interweave, overlap or happen simultaneously; for example, in this lesson, the explanations do not occupy one long block of time, but are shorter and more integrated with the exposure and output stages (see Figure 6.3).

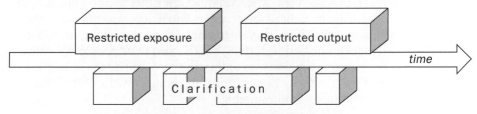

Figure 6.3   Breakdown of 'building bricks' lesson procedure

However, although this may be a more realistic view, it can still be helpful, for 'thinking through' purposes, to plan lessons in terms of sequencing building bricks according to the major aspect of each stage.

Figure 6.4 shows those building bricks plus others that reflect different aspects of the learning diagram we looked at earlier (Figure 6.1).

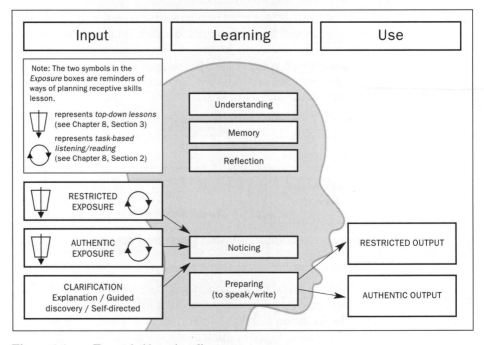

Figure 6.4   Expanded learning diagram

These bricks are purely a working tool to help you plan. Which bricks you choose to label and use is up to you; there is no magic in the number of them. Maybe you'd like to add some of the following to your set, as shown in Figure 6.5.

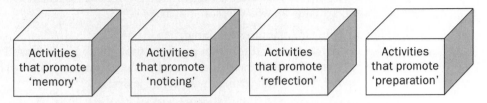

Figure 6.5   Additional blocks

Whatever the components we choose, we now have a way to plan out a number of different lesson shapes in a fairly tangible, approachable way.

Task 67: Alternatives to present–practise

Look at the following lesson sequences.

- Can you imagine how they might look in class?
- How do they differ from the present–practise lesson above?

Lesson 1

Lesson 2

Lesson 3

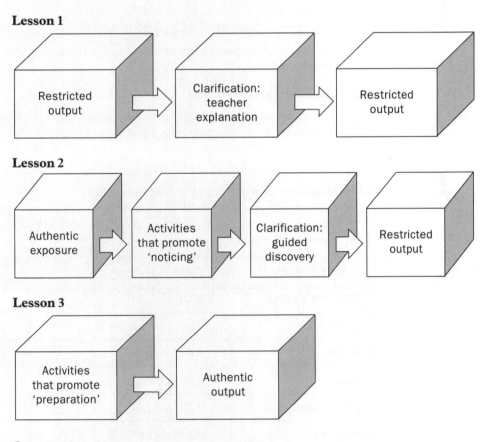

Commentary ■ ■ ■

We'll say more about these lesson components in Chapter 12 on grammar. ■

4 Formal lesson planning

On teacher training courses, trainees are often expected to produce a written lesson plan for each lesson taught. This is not because teachers in the real world always do this for every lesson, but as:

• training in 'planning-thinking';
• evidence to your tutors that you have thought about the lesson;
• a chance for trainers to understand your thinking and find out how to help you better if things go wrong in the actual lesson.

Formal plans often divide into three distinct sections:

• background information about the class, the teacher, the materials and the overall aims of the lesson;
• language analysis of items that will be worked on in class;
• a detailed chronological stage-by-stage description of the intended procedure for the lesson.

In most formal lesson plans, the following are required:

• a clear statement of appropriate aims for the whole lesson;
• a clear list of stages in the lesson, with a description of activities, their aims and estimated timing;

and, if it is a lesson that includes language system work:

• a list of specific target language items (or a statement about how and when they will be selected).

Task 68: A formal lesson plan

Figure 6.6 shows a sample background information page for a lesson written by a trainee teacher. (If you want to try the same format, there is a blank photocopiable form (Resource 13 in Appendix 2), as well as a shorter version (Resource 14).)

Read it and find answers to the following questions:

• Is the teacher on a training course at the moment?
• Which language systems or skills is the lesson mainly working on?
• Imagine you are the trainer observing the class. What will you be most interested to look out for?

Teacher's name	Celia
Observer's name	Mike
Class name	Pre-Intermediate 3
Room	B7
Date	22nd October
Lesson start time	7.30 p.m.
Length of lesson	90 minutes
Observation start time	7.45 p.m.

Length of observation	60 minutes
Observation agenda (observer)	• 2nd contractual in-service observation of school year • Mike says he is interested to see how my confidence has grown since the last formal observation.
Observation agenda (teacher)	• I don't feel very good at 'doing grammar' – so I'm going to do a grammar lesson for the observation! Can you give any advice on what I'm getting right and wrong? • Sometime I feel the pace of the lessons drags a bit. Is it something I'm doing – or is it the students? • Monika and Gabi seem very quiet during the lesson. Could you notice what they do? Give me any ideas, comments or suggestions.
Teaching point (i.e. what you will be working on in terms of language items/ skills)	• Grammar/Speaking: Giving advice and warnings using Type 1 conditionals • Lexis: Everyday household objects and electrical items
Target language items	• *If you touch the dog, it'll bite you.* • *If you use the washing machine after 10 p.m., they'll complain.*
Main lesson aims (i.e. what you hope the learners will achieve/be able to do better after your lesson)	By the end of my lesson learners will be better able to • give advice to other learners about living in a host family; • form accurate oral and written sentences using Type 1 conditionals to express warnings, offers, threats and make bargains in controlled exercises.
Evidence (i.e. how will you know that this has been achieved?)	• Students will respond accurately in drills and in written exercises. • Students will be able to invent sentences of their own following the same pattern.
Personal goals (i.e. what are you trying to improve in your own skills as a teacher?)	• I tend to explain a lot; I'd like to elicit more and guide students to finding out about the language. • My drills are rather dull. I'll try and make these more dynamic.
Class profile	13 students (mainly young adults; 9 female, 4 male) The class is a strong Pre-Intermediate group, though Rebi is noticeably weaker in grammar knowledge than the others. The class works well together and usually participates actively, though →

	some are quiet. Mixhail gets easily distracted and can waste other's time.
Timetable fit	Students have recently been working a lot on talking about the future; talking about hypothetical events will be a useful next step.
Assumptions (about what the students know/ can do)	Students know the present simple and *will* verb forms relatively well.
Predicted problems	• Wrongly using *will/'ll* in the *If* clause. • Pronunciation of the contracted *'ll* form.
Context (to use in teaching)	Story of when I visited the UK and stayed in a family.
Materials used	• Own materials: oral story (based on a story in *Challenge to think*); substitution table; exercises • Box of Cuisenaire rods

Figure 6.6   Lesson plan

Task 69: Finding the right part of a plan

A trainee teacher on an initial training course is using the same background information format for her plan. Decide which headings the following items should go under (e.g. does Item 1 go under the heading 'Main lesson aims', 'Teaching point', ...?).

1 • Reducing my TTT
   • Getting students to listen more to each other

2 Use different prepositions of place accurately in spoken English to describe where things are

3
	on	the table.
	on top of	the cupboard.
It's	next to	the book.
	under	the chair.
	opposite	the window.

4 Students are familiar with some basic household vocabulary, such as *table, fridge,* etc.

5 • Confusion about the meaning of *opposite*
   • Pronunciation of weak forms *to, of, the,* etc.

6 A mouse is loose in the house! Where is it? Frightened husband wants to know.

7 Prepositions of place: *next to, on, on top of, near, beside, under, opposite, behind.*

8 • They will be able to complete the information-exchange activity successfully.
  • They will produce the language accurately and appropriately in drills and in response to questions.

9 My own material: pictures on blackboard

Writing a lesson-plan procedure

Once you've written the background information, the other essential part of a plan is a statement of the intended procedure of the lesson. This is often done as a list of separate stages, with indications of what you will do, what the students will do, how long you expect it to last, what kind of interaction there will be, what the aims of the stage are, etc. It is possible, though not essential, to give a name to each stage, e.g. 'presentation', 'practice', 'feedback', etc. Personally, I find numbering the stages to be sufficient.

How much detail does a plan need? What are the criteria for whether it is a good plan or not? I think there's one key test as to whether your plan is OK or not: could someone else, who has not talked with you about the lesson, pick up your plan and say 'Ah, yes – I see exactly what the teacher intended' and be able to go in and teach your lesson herself?

To achieve this, you need a plan that simply and clearly outlines the intended stages – in enough detail to be 'imaginable' by someone else.

Include:

• the essential steps of each stage;
• classroom management information, such as what sort of groupings you'll use, who will talk, etc.;
• things that may be particular problems or hiccups (e.g. a note about making sure seating is in a particular position, the text of a particularly tricky instruction or a sketch of a difficult board diagram).

For the most part, do not use:

• long prose descriptions of everything that will happen;
• detailed descriptions of routine actions that any competent teacher would do naturally on the spot in class, e.g. 'stand up';
• shorthand notes that may be too cryptic for a reader to unravel;
• word-for-word texts of all your instructions and explanations, etc.

Task 70: Lesson aims and content

Figure 6.7 shows a sample of a staged procedure for a 50-minute lesson. When you have read it,

• write some main aims for the whole lesson;
• list language items you think might be worked on in this class;
• decide what sort of 'story' you think the teacher has planned.

Stage	Procedure (What the teacher will do)	Tasks (What the students will do)	Interaction	Aims	Time
1	Draw a picture on the board of a landscape (forest, villages, river, hills, etc.). Elicit vocabulary.	Name items on picture. Note and practise items that are new. Pronounce lexis with correct stress.	T & Sts	Learners will understand and be able to use lexis necessary for the story in Stage 3.	6 mins
2	Use cut-out paper character (and sticky tape to attach to board) to elicit details of a story of a walk through the land-scape, especially including pre-positional phrases (*over the bridge, around the lake,* etc.). Get students to repeat frequently. Concept-check new items as they appear.	Tell and remember story of the walk. Practise saying pre-positional phrases.	T & Sts	Learners will learn and practise prepositional phrases.	12 mins
3	Ask students to recap by asking students to describe a new route. *How would you get from A to B?*	Students narrate new route.	Pairs	Learners will become more confident and accurate at using the target language.	8 mins
4	Write up ten prompt questions (e.g. *What's the name of the hero? Where does the journey start?* etc.). Ask students to draw their own landscape and invent a story according to the prompt questions.	Students read questions, discuss together and negotiate together to invent a new story.	Small groups	Learners will get practice using target language more creatively to invent a story.	12 mins

5	Ask students to swap groups and show their landscape, then (a) ask 'yes/no' questions to elicit story; (b) hear the story from new partner. Optional: re-swap partners so that people have to now tell a story that was not originally theirs.	Students form new groups. Students ask y/n questions. Students hypothesise stories. Students tell stories.	Small groups	Learners practise forming and asking questions. Learners practise narrating stories using target items.	12 mins

Figure 6.7   Staged lesson plan

Commentary ■ ■ ■

- Here are two possible main aims:
  By the end of my lesson the students will be better able to …
  1 narrate a story about a walk through a landscape;
  2 describe the movement of people using prepositional phrases more accurately.

- The lesson might include some of the following language items:
  Landscape lexis: *trees, wood, forest, stream, river, lake, pond, waterfall, lane, path, river bank, hill, mountain, valley, beach, field, suburbs, garden, fence, wall, island, bridge, building, cottage, street, road,* etc.
  Prepositional phrases: *through the field, down the lane, round the lake, along the river bank, by the river, around the building, over the wall, down the path, around the pond, over the bridge, up to the house, under a tree,* etc.

- A possible story:
  She walked through the field, down the lane, round the lake and along the river bank.
  She sat down by the river for a drink from her thermos.
  Then she looked around and sighed.
  She saw a high wall in front of her.
  She walked all around the wall looking for a way in, but she couldn't find one.
  So she took a ladder out of her pocket*, leaned it against the wall and climbed over.
  In the beautiful garden, she walked down the path, around the pond and towards the house.
  A man was sitting at a desk under a tree playing a game on a computer.
  She stood next to him, watching his game, for a long time.
  On the screen, she saw a girl.
  The girl walked through a field, down the lane, round the lake and along the river bank …

⋆ There's no harm in occasionally shocking your students with a bit of surrealism! It'll make them ask questions – and there's a good chance they'll always remember *ladder* afterwards. ■

5 Lesson aims

For every lesson you teach, and for every activity within that lesson, it is useful to be able to state what the aims are, i.e. what's the point of doing it? what will the students get out of it? It is important to separate mentally:

• the material you use;
• the activities that will be done;
• the teaching point (i.e. the language skills or systems that you will work on);
• the topics or contexts that will be used;
• the aims of the lesson.

On training courses, or when you are being observed by a director of studies or other supervisor, you will often be expected to offer a clear statement of aims before you start teaching a lesson. This can be a useful training discipline, forcing you to concentrate on deciding what activities and procedures are most likely to lead to specific outcomes for the learners. It also enables an observer evaluating your teaching to make that assessment against criteria that you have decided yourself (rather than against their own).

But the pre-lesson statement of aims (like the detailed formal lesson plan) is basically a training tool. Most teachers in their day-to-day teaching do not usually make such a formal statement of what they hope to achieve. Sometimes they may formulate and change the aims while they are teaching; sometimes what was achieved may only really become clear after the lesson has finished.

However, teachers who have been through a training process that required them to do this may be much more aware of why they are doing something in class. They are probably able to make more informed decisions between options, choosing the ones that are most likely to lead to a useful result. Most effective teachers, if gently pushed, will be able to explain what they believe their students have achieved in class. This is an important thing to be able to do; the writing-out of aims on a training course is one route to help you learn to do this. The rest of this section is about aims that have been set before a lesson.

You may have aims of various kinds for the actual running of a lesson, to do with yourself (e.g. 'I will try to talk less'), to do with the classroom ('I will make sure the seating is rearranged appropriately when the activity changes') or to do with individuals ('I will keep an eye on Maria to check that she isn't getting lost'). The most important aim usually concerns intended student achievements: things that they will have learned, skills they will have improved, points they will have reached by the end of the lesson. This is often called the 'main aim' of a lesson.

Task 71: Procedure aims and achievement aims

Some teachers write aims that are only statements of procedure (i.e. what students will do during the class) rather than stating what the teacher hopes the students will achieve by doing them. In the following aims, decide which are procedure aims and which are achievement aims.

1 Students will be better able to ask and answer simple informal questions about a person's life, likes and dislikes.
2 Students will have done a role-play about meeting new clients.
3 Students will be better able to use the phone to order food, call a taxi, etc.
4 Present and practise comparatives.
5 Listen to coursebook recording 16.4.
6 Students will be better able to assess different people's attitudes when listening to a phone-in discussion on the radio.

Commentary ■ ■ ■

Aims 1, 3 and 6 are achievement aims. If you had trouble distinguishing these, keep thinking about this question when you read the sections below. ■

Achievement aims

Although many aims in trainee lesson plans are written as procedure aims, I feel that the achievement aim is considerably more useful for teachers when planning.

Imagine a lesson in terms of a cross-country hike (see Figure 6.8). You may not have been to this part of the countryside before, but you can still imagine something about the journey and predict things you need to prepare beforehand. You know where you probably want to end up, even though you perhaps can't see the end from the starting point. Getting to that end point is your main aim. You may have various decisions to make about the way that you get to that goal: the speed you walk at, the route you take, what map you use, where you will rest, what aids you take to help you, whether you need a picnic lunch, etc. All these decisions are related to the main decision about the aim; if this is not clear, the walk could still be enjoyable, but you will probably pass by fewer interesting sites, meet a number of unexpected problems, and are more likely to get completely lost. And if you have been to this place before, you can make better predictions about the excursion, though never with 100% chance of being spot-on, as so many variables can alter things.

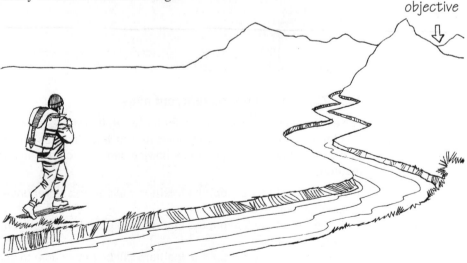

objective

Figure 6.8   Getting to the objective

A lesson might involve learners individually reading a text like the one in Figure 6.9 and writing the answers to some comprehension questions. The **material** is the text itself; the **activity** would be 'learners reading a text and answering questions'. The **teaching point** – the subject matter of the lesson in terms of language skills – is 'reading comprehension of information or advertising leaflets' and 'writing answers to questions'. The **topic** is 'tourist information'.

The **achievement aim** requires a little more thought. You know how the mechanics of the activity will work, but why are the learners doing it? How will doing this activity, using this material, help their English? Aims are the results of the lesson from the learner's perspective. It can be helpful to start with a phrase like 'By the end of the lesson, the learners will have ...' or 'By the end of the lesson, the learners will be better able to ...'

Here are two example aims based on the reading lesson described above:

- By the end of the lesson, the learners will be better able to find specific information in tourist information leaflets.
- By the end of the lesson, learners will have had practice in completing timed exercises on reading comprehension in preparation for their exam next week.

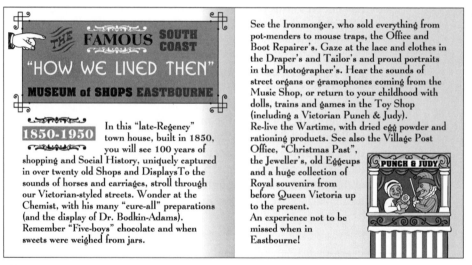

Figure 6.9   Museum leaflet text

Task 72: Same material, different aims

The example above used the leaflet for two quite different aims. Bearing in mind that the text could be used in many different ways in class, in different activities, with different aims, which of the following aims could it be an appropriate piece of material for?

1 By the end of the lesson, the learners will have a clearer understanding of the use of imperative verb forms.
2 By the end of the lesson, the learners will have had practice in listening to and giving instructions.
3 By the end of the lesson, the learners will be better able to understand and use the past perfect tense.

Commentary ■ ■ ■

1   This aim is possible. The activities you devised for using the material would be very different from the ones used when 'reading to find specific information' was the aim. The activities would draw on specific items of language in the text and analyse or focus on them in ways that made the students clearer about their form, meaning and uses.

2   This aim may seem inappropriate at a first glance, but bear in mind that you could use the material in many different ways. If you devised a role-play, giving the text to only some of the students (the 'information office') and asking the other ones (the 'tourists') to find the answers, then the aim would be appropriate.

3   This is a much more unlikely aim; I'm sure it would be possible to invent an activity that used this material and involved work on the past perfect, but there are surely more obvious pieces of material to use. ■

Conclusion so far: a piece of material can be used in many ways, in different activities, with quite different aims. Your decision as to what your aim is will determine the way in which you work with the material. With a piece of text, for example, if your aim is to improve students' ability to read fast, then you might set a time limit to force them to read quickly, or you might turn it into a team game where quick answers win points. But if your aim is to focus on the use of a particular tense, you might want to allow time to discuss the problem, to use the board to draw some time diagrams, etc.

Task 73: Matching material to aims

Here are three aims for three separate activities. Which of the following pieces of material (a, b, c) might it be possible to use in order to achieve each aim?

1   By the end of the lesson, the learners will have had oral practice of six or seven examples of the function of apologising. They will be better able to use them accurately and in appropriate situations.

2   By the end of the lesson, the learners will have revised the use of *in case* and practised using it orally and in writing.

3   By the end of the lesson, the learners will have had written practice in using *going to* to express future events.

If you have a clear aim for a lesson, you can bear this in mind all the way through the class. Knowing where you are going enables you to make moment-by-moment decisions about different paths or options to take en route, while keeping the main aim always clearly in front of you (which you are far less free to do if you have only set aims that are descriptions of intended procedures). Good lesson planning, and especially good specifying of aims, does not therefore restrict you, but in clarifying the end point you intend to reach, sets you free to go towards that point in the most appropriate ways in class. Thus Figure 6.10 complements Figure 6.8 at the start of this section.

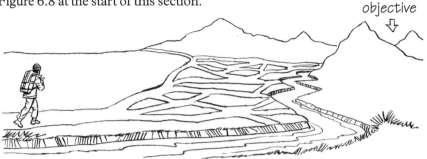

Figure 6.10   Options and objectives

6   A very short section on 'challenge'

Teaching means (a) finding out where the learning is, and (b) going there. It means asking 'Where is the challenge?', not 'How can I avoid the difficult bits?' A struggle on the part of students means that learning is probably going on.

Don't assume that when all students 'get' the thing you are teaching, it means that you have taught well; it may mean you aimed too low or avoided the challenge. Students trying and failing (but making progress) means that more learning is probably going on than when a student 'gets it' immediately.

Teachers generally avoid the struggle when it arises: 'OK, let's stop that and do something different.' They sell the idea of struggle-free learning to their students: 'This isn't difficult'/'This is fun'/'Here's a game'/'This should be easy', etc.

- Maybe we shouldn't plan around 'aims'. The easily achieved aim is no achievement (and how can we know what our students will learn?).
- Maybe we'd do better to try stating what the linguistic challenge will be in each lesson or activity… and then learn to let the students 'wrestle' with this challenge in class.
- Maybe we should stop trying to force-feed information to learners … and rather let learners face up to the problems.

7   Alternatives to formal planning

Just because you may have been trained into using 'traditional' formal lesson plan formats, don't assume that they are the beginning and end of planning. There may be good reasons for not using a standard 'aims-plus-procedure' plan. For example, you may feel:

- you haven't got the time;
- the lesson methodology you wish to use cannot easily be characterised using this format;

- it doesn't seem an economic or helpful way of describing a lesson's way of working;
- it might restrict your freedom to respond to learners in class;
- the lesson content and/or aim will emerge during the class rather than being pre-decided;
- your priority is to create a specific atmosphere, a certain type of rapport, etc.;
- you want to experiment or work on specific aspects of your teaching.

Here are some ideas for other approaches to planning. You may like to choose one or more and try them when preparing lessons.

A brief 'running order'

The simplest type of lesson plan, and one used by many teachers, is a basic 'running order' of activities, perhaps with a note of specific language points or materials that will be used (see Figure 6.11). This plan has the advantage of being something you can do on the bus in to work or on the back of an envelope in the staff room five minutes before going into class!

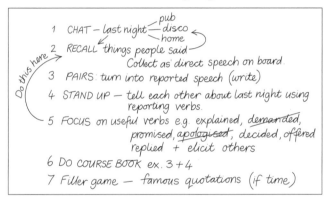

Figure 6.11   Informal running order

Flow chart

Write your procedure notes in sketch boxes, rather than in traditional linear down-the-page fashion. Show a variety of different possible running orders and routes through the stages by drawing lines between different boxes (see Figure 6.12).

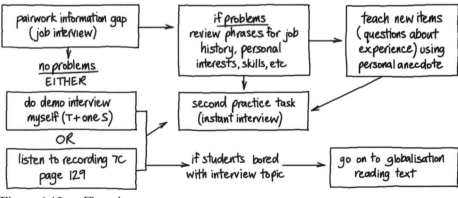

Figure 6.12   Flow chart

Dream through the lesson

Don't write anything. Repeatedly imagine your way through the lesson, perhaps with your eyes closed. Think up possible different routes that you might initiate – or that learners might. See where each leads. (Try this just before you fall asleep at night!)

Focus on the 'critical learning moments'

Rather than planning the entire lesson procedure, before class decide on a number of specific key things you hope learners will gain from the class (e.g. being able to pronounce a set of new words well, being able to replay a difficult recording until they can understand the main message, etc.). For each of these, decide what the 'critical learning moment' will probably be, i.e. which thing you or they do (lasting no more than 30 seconds) that is likely to make the most significant impact on their success – and why. Think through each of these moments very carefully.

Even if you are writing a formal lesson plan, you may still find it useful to mark critical moments with 'C' and perhaps give more detailed information about how these will be dealt with.

Half-plan

This idea is for more experienced teachers, or others who feel confident about their own language awareness and of their ability to quickly think of mini-activities. Put your energy into planning how your class will do skills work (e.g. reading, speaking, etc.). Don't plan any language systems work (e.g. lexis, grammar, etc.). In class, spontaneously work on language issues as they come up if they are useful, interesting and appropriate for students. NB 'Work on' doesn't just mean 'explain' – can you invent on-the-spot practice tasks as well?

Where's the meat?

List the main 'teaching points' for your lesson. Go back and list the inherent 'challenges' in each of these for the students you are working with:

- What do you expect them to find important, difficult, hard to pick up, etc.?
- Where will they make mistakes?
- What mistakes and problems are likely?

Focus 95% of your planning on paying attention to this 'challenge' (NB this refers to the challenge in the teaching points themselves, not in the activities or tasks you use to focus on them). Decide on your teaching strategies to 'get to where the learning is going on'.

Plan the 'critical teaching moments'

Which instructions, explanations, feedback stages, etc. will be 'critical moments' for you, the teacher, which may need to be prepared in detail in advance?

Lesson images

Draw sketch pictures of the class at several key moments in the lesson. Show what learners and teacher are doing. (Not appropriate for a 'sit down and write all the time' kind of lesson.)

The jungle path

… or perhaps don't plan anything!

Most lessons involve you pre-planning a sequence of activities, predicting what language areas will be worked on, what problems are likely to arise and what the students may achieve in the lesson. An alternative approach would be to not predict and prepare so much, but to create the lesson moment by moment in class, with you and learners working with whatever is happening in the room, responding to questions, problems and options as they come up, and finding new activities, materials and tasks in response to particular situations. The starting point might be an activity or a piece of material, but what comes out of it will remain unknown until it happens. You are working more with the people in the room than with your material or your plan.

I imagine a group of people hacking their way through the jungle towards new experiences, new learning. Sometimes the teacher may lead, sometimes the students. Everyone would be encouraged to think, make connections, ask questions and draw conclusions for themselves.

The main pre-planning for a lesson of this kind would involve you using your knowledge of the learners and of the available resources to choose some activities and materials that are likely to prove challenging and raise important questions and issues. You would have an intuitive sense of various potential links between activities, based partly on previous experiences of the outcomes of lessons using similar activities.

In class, some of these activities and materials may be used, some not. You may also feel the need to find other materials as the lesson proceeds, some from a coursebook, some from your head, some from the staff-room library, etc. Although you may be clear about a number of possible directions the lesson might take, it will be impossible for you to state the lesson's aims until after it has finished.

After a lesson like this, many teachers are surprised to find that they come out feeling that they have taught particularly well; this may be to do with the fact that they have had to listen and respond to students far more carefully than they usually do.

Here is an example lesson description:

Lesson A

1 You take a communication game (concerning different attitudes to smoking) into class. The students do this in pairs.
2 When they have finished, some students ask about some language problems they had. The students discuss and work out some answers to the problems.
3 You invent a quick practice exercise that will focus on one of the language points.

4 When that has finished, a student asks about the pronunciation of some words in the exercise. You work through some examples on the board and then tell them to turn to a page in their coursebook where there is a game to help raise students' awareness of word stress. The class decides that they don't want to do this now, but will do it for homework.

5 Some students remind you that they haven't yet discussed smoking as a whole class and they'd like to hear what some of the rest of the class thought, etc.

Here are two common examples of a 'jungle path' lesson where you start without any materials:

Lesson B

You ask 'How was the weekend?' (or a similar question) and, after listening to a number of answers, lead this into a discussion based on something a student said. At some point, you select particular items of language that a student has used, focus on these (perhaps considering grammar or pronunciation), invent a simple exercise that will help students work on this, etc.

Lesson C

A student asks a question at the start of the lesson. This leads into some work on the board (perhaps you set the class a problem to solve that will help to clarify the language difficulty). While the students are working on the puzzle, you go to the staff room and collect a further exercise on the same language area. You return and offer the students the new exercise, but they say they feel clear now about the language item. However, there is another question which has arisen ...

A fourth example demonstrates how a competent and confident teacher might hand over responsibility and decision-making entirely to the class:

Lesson D

You start the lesson by asking 'What shall we work on today?' You then wait while the class decides, taking care not to manipulate them into deciding something that you want them to do. Once the decisions are made, you do whatever you have been asked to do.

The 'jungle path' lesson can look artless to an observer, yet to do it successfully requires experience. It is not simply a 'chat' or an abdication of responsibility, though in inexperienced hands it might well be simply a muddle and a 'lazy' alternative to careful planning. In fact, for a competent teacher, it involves working minute by minute with the class, actively planning and replanning as you go, constantly basing the work around the students and their needs, statements, problems, questions, etc.

When doing this, you need to be aware both of the people in the room and of the wide variety of options open to you. You need to be able to make decisions, moment by moment, about which route is the best one to follow. You need to be familiar with all the resources of material and information available to you.

The need for teaching experience and awareness of resources available suggests that lessons of this type are more appropriate for teachers who are already fairly competent in planning and executing more traditional lessons. For this reason, it is the lesson you don't normally learn to do on teacher-training courses!

8   Planning a course

'I can plan a lesson. But how can I plan a day, a week, a month, a term, a year?'

There are two main considerations:

- What will I teach (i.e. what is the syllabus)?
- How will the separate items be sequenced (i.e. what is the work plan or timetable)?

What will I teach?

On a day-to-day basis, there are a variety of reasons for the selection of lesson content.

Task 74: Selecting lesson content

Look at the following list of reasons. Which seem to you the most important ones to consider when selecting content to work on?

- I'm following a required school syllabus.
- It's the language featured in the next coursebook unit.
- The students requested it in a Needs-analysis form
- The main class teacher asked me to do it.
- I understand this bit of grammar myself!
- I think this will be useful for them.
- This is appropriate for their level.
- A student has asked me about it.
- I always teach this item at this point in the course.
- I don't want to work on the language item the book has next.
- I've noticed that the students seem to need this structure.
- I like teaching this language item.
- We negotiated and agreed that we would study this now.
- I think they might enjoy my lesson about this.
- They have problems with this.

Commentary ■ ■ ■

There are many valid reasons for choosing what to teach. I would tend to value those that directly respond to learner needs (e.g. 'I think this will be useful for them') over those that are only (or primarily) following a pre-set list (e.g. 'It's the language featured in the next coursebook unit'). Having said that, many teachers work in contexts where they are expected to work on specific things on certain days. In some schools, for example, the management may even require that different classes work on the same areas in lessons at the same time. ■

The syllabus

A syllabus provides a long-term overview. It lists the contents of a course and puts the separate items in an order. In some schools, the syllabus may simply be the coursebook – 'Get to Unit 17 by half term' – whereas in others, there may be a much more detailed requirement.

A syllabus can be mainly grammatical or functional or lexical. Alternatively, it may be based on skills work (e.g. speaking and listening), or it may contain a mixture of work on systems and skills. Some syllabuses describe course content in terms of topics or tasks.

Having a syllabus can be a great help, setting out clearly what you are expected to cover with your class. It can be a burden, too, if it is unrealistic for your students in terms of what they need or are likely to achieve within a certain time.

Task 75: Your syllabus

What syllabus are you currently working to? Is it prescriptive? detailed? non-existent? useful? How does it affect what you do? Who decided on it? How much say have you had in it? How much say have your students had?

The Common European Framework

An important document called the *Common European Framework* (CEF), published by the Council of Europe, has had a lot of influence over syllabus design in Europe. It describes possible course content in terms of what learners need to **do** with language to communicate in the real world, a radical departure from many syllabus that describe what people need to **know**. The CEF organises the content into a clearly defined level system. With more schools and educational establishments taking up the CEF, it now provides a common basis for discussion and reform in language teaching, course design, testing and materials writing. From the students' perspective, there is more chance that the level and qualification they achieve in one country will be understood in any other country they go to.

Timetables and work plans: How will the teaching content be sequenced?

In school management, **timetabling** refers to the preparation (by a head teacher, head of department or director of studies) of an overview master plan of which classes are with which teachers in which rooms at which times.

For a teacher, **timetabling** refers to the day-to-day, week-to-week decisions about how to interpret a syllabus into a series of lessons. You could also call this a **work plan** or a **scheme of work**. It is usually wholly or partly the teacher's job.

The process of making a work plan typically involves looking at a school syllabus or a coursebook contents page and trying to map out how you will cover the content in the time available, i.e. selecting items from the syllabus and writing them as a dated list, under headings or by placing into appropriate spaces on a blank timetable grid (i.e. a diagrammatic or diary-like page representing a day, week or month with spaces for lesson notes). The work plan is your translation of the syllabus requirements into a balanced and interesting series of lessons.

Work plans are usually written out in advance, prepared by the teacher responsible for teaching a subject with a particular class. You may be required to show it to your supervisor or head of department, and you may have to get formal approval for what you intend to do (some schools require them months ahead). In some places, a head of department or director of studies may provide you with a pre-written work plan, though this is unusual. If you are not required to hand in a work plan far ahead of time, you have the option of working it out in negotiation with your class. In some schools, you may be expected to fill in retrospective work plans showing what you actually taught, rather than what you intended to teach.

A work plan enables other teachers to understand what work is being done in your class. The information it provides may be especially important if another teacher shares your class with you, if you are ill or absent one day, or if your manager is concerned about your class in any way. It is also useful for your students to see what they will be doing. The work plan should give others a clear idea of what work was planned for a particular lesson and also show how that fits into the overall shape of the week and the course.

A work plan may be more or less detailed:

- A **skeleton work plan** lists only general headings or labels (e.g. Tuesday 9.00 listening; 10.30 grammar and speaking) or perhaps coursebook page numbers. This type of work plan is used for planning the overall shape of a week or course; it helps to ensure that there is balance and variety in a course.
- A **detailed work plan** contains more information, specifying exactly what is to be done (e.g. 'input on present perfect simple plus oral practice using coursebook Unit 7E; listening Exercise 3 page 56'). A detailed work plan is for your own planning, for keeping an accurate record of the course and for informing others (e.g. your director or another teacher) about what you are doing in class.

Task 76: Interpreting skeleton plans

Figure 6.13 shows two excerpts from different skeleton work plans prepared for a mid-level full-time English course with young adults who need English for general and social purposes. Evaluate the two work plans, thinking about:

- whether you would be comfortable using it as your own work plan;
- what conclusions you can draw about writing work plans for a course that might help you plan your own.

Work plan 1	Monday	Tuesday
9.00–10.30	Grammar	Grammar
	Vocabulary	Vocabulary
10.30–12.00	Grammar	Grammar
	Vocabulary	Vocabulary
1.30–3.00	Pronunciation	Written exercise
	Grammar	Grammar
	Speaking game	Song

Work plan 2	Monday	Tuesday
9.00–10.30	Speaking	Grammar (review yesterday's work)
	Listening (coursebook)	
	Vocabulary game	Speaking: role-play
10.30–12.00	Grammar	Listening (radio news)
	Pronunciation	Reading (newspaper)
	Check homework	
1.30–3.00	Listening (song)	Writing (preparing a class newsletter)
	Speaking	

Figure 6.13   Work plans 1 and 2

Commentary ■ ■ ■

Work plan 1 looks problematic. It is clearly biased strongly towards work on language systems, and especially towards grammar and vocabulary. Work on the skills of listening, speaking, reading and writing is minimal or non-existent. The last lesson of the day seems to include a game or a song as a sort of 'bonus' or 'extra' rather than integrating speaking and listening work into the course. Whereas some element of systematic work and routine can be beneficial, there does seem to be a very predictable shape to this course (if it's nine o'clock, it must be grammar), that could prove demotivating in the long run.

Conclusion 1: a balance of activities on a timetable is important. Include work on language skills and language systems in appropriate proportions for your students' needs.

Conclusion 2: variety is useful. Choose varied topics and include varied activities. Don't always start the day with the same kind of work.

Both of these problems seem to find some answers in Work plan 2. There is an interesting balance of work on skills and systems; there is variety, both in terms of what is done and when it is done; there is also some sense of separate activities adding up to something bigger – for example, in the three related activities based around 'news'. There is attention to links between work done on different days (the homework checking, for example, or the review of the previous day's work). If the aims of the course are in the area of 'general English', then this timetable seems to offer more chance of achieving them than the mainly grammar and lexis-based programme of Work plan 1.

Conclusion 3: it is important to plan activities that will add to a sense of moving forward; of growing achievement and progress.

Conclusion 4: it is essential to consider the aims of a course; a course leading to a written grammar exam will have very different timetables from a general English course. ■

Task 77: A task-based plan

Figure 6.14 shows a different kind of skeleton work plan for a similar course.

- How does it differ from the two you have just looked at (Figure 6.13)?
- How do Monday and Tuesday differ?

Work plan 3	Monday	Tuesday
9.00–10.30	Introduce task.	Introduce task. Language help and planning. Review and feedback on task.
	Language help and planning.	
	Task.	
10.30–12.00	Review and feedback on task.	Introduce real-world task. Task. Read follow-up material. Listen to competent language users doing task.
	Research to enrich task performance.	
	Language help and replanning.	
	Listen to competent language users doing task.	
1.30–3.00	Repeat task.	Introduce real-world task. Task. Language review and feedback on task. Repeat task.
	Review and feedback on task.	
	Follow-up reading.	

Figure 6.14   Work plan 3

Commentary ■ ■ ■

This is an interesting variation. Instead of listing language skills and systems, it plans the days in terms of preparation for and undertaking of real-world tasks plus follow-on stages. In other words, it is thinking about language study in terms of things the learners might do in real life. (Examples of real-world tasks might include 'phoning and asking for information', 'asking for directions and finding a location', 'making a short public speech', 'writing a job application letter', etc.).

On Monday, the whole day is given over to a long cycle based around a single major task. On Tuesday, a number of shorter task cycles are done. The selection and sequence of stages in each case is a little different. ■

How can you go about making a detailed work plan?

Preparing a work plan can seem a very daunting challenge – there are so many factors to consider and evaluate. You'll need to draw on all your knowledge, skills and intuition to make it work. Figure 6.15 shows one possible eleven-step method for planning. It starts by making a skeleton and then expands on this to make a more detailed plan.

1	**Decide the duration**	Decide how long you want to plan for (the whole course? one week? a term? etc.)
2	**Consult the syllabus**	If you have a syllabus, consult it to see the intended course content. Check what work has not been done.
3	**Review learner needs**	Review any Needs-analysis data you have gained from your students.
4	**Decide the aims**	Write down a number of things learners should achieve in the course (or part of the course): these are the course aims.
5	**Choose the components**	Decide if you want to plan in terms of (a) language systems and skills, (b) tasks, (c) something else (e.g. exam items? texts? topics? etc.).
6	**Prepare a grid**	Draw a blank grid showing the number of lessons you have to plan for. Each grid cell should have enough space for you to write in some lesson information.
7	**Make cards**	Cut up a number of rectangles of paper, each the same size as the cells.
8	**Select activities**	Think of some activities that are appropriate for your learners and help lead towards the course aims you set. Write these down, one item to each piece of paper.
9	**Arrange the cards**	When you have a number of filled-in pieces of paper, lay them on the blank grid. Play around with them, move them, order them, rearrange them until you start to feel that certain sequences work effectively.

Row 6 grid:

	Mon	Tue	Wed	Thu	Fri	Mon	Tue	Wed	Thu	Fri
9.30										
11.30										
2.15										

Row 9 grid:

	Mon	Tue	Wed	Thu	Fri	Mon	Tue	Wed	Thu	Fri
9.30	■		■	■		■				
11.30	■	■	■					■		
2.15		■				■				

10	**Complete the skeleton**	Fill in more scraps to complement and complete the grid, making a coherent skeleton timetable.
11	**Flesh out the timetable**	Remove the cards one by one and write in a more detailed description of what you intend to do on the timetable grid underneath it.

Figure 6.15   Eleven steps to planning a work plan using a blank timetable grid

The detailed timetable shown in Figure 6.16 is based around tasks and was planned using this method. It directly reflects some wishes and needs mentioned by students. When you read it decide:

• whether it seems to provide coherent, balanced days;
• whether you think planning work around tasks might be more useful to you than planning around language systems and skills.

Work plan 3	Monday	Tuesday
9.00–10.30	Discuss differences between various locations in the world. Read texts and compare lifestyles in these places.	Plan a possible class newsletter.
10.30–12.00	Decide on criteria for choosing a holiday. Choose a holiday by reading brochures and advertisements.	Compare a range of published magazines and notice features you could use in your own magazine.
	Write a booking form for a holiday and car hire.	Write a newsletter article.
	Deal with problems and reach a satisfactory outcome.	Read and give feedback on other students' articles.
1.30–3.00	Buy a train ticket (role-plays).	Use the Internet to research some jokes to add to the newsletter.
	Find your train by listening to station announcements.	Prepare a final draft of the newsletter.
	Meet and socialise with other guests at your hotel.	

Figure 6.16   Work plan 4

Work plan 5 (Figure 6.17) is a more traditional one, based on systems and skills. It was written by a teacher in Spain who meets her class for two hours each week on a Tuesday evening; this timetable covers one month, the second month of a six-month course for adults who want to improve their general English for a variety of reasons (but no one is planning to take an exam). Their level is elementary (i.e. they are not beginners; they know a number of structures and can create a number of sentences themselves, though often inaccurately).

Task 78: Understand a work plan

Place the following items into one of the numbered spaces on the work plan.

a   Speaking: in groups, they design their ideal home.
b   Students do oral pairwork activity: 'Finding out about what they've done in their lives'.
c   Class discussion about the course so far.
d   Students, in groups of three, compare how they spent the last week, filling in a diary for the other group members.

Work plan 5

Week 5
Talking about experiences the students have had: class discussion.
Teacher focus on use of present perfect; clarify form and use.
1 ....
Unit C6: students do listening Exercise 3 and written Exercise 7.
Homework: keep a simple diary this week.
Week 6
Teacher uses clock to revise telling the time and talking about the time (four lessons ago).
Teacher asks students for any other expressions involving time they know (write, e.g. *at the weekend* on board; focus on use of *on, in, at*.
2 ....
Unit C10: students do written Exercise 3.
Game: past participle quiz (revising last lesson).
Homework: Unit C10 Exercises 1, 2.
Week 7
Vocabulary: around the house. Use large poster to find out which words they know and which would be useful to learn.
Listening: Students must fill in this information on a picture of the house.
3 ....
Week 8
4 ....
Negotiating/planning the next month.
Students work in groups to write a test that they will take next lesson.
Listening: pop song. Task: listen and fill in the blank spaces in the text.

Figure 6.17   Work plan 5

Commentary ■ ■ ■

1 b   2 d   3 a   4 c

Activity b seems to go well with grammar work on the present perfect tense, so space 1 is appropriate. Similarly, activity d will offer a number of opportunities to practise using the time expressions studied in week 6's lesson (space 2). The 'home designing' activity (a) links in with the other activities in week 7. The discussion about the course so far (c) would make a good starting point for planning the following month. ■

Topic-based work plans

Many teachers plan a day's – or a week's – work around a single topic, looking for ways to link the course aims with the ongoing theme. Having a single theme may help to give a sense of coherence to the work. This can help you find good ideas, as instead of struggling to find 'any idea' for teaching something, you can focus your creative thinking onto a specific topic area. For example, the topic of 'celebrities' might allow you to incorporate a number of useful lessons that focus on skills, systems and real-life tasks, e.g.

* Grammar: present perfect – saying what celebrities have done/haven't done in the lives;
* Speaking: discussion: 'Is it good to be famous or not?';
* Writing: writing a fan letter to a star;
* Reading: biography of a celebrity;
* Lexis: items connected with a luxury lifestyle.

Task 79: Choosing teaching content for a topic area

You are going to use the topic of 'islands' with a general English class around Elementary level. What teaching content could you use that will link neatly with this theme?

9   Unrealistic requirements

Teachers are often faced with planning a course when there are syllabus requirements they don't agree with or teaching material that they don't like. There is a fine balance between doing what you are required or expected to do and doing what you believe is appropriate, useful or needed.

There is obviously no single, magic answer to problems of this kind. However, it is often possible to do what is expected of you, to reach the goals you have been told to reach, to use the pages of the book you have been told to use, to get students through tests they need to pass, to make the end point of the lesson, the day, the course exactly where it is supposed to be, but still to make the journey there surprising, interesting and exciting. The parabola ends up at the same point, but follows a much more interesting route.

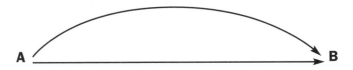

Some examples:

- Your boss has told you that the only aim of your course is to get students to pass a (very boring) written grammar and essay exam at the end of term.

The straight line approach is to spend all the class time doing grammar and written work. The parabola is to follow a balanced syllabus that includes a lot of speaking, listening and other skills work of all kinds, as well as grammar and vocabulary. Sometimes the parabola is the shortest road; you may find that the students make much better progress and get better results than students who only follow the straight line.

- You have been told that you must 'do' two pages of the coursebook every day. The whole book must be covered by the end of the term.

The straight line would be to work through everything in the coursebook as it is written, doing each exercise in order, in the way that the coursebook writer tells you to. The parabola is to use the two pages every day as required, but really exploiting them using them as resource material, inspiration. Change the order! Get students to cross out boring exercises! Design better pictures for a text! Debate with the students how to use the book! Agree with students to speed through six pages in one day (and free yourself for two days)! Supplement with lots of your own goodies! Turn texts into dictations, information gaps, listenings, games, etc.!

Straight lines are boring! Be bold – travel by parabola! Don't assume that an edict from above completely closes down all your options.

10 English and teaching in the world

When considering what we teach and how it will impact on our students, we are naturally often wound up mainly in the small details of what will happen when and how to do it. It is important, all the same, to also be able to step back and refresh our wider perspective on the role our teaching has on our students' lives and on the life of the world. There are some questions worth asking which could have a direct and important impact on our day-to-day decisions about what we plan.

English as an international language

Task 80: Your students' interaction needs

Do the students you work with need English to communicate with English mother-tongue speakers? Or are they more likely to be using English as a language to interact with other non-native users?

Commentary ■ ■ ■

In many places, language teaching has for some time seemed quite UK-centric (or US-centric), with coursebooks drawing a lot on UK/US culture and with language samples mainly using one variety of pronunciation. There may also be an unstated assumption that learners will visit the UK or USA and need English mainly to communicate with locals there.

But many learners who study the language have no intention of going to these places, and they may well not be learning English to communicate with native speakers, but in order to use it as a lingua franca, enabling them to meet (and maybe do business with) people from all over the world. ■

Significantly more people around the world will have English as a fluent second (or third) language than use it as native speakers. Teachers and researchers are increasingly asking what kind of English we should be teaching and what language samples (e.g. what pronunciation models) are appropriate to offer our students.

World Englishes

Task 81: Englishes

'English is English, isn't it?' What is the meaning of the plural form in the subheading above?

Commentary ■ ■ ■

There are many varieties of English around the world, each having grammar, vocabulary, pronunciation, etc. arising from and appropriate to the local context. Varieties often incorporate expressions and pronunciation features from other local languages. These Englishes may have an official role (e.g. language of secondary education) or they may be used only by a minority group or by people who normally speak their own tongue, but select English at certain times or in certain places (e.g. by Czech teenagers meeting to play fantasy board games).

Some internationally known varieties, such as UK English, may be viewed in some contexts as more prestigious, while local varieties can be undervalued or looked down on. They are often known by a local, jokey, nickname, e.g. Singlish (Singapore English) or Hunglish (Hungarian English). ■

This all raises important questions such as 'Who owns English nowadays?' 'Is it right to view some varieties as inferior and others as better or more correct?' and 'Is the imposition of one variety of English colonialistic?'

Task 82: Choosing which variety of English to teach

Imagine you are a Brazilian teacher of English who has just started a contract to work in a rural school in Tanzania. What variety of English is it appropriate to base your teaching on – your own? East African English? UK English? US English? An international English?

Commentary ■ ■ ■

'What can I teach?' is a question that many teachers face, especially if they take on work outside their home country. There is no simple answer, and there may be many constraints on what you choose (e.g. which coursebook you have). ■

My brief, perhaps simplistic, answer is that I think you need to be aware of:

- what your students need and expect;
- what you are realistically able to do;
- the impact your choices might have in the long term, personally, locally, nationally and globally.

Your learners' needs, such as having to take an exam that requires a certain variety of English or needing to communicate in a particular context, are probably paramount concerns.

One approach I have seen a number of teachers adopting is that of being completely open about acknowledging the range of Englishes available and raising it for discussion and choice; for example, after playing a recording, saying 'Well, the person on the recording said … but, myself, I say … and here in this town, I've noticed that people say …'.

Appropriate methodology

Task 83: The impact of my teaching

In reading this book, have you come across ideas or techniques that have made you stop and think 'That's completely unsuitable for my students' or 'That is just impossible in this locality/culture'?

Commentary ■ ■ ■

I rather hope you have, because the book isn't intended to offer any all-purpose solutions, but to suggest some possibilities and encourage you to enquire into how they might fit with your own teaching and its context. The kind of techniques and teaching strategies discussed in this book represent my version of what seems to me current good practice and thinking. But it is one person's view based on my experience in the kinds of schools and countries I have worked in. It may well not be appropriate methodology in other schools, other places, other cultures. ■

There may be serious dangers in trying to 'export' en masse an approach that works in one place and assuming it will also work elsewhere. The right methodology is the right methodology for a context. It isn't a universal answer.

This is not to say that the right methodology is automatically whatever the status quo happens to be or what conservative thinkers in a locale believe to be best. Some teachers or managers may have a stake in maintaining things just as they are and reject any innovation or suggestion for improvement. In these cases, the teacher who feels that they have something important to offer has a difficult dilemma as to whether it is right to implement their innovation and how to do it most effectively.

Global issues

Beyond concerns about language and methodology, maybe teachers should also be asking about their role on the planet as a whole.

Task 84: Organising a discussion class

You might like to try out some of these questions on yourself.

- What cultural impact does my teaching of English have on the development of the country and on the use of its own languages?
- Should I be concerned about the impact my teaching has on the world, the peoples of the world and the global future?

- If I believe that some aspect of language education locally, nationally or globally is bad (or not helpful) for my students (e.g. the exams they have to take are poorly designed or not related to any real needs), should I tell them, keep quiet, campaign behind the scenes, etc.?
- How aware am I of the impact of what I do and say on other people's lives and happiness?
- How much should I take a role in educating learners, not just in language but also in raising awareness about prejudice, exploitation, environmental issues and interdependence? Is this part of my job?
- What right do I have to take a stand on issues I believe in?
- Can I play a role in establishing new sets of values among learners? (and should I? and whose values am I promoting, anyway?)

Chapter 7 Speaking

1 Conversation and discussion classes

Task 85: Organising a discussion class

You have been asked to include a regular discussion lesson or conversation class in your course. How could you organise this and why might it be useful for learners?

Commentary ■ ■ ■

This suggests a lesson in which you and the learners mainly talk together. The learners will get a chance to become more fluent and confident. A lesson of this kind is based on a belief that giving an opportunity and encouragement to speak will be a useful thing to do in class, and that (you hope) students can 'learn to speak by speaking'.

Fluency and confidence are important goals. There is no point knowing a lot about language if you can't use it (which, sadly, has been the experience of many language learners in the past – able to conjugate a verb, but unable to respond to a simple question).

How could a lesson like this be organised? The following points give some suggestions (summarised in Figure 7.1).

- **Topic and cues**
  At its simplest, you (or learners) would possibly bring to class a topic (e.g. 'banning smoking' or 'globalisation'), as well as a cue (e.g. in the form of a short newspaper article or a provocative question) that will serve to help spark conversation. Most of the lesson would then be taken up with discussing this, stating and comparing views. There might be little or no explicit 'teaching' of grammatical or vocabulary points. In planning the lesson, it would be a good idea to prepare a number of further cues (e.g. a follow-on article or question) to keep in reserve in order to move the discussion forward if it starts to drag.

- **Structuring talk**
  Your main role will be to structure the talk, making sure that all learners get a chance to participate, trying to prevent it getting boring, occasionally adding to the discussion himself in order to keep it interesting. It is likely that you will generally want to reduce your own participation level; the more you talk, the less space there is for learners to say something.

- **Avoiding the talk-talk loop**
  There is a danger of getting locked into a 'talk-talk loop', in which you say something, but because there is no response from the learners, you say something else, and again with no response you add something else, etc. It takes a little courage initially, but you will usually get far more conversation out of a class by asking one clear question and then shutting up – and patiently allowing even quite a long silence, while learners formulate what they want to say. Repeatedly adding new comments or new questions can have the opposite effect to that intended, confusing the class and closing down people who were planning to speak.

- **Open questions**
  A key technique will be to use 'open questions' (e.g. *where, what, who, why, how, when* questions that require a longer answer) rather than 'closed' questions (e.g. verb-subject questions that require nothing more than 'yes' or 'no'). For example, instead of 'Is noise pollution a bad thing?' (answer = 'yes' or 'no'), you could ask 'What do you think about noise pollution?' Focusing on specific issues is even more likely to encourage reactions, for example 'When they make that noise with the drill outside, how do you feel?'

- **Playing devil's advocate**
  One useful intervention you can make is to sometimes play 'devil's advocate' (i.e. deliberately taking an opposing or contrasting viewpoint in order to spur on conversation). ■

Planning it
You need: a relevant topic; an initial cue; follow-on cues

Teaching it
Techniques: Open questions
                   Monitor participation levels
                   Invite people in
                   Avoid the 'talk-talk' loop
                   Listen more than talk
                   Play devil's advocate where appropriate

Figure 7.1   A basic discussion lesson or conversation class

Task 86: Fluency and confidence aims

The aim for the conversation class is for learners to 'become more fluent and confident'. Why might learners need this (i.e. what may have prevented them becoming fluent)?

Commentary ■ ■ ■

Very often, when people study a language, they accumulate a lot of 'up-in-the-head' knowledge (i.e. they may know rules of grammar and lists of vocabulary items), but then find that they can't actually use this language to communicate when they want to. There seems to be some difficulty in moving language from 'up-there' knowledge to actively usable language. For many learners, their 'passive' knowledge is much larger than their 'active' language. Without experience in using the language, learners may tend to be nervous about trying to say things. Partly they may fear seeming foolish in front of others; they may worry about getting things wrong; they may want to avoid your comments or corrections; and so on. In addition to these, it may simply take a long time to 'put the pieces' of a communication together, leading to long embarrassed pauses while the learner tries to find out how to say what they want to say, perhaps while a ticket queue waits behind or a group of embarrassed friends look on. ■

Fluency and confidence

One of the best ways for you to help learners activate this knowledge is to put them in 'safe' situations in class where they are inspired and encouraged to try using language from their 'store'. These would not mainly be activities that teach 'new' language; rather, they would allow learners to try out language that they already understand and have 'learned', but not yet made part of their active personal repertoire. Generally speaking, you are likely to want to create activities in which learners feel less worried about speaking, less under pressure, less nervous about trying things out. It's a fine balance though, as you also want learners to feel under some pressure to take a risk and use language that they may have been avoiding using until now.

Many activities in class are suitable for fulfilling these 'fluency and confidence' aims, but for the moment, let's stick with the class discussion such as might happen in a 'conversation class'.

Task 87: Activities that lead to fluency and confidence

This is a lesson aim: 'Learners will become more fluent – speaking more confidently with less hesitation'. Which of these activities might help fulfil this aim?

- Learners repeat sentences you say.
- At the start of the lesson, learners chat with you about their weekend plans.
- Learners look at a list of hints and tips for making business presentations.
- Learners listen to a recording and practise repeating words with the same difficult vowel sound.
- Learners work in pairs and agree their list of the best five films of all time.
- Learners listen to and study a recording of a social conversation.
- Learners prepare a monologue about their hobbies and then give a five-minute speech to the whole class.
- Learners learn by heart a list of useful chunks of language they can use in conversations.

Commentary ■ ■ ■

Arguably, all of these contribute in some degree towards the aim, though lesson stages that focus mainly on language repetition or language study are at best contributing foundation skills and knowledge rather than directly working on fluency itself. The activities that are primarily focused on encouraging fluency are the second (the chat) and the fifth (the discussion about films). ■

Task 88: Problems in organising discussions

You are a student in a foreign language class. A new teacher comes in, stares at the class and says 'Today we're going to talk about oil pollution. What do you think?'

- How do you feel as a student?
- Why might you not feel like taking part in the discussion?

Following the teacher's question, the students look down at their tables, make faces at each other and keep silent. The teacher tries to encourage them to speak, and, in doing so, talks more and more himself. At the end, no student having said a single word, he sits down exhausted and mumbles to himself, 'Well, that seemed to go OK.'

- What advice would you give the teacher when planning future lessons of this type? (i.e. How can you enable as much student participation as possible?)

Commentary ■ ■ ■

The truth is that a lesson like the one described in this task is more likely to produce silence or a desultory sentence or two than a scorching debate.

Why this happens is not too hard to fathom. Imagine yourself as a student in that lesson. Probably you have no interest in the subject, no relevant knowledge or experience, no motivation, no desire or perceived need to speak about it and worst of all, a slight panic: 'The teacher wants me to say something and I haven't had time to think'. Hence, as a result of all of these, there is nothing to say.

If we want to get students talking, we need to answer all these objections. If the subject is relevant and interesting, if the students already know about or are provided with information to give substance to the topic, if they feel motivated to talk about it, if they feel that they really want to say something, there is a good chance of something interesting happening.

To achieve the main aim (of working on fluency), we often want to find ways of enabling as many students as possible to speak as much as possible. Sometimes an all-class speaking activity is useful, but if it takes up the whole lesson, it actually offers very little speaking time to each individual student. It's usually a good idea to organise speaking activities in pairs, threes and small groups, as well as with the class as a whole. ■

Task 89: Ways to start a lively discussion

Which of these activities (all based on the idea of discussing recent news) is likely to give learners a good opportunity to speak and encourage as many to speak as possible?

- Small talk at the start of the lesson: the whole class chats about recent events, etc.
- You write a controversial question based on the day's news on the board. The class work in groups of four or five students to discuss it.
- Pairs of learners have different pictures cut from today's newspaper (which they don't show each other). They compare their views, initially describing their two pictures.
- Everyone is given the name of a famous person (which they keep secret). The whole class stands up and walks around (as if at a party), meeting, chatting and answering questions about recent events 'in character'.

Commentary ■ ■ ■

All these activities seem to likely fulfil the goals to some degree – and, by the way, also make use of four common groupings (whole class seated, whole class mingling, pairs, small groups).

In terms of the numbers of people speaking, it is mathematically true that the whole-class activity will allow a smaller number of people to be speaking at the same time, whereas the last activity, in which participants work individually, is likely to provide opportunity for the most speaking by the largest number of people. Whether learners feel encouraged to speak also depends on how motivated they feel by the task. Having a clear, concrete task (e.g. describing a photo or answering a specific question) may offer a more manageable starting point than a general invitation to 'state your view'. Similarly, having a 'role' may give learners permission to speak more freely, taking away some of the nervousness associated with formulating one's own view. ■

A few keys to getting a good discussion going

- **Frame the discussion well**
  Don't just jump in the deep end (as the oil pollution example above did – 'Here's the topic, now TALK!'). It usually helps to find ways to lead in at the beginning and ways to close at the end. A lead-in may be no more than a brief focus on a picture; it could be a text that everyone reads and which naturally flows into the topic. It could be a personal recollection from you.

- **Preparation time**
  Your students may need some quiet time before the speaking activity, not to write out speeches (this is to be a speaking activity, not a reading aloud one), but perhaps to look up vocabulary in their dictionaries, think through their thoughts, make a note or two, etc.

- **Don't interrupt the flow**
  If at all possible, avoid classroom management techniques that interfere with the natural flow of conversation. I'm thinking particularly about learners having to put their hands up before they speak. Try alternatives such as keeping a watchful eye on the class and noticing those small movements and looks that suggest someone wants to speak, and then invite them to speak with a gesture or by a natural comment such as 'Dasha, what do you think?'

- **Specific problems are more productive than general issues**
  Rather than giving the students a general topic to discuss, try setting a specific, related problem. This is often more challenging, more interesting and more realistic. In the oil pollution example, you could divide the students into two groups: managers of Reddo Tankers (a large multinational oil shipping company) and GreenEarth (a conservationist group) and tell them that they must decide (and agree) how to minimise the risk of pollution in future. Make it more interesting by giving them some resource data, e.g. a page or two of essential information about the company, recent accidents, graphs, local newspaper articles, maps, etc.

- **Role cards**
  Giving students brief role cards sometimes helps, e.g. 'You are a motorist who uses Reddo petrol. Explain how you want to support "green" issues, but also need to drive your car.' It can often be easier to speak in someone else's character than in your own. (See Section 3 for more role-play ideas.)

- **Buzz groups**
  If a whole-class discussion seems to be dying on its feet, try splitting the class up into 'buzz groups', i.e. quickly divide the class into small sets of four or five students. Ask them to summarise the discussion so far, particularly

considering if they agree with what different people have said. After a few minutes (with students still in groups), ask them to think of three comments or questions that would be interesting to share with the whole class. Then bring the whole class back together and continue the discussion. The entire buzz-group stage may take only about three or four minutes, but can help inject a lot more energy into a discussion.

- **Break the rules**
  Don't feel that you can never bend the above rules; sometimes it may make sense to go straight into the discussion (perhaps because you want them to get some practice at unprepared speaking, or because the subject is burning so strongly that it just demands to be started immediately).

Task 90: Using material to generate discussion

Find a way to use this material in a discussion lesson. How would you introduce it? Would you need other materials? If so, what?

Commentary ■ ■ ■

A discussion could be based around a decision as to which of the three buildings should be built on the vacant site. The discussion would probably be a lot more interesting if the speakers had a real involvement in the issues. Role cards might be useful, say, for 'architects', 'local residents' and 'town council'. Some lively arguments could result.

The whole activity could be introduced with some consideration of what the students associate with the seaside, what they imagine local residents feel about holidaymakers, retired people moving down, etc. ■

Task 91: Devising a discussion activity

The subject is 'pop festivals'. Devise a discussion activity suitable for a range of levels.

Commentary ■ ■ ■

One possible idea: In groups, plan a pop festival for our town. Who should be invited to play? Where would it be? What problems might there be? How will we keep the locals happy? etc. Finally, design an advertisement poster to include important information and encourage visitors to come. At the end, the separate groups pin up their posters around the walls and visit each other's. In the role of potential visitors and festival organisers, they ask and answer questions. ■

2 Communicative activities

The discussions and conversations in Section 1 are examples of communicative activities, i.e. classroom activities designed to get learners to speak and listen to one another.

We typically communicate when one of us has information (facts, opinions, ideas, instructions, etc.) that another does not have. This is known as an 'information gap'. The aim of a communicative activity in class is to get learners to use the language they are learning to interact in realistic and meaningful ways, usually involving exchanges of information or opinion.

Task 92: Communicative activities

Consider the definition above and tick which items on the following list are communicative activities.

1 Repeating sentences that you say
2 Doing oral grammar drills
3 Reading aloud from the coursebook
4 Giving a prepared speech
5 Acting out a scripted conversation
6 Giving instructions so that someone can use a new machine
7 Improvising a conversation so that it includes lots of examples of a new grammar structure
8 One learner describes a picture in the textbook while the others look at it.

Commentary ■ ■ ■

By my definition, only Activity 6 above is a communicative activity; it is the only one that involves a real exchange of information. Repetition, drills, speeches, etc. all give useful oral practice, but they do not provide communication. In Activity 6, one person knows something that another doesn't know and there is a need for this meaning to be transferred. I exclude Activity 8 because the communication is meaningless: why (other than in the classroom) would we listen to someone describing something we can see for ourselves? Activity 8 is a display activity, showing off language learned, but there is no real communication here. We can, however, transform it very easily: if a learner describes a picture that the others cannot see and the listeners have a task, say of drawing a basic sketch of that picture, then there is real communication, and the 'describers' and 'artists' will interact with a specific purpose. This classroom activity effectively mirrors activities that learners might be involved in when using the language in the outside world, listening to a description of something over the phone, for instance.

Activity 7 is excluded from the list because, in real communication, the language that the students use is largely unpredictable. There may be many ways to achieve a particular communicative goal. Communicative activities are not simply grammar-practice activities, for although you could offer likely grammar or vocabulary before the activity, the main aim for the students is achieving successful communication rather than accurate use of particular items of language. ■

Some common communicative activities

Here are examples of some popular general types of communicative activities you may wish to try out. Note that, in every case, we are primarily concerned with enabling and encouraging communication, rather than with controlled use of particular items of language or with accuracy.

Picture difference tasks

In pairs, one student is given picture A, one picture B. Without looking at the other picture, they have to find the differences (i.e. by describing the pictures to each other). See a complete example activity in Chapter 3, Section 3.

Group planning tasks

The first example is 'planning a holiday'. Collect together a number of advertisements or brochures advertising a holiday. Explain to the students that they can all go on holiday together, but they must all agree on where they want to go. Divide the students into groups of three and give each group a selection of this material. Their task is to plan a holiday for the whole group (within a fixed budget per person). Allow them a good amount of time to read and select a holiday and then to prepare a presentation in which they attempt to persuade the rest of the class that they should choose this holiday. When they are ready, each group makes their presentation and the class discusses and chooses a holiday.

The second example is 'Survival'. Tell a 'lost in the forest' story (Resource 15 in Appendix 2). Make it dramatic (invent the details). Include a disaster of some kind, e.g. minibus crashes miles from anywhere, injuries, etc. Give them the map and the notes. Students must plan what they should do to have the best chance of survival.

List sequencing tasks (also known as 'Ranking tasks')

Prepare a list of items that learners can discuss and place in a particular order according to their opinions, e.g.

* What's the most useful invention?
* What's the best improvement that could be made to our town?
* What are the worst programmes on TV?
* Who's the most important person of the last 100 years?
* What are the qualities of a good language course?

Pyramid discussion

A 'pyramid discussion' is an organisational technique that works particularly well with simple problem-based discussions and especially with item-selection tasks, e.g. 'What are the four most useful things to have with you if you are shipwrecked on a desert island?', or list sequencing tasks, e.g. 'Put these items in order of importance'. Here's how to do it:

1 Introduce the problem, probably using a list on the board or on handouts.
2 Start with individual reflection – learners each decide what they think might be a solution.
3 Combine individuals to make pairs, who now discuss and come to an agreement or compromise. If you demand that there must be an agreed compromise solution before you move on to the next stage, it will significantly help to focus the task.
4 Combine the pairs to make fours; again, they need to reach an agreement.
5 Join each four with another four or – in a smaller class – with all the others.
6 When the whole class comes together, see if you can to reach one class solution.

What's the point of doing a discussion in this way? Well, most importantly, the technique gives students time to practise speaking in smaller groups before facing the whole class. Even the weaker speakers tend to find their confidence grows as the activity proceeds and they are able to rehearse and repeat arguments that they have already tested on others. Learners who would usually never dare state their views in front of the entire class will still get a number of chances to speak, and because they have practised a little, may even get up the courage to say them again to everyone. It also tends to lead to a much more exciting and well argued whole-class discussion. The smaller groups are seedbeds for a variety of ideas and opinions; if we jumped in the deep end with the whole-class stage, we would probably get silence or possibly just one or two students dominating.

Board games

Many commercially available board games lead to interesting speaking activities, though you do need to check them out and ensure that they represent 'good value' in terms of how much useful language they generate. Its also quite easy to create new board games specially designed for your class and their interests. I find it very useful to have one blank board game template (there's a copy in Resource 6 in Appendix 2). It is then relatively quick to write in a number of interesting questions or statements in each square round the board. Learners play the game in groups, moving their pieces and either giving a monologue or discussing squares they land on.

Puzzles and problems

There are many published books nowadays filled with logic puzzles and problems. Many of these make interesting discussion tasks, maybe following a structure of (a) letting learners spend a little time individually considering the problem, then (b) bringing students together in a group to try and solve the puzzle together. Alternatively, some puzzles work well with the same stage a), but then for stage b) having a full class 'mingle' (all learners walking around, meeting and talking), during which learners can compare their solutions with others.

How to organise learners in speaking tasks

Getting the physical arrangements right is often a big part of getting a speaking activity to work well. That may seem an obvious enough comment, but it's interesting how often teachers set up a group speaking activity and then, for example, leave students sitting in shoulder-to-shoulder lines.

It's hard to talk to someone you can't make eye contact with (though sometimes you may want to play around with this idea, for example, deliberately keeping students apart when practising 'phone calls').

Learners usually need to be able to:

• make eye contact with those they are speaking to;
• hear clearly what the other person/people are saying;
• be reasonably close together.

Different variations of seating/standing arrangements can be useful. Check ideas in Chapter 5, Section 3. Plan the arrangement carefully to match the requirements of the specific activity; for example, you may want an arrangement that allows students to talk secretly without other teams overhearing (e.g. making plans for a confrontational 'public inquiry' meeting to be held later in the lesson).

3 Role-play, real-play and simulation

Role-play

In role-play, learners are usually given some information about a 'role' (e.g. a person or a job title). These are often printed on 'role cards'. Learners take a little preparation time and then meet up with other students to act out small scenes using their own ideas, as well as any ideas and information from the role cards.

A simple role card could do nothing more than name the role, e.g.

or

or alternatively they could offer guidance as to what to do rather than the role itself, e.g.

Buy a train ticket to Brighton.	Complain that your train has been delayed for two hours.	Find out when your son's train from Paris will arrive.

Role cards often contain some of the following information:

Background information
Your name
Your job
Your sex
Your age
Personal appearance, clothes, etc.
Your character
Your interests

Points relevant to the task
Pieces of information you know (that maybe others don't)
Your opinions about the issue/problem/situation/people/etc.
What you want to happen, be decided, etc.
Items of language you may need

A good set of role cards is often designed so that the participants will have distinctly different points of view and natural disagreements. They can lead to excellent discussions – and arguments – without anyone having to feel bad at the end because they got angry.

Role cards can be designed to offer students opportunities to practise specific pieces of language (maybe grammatical points, functional areas, lexical groups, etc). The following set of cards is designed to give pairs of in-company business students a chance to practise using modifiers with adjectives (e.g. *quite big, rather fast, extremely intelligent*). Students will certainly need a good amount of time to prepare both ideas and language before tackling a role-play such as this. (As role card 1 requires more preparation time, you could ask both students in a pair to prepare role card 1, then do the role-play twice, swapping roles after the first, so both students can take both roles.)

Role card 1

Your company has designed a range of revolutionary new products, completely different from your usual ones.

You are having a meeting with one of your best customers. Decribe the new products to him/her.

Role card 2

You are having a meeting to hear about some amazing new products from an important supplier.

Ask a lot of questions and find out as much as you can about the products.

Task 93: Writing role cards

Here are three role cards that very briefly set out particular viewpoints in order to encourage a small group discussion on vegetarianism and meat eating. The fourth card and fifth cards are missing. Write them.

1 You believe that meat eating is natural for humans and that vegetarians are missing out on an important part of their diet.
2 You have been vegetarian for six years because you believe it is healthier.
3 You like the taste of meat, but don't eat it for moral reasons, as you feel it is wrong to kill animals.

Commentary ■ ■ ■

There are many possibilities. The extra cards could represent a vegan, a religious viewpoint, a scientific view, a 'they're all crazy' view, a chef, a butcher, etc.

Role-play also gives you the possibility of introducing some more bizarre or interesting variations to a discussion, e.g. 'You are a chicken. You feel very strongly that you are being exploited by the meat industry.' In a role-play about pollution, you might have a card saying 'You are the planet Earth. You don't think people are listening to you.' ■

As well as initiating general discussion on issues, role-plays can also be set in specific contexts, providing a starting point for speaking practice and also for practice of specific language items.

Task 94: Adding a missing role card

Same task again. Here are some role cards. What do you think the missing card might have on it?

1 You are a store detective. You can see a suspicious-looking person at a clothes rail who appears to be putting something into her bag. Go over and firmly but politely ask her to come to the office.
2 You bought a sweater from this shop yesterday, but you have brought it back because it is too small. You want to go to the assistant to return it and get your money back, but before you do, you start looking at the other sweaters on the rail and comparing them with the one you got yesterday, which is in your bag.
3 You are a shop assistant. You have just noticed a customer coming in who was very rude to you yesterday. She wanted to buy a sweater, which you told her was the wrong size, but she insisted was right. Finally, she bought the sweater and stormed out of the shop. You hope she isn't going to cause more trouble.

Commentary ■ ■ ■

Possibly:

4 You are the manager of a large department store. The police have just phoned you to warn that a number of shoplifters are operating in this street. You decide to have a walk around your store and warn the assistants and the store detective to keep their eyes open.

This role-play provides scope for use of functional language (apologising, refusing, disagreeing, denying, etc.), as well as practising 'shop' vocabulary in a useful and interesting way. The potential for dramatic conflict is built into the cards, though the participants could, if they wished, avoid this completely. ■

Running a role-play: some guidelines

- Make sure the students understand the idea of 'role-play'. Do they know what's going to happen? Do they know what is required of them? Are they comfortable doing that or not?
- Make sure the context or situation is clear.
- Do they understand the information on their own card? Allow reading/dictionary/thinking time (during which you go round and help if necessary).
- Give them time to prepare their ideas before they start – maybe encourage note-making – but when the activity starts, encourage them to improvise rather than rely on prepared speeches and notes. The preparation work they have done will inform their role-play, but could simply get in the way if they over-rely on it. (It may help to take away the cards when the role-play starts.)

Real-play

A powerful variation on role-play is **real-play**. In this case, situations and one or more of the characters are drawn not from cards, but from a participant's own life and world. Typically, one of the learners plays him/herself, but in a context other than the classroom. This person explains a context (e.g. from his/her work life) to other learners, and then together they recreate the situation in class. The real-play technique allows learners to practise language they need in their own life. It is particularly useful for business and professional people.

Rather than a set of role cards, the most useful tool for real-play is a blank framework – in effect, a card that allows learners to create their own real-play role card. In class, I start by asking learners to choose a problem or situation that they might want to work on, and then guide them how to fill in their cards. Some frameworks will need to be worked on individually, some (if they are mutually dependent) in pairs or groups.

The following framework is for a two-person real-play (A and B). Each learner needs one framework card. They start by agreeing which person's situation they will work with first (e.g. A's), and then A (the initiator) will explain a work situation to B. Both will fill in their own framework role card as appropriate.

Real-play: work situations involving two people	
Who are the two people?	
Where are you?	
What are you talking about?	
Why are you talking?	
What happened just before this?	
Is any other information important?	
What are some points that will come up in the discussion?	
What would be a good result ?	

When they are prepared, learners improvise a conversation as if it was a normal role-play, quite possibly with someone else playing the role of the initiator (rather than playing it herself). When it's finished, it may then be useful for the initiator to give feedback on how the characters and events seemed, to 'fine-tune' it (e.g. 'My mother used to speak much louder than that'), in preparation for a second go at doing the role-play, possibly – and revealingly – with swapped roles. You can also provide helpful feedback and language help, perhaps suggesting some typical phrases that might be used. After the second role-play, it may be useful to review the task using a form like this:

Real-play: review
Was the discussion like the real thing?
What were some interesting things that happened/that you said?
What have you learned from this? Will the task help you in real life?

Here is a brief description of a sample real-play activity:

In a Business English class, a receptionist at a company said that she found it difficult to deal with foreign visitors who wanted to ask a question rather than just be directed to a person's office. She described a recent time when this had happened and then real-played this with another student (who played her, while she played the part of the visitor). She found it helpful to watch her colleague playing her own role, as he did some things quite differently from her and used some interesting expressions. The teacher was also able to suggest some ideas and language. Then they repeated the real-play (with her playing herself). She said afterwards that she felt a little more confident about such situations.

Simulation

Simulation is really a large-scale role-play. Role cards are normally used, but there is often quite a lot of other printed and recorded background information as well – newspaper articles, graphs, memos, news flashes, etc. – which may come at the start of the simulation or appear while the simulation is unfolding, causing all participants to take note of the new data and possibly readjust their positions. The intention is to create a much more complete, complex 'world', say, of a business company, television studio, government body, etc.

This is a brief description of an example simulation:

The participants are all members of a UFO-spotters society at their annual meeting. They are deciding how they could better publicise their cause to the public. At the start, they have some facts about UFO incidents and some government statements (collected from magazines and the Internet). At an appropriate point in the simulation (probably about one-third of the way through), you introduce a news flash that a UFO has landed in Siberia. This obviously changes the direction of the meeting! Later interventions include a request to interview members of the society and, at the end, news that the UFO was another fake.

4   Fluency, accuracy and communication

Imagine a switch inside your head – it swings between two settings: 'working mainly on accuracy' and 'working mainly on fluency' (see Figure 7.2).

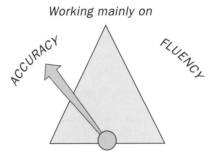

Figure 7.2   Accuracy/fluency switch

It's probably a huge simplification, but I suspect that something like this is at work in my head through most of my language teaching, changing its setting from activity to activity, stage to stage – and, in some teaching, changing moment by moment in response to things happening in class. And I think that initially getting that switch installed and working may be a key skill for anyone learning to be a language teacher.

Certainly there are activities in which you are arguably working on both accuracy and fluency in relatively equal measure, but many everyday language-teaching lesson stages are focused on one more than the other, and at any one moment, in any one activity, it is likely that you will be aiming to focus on accuracy rather than fluency, or fluency rather than accuracy.

It is therefore important for you to be clear about what is involved in accuracy-focused work as compared with fluency-focused work. And it's especially important to be clear about the differing aims – and consequently different classroom procedures – of the two.

Task 95: Student views on speaking tasks

Here are some things you may hear your students say (or imagine them thinking!). Take sides. Rehearse your arguments and replies to some or all of the comments.

- But I don't want to talk to other students. They speak badly. I just want to listen to you speak.
- I speak a lot, but what is the point if you never correct me? I will never improve.
- You should be teaching us – not just letting us talk. That's lazy teaching.
- I don't need to speak. Teach me more grammar. I will speak later.
- There's no point doing this task if we use bad English to do it.
- This is just a game. I paid a lot of money and now I have to play a game.

Commentary ■ ■ ■

There are times in class when a focus on accuracy – and therefore a greater use of instant correction – may be appropriate.

There are other times when the focus is on fluency. At these times, instant correction may be less appropriate and could interfere with the aims of the activity.

You need to be clear about whether your main aim is accuracy or fluency, and adapt your role in class appropriately.

Having said all that, there may still be a kind of correction that fulfils the 'non-interfering' aim of fluency activities, yet offers substantial concrete help to the learner who is coming to terms with language items. We will look at this under the heading of 'scaffolding' a little later in this section. ■

Running a fluency activity

If the main aim is to get the students to speak, then one way to achieve that would be for you to reduce your own contributions. Probably the less you speak, the more space it will allow the students. It could be useful to aim to say nothing while the activity is underway, and save any contributions for before and after. In an activity mainly geared towards encouraging fluency, you are likely to monitor discreetly or vanish (see Chapter 5, Section 5).

The activity route map from Chapter 3, Section 1 (see Figure 7.3) works well for a fluency activity, and we can add a column for likely teacher involvement:

	Stage	Teacher involvement
1	Before the lesson: familiarise yourself with the material and activity	
2	In class: lead-in/prepare for the activity	Teacher centre-stage
3	Set up the activity (or section of activity), i.e. give instructions, make groupings, etc.	Teacher centre-stage
4	Run the activity (or section): students do the activity – maybe in pairs or small groups – while you monitor and help.	Teacher out of sight, uninvolved
5	Close the activity (or section) and invite feedback from the students.	Teacher centre-stage again
6	Post-activity: do any appropriate follow-on work.	?

Figure 7.3   Activity route map

A useful thing for you to do during Stage 4 above is to take notes (unobtrusively) of interesting student utterances (correct and incorrect) for possible use later on (at the end of the activity, the next day, next week, etc.).

Ideas for correction work after a fluency activity

- You write up a number of sentences used during the activity and discuss them with the students.
- You write a number of sentences on the board. You give the pens/chalks to the students and encourage them to make corrections.
- You invent and write out a story that includes a number of errors you overheard during the activity. You hand out the story the next day and the students, in pairs or as a whole group, find the errors and correct them.

- You write out two lists headed 'A' and 'B'. On each list, you write the same ten sentences from the activity. On one list, you write the sentence with an error; on the other, you write the corrected version. Thus the correct version of sentence 3 might be on either list A or list B (the other list has the incorrect version). You divide the students into two groups, 'A' and 'B', and hand out the appropriate list to each group. The groups discuss their own list (without sight of the other list) and try to decide if their version of each sentence is correct or not. If it is wrong, they correct it. When they have discussed all the sentences, the groups can then compare the two sheets (and perhaps come to some new conclusions).

Scaffolding

I suggested earlier that, during a fluency activity, there may be a way to offer spontaneous correction that:

- does not interfere too much with the flow of conversation;
- offers useful language feedback;
- actually helps the speaker to construct his conversation.

'Scaffolding' refers to the way a competent language speaker helps a less competent one to communicate by both encouraging and providing possible elements of the conversation. It is the way a primary-school teacher might help a young child to communicate, or the way a chat-show host might draw out a guest. The listener offers support – like scaffolding round a building – to help the speaker create his own spoken structure.

Scaffolding in class isn't a normal conversation in the sense that the teacher/listener is not aiming to contribute any personal stories or opinions of her own; the aim of her own speaking is solely to help the speaker tell his story.

Here are some notes on techniques that might be appropriate:

Scaffolding techniques

- Showing interest and agreeing: nodding, 'uh-huh', eye contact, 'yes', etc.;
- Concisely asking for clarification of unclear information, e.g. repeating an unclear word;
- Encouragement echo: repeating the last word (perhaps with questioning intonation) in order to encourage the speaker to continue;
- Echoing meaning: picking on a key element of meaning and saying it back to the speaker, e.g. 'a foreign holiday';
- Asking conversation-oiling questions (ones that mainly recap already stated information), e.g. 'Is it?' 'Do you?' 'Where was it?' etc.;
- Asking brief questions (or using sentence heads) that encourage the speaker to extend the story, e.g. 'And then …' 'He went …' 'She wanted …' etc.;
- Unobtrusively saying the correct form of an incorrect word (but only if having the correct word makes a significant positive contribution to the communication);
- Giving the correct pronunciation of words in replies without drawing any particular attention to it;
- Unobtrusively giving a word or phrase that the speaker is looking for.

Task 96: Identifying scaffolding techniques

Which scaffolding techniques can you identify in this short transcript of a lesson at Elementary level, where a learner wants to tell his teacher about a TV story he saw concerning the rather unlikely sport of 'extreme ironing'.

STUDENT: It is like sport …
TEACHER: Uh-huh.
STUDENT: … but is with 'eye ron'.
TEACHER: With an iron?
STUDENT: Yes, is 'eye ron' sport. They … er …
TEACHER: What do they do?
STUDENT: Er, yes. It is like sport ex … ex …
TEACHER: An extreme sport?
STUDENT: Yes. They use 'eye rons' in extreme place
TEACHER: Ha – irons in extreme places? Where?
STUDENT: Ah, like onto a mountain.
TEACHER: On a mountain!
STUDENT: Yes (*laughs*), on a mountain or river.
TEACHER: What do they do?
STUDENT: They iron and in tree on top.
TEACHER; At the top of trees?
STUDENT: Yes.

5   Different kinds of speaking

How can we teach speaking? Is it enough to give learners communicative activities that require them to speak (trying out using grammar, phrases, vocabulary they already know, etc.) or is it possible and necessary to teach specific skills? So far, we haven't really taken into account that there may be 'skills of speaking' that also need to be studied and practised.

In order to answer these questions, we need to consider what is involved in successful speaking, and particularly consider the nature of different 'genres'.

Task 97: Defining 'genre'

What does the word 'genre' mean? Why might 'genre' be an important consideration when teaching language?

Commentary ■ ■ ■

In everyday life, people speak in a variety of ways, depending on who they are with, where they are, the nature of the situation, etc. To take two extreme examples, giving a sermon in church is a very different kind of speaking from enquiring about car insurance over the phone. These are two different genres. A genre is a variety of speech (or writing) that you would expect to find in a particular place, with particular people, in a particular context, to achieve a particular result, using a particular channel (e.g. face to face, by phone), etc. A genre is often characterised by specific choices about style, manner, tone, quantity, volume, directness, choice of words, formality, type of content, etc. Quite apart from the detailed content and specific words of the sermon or the phone call, there is likely to be a generally recognisable 'sermon-ness' about the sermon and a 'enquiry-on-the-phone-ness' about the call. That's not to say that we can't also knowingly choose to ignore or undermine the genre, e.g. by giving a sermon in the style of a comedy sketch (in fact, substituting one genre for another)! ■

Task 98: Varieties of speech genre

Make a list of about ten distinctly different real-life types of speaking, e.g. making a public speech.

Commentary ■ ■ ■

Some possible answers:

* Giving an academic lecture
* Telling a joke
* Greeting a passing colleague
* Making a phone enquiry
* Chatting with a friend
* Explaining medical problems to a doctor
* Giving military orders
* Negotiating a sale
* Giving street directions
* Making a business presentation
* Communicating 'live' during an Internet game
* Explaining a grammatical point

■

Being more specific about genre

A term such as 'making a public speech' is still relatively imprecise. It could refer to a wide variety of quite different kinds of task, from thanking some colleagues for a birthday present to standing up as best man at a wedding reception to presenting a one-hour talk at a conference of 3,000 people.

It is possible to specify types of speaking more precisely than by simply naming a genre if we add information about **why** the speaking is being done, **where** it is being done and **who** is listening or interacting with the speaker.

Task 99: Analysing a genre

Take three of the general items in your list from Task 98. For each item, choose a specific example that you can picture clearly and analyse it using the grid in Figure 7.4. Two examples have been filled in to help you. (NB You are not analysing all examples of each genre, just one specific one; for example, the lecture specified here may be very different if any of the variables (why, who, where, one-/two-way) were altered.)

Genre	Purpose	Setting	Audience	Response
What general kind of speaking is it?	Why is this speaking done?	Where is it done?	Who is listening?	Does the speaker get a spoken response from listener(s)? ● one-way (no response)? ● two-way (reciprocal communication)? ● multiway? (more than two communicate)?
An academic lecture	To inform people of facts about 17th-century British history	Lecture theatre at Budapest University	Room of students listening, note-taking, etc.	Mainly one-way: response only in terms of posture, expression and possibly a question or comment
A stand-up conversation at a formal party	Making contacts; finding new clients	Living room of a private house in Nairobi	One or more other professional people of similar social status	Multiway: a varying number of people speak

Figure 7.4   Genre-analysis grid

Why is genre important?

Imagine that you are nineteen years old and about to meet your girlfriend's/boyfriend's parents for the first time. I'm sure that a lot of words and phrases would be buzzing through your head as you try to select just the right thing to say. However, even before you make a decision as to the exact words to say, you probably first have to make a bigger decision as to the generally appropriate way of talking to them. Will you adopt a hip, street-talk style? A very formal, wordy greeting? Will you make a speech? Rap a spontaneous poem? Will you be informally polite and friendly? It's possible that you can make this decision subconsciously in a fraction of a second, but having made it, it colours everything else you decide to say when you open your mouth. It determines the choice of grammar, words, how much you talk, how polite you are, how much you speak and how much listen, etc. Of course, you can adjust your 'genre' as you take part in the conversation, but again your new choice will colour all you say, and generally it is unlikely that you'll decide to switch dramatically into a genre that you earlier rejected as entirely inappropriate.

From this example, it's apparent that choice of genre is a vital decision a speaker makes before she proceeds with almost any speaking act. A learner of a language needs to learn not just words, grammar, pronunciation, etc., but also about appropriate ways of speaking in different situations – which may be significantly different in the target language culture compared with their own. For this reason, offering a range of communicative 'fluency' activities to our learners is probably insufficient as a course in speaking. We must think about the range of speaking acts that a learner may be faced with and give them chances to practise selecting appropriate genres and planning the appropriate language needed for a variety of different speaking situations and audiences.

Successful speaking involves fluently communicating information or opinions in a clear unambiguous manner in an appropriate way for a particular context.

Task 100: Deciding which genres are useful for your students

Here are a number of common speaking genres. Which ones would be most useful to work on with a class of students you are familiar with?

a Meeting people at an informal party
b Discussing new sales at a business meeting
c Telling a joke in a café
d Leaving an answerphone message
e Asking a switchboard operator if you can speak to someone in a company department
f Buying a train ticket at the station
g Asking for directions on the street
h Agreeing the price for a business deal
i Checking in at the airport
j Making a dentist's appointment over the phone

Task 101: Factors involved in speech acts

If your learners had to take part in the speech acts in Task 100 above, what sort of things might prove difficult for them? The table in Figure 7.5 lists some of the skills and strategies that competent language users might employ when speaking.

Choose three of the genres from Task 100. For each one, select four or five items from the table that seem to be most important for successfully establishing and maintaining communication. For example, if I consider (a) Meeting people at an informal party, I might decide that the following were most important (and tick them in the table):

• Being aware of appropriate topics and style for the context (e.g. business meeting, social chit-chat)
• Speaking spontaneously with limited/no preparation time before speaking
• Coping with unpredictable responses
• Showing interest in the person speaking

These are only possible answers. Different people might select other items.

	a			
Pronunciation				
Speaking clearly, with comprehensible sounds				
Using fluent, connected speech with appropriate word-linking				
Using stress and intonation to emphasise, draw attention to things, express emotion or attitude, etc.				
Using an appropriate pace				
Context				
Choosing and maintaining a suitable level of formality/informality				
Choosing and maintaining a suitable level of politeness				
Being aware of appropriate topics and style for the context (e.g. business meeting, social chit-chat)	✓			
Coping with a stressful speaking context (e.g. other people waiting, limited time to speak)				
Speaking spontaneously with limited/no preparation time before speaking	✓			
Coping with uncertainty about the language level of other people				
Organising information				
Structuring speech as you talk				
Giving neither too much nor too little information				
Not offering irrelevant information				
Conveying clear, accurate information				
Clearly sign-posting to your listener(s) the structure and stages of what you say				
Interaction				
Establishing a relationship before and during communication				
Coping with unpredictable responses	✓			
Turn-taking				
Listening				
Listening and responding appropriately in line with the progress of a conversation				
Showing interest in the person speaking				
Reaching a negotiated/compromise conclusion	✓			
Coping with a variety of content (facts, opinions, arguments, anecdotes, etc.) simultaneously				
Speaking strategies				
Holding the floor when you wish to continue speaking				
Interrupting politely				
Starting new topics or changing topics				
Language items				
Fluently forming accurate structures to express required meaning				
Knowing fixed phrases used in specific situations				
Creating effective questions				
Having sufficient lexical resources to express meanings				

Figure 7.5   Grid for assessing speech acts

How can you organise a speaking lesson based around this idea of helping learners to work better within a given genre? Broadly speaking, you have two options:

1 You can work on the individual micro-skills (e.g. things such as those in the table in Figure 7.5) using games and practice activities;
2 You can work on a bigger scale, getting learners to deploy a range of these micro-skills while completing a genre-based task.

Task 102: Practising micro-skills

Take the micro-skill of 'interrupting politely' (in an informal social conversation). Can you think of a game or practice activity that might raise students' awareness of this or help them improve their skills in this area?

Commentary ■ ■ ■

Here are two sample games and activities:

1 Learners work in small groups. Each person takes a card with a topic word on it (e.g. 'swimming'). One person in each group must start speaking on their given topic. Others attempt to interrupt and change the topic politely to their topic, while all work to maintain a balanced 'café' conversation.
2 Hand out a list of expressions for interrupting politely (e.g. 'By the way …'), but including some unlikely or incorrect ones (e.g. 'Now I want us to talk about …'). Learners select the correct items from the list. (Then have a conversation using them.) ■

Task 103: Stages in a speaking lesson

You have decided to work on 'making a business appointment over the phone' (or another similar speaking task). One important stage of the lesson will be when learners try doing the speaking itself (simulating it in pairs, probably, rather than making real phone calls!). What other stages do you think there might be in the lesson?

Commentary ■ ■ ■

The following are some likely elements:

Once you have explained the specific speaking task, the learners may need to:
• plan how they will do the task;
• rehearse parts (or all) of it;
• hear examples of competent speakers doing the same task;
• get input from you on possible structures, phrases, vocabulary, etc.;
• reflect on how well they did the task after they finish;
• replan or revise their original ideas;
• have another go at doing the task a second (third?) time.

At various points, the learners may want correction and advice on how to do it better. ■

Here are those elements arranged into a basic lesson sequence, together with a worked example for 'making a business appointment over the phone'. The stage marked with a star could come at any point of your choosing.

Basic lesson sequence

1 Set task
2 Plan the speaking
3 Rehearse the speaking
4 Do the task
5 Feedback/Review the success
6 Add/Correct/Revise
7 Redo the task
☆ Exposure to example

Worked example

1 Set task: Tell learners that they must phone a business contact to make an appointment for a meeting to discuss future plans.
2 Plan the speaking: Ask learners to work in pairs to decide what the caller will say and how the receptionist will respond. Learners should not write out a whole script, but can make notes of particular phrases.
3 Rehearse the speaking: Learners practise in pairs. You listen in and suggest corrections and improvements.
4 Do the task: Make new pairs. Without further discussion, learners 'phone' each other and do the task.
5 Feedback/review: The pairs meet and reflect on whether the task was done well. Maybe the whole class also discusses the question and you offer notes. You may draw attention to specific language that learners could use and specific ways of interacting appropriate to the genre.
☆ Exposure to example: Play a recording of competent speakers doing the same task. The class is asked to take down notes about language they use.
6 Add/correct/revise: The pairs work out how they could improve their task next time.
7 Redo the task: Makes new pairs. The task is done again.

Chapter 8 **Receptive skills: listening and reading**

1   Task-based listening

Even if someone knows all the grammar and lexis of a language, it doesn't necessarily mean that they will be able to understand a single word when it is spoken. Amongst other things, it may seem to them that:

- people speak too fast to follow;
- they can't tell where words start and stop;
- people pronounce words they just don't recognise;
- they can't work out details of what is being said;
- they can't get even a general sense of the message;
- they don't know what attitudes people are expressing;
- they can't pick out those parts that are most important for them to understand.

So, how can you help your students to become more skilful at listening?

Task 104: An unsatisfactory listening lesson

The following is a transcript of a short telephone conversation from the recording accompanying a contemporary coursebook. Although it has been specially recorded for students of English, it sounds reasonably authentic, i.e. it sounds spontaneous rather than scripted; the people are speaking at normal speed and are not making unnatural efforts to enunciate or exaggerate stress and intonation.

RECEPTIONIST:	Sayers Recruitment and Training. Can I help you?
RUBY:	Hello, yes, erm, I'm, er, I saw your advert and I'm looking for a job, I mean, I'm interested in a new job, and …
RECEPTIONIST :	Ah, yes, you need to speak to Mrs Sayers, but I'm afraid she's not in the office right now. Could I take your name and number, and I'll ask her to call you back?
RUBY :	Er, yes, yes. The name's Ruby, Ruby Tuesday and my number is 0308 557 1919.
RECEPTIONIST :	Thank you, Miss Tuesday. I'll pass on your message.
RUBY :	Thanks. Bye.
RECEPTIONIST :	Goodbye.
from *Straightforward Pre-Intermediate*	

Here is the opening of a lesson procedure using this material intended to help improve students' listening skills:

- Say to students: 'Listen to this.'
- Play recording once.
- When finished, quickly ask individual students the following questions:
  1 Who does Ruby want to speak to?
  2 What had Ruby seen?

   3 What's the full name of the company?

   4 What words did the receptionist use to explain that she would tell the other person?

- Look coldly at students who get the answers wrong and tell them that they should have listened harder.

Apart from the insults, in what other ways might this plan be unsatisfactory?

Commentary ■ ■ ■

This lesson is a parody of some of the language lessons that I was on the receiving end of as a student in school. I remember feeling quite nervous about them.

While I was listening, I knew that some comprehension questions were going to come at the end, but I never knew what the questions might be or who would be asked to answer them. The questions, anyway, seemed pointless; they were not necessarily what I would listen for if I heard the conversation in real life; it was as if the teacher was focusing me on the difficulties rather than showing me that it was possible to achieve a lot despite the difficulties. The questions seemed more of a memory test than anything else. When the recording was played, I struggled to listen to everything, and to remember all I heard, and in consequence actually remembered very little.

In fact, it's actually not necessary to understand every word in order to understand the information you might need from a recording. We need to show students this important fact – help them to worry less about understanding everything and work more on catching the bits they do need to hear. Often, when listening in everyday life, we may need to listen to:

- get a general overview of the main story or message of a conversation;
- catch specific details such as names, numbers, addresses, etc.

There is really nothing in the above lesson plan to help a student learn to listen better; either he can already listen and remember the required answers, or he cannot. But if he wants to improve his listening, then he needs a different approach. ■

Task 105: Using a printed text with listening tasks

Here is a second version of the same lesson plan:

- Hand out a copy of the text of the conversation to all students.
- Play recording.
- When finished, ask individual students the following questions:
   1 What does Ruby want to do?
   2 How does the receptionist help her?'

There still seems to be another problem with this. What?

Commentary ■ ■ ■

The questions are a lot more sensible, and the general tone is certainly less threatening! But the problem now is that the students don't actually need to listen at all. Giving out the text turns it into a reading exercise. Reading is usually easier for most students than deciphering the stream of speech, and most students will probably work out the answers from the printed page rather than by listening. ■

If I sum up my feelings about Tasks 104 and 105, I get a checklist like this:

1　The activity must really demand listening.
2　It mustn't be simply a memory test.
3　Tasks should be realistic or useful in some way.
4　The activity must actively help them to improve their listening.
5　It shouldn't be threatening.
6　Help students work around difficulties to achieve specific results.

One way to achieve these goals is simple enough. By giving students the questions before the recording is played (rather than after), you will give students the opportunity to listen with a clear aim in mind. In everyday life, we usually have some purpose in mind when we listen: to find out today's weather, to learn something, to be entertained, to discover what John did next, etc. By giving the learners a clear purpose in listening, you turn the exercise from a memory test into a listening task.

Task 106: Redesigning a listening procedure

Look again at the lesson procedure in Task 105. Redesign it to take the checklist above into account.

Commentary ■ ■ ■

A simple plan would be as follows:

• Set questions.
• Play recording.
• Check if the students have found the answers.
• If not, play the recording again as often as necessary. ■

This 'question first' technique is often characterised as 'task before audio'. The word 'task' reminds us that the activity the students are asked to do may be something more useful, more realistic, more motivating than simply finding answers to comprehension questions.

Task 107: Selecting listening tasks

Think of a task (other than finding answers to comprehension questions) to set students before listening to the telephone enquiry at the start of this section.

Commentary ■ ■ ■

Some ideas:

• Students must decide whether the conversation is between two friends, two colleagues or two people who don't know each other.
• From a selection of telephone numbers in the book, students pick out the correct one said by the receptionist.
• Students have a newspaper page with five advertisements on it. They must decide which one is the one connected to this recording. (They might need to check company name, contact person's name, type of advertisement, etc.).
• Students have a copy of the receptionist's notepad and must check it to see if she has made any errors (e.g. getting Ruby's name wrong).
• Students have a copy of the dialogue, but with sentences in the wrong order; they must listen and arrange them in the correct order.

The most useful tasks may be ones that require students to listen in similar ways to how they might hear such a conversation in real life. In the case of a phone enquiry like this:

- if they are the receptionist, they need to understand the general nature of the enquiry (e.g. someone looking for a job, not wanting to offer a job) and get accurate information from them (name, number, etc.);
- if they are the caller, they might need to clearly understand any people's names or numbers they need to know and, more generally, what will happen with their enquiry (e.g. do they need to phone back again later?). ∎

Choosing the right task

Remember the broad distinction between different kinds of listening:

- to get a general overview of the main story or message of a conversation;
- to catch specific details such as names, numbers, addresses, etc.

This can be reflected in tasks. Do you want students to gather specific details or to catch the gist? You can, of course, do both, but remember that it's usually better to divide these different kinds of listening into separate replays of the listening material, e.g. set the first task, play the recording, get feedback; then set the second task, play it again, get feedback. (There is more on sequences of tasks in the next section.)

Remember, too, not to overburden students – if you are asking them to listen and write (e.g. note down names, times, etc.), then this is using two skills at once. Unless note-taking is a specific skill being practised, it is often better to limit the amount of writing demanded of students, especially at lower levels.

Having said all this, we must still wonder how useful, relevant or interesting it will be for your students in your location to listen to a recording of people discussing a recruitment advertisement. If you are teaching in an English-speaking country – or if your students are planning to work there – the lesson may seem more relevant than to students who are unlikely to do this at any point soon. The recording raises a few other doubts:

- In real life, you would only listen to this kind of conversation between two people if you were eavesdropping. This is arguably not the most useful listening skill we need.
- Most listening we do in real life will be interactive rather than on recorded media. We will have opportunities to respond, affect the course of the conversation, ask for clarification or repetition, etc., and we will have the chance to see the speakers, which will allow us to get additional help from gestures, facial expressions, etc.
- In real life, although we sometimes have a clear purpose in listening, we usually won't be directed and guided by tasks that help us know what we should listen for.
- Are we really helping students to become better listeners by using recordings like this?

Despite all these doubts, a task-based approach to listening using recorded material does seem to be generally helpful in improving students' abilities. And I'm sure it's better than the memory test we started with.

2 The task–feedback circle

Many teachers use a graded sequence of tasks as a route map through a listening lesson. By starting with a simple task, letting students do it successfully, then moving on to set a more difficult task on the same recording, etc., the teacher can virtually let the class find its own level, i.e. you stop setting new tasks when you find the point at which they are beginning to find it too difficult.

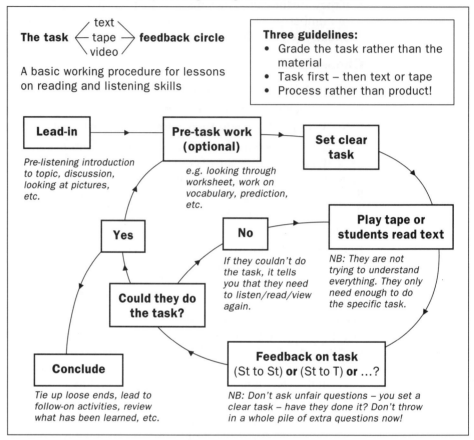

Figure 8.1   The task–feedback circle

The task–feedback circle (see Figure 8.1) can help you plan useful listening lessons if you simply follow it round. Go round the circle three or four times – or as many times as your students need. It's important to note that it involves not only setting a sequence of tasks and checking whether they can do it, but also replaying the recording again and again (and again).

Many teachers plan their sequence of tasks from 'general' overview tasks (such as 'How many people are speaking?' 'Where are they?' 'What are they discussing?' etc.) towards much more detailed, tightly focused tasks (such as 'What were the reasons for leaving on Tuesday?') ending up with language-study issues (e.g. 'What positive words does he use to describe the company?' 'What tenses are used in the story?' etc.) (see Figure 8.2). A possible rationale for this is discussed in the next section.

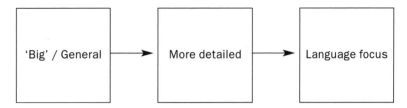

Figure 8.2   Task sequence

As a general planning aid, the task–feedback circle and the 'big to small' task sequence will work well for many standard coursebook and classroom recordings, e.g. where there is a radio discussion, an overheard conversation, a lecture, etc. or any text where it is useful to comprehend both general overall message and smaller details.

In some cases, this might seem an inappropriate approach, for example, with texts where in real life we would only listen inattentively to the bulk of the text and just focus briefly to gain a small piece of information from a part of it that directly interests us, for example when listening to train announcements in a station or listening to a weather forecast. In such cases, it may be more useful to start straight in with a detailed question such as 'What platform should you go to for the Budapest train?' It's worth noting, though, that even in this case, you probably still need some top-down 'background' scene-setting so that listeners realise they are in a station, trying to catch a train, are going to hear an announcement, etc.

To make sure that a lesson is genuinely useful for students, we need to consider why someone might listen to such a text in real life – and what kinds of skills or strategies they'd use. We then need to design tasks that either (a) closely reflect what they might need to do in real life or (b) help them improve skills that will be useful to them in future.

Most tasks fall into one of these categories:
- Take part in a conversation;
- Answer questions;
- Do/choose something in response to what you hear;
- Pass on/take notes on what you hear.

Here are some brief examples of a range of these tasks.

Listen and …
- choose the correct picture;
- follow the route on the map;
- walk/sit/move according to the instructions;
- choose the best answer for each question from the four options;
- say a reply to each comment you hear;
- decide which person is saying which sentence;
- match the pictures of people with this list of opinions;
- note down the leader's suggestions about where the camp should be;
- collect all comments made about shops;
- tell your partner what Mikhail thought about the hospital;
- draw a picture of the alien;
- build a model of the office with Cuisenaire rods;

- decide whether they like the present or not;
- pick up and show the correct picture;
- note the exact words Zsuzsa uses to refuse the offer;
- take down the message, address and phone numbers;
- follow the instructions to make an origami model;
- listen again until you have learned the poem by heart;
- argue against the proposition.

Some listening tasks are obviously more difficult than others. An important point (and typically a difficult one for newer teachers to come to terms with) is that the students getting the right answer is not necessarily the most important thing! A student who finds all the correct answers on first hearing and with no difficulty has simply not been challenged by the recording. It reflects over-simple tasks and shows that little progress in listening has been made.

The effort that a student puts into listening and searching for an answer that is not easily found is, however, very useful work. Whether she finally gets the right or wrong answer is to some degree irrelevant, because in trying to get the right answer, she is stretching her powers of listening to the limit. For this reason, she will probably need to hear the recording played three, four or more times in order to get close to the target. Thus the guideline is 'process rather than product', meaning that the going is more important than the getting there. I'm not saying that getting wrong answers is good, but I am trying to steer you away from thinking that right answers are the only goal. The goal is to work on the listening itself.

Some guidelines for listening skills work in class

- Keep the recording short: two minutes of recorded material is enough to provide a lot of listening work.
- Play the recording a sufficient number of times. (This is one point that teacher trainers and supervisors often comment on when they observe teachers' lessons: the teachers did not give the students enough opportunities to hear the recording. The students found the material a lot more difficult than the teacher realised.)
- Let students discuss their answers together (perhaps in pairs).
- Don't immediately acknowledge correct answers with words or facial expressions; throw the answers back to the class: 'What do you think of Claire's answer – do you agree?'
- Don't be led by one strong student. Have they all got it?
- Aim to get the students to agree together without your help, using verbal prodding, raised eyebrows, nods, hints, etc. Play the recording again whenever they need to hear it, to confirm or refute their ideas, until they agree.
- Play little bits of the recording (a word, a phrase, a sentence) again and again until it's clear.
- Give help if they are completely stuck – but still with the aim of getting them to work it out if at all possible (e.g. 'There are three words in this sentence' or 'Listen to what she says here') rather than giving them the answers.
- Consider giving the students control of the CD player or tape recorder – to listen when and to what they wish.

- Don't cheat them by changing your requirements halfway, i.e. don't set one task, but then afterwards ask for answers to something completely different!
- Don't let them lose heart. Try to make sure the task is just within their abilities. It should be difficult, but achievable. The sense of achievement in finishing a task should be great: 'It was difficult, but we did it!'

The last technique above leads us to another guideline: 'Grade the task, rather than the recording.' This means 'Don't worry too much about what student level the recording is suitable for, but do make sure your task is set for the right level.' In theory, it is possible to use any recording – for example, a recording of this morning's radio news – with any level. At beginner level, I could ask them to catch the names of every famous person they heard. It would be challenging and stimulating for a beginner to feel he has got something out of an authentic news recording! At a much higher level, I could expect them to be able to understand most of the recording and do a sophisticated task like picking out unstressed words. In both cases, it is not the recording that sets the level of the lesson; it is the task.

In practice, of course, some recordings are naturally going to seem more appropriate for specific levels of student. Thus a recording of someone asking for directions in the street is more likely to be usable at a lower level than, say, a discussion on complex moral issues.

Task 108: Ordering stages in a listening lesson

Here is a lesson to exemplify the techniques described above. The recording is a conversation between two people in a bus station. At one point, we hear the announcer list the buses about to depart. The lesson plan is out of order; put the items back into their original order.

a Play recording; students then compare answers in pairs; tell me their answer. If correct, continue; if not, play recording again, etc.

b Play recording; students then compare answers in pairs; tell me their answer. If correct, continue; if not, play recording again, etc.

c Show picture of bus station. 'Where do you think this is?' 'What's happening?' etc.

d Lead into a communicative activity based around the topic of travel problems.

e Set task: 'How many people are speaking?' 'Where are they?'

f Introduce topic: long-distance buses; discuss a little: 'Anyone been on one in England or the United States?'

g Set task: 'Here is your bus ticket' (different destinations for different students). 'Which bus number must you catch?'

h Set task: 'Why is the old lady worried?' 'What suggestion would you make?' (The task requires listening to and interpreting a longish section of the recording.)

i Play recording; students then compare answers in pairs and give their answer. If correct, continue; if not, play recording again, etc.

Commentary ■ ■ ■

The original order is: c, f, e, i, g, a, h, b, d. The stages a, b and i are, of course, interchangeable. This order shows a logical progression from an introduction to a very simple first task (to give students confidence), through to a more difficult task (requiring recognition of the pronunciation of a town name and a bus number) and finally to a demanding task involving interpretation of a much longer piece of speech. By the time students start to listen intently for this, they will already have heard the recording a number of times, and the final task should therefore be that much easier. Even the weakest student will also go away with a feeling of having achieved something (e.g. one of the earlier tasks), even if he couldn't get the last one perfectly. ■

3 How do we listen?

When we listen, we use a variety of strategies to help us pick up the message. Some of these are connected with understanding the 'big' picture, e.g. gaining an overview of the structure of the whole text, getting the gist (the general meaning), using various types of previous knowledge to help us make sense of the message, etc. Listening in this way is sometimes termed 'gist listening' or 'extensive listening'. Other strategies are connected with the small pieces of the text, e.g. correctly hearing precise sounds, working out exactly what some individual words are, catching precise details of information, etc. This is often called 'listening for detail'.

Task 109: Starting points for listening lessons

When working on listening in the classroom, do you think it makes more sense to start with work on the 'small pieces' (e.g. sounds and words and details) or on the 'big pieces' (e.g. background topics, the overall structure and organisation of a text, the general meaning, etc.)?

Commentary ■ ■ ■

The two views described here are known as top-down and bottom-up. The next section introduces them. ■

Top-down and bottom-up

It used to be believed that listeners built up their understanding of a text by working out what each individual sound was, then adding these up into a word, understanding the word, checking the meaning of that word with the words around them, etc. (a bit like building up a wall from the individual bricks). Although this theory, known as 'bottom-up' (i.e. building up the messages from the individual small pieces), may initially sound appealing, it is virtually impossible to do.

Spoken English probably comes at you too fast to be able to adopt such an item-by-item approach on its own. It seems likely that we make use of 'bottom-up' skills more to fill in missing gaps rather than as a general approach to comprehension word by word.

The alternative theory is that when we listen to a new dialogue, we start processing the text using skills associated with a second theory ('top-down'), i.e. making use of what we already know to help us predict the structure and content of the text, and getting a general overall impression of the message.

Task 110: Factors that help you listen

Imagine that you are going to listen to (and take part in) an important conversation in a foreign language you half-know. You are, naturally, a little nervous. Will it be easier for you to follow the dialogue if you:

- have some idea what the topic being discussed will be?
- know something about that topic?
- know the typical sequence of exchanges that is used in a dialogue like this?
- can predict issues likely to be raised?
- are quickly able to get an overview of the general direction of the conversation?
- know any general rules or guidelines for what can/can't be said in conversations of this type?
- understand the attitudes of the participants?
- know some words/phrases that are commonly used in conversations of this type?

Commentary ■ ■ ■

I think the answer to each of these is probably 'yes'. We don't come to a new piece of listening completely from a 'zero' starting point. We bring our previous knowledge to it, even before it's started. Making a good prediction of the content or the shape of a listening text will definitely help us to make better sense of it when it happens. Rather than having to start from scratch, the listening may fall neatly into an imagined framework we have already set out for it. Of course, we can't be ready for everything, but anything that we have correctly expected frees up our energy to pay attention to things that require more intensive listening. This is summed up in Figure 8.3. ■

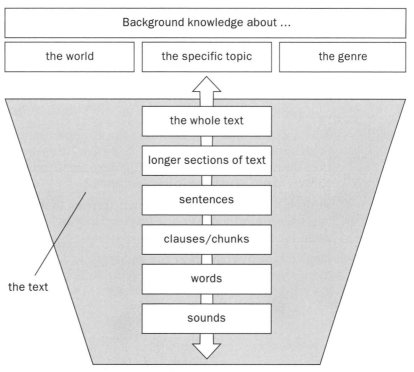

Figure 8.3   Geography of a listening text

Task 111: Top-down and bottom-up

Do the following represent use of top-down or bottom-up strategies?

1 Before we start listening, we can already predict some possible words and phrases that might be used because of our knowledge of lexical sets associated with the topic.
2 We listen carefully to a recording a number of times so that we can find a word we can't catch clearly.
3 When we don't clearly catch some of what people say, we hypothesise what we have missed and reinstate what we think was there, based on our knowledge of similar conversations.
4 We know the typical pattern some interactions follow (e.g. the typical sequence of exchanges when ordering a taxi on the phone), and this helps us to understand these when they are spoken.

Commentary ■ ■ ■

Strategy 2 is bottom-up. Strategies 1, 3 and 4 are examples of top-down strategies, and we do a lot more of this kind of processing that you might expect. Using background knowledge, prediction and 'filling-in' gaps are all important listening skills. ■

Top-down and bottom-up in the classroom

When we listen, we probably adopt a continually varying combination of top-down and bottom-up strategies, so work on both areas is useful to learners. I suspect that when I listen, I often process chunk by chunk, catching the general meaning of a small segment of text and, if necessary (e.g. if something isn't clear), go back over and review the temporarily stored segment (from short-term memory) and analyse more carefully what its components were.

You need to decide your own personal theory about how people listen so that you can plan lessons to reflect this. Many teachers nowadays believe that we mainly listen 'top-down' in real life, and so structure lesson sequences starting with top-down work.

A typical classroom listening lesson (for example using a radio phone-in programme on traffic congestion) might involve a sequence of tasks that move from the top to the bottom part of the diagram shown in Figure 8.3. (NB You are unlikely to use all of these in a single lesson.)

Figure 8.4 shows a possible route map through such a lesson, starting from the 'big' background and overview tasks and moving towards the 'smaller', more detail-focused and language-focused issues.

Don't take such a map as a fixed 'right way' to do things; but it's certainly worth trying out as an experiment if you generally approach listening (or reading) texts in a different way, say by jumping straight in with a focus on detail.

Procedure	Why?
Discuss the general topic	Learners start to think about the topic, raising a number of issues that will be discussed later on the recording. This preparation may help them to hear these things being discussed later.
Predict the specific content	Students hypothesise specific issues that may be raised.
Predict the structure	Students consider/discuss possible organisational structures for a phone-in (who speaks? what kind of questions? typical exchanges? etc.). This may help learners to recognise the content more easily.
Gist listening for overview	Learners get an overall impression of the content without worrying about small items or individual words.
Gist listening for attitudes	Learners interpret intonation, paralinguistic features (sighs, etc.).
More careful listening for complex meanings	By catching and interpreting smaller parts of the text, learners fine-tune their understanding.
Listening to pick out specific small language details	This focused work (e.g. on pronunciation) may raise learner awareness (e.g. of weak forms) and thus help students to listen better in future.

Figure 8.4   Possible route map for a listening lesson

Task 112: Planning a top-down procedure

Find a listening text (e.g. in an upcoming unit of your coursebook). For the moment, ignore any tasks and exercises printed in the book. Plan an original **top-down** lesson using the procedure above.

4   Listening ideas

In this section, I'll suggest some ideas for more adventurous listening activities.

News headlines

One interesting and popular example of a lesson using the task–feedback circle (see Section 2 of this chapter) is to use up-to-date material recorded off the radio. Many teachers regularly record the news headlines each morning for classroom use. Resource 16 (Appendix 2) gives a complete lesson procedure that you can use with any recording of the day's news headlines (NB headlines only, not complete stories; the recording should be less than a minute long). This lesson would be suitable for most classes at Intermediate level or above. Remember to set tasks before each listening and to replay the recording as often as necessary in order for the students to find the answers to one task, before moving on to the next.

Jigsaw listening

No wonder this technique is a teachers' favourite! You can run listening activities that allow learners to work at their own speed, controlling the CD player or tape recorder themselves and repeatedly playing parts of a text until they are really happy with their understanding of it. It also involves a lot of message-oriented communication and useful group co-operation.

Here's the basic idea:

* Working in small groups, learners listen to separate small parts of a longer recording, i.e. each group hears different things.
* They then meet up, perhaps in pairs, threes or fours, with people from groups that listened to other parts of the recording.
* They report to each other on what they have heard and compare ideas and reach a conclusion or consensus or complete some specific task. The task might be simply to construct a full picture of the recording's contents.

To run a jigsaw task, a little technical preparation is required:

* You'll usually need a separate CD player or tape recorder for each group to listen on and the same number of separate recordings.
* To make sure that students cannot accidentally hear parts of the recording from other groups' sections, you might need to rerecord and edit some recordings (if your coursebook doesn't offer ready-made materials).

Jigsaw task ideas

Three (or more) slightly different viewpoints of a single event, each on a separate recording. The task is to work out what actually happened. Useful additional materials might be a location map or diagram of a room. Example events:

* witnesses of a crime
* accident reports
* finding where someone might have lost their purse
* working out exactly who was at a meeting ('I met Jay and Frieda …', etc.)
* working out the sequence of events (what happened first, second, etc.)
* a news story with additional (or varying) details in each separate section
* a description of a place or people (to get the complete picture, students will need to put together information from all sections)
* a party
* an office
* a factory process
* 'diary' information from three people (e.g. when/where they are doing things); the listening task could be to choose a time and place for a meeting.

The Tape Gallery

A variation on jigsaw listening. Find about ten interesting short jokes, stories, advertisements or poems (not more than a minute long) and record yourself reading them, each onto a different cassette or CD. Borrow two or three extra tape recorders/CD players and place them at different locations around the room. Put two or three of your cassettes/CDs next to each machine. Make sure learners know how to operate the machines. Then invite learners to wander freely around the different places, changing tape/CD or location at will, with the aim of choosing their favourite recording. Make sure they play recordings softly and that they don't all gather round one machine, but otherwise leave the control of the activity to them. Afterwards, get feedback on what they enjoyed or learned.

Home recording

Many teachers have found that it's interesting and useful to make their own short recordings for classroom use. This gives you the chance to offer listening topics directly relevant to your course or of interest to your learners. A popular tactic is to 'interview' one or two other teachers in the staff room.

When you ask colleagues if they can help, warn them how much time it might require. It's often possible to do the whole process of briefing, rehearsal and recording in about ten minutes.

You can have completely unscripted, improvised, 'natural' conversations, but it often works better if you give your speaker(s) a briefing on:

- what you want them to talk about;
- any particular points that should be mentioned;
- language items you would really like included (e.g. 'Please use lots of present perfect!') or avoided (e.g. 'Don't use the past progressive if you can help it');
- how fast and clearly you want them to speak (e.g. normal speed or slower?).

One useful strategy is to offer speakers a set of brief written notes – just the key words – to help them remember the structure of the conversation. Alternatively, you could fully script the text of recordings, so that the speakers just read this aloud. It's usually worth doing one quick rehearsal or 'read-through' before recording.

NB Making a home recording will take some of your time and it can be quite hard to make a voice recording of good enough audio quality to stand up to playing in some classrooms.

Live listening

One activity that has grown in popularity in recent years is 'live listening'. The basic idea is straightforward: students get to listen to real people speaking in class, rather than to recordings. Here's a way of trying this:

- When you find that your coursebook has a fairly dull listening text coming up, instead of using the recording, invite a colleague with a spare five minutes to come into your class.
- Make sure the class has a clear task while listening, e.g. to note down the main points that each speaker makes.
- Sit in front of the learners and have a live 'ordinary' conversation on the same topic as the book.

Though there is certainly a lot of value in getting a variety of visitors with different vocal styles into your class, you can do live listenings on your own, too: reading or improvising conversations in your own voice, or 'acting' a range of characters yourself. The following activity could be done using a visitor or by yourself.

Guest stars

Prepare notes for a short monologue in character (e.g. as the Queen or Britney Spears). In class, announce that a guest star is coming today, but don't say who it is. Go out of the room and return 'in character' (or invite another colleague in). The 'guest' then chats naturally for a minute or two in character, about her life, a typical day, how she feels, etc. The learners should listen and not shout out who they think it is, but instead write down their guess. At the end of the monologue, let them compare their guesses in small groups (giving reasons) and then check with you. When they know who the guest is, they could briefly ask a few more interview questions to the character. Repeat the activity with different 'guests' as a regular slot in your lessons. (Maybe students could play the 'guest', too.)

5 Approaches to reading

Reading to oneself (as opposed to reading aloud) is, like listening, a 'receptive' skill, and similar teaching procedures can be used to help learners. The task–feedback circle works equally well with reading texts, and many of the guidelines given in Section 2 are also easily adaptable.

The most obvious differences are to do with the fact that people read at different speeds and in different ways. Whereas a recording takes a definite length of time to play through, in a reading activity, individuals can control the speed they work at and what they are looking at.

Task 113: Difficulties when reading a foreign language

What are your own main problems when trying to read a text in a language that you don't know very well?

Commentary ■ ■ ■

Maybe:

- I don't know enough vocabulary.
- I need the dictionary all the time.
- It's very slow – it takes ages just to get through a few sentences.
- I often get to the stage where I understand all the individual words, but the whole thing eludes me completely.
- Because it's slow, the pleasure or interest in the subject matter is soon lost. ■

Many learners approach reading texts expecting to read them thoroughly and to stop only when they have understood every word. Clearly, there is value in this as a way of improving their vocabulary and their understanding of grammar, but, as with listening, this kind of approach does not necessarily make them into better readers, because this plodding, word-by-word approach is not the way that we most often do our reading in real life. In order to make students better readers, we need first of all to raise their awareness that it's not always essential to understand every word, and that practising some different reading techniques in English may be very useful to them. And if their basic strategy is to read slowly and ponderously, then a good first strategy could be to help them learn to read fast; not worrying about understanding every word; not, perhaps, even understanding most words, but still achieving a specific and useful goal.

Task 114: Selecting an appropriate reading task

Imagine that you have given students a copy of a tourist leaflet publicising a nearby town and advertising local attractions, museums, special events and with information on prices, opening times, etc. What would be a suitable task to get students to read this quickly (rather than read every word)?

Commentary ■ ■ ■

You probably want tasks that encourage students to search for specific small sections of text which they then read more carefully to find a required piece of information. These might be factual, information questions such as 'When does the Military Museum close?' 'Can I take my dog into Chapultepec Park?' 'What is a good souvenir to take back from this region?' 'How much would it cost for a family of four to go swimming at the lido?' 'What are the newest animals in the zoo?'

Students doing this will be reading the material in a similar way one to how people might read it in everyday life. ■

Skimming and scanning

Many activities designed to increase reading speeds are variations on the following two ideas:

• Read quickly and get the gist of a passage.
• Read quickly and find a specific piece of information.

The first of these is also known as **skimming**. A typical skimming task would be a general question from the teacher, such as 'Is this passage about Jill's memories of summer or winter?' or 'Is this story set in a school or a restaurant?' The learners would attempt to find the answer quickly, without reading every word of the passage, by 'speed-reading' through some portions of the text. Skimming is mainly concerned with finding key topics, main ideas, overall theme, basic structure, etc.

The second of the ideas is also known as **scanning**. A common scanning activity is searching for information in a leaflet or directory, and a typical scanning task would be 'What time does the Birmingham train leave?' or 'What does Cathy take with her to the meeting?'

Skimming and scanning are both 'top-down' skills (see Chapter 8 Section 3). Although scanning is involved with details of the text, the way that a reader finds those details involves processing the whole text, moving her eyes quickly over the whole page, searching for key words or clues from the textual layout and the content that will enable her to focus in on smaller sections of text that she are likely to get answers from. Skimming and scanning can be summarised as follows:

Skimming	Fast reading for: key topics, main ideas, overall theme, basic structure, etc.
Scanning	Fast reading for: specific individual pieces of information (e.g. names, addresses, facts, prices, numbers, dates, etc.)

Task 115: Choosing useful reading activities

Which of the following seem to be useful reading activities and which not? Why? Briefly work out an alternative procedure for the less satisfactory ones.

1 The class reads a whole page of classified advertisements in the newspaper, using their dictionaries to check up all unknown words.
2 Students each have a copy of the *Guardian Weekly* newspaper. Ask them to find the word *over* somewhere on the front page.
3 Place a pile of local tourist leaflets on the table and explain that students, in groups of four, can plan a day out tomorrow.
4 Students read a short extract from a novel and answer five multiple-choice comprehension questions about fine points of detail.

Commentary ■■■

One test for useful reading (or listening work) might be to check how far tasks reflect real-life uses of the same text. If a text is used in class in ways that are reasonably similar to real life, it is likely that the task will be effective.

Procedure 1 seems unsatisfactory because it is an unrealistic use of the advertisements; in real life, no one would read them in such a way. A more realistic task would require them to scan the ads for specific items (as we do when we want, say, to buy a second-hand TV). So 'What is the best TV I could buy?' would be a far more realistic task.

Procedure 2 is similarly strange. This is a scanning exercise, but an entirely unrealistic one. We might well scan the front page of a newspaper looking for names of people or countries that we wanted to read about or headings that directed us to information we needed (such as weather), but it seems unlikely that we would search for a single word like *over* (though as a game, it could be fun). For a more useful scanning task, students could be asked to find where specific articles are or find certain factual information. Skimming tasks would also be useful, to get the gist of an article for example.

Procedure 3, although it perhaps appears a little strange initially, is in fact a very interesting reading activity. The students will be using the leaflets for precisely the purpose for which they were written, and will be reading them in order to obtain a whole range of appropriate ideas and information: seeing what's available, checking opening times, prices, etc. As a bonus, there will be a lot of speaking as well as reading.

Procedure 4 describes an exercise commonly found in exams. It is clearly useful as a demanding way of testing comprehension, and is useful for studying the fine shades of meaning a writer conveys. It is, however, important to ensure that this kind of activity is not the only reading work done, partly because it seems to be confirming to students that this is the normal (or only) way to read a novel. Students also need to be shown approaches to a novel that allow them to read fluently, at speed, without worrying about catching every nuance. ■

Real-life purposes are not the only way of measuring the usefulness of classroom reading work. Often we might want to train students in specific reading techniques or strategies, things that will help their future reading, even if the immediate classroom work doesn't itself reflect a real-life purpose.

Top-down reading

As with listening lessons, many reading lessons move from 'big' to 'small', i.e. 'top-down' – from overview to details. Using the task–feedback circle as a starting point, we can plan a route map for a basic reading lesson (Figure 8.5).

Pre-text	1	Introduction and lead-in, e.g. get the learners interested in the topic, initial discussion of key themes, make an explicit link between the topic of the text and students' own lives and experiences, focus on important language that will come in the text
	2	First task (pre-reading), e.g. predict from some extracted information (illustration, key words, headlines, etc.), read questions about the text, students compose their own questions
Text	3	Tasks to focus on fast reading for gist (skimming), e.g. check text against predictions made beforehand, guess the title from a choice of three options, put events (or illustrations) in the correct order
	4	Tasks to focus on fast reading for specific details (scanning), e.g. find single items of information in the text
	5	Tasks to focus on meaning (general points), e.g. answer questions about meaning, make use of information in the text to do something (make a sketch, fill out a form, find out which picture is being described, etc.), discuss issues, summarise arguments, compare viewpoints
	6	Tasks to focus on meaning (finer points, more intensive comprehensive understanding)
	7	Tasks to focus on individual language items, e.g. vocabulary or grammar exercises, use of dictionaries, work out meaning of words from context
Post-text	8	Follow-on task, e.g. role-play, debate, writing task (e.g. write a letter in reply), personalisation (e.g. 'Have you ever had an experience like this one?')
	9	Closing, e.g. draw the lesson to a conclusion, tie up loose ends, review what has been studied and what has been learned

Figure 8.5   Possible route map for a reading lesson

Here are some specific ideas for reading tasks

- Put these illustrations of the text in the correct order.
- Put these cut-up paragraphs in the correct order.
- Find words in the text that mean the same as the words in this list.
- Read the text and find the mistakes in this illustration (or draw your own).
- Read the text and make a list of particular items (e.g. jobs that need doing, the author's proposals, advantages and disadvantages, etc.).
- Give a headline to each section of the article (or match given headlines with the sections).
- Find appropriate places in the text to reinsert some sentences that have previously been separated from the text.
- Write a reply.
- Look at the title and the illustrations (but not the text). Predict which of the following list of words you will find in the text.
- Solve the problem.
- Discuss (or write) the missing last paragraph of the text.
- Discuss interpretations of, reactions to, feelings about the text.
- Make notes under the following headings: ...
- Before you read this text, make notes about what you already know about the subject.
- Act out the dialogue, story, episode, etc.
- Put this list of events in the correct order.

For ideas on using reading to help teach grammar, see Chapter 12.

6   Extensive reading

A lot of classroom work (with coursebooks, exercises, texts) involves **intensive reading,** i.e. reading texts closely and carefully with the intention of gaining an understanding of as much detail as possible. This is often a stop/start kind of reading, involving going back over the same (usually short) text a number of times to find more and more in it, making sure that the words have been correctly interpreted. This is how a competent language user might read an instruction manual for a piece of flat-pack furniture or a leaflet with guidelines on whether they have to pay income tax or not. It's not the way she would typically read a chapter from a novel or a magazine article, although, in classrooms, it is often how students are asked to process such material (with true/false and other comprehension questions to check if they can pick up specific points).

In everyday life, we tend to do much more **extensive reading,** i.e. fluent, faster reading, often of longer texts, for pleasure, entertainment and general understanding, but without such careful attention to the details. When we don't understand words or small sections, we usually just keep going, maybe only coming back when there has been a major breakdown in our understanding.

There is a great deal of evidence that extensive reading has a powerful impact on language learning. The more someone reads, the more they pick up items of vocabulary and grammar from the texts, often without realising it, and this widening language knowledge seems to increase their overall linguistic confidence, which then influences and improves their skills in other language areas, too (though this is probably only true in cases where the material they read is self-chosen and is genuinely relevant and interesting to them).

So, there are strong arguments for actively encouraging students to read a lot in the target language, both in and outside the classroom. We can help by:

- providing a library of readers (see below), magazines, newspapers, leaflets, etc.;
- training learners how to select suitable reading material and in ways to read it;
- creating a 'book club' environment that encourages learners to choose what books to purchase, talk about favourite books, share them with each other, write brief recommendations, etc.;
- allowing sections of classroom time purely for students to read; some teachers who have five or six lessons a week set aside one of these lessons as quiet reading time.

A library doesn't need to be large. It can be something as simple as a small box of books and magazines. However, it's important to include items that are relevant and suitable for your class. Unabridged old copies of worthy classics are probably not a good choice. Better to have a few recent magazines on themes that students like (e.g. films, pop stars, computer games, etc. for a teen class) and a small set of graded readers.

Readers

'Readers' are books of stories (or other content) published specifically for learners to get extended exposure to English. They often have their grammar and vocabulary 'graded' to named levels (e.g. Elementary) so that learners at that level should stand a reasonable chance of successfully reading them. Many state the size of vocabulary used and have footnotes or glossaries of words outside their stated word limit. The main aim of readers is to provide opportunities for extensive reading for pleasure. For this reason, be careful about integrating comprehension checks, tests and exercises into your teaching. As far as possible, let students read, enjoy and move on, rather than read and then have to do lots of exercises afterwards. There are ideas for some creative extensive reading activities at the end of this section.

Task 116: Reading round the class

Readers can be read outside class or can be used in 'quiet reading' class time. Some teachers use them in class for reading aloud, with different students reading short sections one after the other. This reading aloud 'round the class' is something many of us recall from our schooldays. Why might this popular technique not be effective?

Commentary ■ ■ ■

- I read faster than he speaks.
- It's so boring.
- She makes mistakes.
- I've already read to page 37 myself.
- He can't pronounce it and he gets embarrassed.
- I'm so nervous about reading, I miss the story.
- I can't follow the story with all these different people speaking.
- I prefer to read to myself.

- It's going to be 35 minutes till my go.
- It gets in the way of me hearing the voices of the characters.
- It's not good practice for speaking – I'd never talk like that! ■

Obviously a fluent reader with the ability to inject life and feeling into the reading is a wonderful bonus. Most students, however, do not fit this description, and round-the-class reading tends to be a slow, tedious turn-off rather than a rouser of enthusiasm.

Some alternatives to reading aloud round the class

Here are some alternatives to try:

- You reading;
- You reading narrative, but students reading character dialogue;
- You (having read the chapter yourself before class) telling the story in your own words, without notes, in the most spell-binding way you can; later, you get students to do the same with other bits;
- Students reading to each other in small groups or pairs, stopping, changing, discussing and helping each other whenever they want to;
- Students reading silently, then, without discussion, acting out/improvising a scene based on what happened;
- Students silently speed-reading a chapter (say in two minutes) then reporting back, discussing, comparing, etc. before silently reading it more carefully.

Extensive reading activities

The following ideas are some slightly more unusual activities based around interpreting and enjoying readers in class:

- Don't always start at the beginning! Try jumping in at the middle and reading one page. Predict what happened before, who the people are, where they are, etc. Or use a contents page similarly.
- Use a key section of the story as a dictation.
- Create a situation quite separate from the story of the book and allow students to improvise to see how the characters would behave in a totally different environment or time. The Forsytes watching TV together? Jane Eyre applying to get a temporary secretarial job? Not quite as silly as it sounds – this is a very exciting way to investigate character.
- Students draw the picture of the scene. When finished, they compare and discuss their different interpretations.
- Interviews: one student is a chat-show host or a newspaper reporter and interviews another student in the role of a character. 'So why did you do that?' 'What do you really think about Joseph?' etc. Or get all the characters together and interview them. Similarly, put the characters 'on trial' in a courtroom: 'Whose fault was it?'
- Map the story (or one chapter). Draw lines on it to show different characters' movements. Or map out the relationships between characters. A good classroom poster?
- Keep a character's diary.
- Review the book for a TV programme. Meet the author. Discuss, argue. Phone-in callers can ask questions.
- Would it make a good film? The students are the board of directors for a film

company. They need to decide whether the book is film material or not. How does the story need to be changed? How can they make it more exciting? Who should direct it? Who should play the parts? Make an advertisement poster for the film.

- What did the front page of the local newspaper look like on the day when ...?
- Choose a page or paragraph from the next chapter in the book and blank out some words. Students need to guess what is going to happen by trying to find the missing words.
- Redesign the cover of the book. Write the 'blurb' on the back cover.

Chapter 9 Writing

1 Helping students to write

Task 117: Writing in real life and in the classroom

List some things you have written in the past two weeks. What are the implications of your list for the English language classroom?

Commentary ■ ■ ■

The role of writing in everyday life has changed quite dramatically over recent decades. When selecting work for students, you need to be clear about whether it is useful practice. These issues are discussed in the next section. ■

Writing in everyday life

Whereas, in the early 1990s, many people wrote very little day by day, the advent and popularity of e-mail, web forums, Internet messenger services and text messaging has meant that there is now a huge increase in written communication. Whether this growth and popularity will continue as new technology offers easier, cheaper and faster video and voice connections is not clear.

This new kind of communication has its own peculiar rules and rituals, and in some cases has evolved its own shorthand, abbreviations and lexis, often because of the perceived need to write quickly or within a limited word/character count. You can buy little dictionaries of text-message conventions and abbreviations. There are also new ways of expressing oneself. I can now communicate instantly across the world and use a little picture of a cartoon face to express my reaction to something written by my friend. Is that writing?

Beyond these new ways of communicating, many people actually do very little writing in day-to-day life, and a great deal of what they do write is quite short: brief notes to friends or colleagues, answers on question forms, diary entries, postcards, etc. The need for longer, formal written work seems to have lessened over the years, and this is reflected in many classrooms where writing activities are perhaps less often found than those for other skills.

Writing in the classroom

Despite the points raised above, there may still be good reasons why it is useful to include work on writing in a course:

- Many students have specific needs that require them to work on writing skills: academic study, examination preparation and Business English are three common areas where written work is still very important.
- At the most basic level, your students are likely to be involved in taking down notes in lessons such as yours; this is a skill that is worth focusing on.
- Writing involves a different kind of mental process. There is more time to think, to reflect, to prepare, to rehearse, to make mistakes and to find alternative and better solutions.

- It can give you a break, quieten down a noisy class, change the mood and pace of a lesson, etc.

Much writing work in the classroom falls on a continuum of how much restriction, help and control is offered, from copying to unguided writing.

1	**Copying**	Students practise forming letter shapes in a handwriting book, note down substitution tables from the board, copy examples from a textbook, etc.
2	**Doing exercises**	Students write single words phrases, sentences, etc. in response to very tightly focused tasks with limited options and limited opportunities for creativity or getting things wrong.
3	**Guided writing**	You guide students to write longer texts in quite restricted or controlled tasks by offering samples, models, possibly useful language items, advice, organisational frameworks, etc.
4	**Process writing**	Students write what they want to, with help, encouragement and feedback from you and others throughout the process of choosing a topic, gathering ideas, organising thoughts, drafting, etc.
5	**Unguided writing**	Students write freely without overt guidance, assistance or feedback during the writing process, though a title or task may be set, and work may be 'marked' later.

Accuracy tends to be more of a concern towards the top of the scale, fluency increasingly important towards the lower part. 'Copying' and 'doing exercises' are making use of writing in order to help students learn something else, e.g. grammar, but do not significantly help students become better 'writers'.

Teaching the skill of writing

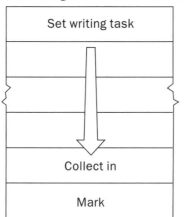

Is it possible to teach the 'skill of writing'? How could we do it? For many teachers, the answer seems to be mainly by setting a writing task, leaving the students to do it (perhaps as homework) then collecting it in and marking it (Figure 9.1).

Figure 9.1   Setting a writing task

Some teachers doubt if there is any useful in-class work that could be done on writing, believing that it is essentially an individual activity. However, there are many possible steps that could go into the middle area of the diagram in Figure 9.1. A student can learn to become a better writer by (a) being actively encouraged and helped to follow through a series of preparatory steps before the final text is produced, and (b) becoming more aware of that preparation process, so that it can be done more independently and transparently in future. For example, we could help learners:

- choose a topic;
- choose a genre;
- get ideas;
- discuss ideas with others to get new perspectives;
- select between ideas;
- sequence ideas;
- make notes, diagrams, etc. to help organise ideas;
- find grammar and lexis suitable for the text;
- do practice exercises on language items that will be useful;
- study sample and model texts similar to what they want to write;
- plan the organisation of their text;
- draft a rough text;
- get feedback on content;
- get feedback on language use;
- co-write sections of text in groups;
- make alterations and rewrites;
- write a final version;
- find appropriate readers.

Activities designed to work in these areas in class come under the headings of 'guided writing' or 'process writing' work (which in practice tend to overlap quite a lot).

Planning classroom writing work

A typical route for classroom work on helping students to write (where the teacher has already selected the topic or title) might involve some or all of the following steps:

1	**Introduce the topic**	Get students interested, maybe by reading a text (article, letter, advert, etc.) showing pictures, discussing some key issues, etc.
2	**Introduce and summarise the main writing task**	Make sure students are clear what they have to do. They need to know the genre (magazine article? letter? formal report? etc.), who they are writing for and why. Avoid bland, 'genre-free text for no particular audience' writing tasks.
3	**Brainstorm ideas**	Whole class: use the board to collect as many ideas as possible. Small groups: speak and take notes.

4	**Fast-write**	A very good way to overcome 'blank page' terror and get ideas flowing is to 'fast-write' (see instructions in the next section).
5	**Select and reject ideas**	What's worth leaving out?
6	**Sort and order ideas**	Start to plan structure of text by arranging ideas.
7	**Decide on specific requirements: style, information, layout, etc.**	How is the text to be laid out, paragraphed, organised? Are there any special rules (e.g. if it's a letter, report, etc.)? Are there things that must be included or stated in a certain way?
8	**Focus on useful models**	Help students to study one or more samples of written texts similar to the one they are writing. Focus on content, message, organisation, grammar, phrases, etc.
9	**Plan the text**	Use notes, sketches or cut-up cards to start organising a possible shape for the text.
10	**Get feedback**	At various points, you, other individual students or groups can read and make helpful comments and suggestions about a text. This help may be on the content and message, the organisation, the language, etc.
11	**Prepare draft(s)**	Students often benefit from preparing a draft version before the final one. This gives them the chance to get reader reactions and corrections.
12	**Edit**	Students carefully go through their own text, checking if it says what they want it to, if it reads clearly and smoothly, if its language is correct, etc.
13	**Prepare final text**	Based on feedback, students write a finished text.
14	**Readers!**	Rather than simply 'mark' a text, it's great when students can respond to it in some more realistic ways.

In many cases, the tasks we set our students will determine the kinds of activities and lesson stages that are appropriate. When selecting writing tasks, remember that the old school 'write a story about …' represents only a very small (or non-existent) part of a normal person's writing. While 'creative writing' is often a great activity, we need to make sure that learners mainly get practice in the range of real-life writing tasks that they will face. As far as possible, select the tasks most relevant for their needs. Here are some general ideas for real-world writing tasks. You may be able to use these to help you generate more focused ideas of your own that are relevant to your learners.

Write real letters/e-mails	Think of real people to whom students can write, e.g. to Members of Parliament, to prisoners, to manufacturing companies, to fan clubs, to local newspapers, to other schools, etc. Send them. Get replies. Write back.
Publish your own newsletter, magazine, handout, etc.	Class magazine, school magazine, fan newsletter, local news, campaigning on environmental or political issues, etc.
Advertise (ideas, school events, products, etc.)	Advertise around the school, around town; send in your ads to local papers, etc.
Send comments, replies to discussions, reviews, etc. to web sites	There are now a wide number of discussions, message boards and newsgroups specifically for students or for special-interest groups. Many shop and consumer sites invite reader reviews of books, products, events, etc.
Write questionnaires and then use them out in the street	These can be written in English or in the learners' own language. Write up the results. Publish them!
Long-term projects	These are a good way of integrating writing with other work. The aim could be a file or book at the end (see Chapter 16, Section 14).
Apply for things, fill in forms register for things, etc.	This can be done directly online if students have Internet access or printed out on paper.

Here are some examples of a few specific tasks:

- Write a guide book entry about your part of town.
- Write feedback and evaluation of a new product.
- Fill in a car-hire booking form.
- Write a review of a new game on a computer forum message board.
- Write a postcard to a manufacturer requesting an information leaflet about their work.
- Write (and design) computer presentation slides.
- Write an academic essay summarising arguments for and against a viewpoint.
- Write your personal profile for inclusion in a class souvenir booklet.
- Write a poem about your strongest childhood memory.
- Write a letter in reply to a job application to arrange an interview.

2   Writing in class

In this section, we will look in more detail at some classroom activities and strategies mentioned in the previous section.

A   Ideas for generating ideas

Brainstorming

It can be hard to get enough good ideas to write about. Brainstorming is a way to get the 'ideas creation engine' running. It means 'opening your mind and letting ideas pour out'. It also means not engaging that 'checking' part of your brain that too quickly dismisses things as stupid or useless (because we lose out on a lot of potentially good ideas because we reject them too soon). For this reason, it seems helpful to separate the ideas collection and the (later) critical review of those ideas

Here's a way to brainstorm in class:

* Write the topic or title in a circle in the middle of the board.
* Tell students to call out anything that comes to mind connected with the topic.
* Write up everything on the board.
* There should be no discussion or comments (especially derogatory ones!) – just ideas.

So what will happen? People will call out ideas. You'll write them up. It may take a while to get going, but after a bit, the ideas will probably start flowing. After a reasonable period of time (i.e. however long it takes to fill the board with thoughts), you can stop. Now there is a lot to look back over. Invite students to select ideas they like and can use, or maybe allow some discussion time in groups to continue the sifting process. Everyone should have something they can make use of.

Text-starts

A lot of real-life writing involves looking at other texts and summarising, reporting, responding to them, selecting ideas from them, commenting on them, etc. Supplying 'text-starts' can be a good way to provide useful writing work for students and practises reading/writing skills that are useful in professional life and academic research. The actual content of the texts provides a lot of 'support' for the writer (especially the one who worries that she must be 'imaginative' to write) in that there is something concrete to deal with and many ideas are already formulated and mainly need a response or opinion, rather than original thought.

Some ideas:

Resource material	Writing task
Information about a holiday location (pictures, description, list of attractions, etc.)	You are the copy-writer for the local tourist board. Write a two-paragraph advertisement for the place to encourage more visitors to come.

Resource material	Writing task
Full data and illustrations of three different up-to-date household products or gadgets. Possible extra information about consumer trends, the economy, etc.	You are a senior manager and will attend a meeting to decide on one new product to produce. Write a brief report on each product, then outline your recommendations as to which one to choose, with reasons.
A map of a town. Short descriptions of 'ghosts' that are said to haunt specific buildings and locations.	You are a local tour guide who has decided to start a 'Ghost walk' for tourists around town. Plan a route for the walk. Write a short article for the local paper to publicise it.
Seven e-mails to your company pointing out problems with the delivery service.	You are head of the delivery department. Write an e-mail to the director summarising the problems and making recommendations.
A number of articles from different sources on the same news item; a letter from your friend asking if you've heard about the item and what you think about it	Write a letter to your friend.
History articles, encyclopaedias, websites, etc.	Prepare a wall poster to interest and inform your friends about a historical topic.

Fast-writing

For many writers, the single most difficult thing is simply to start writing. The blank page sits in front of you, and it can become very hard even to put down the first word. The longer you fail to write, the harder that first sentence becomes. Instead, imagine that your students could have a whole page of their own writing to start from; not a final version, but something on which to base their new writing. This is what fast-writing aims to achieve. Even if only a word or a line from this first attempt makes it into the final text, it is has served its purpose, like the ignition key on a car, getting the writing started.

Tell students that they need a few pieces of blank paper. The rules are that when you say 'start', they should:

- start writing about the topic;
- not stop writing;
- not put their pen down at all;
- not worry about spelling, grammar, etc.;
- write 'um, um, um' or 'rubbish' or something else if they can't think of what to write;
- not stop to go back and read what they have written;

- keep writing till you say 'stop' (which will be after five/eight/ten minutes or however long you think is appropriate for your group).

At the end, they will have a page or more of writing. A lot of it will be rubbish! But there will also often be ideas and ways of saying things that are well worth retrieving. Give the learners enough time to really look back over what they have written. Tell them to be ruthless and cross out a lot of the writing, but also to retrieve some good pieces. They can then use these as starting points for the new writing.

It's a surprisingly useful task. Often we don't know what on earth we are going to write until we start writing it. Fast-writing is one way to start that finding-out process.

B Ideas for helping writing

Structuring and organising

Some simple strategies may help learners find an order for their ideas. 'Card planning' involves learners writing down the main themes of their text as notes onto separate cards. They then arrange the cards in various orders until they get a sequence that seems to work. Similarly, learners could draw a sketch diagram showing how their text will be put together, using lines and arrows to link separate items.

Looking at sample texts

It is often helpful if students see samples of the kind of texts they are working on. If you offer this as an activity early on in the lesson sequence, it is likely that this sample will be viewed as a kind of model on which to base their own work. The final product may then be substantially similar to the original, especially in layout and organisation, but with substitutions of content. If you offer samples later on in the writing work, learners will probably see the text as something to give them extra support and ideas, but may not significantly alter their own overall structure and content.

What can you study in a sample text?

- The layout
- The overall message
- How the items are organised
- Specific phrases and sentences used
- Distinctive grammatical features
- The style and tone
- The effect on the reader

Getting feedback on drafts

Feedback on writing isn't something to save up until the entire text is fully completed. In fact, it is of very little use then, as the thing is over, and students will probably just want a complimentary comment and then to forget it. The most useful comments are those that will have an impact as the writing is evolving; these will be useful from as many different readers as possible, from fellow students just as much as from you.

Organise pairs of students to read each other's work, or groups to give comments. Feedback could be done in answer to specific questions or according to a feedback form of some kind or more freely as general response and comments. As a result of feedback, students can write a new draft of their work, which can then be submitted again to readers for comments. This cycle of feedback and comments can lead to excellent results and really helps writers get a clearer idea of what a reader finds in their work.

Using computers

If you like the idea of redrafting and feedback, you may want to give thought to whether the writing is on computer. Using a word-processing package on a computer has significant advantages for student writing over pen and paper:

- It is readable (no handwriting jungles)!
- Multiple copies can be printed out for as many readers as needed.
- Suggestions and edits can be written on to hard copies and then editing can be done on the computer – no need to rewrite from scratch.
- It can be e-mailed directly to other students or to you.

Some specific features of word-processing software may be useful. If your students are relatively unfamiliar with computers, you may want to teach them how to:

- select text; change font and font size; apply underline, bold, italic, etc.;
- use basic 'cut', 'copy', 'paste' editing features;
- set the spell-check language and options for 'check spelling as you type';
- regularly save back-up copies so that six hours of vital work is not lost after one mistake;
- use (and be wary of) any grammar checking facilities;
- use a 'comment' feature, allowing different readers to leave notes in the body of the text that the writer can then review and use later on;
- program simple macros (i.e. mini-programs that can do frequently repeated actions at the press of a button). For example, I have found that having a word-count macro is very handy on the main toolbar.

3 Responses to writing

Task 118: Successful writing

In real life, when we write something, how can we measure if the writing was a success?

Commentary ■ ■ ■

Well, it's certainly quite rare for us to hand it to someone else, wait a few days and then get it back with a short comment and/or a mark written at the bottom. Yet this is a fairly common response in classroom situations. Such marking may sometimes be helpful or required, but often isn't the most useful way to help our learners become better writers. ■

Audience and purpose

In real life, we can judge if our writing was successful by whether it did what we wanted it to do. For example:

- if we wrote a complaint e-mail to an Internet bookshop, we would feel successful if they replied, seemed to understand our problem and took steps to deal with it;
- if we wrote a story about a happy incident in our childhood, we might feel we had succeeded if other people read it and enjoyed it, and perhaps wanted to talk to us about it and ask questions or respond with their own stories;
- if we wrote a report about sales prospects in Slovakia for a board meeting, we might feel that we had achieved our goal if other people at the meeting found the information clear, succinct and complete and were able to make use of it in the discussion.

The fact that writing can achieve such things is part of what motivates us to put care into our writing. And in cases where we are not able to get such immediate, direct, tangible feedback, we may need to be particularly careful in rereading and editing a text before we send it away to a reader. This 'delayed response' nature of much writing can be part of what makes it hard to do. Good writers need to become careful readers of – and reflectors on – their own work. The existence of **audience** and **purpose** are worth bearing in mind in class.

Setting relevant writing tasks

Rather too many classroom writing tasks are directionless and audienceless. If students are only writing 'to please the teacher', there is probably relatively low motivation, and the quality of writing may be compromised, as students will have no clear perception as to why the work is being done. So how can we provide audience and purpose? Here are some key strategies:

- If you have done a Needs analysis with your students, base writing work on stated needs, i.e. using task types, contexts and situations directly relevant to students.
- Even before students start writing, think carefully about what will happen with the finished piece of text. If students know who will read their text and what that reader may need or expect from it, then they have a clear idea of the purpose of the writing, which will strongly affect many other decisions they take in the writing.
- Make sure you do not mark and give feedback only on accuracy of language. Include attention to the question of whether the writing is **appropriate** for the task type and is well targeted at the probable reader.
- Even if you feel that you have relatively little idea of your class's needs (for example, if your class is studying on a short general English course), you can still select writing tasks that are likely to reflect things that many students may need to write in real life.

Task 119: Reflecting real-life writing purposes in the classroom

Think up some ideas for real-life writing purposes that could be reflected and recreated in classroom writing activities, e.g.

Real-life purpose: You want to persuade someone to change their mind and come to your party.

Possible classroom task: You write a letter.

Commentary ■ ■ ■

Here are a few more:

Real-life purpose	Possible classroom task
You want to sell your second-hand bike.	You write a noticeboard ad or newspaper small ad.
You want people to vote for you in the class election.	You design and write a poster or election leaflet.
You want to inform a colleague who phoned and when.	You write a memo.
You want to book a suitable hotel for a visit to Vienna.	You fill in an Internet booking form.
You want to make people laugh.	You write three jokes in the class magazine.

■

Marking

If you are required (or wish) to provide some more traditional marking/feedback on written work, what are the options?

Task 120: Alternatives to traditional 'marking'

Your students have done some written work. You now collect in the papers, underline every mistake in red pen and write a mark or grade at the end. That's one option, but why may it not always be a good idea? What alternative options can you think of?

Commentary ■ ■ ■

Getting back a piece of work with a teacher's comments and corrections on it can be helpful. It can also be discouraging, especially if there is too much information, if the information is inappropriate or hard to interpret, or if the general tone is negative rather than positive. The red pen particularly has associations for many people with insensitive and discouraging correction and judgement. Some alternatives are listed below. ■

Variations on traditional teacher marking

Earlier in this chapter, we looked at options for getting students to look at each other's work – and they could even 'mark' it. However, many learners will expect the teacher to look at their work and may feel let down if it is only evaluated by other students. Here are some other options available to you:

- Use a green or a blue pen!
- Discuss the marking criteria with students. Agree a mark or grade.
- Write the correct answers in the margin.
- Use correction codes in the margin (see Figure 9.2).

- Underline all errors of one type (e.g. all verb-tense mistakes, all spelling mistakes, etc.).
- Write a letter in reply.
- Write nothing. Discuss the work with the individual students.
- Only write a comment about the **meaning** and **message** of the piece.
- Create a composite essay using good bits and problematic bits from a number of students' work. Photocopy it and hand it out for students to discuss and correct, together or in groups or individually, perhaps for homework.
- Use errors from a number of different students' writing to devise an exercise, quiz, game, etc. Or get students to create the exercise themselves based on their own mistakes (more challenging than simply copying out correct answers).
- Give a dictation based on sentences from their work.

In all of these options, there is one important guideline to bear in mind: tell students (or agree) before the writing what will happen afterwards (e.g. 'I'll be marking tense mistakes only').

Task 121: Correction codes

Some teachers like to use 'correction codes' for marking students' work.

1 In the text below, what does each code mean?
2 Why might correction codes be more useful to a learner than if the teacher had written the correction in?
3 Why have some mistakes been ignored?

Harry Greenman

The spaceship landed. A door opened. Harry the Greenman
˅   stumbled and fell out of the spaceship – He mumble something
ww sp that any body could understand but than a bit louder. "My name
    ⋏ is captain Greenman and I want study your language. Who
       is Director of this school?"
       Frank, a tall man gave to understand that he is the boss and they
sp   arranged some lessons. Next morning Frank thaught some
ww ˅   grammar. But the lesson was very bored. Captain Greenman felt
       asleep. Frank was very angry and threw the greenman back in
wo   the spaceship. Suddenly came another creature out. It was Mrs
       Greenman. She hit the director and turned back into the
       spaceship.

Commentary ■ ■ ■

Codes can indicate where an error is and what type of error it is. However, they leave the learners to do some work in order to find the corrections for themselves. This may seem preferable to handing them the correction 'ready made'. It is, of course, essential that the students understand your own set of codes! In the above example, V = verb problem (possibly incorrect tense); WO = word order; WW = wrong word; ⋏ = missing word; SP = spelling.

It often seems inappropriate to point out every error; it can be dispiriting to get back work with a large quantity of marks on it. You probably need to decide which errors you think are most important or useful for the student to work on at the moment and then to draw attention to these. ■

Task 122: Evaluating written work

Here are two pieces of student writing.

1 Note some of the students' language or writing problems.
2 What classroom work might help these learners to become better writers?

MY BARENTS. SAYED GOOBY
MY. WHANT GO EARBORT. I AM
GONNING FLY. MENY HOWRES.
WHANT ARIV ON SUNNEDAY GONNING
LONNDEN

It was my birthday. I had really nice birthday party.
It was party with my friends. I had lovely chat
with friends. Although I was eating something
at the party, I couldn't. I just drank. I had an
absolutely wonderful time.

Next morning climate was fine. Whereas my feeling
was awful with headache. I couldn't work properly.
I had bad condition. Eventually I did big mistake.
Customer complained at me.

At that evening I met to my friend. My friend
and I had dinner. Needless to say, I didn't enjoy any
more. It was absolutely bad mood. I had promised
never to do anything like that again.

Commentary ■ ■ ■

The first text has a number of serious problems:

- orthography: poor formation of letters, no lower-case letters;
- punctuation: incorrect use of full stops, no other punctuation;
- spelling: many mistakes in moving sound to spelling;
- layout: no attempt to lay text out;
- language: student does not have enough control of basic lexis or grammar.

These problems really prevent the writer getting his message across. The writing task set seems to have been inappropriately difficult for his level (i.e. 'free' writing as opposed to guided sentence making), and it looks as if insufficient help was offered in preparation for writing. It would probably be pointless to try to work through a correction or rewrite of this letter; what the student needs is a lot more practice work on a range of lexis and grammar items. He also needs some real support and guidance when attempting any future writing task and probably some practice work on forming the shapes of letters and using these in written sentences. A discussion of the subject matter of the text with the student (i.e. content rather than language) might be fruitful. It may be that the writer's intended meaning is clearer in spoken English than in written English.

The writer of the second text clearly has a much greater command of English. We can identify some grammar problems (e.g. missing articles: *a* and *the*) and some lexis problems (e.g. *climate* instead of *weather*). We can also notice some effective and correct uses of grammar, lexis and 'chunks' of language (e.g. *Needless to say, I didn't…*). Importantly, the message that the writer wants to convey is usually quite clear; she comes over as an individual with something specific she wants to tell us.

There is, however, another problem: the text doesn't seem to flow in the way we expect a story to. There are a lot of short sentences. The repetition of words (e.g. *party, friends*, etc.) gives the story a stilted, unnatural feel. It takes us a lot of reading to discover a small item of new information; even a sympathetic reader might soon become bored.

As well as offering some practice of specific language items (e.g. articles), we could also help the writer work on ways to make a written text more natural and readable: using pronouns to replace nouns, using synonyms to avoid repetition, varying the length of sentences, using conjunctions, using metaphor, etc. These are some examples of writing skills that can be focused on in the classroom. ■

Task 123: Writing a response to a student's written work

The writer of the second text in Task 122 is your student. Write a response to her.

Chapter 10 **Language analysis**

1   Analysing grammar: an introduction

Before teaching a grammatical item, it is essential that you understand it well. This usually involves some research and careful thinking. Even after many years teaching, the night before a lesson I still find myself checking my grammar books, books on usage, a dictionary or two – and then making a few notes. Different teachers will consider different things, but my own thinking and research typically includes the following steps.

- **Select** the grammar items I want to teach.
- **Fine-tune** the selection: am I clear about precisely what is/isn't included, e.g. if it's a verb tense, am I dealing with one meaning or more than one? Positive form? Negatives? Questions? Exceptions? Typical student problems? etc.
- **List** situations, places and relationships in which the language is typically used.
- **Brainstorm** between five and ten typical everyday sentences that use the grammatical item in a natural way.
- **Select** one of these sentences as a 'target sentence': it should be realistic and natural. (Choosing one target sentence helps me focus my planning so I know exactly what language I am aiming to work on; it doesn't mean that my students will only meet this one example of the language item.)
- **Decide** on a situational context (that I could describe, draw, mime, etc.) or a possible text (reading or listeing) that I could use to focus on the language.
- **Analyse** the form of the target sentence.
- **Analyse** the meaning – with concept questions – of the target sentence.
- **Analyse** the pronunciation of the target sentence.
- **Analyse** typical student problems likely with the target sentence.
- **Decide** what I hope learners could achieve in a lesson on this item. Write this as a 'main aim' for the lesson.

In this chapter, you'll find a basic introduction to analysing language. Even if you know relatively little about grammar, the next section will show you a way to analyse grammatical form for teaching purposes that doesn't depend on knowing grammatical terms. Section 3 then gives a brief introduction to the actual terminology.

2   Analysing language: grammatical form

Traditionally, a form analysis for classroom teaching purposes has been based around sentences, and most grammar studied in coursebooks is still at sentence level. This is despite the fact that, in recent years, researchers have shown increasing interest in language beyond sentence level.

Here is a sentence: *I'm playing tennis with Paul this evening.* What do I need to know about this sentence? What do my students need to know? If I take the sentence apart, what have I got?

Firstly, there are a number of words – vocabulary items – that I need to know the meaning of: *playing, tennis, with, evening,* etc. In fact, the whole sentence is in one sense nothing more than vocabulary – words in a particular order. Some words commonly go together: you *play tennis* (you don't *do tennis* or *make tennis*). Similarly, you play tennis *with* someone not *at* someone, and not (in this case, at any rate) *opposite* someone. These 'going together' patterns (or 'collocations') need to be understood and learned.

Similarly, we might say that *I'm* often goes together with a verb ending with *-ing* (i.e. it's not usual for *I'm* to be paired with a present participle). This pattern of *I'm + -ing* is, in fact, a regular pattern that we can use with many other verbs. If I understand how to construct *I'm play + -ing*, then I can soon learn to use other verbs: *I'm working, I'm eating*, etc. I can also learn that changing the pronoun and the *'m* (to *'s* or *'re*) has other generalisable results. The pattern itself generates a wide range of different possibilities quite separate from the vocabulary it uses. By changing the vocabulary, I can utilise the pattern to talk about a variety of different things. We have now, of course, started to look at the area of grammar.

Grammar is concerned with the **form** of the language: that is, the patterns, the regularities, the nuts and bolts you connect together in different ways. Some common items have names: the past progressive tense, reported speech, uncountable nouns, relative clauses, etc.

In the sentence *He was going to arrive at ten o'clock*, we can isolate *was going to* as a grammatical item. It has a consistent meaning that remains, even when we change the other items that surround it: *Mike was going to clean the whole garage, The agency was going to cancel all contracts.* There is only one variation in form: *was* sometimes becomes *were*, and it is not too hard to pin down the reason why this happens. It is also clear that *was going to* must normally be followed by a particular kind of word. For example, *bookshelf, underwater, laughed, cooking* and *by* are not usually possible, whereas *swim, laugh* and *cook* are. We can now summarise our understanding of this piece of grammar as follows:

....	was were	going to	arrive cook swim	(..........)

The same sentences could be summarised in grammatical terms as follows:

subject + *be* simple past + present participle *go* + *to* + infinitive

I find the first version both easier to understand and easier to manipulate and use; knowing that *arrive* and *cook* are infinitives is sometimes essential, but, at least at low levels, students seem to find 'patterns' (as in the table) more user-friendly than grammatical terms.

Task 124: Analysing grammatical patterns

Summarise the underlined grammar patterns using either a table or grammatical terminology.

a Michael <u>used to work</u> in Moscow.
b <u>I'll have finished</u> by midnight.
c How many records <u>have you got</u>?
d <u>Did you fly</u> over the Alps?
e <u>I'm playing tennis</u> with Paul <u>this evening</u>.

Substitution tables

The following example is clearly related to the patterns we saw above:

Has	Mary John he	bought eaten read	the	book chips chocolate story magazine	?
Have	you they your friends				

This is a **substitution table**. By reading from left to right, choosing one word from each section, you can make a large number of grammatically correct sentences (although the meaning may require a little thought). A table such as this could be both a stimulus to practice activities in the classroom and a way of recording the studied grammar in notebooks. After working on new grammar, I often get learners to help me construct a substitution table on the board, which all the class can then copy into their books.

Simple variations on a table can alter the level of challenge involved: for example, removing the horizontal line in the substitution table above makes an activity one that requires more thought on the student's part.

Similarly, blanking out a column or leaving spaces in a column and getting students to invent words to go there adds to the difficulty (and probably the interest):

Has	Mary John he			book chips	?
Have	you they your friends		the		

Oral practice in the form of drills (see Chapter 12, Section 2) is often based around substitution tables.

Task 125: Writing a substitution table

The following substitution table is for *Wh-* questions (*Who, Where, When, Why, How, What*) in the past simple tense.

Where What How When Why	did	you he she Caroline the teachers	go eat see do run	?

Use a grammar book to help you write a substitution table for *Wh-* questions using the 'interrupted' past progressive tense (e.g. *What was he doing when the guests arrived?* etc.).

3   Welcome to English Grammar

This introduction to grammatical terminology can only provide a starting point and a few signposts. It may be of use to you if you feel you are starting out without any bearings at all. It's likely to be most relevant to native English speakers who have never studied their own language much and feel adrift amongst the quantity of terminology. But bear in mind that this isn't any more than a quick summary. To do any teaching of grammar, you'll need to use grammar books and other reference sources.

Verbs

Task 126: Recognising grammatical items 1

Find at least one example of each of the following in the text below: a past participle, a base form, an auxiliary verb, an imperative and a multiword verb.

> Broadband Internet has become much cheaper over the last few years. Take our special offer up in the next seven days, and we'll throw in a free three-month subscription to the best virus-protection service.

Commentary ■ ■ ■

Past participle: *become*
Base form: *throw*
Auxiliary verb: *has, will*
Imperative: *take*
Multiword verb: *take … up, throw in*   ■

Verbs are usually listed in coursebooks and grammar books in three columns which show:

1) the base form, 2) the past form, 3) the past participle.

- The **base form** is used to make the **present simple** (e.g. *they walk* or *she runs*).
- Putting the word *to* in front of the base form makes an **infinitive** (e.g. *to run*). Infinitives without *to* are called **bare infinitives**.
- A **present participle** is made by adding *-ing* to the base form (sometimes requiring spelling changes). It is used in progressive tenses (e.g. *we're **arriving*** or *he was **singing***).
- The **past form** is used in the past simple tense (e.g. *I **coughed***). There are regular past forms (ending in *-ed*) and irregular ones (with various forms).
- The **past participle** is used in perfect tenses (e.g. *he's **gone*** or *they had **begun***).

The most commonly studied tenses and verb forms are:

- present simple
- present progressive (also called present continuous)
- present perfect
- past simple
- past progressive (also called past continuous)
- past perfect
- *will*
- *going to*
- *used to*

Many tenses require use of **auxiliary verbs**. These are short verbs such as *do, be* and *have* which are used together with other **main verbs**. For example, *We're making bread* includes the auxiliary verb *are* (contracted to *'re*) and the main verb *making*.

Modal auxiliaries are the auxiliary verbs *may, might, must, shall, should, will, would, can, could* (plus some other **semi-modals** such as *ought to* and *have to*) that show the speaker or writer's attitude or interpretation of the topic being discussed.

When teaching verbs, you need to make sure that you cover not only **positive statement forms**, but also **negatives** and **questions**. Students also need to know how to form **imperatives** (telling someone to do something), **passives** (focusing on the thing done rather than the doer) and **conditionals** (*If …*, etc.).

Many English verbs are not simply single words but **multiword**, comprising a main verb and one or more **particles**. For example, the sentence *Her flight took off at 3.40* includes the multiword verb *took off*. Students and coursebooks often classify these as **phrasal verbs** or **prepositional verbs**.

Nouns and noun phrases

Task 127: Recognising grammatical items 2

In the text below, find at least one uncountable noun, a pronoun, a compound noun and a noun phrase.

> Hey! When you said it was just a little studio flat, I never expected this! There's so much light, and that panoramic view over the river is just amazing!

Commentary ■ ■ ■

Uncountable noun: *light*
Pronoun: *you, it, I, this*
Compound noun: *studio flat, panoramic view*
Noun phrase: *just a little studio flat, so much light, panoramic view over the river* ■

An important grammatical distinction with English nouns is whether they are **countable** (i.e. we can count them: *one pencil, two pencils*, etc.) or **uncountable** (i.e. we can't count them: ~~one weather, two weathers~~). Some nouns (e.g. *paper*) can be countable with one meaning and uncountable with another.

Compound nouns are made of two or more words, e.g. noun + noun or adjective + noun, but act as if they were a single, one-word noun. Examples are *streetlight, first-aid kit, video recorder.*

Noun phrases are combinations of words that act as if they are nouns (i.e. we could substitute a noun for them). For example, in the sentence *I saw a really strange animal with vertical black and white stripes all down its side*, all the words after the first two make up a noun phrase which could be substituted (with some loss of information) by the words *a zebra*.

Pronouns can be used instead of nouns or noun phrases, usually in cases where we already know what is being referred to, e.g. in the sentence *John saw it*, the word *it* is a pronoun.

Prepositions

Task 128: Recognising grammatical items 3

How many prepositions can you find in this sentence?

> Put the ladder next to the cupboard, the toolbox under the stairs and the hamster in her cage!

Commentary ■ ■ ■

next to, under, in ■

Prepositions are generally short words (or phrases) that tell us about:

- where something is (prepositions of place), e.g. **on** *the table*, **at** *the bus stop*, **against** *the wall*;
- the movement of something (prepositions of movement), e.g. **towards** *Madrid*, **over** *the bridge*;
- when something happens (prepositions of time), e.g. **at** *half past eight*, **on** *Christmas Day*, **in** *the afternoon*;
- relationships between things, such as cause and effect, e.g. *because of*.

Many words require the use of a specific preposition. For example, in the sentence *Mike listened to the news*, the verb *listen* requires the preposition *to*. You listen *to* the news not *at* or *over* it.

Prepositions also occur as particles in multiword verbs (see above).

Task 129: Recognising grammatical items 4

Find a comparative, an ungradable adjective, an indefinite article, an adverb of frequency and a relative pronoun in the following text.

> He gets to the café at about ten and always takes
> the corner seat upstairs. It's smokier and rather cold,
> but from his point of view, it's a brilliant choice – the only
> seat that has a view over the whole street.

Commentary ■ ■ ■

Comparative: *smokier*
Ungradable adjective: *brilliant*
Indefinite article: *a*
Adverb of frequency: *always*
Relative pronoun: *that* ■

Adjectives

Adjectives give us more information about a noun or a noun phrase; for example, in the sentence *There's a tall tree next to the hostel*, the word *tall* is an adjective.

When we compare things, we use the **comparative** form of an adjective. For most words, this is made by adding -*er* to the adjective, e.g. *taller* (sometimes with spelling changes). Longer adjectives make the comparative with *more*, e.g. *more delightful*. There are a few irregular comparatives, e.g. *worse* is the comparative form of *bad*.

To say that something is 'the most' or 'the least', we use the **superlative** form. For most adjectives, you add -*est* (sometimes with spelling changes) and put *the* before the adjective. Longer adjectives make superlatives with *the most*, e.g. *the most astonishing*. Again, there are irregular ones, e.g. *the worst*.

Some adjectives are **gradable**, i.e. we can use them with **modifiers** to say there are different amounts or degrees of something, e.g. *It's **a bit** hot, It's **rather** hot, It's **very** hot, It's **extremely** hot,* etc.

Some adjectives already show extreme conditions or describe things that can only be one way or the other with no intervening area. These cannot normally be graded in any further way, i.e. they are **ungradable**. Examples are *excellent, huge, essential*.

Determiners

Determiners are words that come in front of nouns or noun phrases. The term includes **articles** and **quantifiers**.

The is the **definite article**. *A* and *an* are the **indefinite article**.

Uncountable nouns never take the indefinite article.

When we have new information to state, we generally introduce it the first time with the indefinite article. The definite article is used when our listener or reader already knows what we are talking about; the noun it introduces is not new information. The following sentences show examples of both: *There is a very interesting library just outside Budapest. The library has over two million books.*

Beyond this, the guidelines for use are quite complex!

Quantifiers tell us how much of something there is, e.g. *lots of cake*, *a few boys*, *some apples*, *not much interest*.

Adverbs

There are some easily recognisable kinds of adverbs. They are words that:

- tell us how something is done (adverbs of manner), e.g. *quickly, angrily*
- tell us when something is done (adverbs of time), e.g. *soon, nowadays*
- tell us how often something is done (adverbs of frequency), e.g. *regularly, usually*
- tell us where something is done (adverbs of place), e.g. *there, nearby*
- tell us how much there is of something (adverbs of degree), e.g. *very, rather*
- indicate an opinion or attitude, e.g. *luckily, surprisingly*

I never get on with adverbs. They always seem like the word class for everything that no one knows how to classify. If you can't work out what word class something is, it's probably an adverb!

Relative clauses

Relative clauses are parts of sentences that tell us more information about someone or something, e.g. in the sentence *Can you see the car that's parked outside the church?* the relative clause *that's parked outside the church* tells us more information about which car is being discussed.

Relative clauses often start with a **relative pronoun**, e.g. *that, who, which, when, where, why, what, whose*.

Where to go from here

- Don't try and sit down with a grammar book and learn it; better to integrate your learning with your teaching. If you are going to teach the past perfect tomorrow, then sit down and research it tonight. Read and take notes. Make friends with the item.
- Slowly build up your grammar knowledge in this way, lesson by lesson, item by item.
- Make good use of the notes in Teacher's Books that accompany all major coursebooks. There are often a lot of helpful hints about the lesson's grammar. But don't rely on only this information. You must get and use your own grammar references as well.
- I often find that I need to refer to two or three different sources to really get my head around an item of grammar. It's interesting that grammatical description isn't fixed and set in stone. Different books can take very different angles on things, often classifying in different ways and giving different names. You need to gather and sort all this out in your head and decide what is most useful and helpful from your perspective.
- Having researched and got comfortable with a new grammar item, let it settle in your head and then think coolly and calmly as to what small part of that you can deal with in a single lesson.

- Some new native-speaker teachers get 'grammar drunk' when they start teaching. Having previously known little about their own language, they do their research and then find it so exciting that they go into class wanting to tell their students about all that they have learned. Remember, you need to know as much as you can about grammar. But your students cannot absorb it all in one go. Good research should not lead to a 40-minute lecture on 'Everything I know about the present perfect'.

It's worth noting that there are different kinds of resource book that may be helpful, including:

- Traditional grammars, written mainly for academics or native speakers, can be a bit overwhelming for the teacher.
- Pedagogic grammars are written specifically for teachers. These often include helpful notes about typical errors and student problems.
- Usage books are guides to how the language is used. They refer to grammatical points, but also include information on vocabulary and pronunciation issues, style, idioms and so on. The items may be organised alphabetically or according to meanings or functions rather than by grammatical class.
- Student grammars and workbooks often present bite-sized (or one-page-sized) nuggets of grammatical information alongside exercises to practise those points. Students often like working through these, exercise by exercise, at home. They are also a useful resource for teachers because of their clear, straightforward and short explanations, often with usable teaching examples and contexts.

4 Analysing concept: the meanings of words

Meaning isn't as precise as we might feel it to be. At what point exactly does a *stream* stop being a *stream* and become a *river* or a *brook* or a *creek* or something else? Are there fixed and definable differences between these meanings, or is there a degree of 'fuzziness' here? Is it partly down to personal interpretation, to our own feelings?

Even where the dividing lines between one meaning and another seem clear, are they in the same places in other languages? Does language X interpret and name things in the world in the same way as language Y? Does it, for example, see *leaflet*, *booklet* and *brochure* as different things or as one thing – or even subdivide them further into more names? Translations of words cannot be exact because different cultures have interpreted the world around them in different ways.

These are obviously difficulties for learners and teachers. In order for us to help our learners, it's going to be important for us to analyse the meaning of lexical items as effectively as we can. In this section, we'll consider three ways of doing this, looking at the components of meaning of lexical items, the meaning of lexical items in context, and meaning in relation to other words.

A Components of meaning

Imagine that a student is reading a text and come across the sentence *Liz took her wellingtons off.* He asks you 'What does *wellingtons* mean?'. Well, what **does** *wellingtons* mean? A dictionary written for native speakers says:

> **1** Also called 'gumboots'. Brit. knee-length or calf-length rubber or rubberized boots, worn esp. in wet conditions. Often shortened to 'wellies'.
>
> **2** Military leather boots covering the front of the knee but cut away at the back to allow easier bending of the knee.
>
> [C19: named after the 1st Duke of Wellington]
>
> *(Collins English Dictionary)*

OK, that's clear, and relatively easy for a good user of English to follow, but it is more problematic for a learner, for a number of reasons:

- The definition is written in language more complex than the item being defined: if the reader doesn't understand *wellingtons*, then it is possible that he will also not understand *knee-length, calf, rubber, rubberized, worn, esp., shortened*, etc. The whole entry is in a 'dictionary style', which may be hard to interpret.
- There is no distinction between the everyday meaning (1) and the much rarer second usage (2).
- There are no examples of how these words might be used.
- Common, everyday knowledge, feelings and reactions that we carry around in our head are ignored, e.g. wellies are often black or green; wellies are associated with farmers, ramblers, fishermen, etc.; wellies can get very smelly; you have to pull them on, etc.

In a classroom where a student has just asked 'Teacher, what means *wellingtons?*', I can help the student understand the meaning by:

- avoiding language more complex than the word I'm trying to explain;
- focusing on the most important usages;
- using examples;
- using my own and the student's knowledge and feelings to focus on what we understand by this word.

One way to make language less complex is to avoid words that the students are unlikely to understand. Another way is to avoid complex grammar. Another way is to keep your sentences short. In the example below, I have combined information from the dictionary definition with my own knowledge, and then segmented this information into small, bite-sized chunks, each chunk very simply stating *one feature* of this information in simple language:

Wellingtons

You wear them on your feet.★
You wear them when it rains.
You wear them in the snow.
They're made of rubber.★
You wear them when you walk in or near water.
You wear them when you walk in mud.★
Farmers often wear them.
Fishermen often wear them.
Walkers often wear them.

You wear them when you don't want your feet to get wet.
You wear them so that your feet will be dry.
They are difficult to take off.
They are often black or green.
They are quite tall.
Sometimes they are smelly!
My socks come off in them.

I have put an asterisk beside the three sentences that seem to carry the essence of what wellies are; I would use these sentences if I had to explain the meaning to a foreign student. However, a combination of any four or five of the sentences above would probably give a student enough information to understand what *wellingtons* are. After all, in many cases, we won't be teaching the student what *wellies* are (they may well have them in their own country); we are simply trying to allow them to recognise that these new words are the English way of describing something that they know in their tongue. (Conversely, some students may not know what they are, and we may have to teach a new concept as well as a new word.)

Task 130: Analysing meaning

Segment the meaning of the following words into their component parts, using language that is less complex than the words themselves: *a calf, a watch, a clock, a poster.*

Commentary ■ ■ ■

a calf	It's an animal. It's a cow. It's young.
a watch	It tells you the time. You wear it on your arm.
a clock	It tells you the time. You see it on a wall, or a table, or a cupboard.
a poster	It has a big picture or an advertisement.
	It's made of paper.
	You can put it on a wall in your house.
	You can see very big ones on buildings or beside the road.
	Many advertise cars, beer, cigarettes, airlines, fizzy drinks, etc. ■

B Meaning in context

Task 131: Finding missing words

In the following short text, fill each gap with any appropriate word.

> There was _____ traffic all the way from the airport to town and, when we eventually arrived at the hotel, it was _____ late. Luckily, we had phoned up that morning and _____ a room, so the receptionist was _____ us.

Commentary ■ ■ ■

Unless you decided to be poetic or dramatic or to create any other specific effect, you will probably have found that each gap suggested a small set of likely alternatives to you, perhaps: *heavy*; *quite/rather/very/really*; *reserved/booked*; *expecting*. These are not 'right' answers, they are simply some of the most common or natural words for these contexts. You probably chose some of them because they seemed to 'go together' naturally (e.g. rather than *crowded traffic*). Others you may have chosen because of the meaning of the text (e.g. *too late* might have seemed grammatically possible, but in the context of the second sentence, it made no sense). ■

Collocation

When words typically 'go together' with certain other words, we can say that they **collocate**. Thus *heavy* collocates with *traffic*; so do *jam, cop* and *light*. Such collocations are an essential key to using English well. It may be that knowledge of collocations is more useful to a student than an understanding of the fine differences of meaning between words. Perhaps it doesn't really matter exactly what the detailed meaning of *book a room* is (i.e. does it happen differently in different countries?); it's much more important to understand its general meaning and to know that it is the normally used word in this context.

We can help students better understand meaning in context by:

- pointing out collocations when they occur;
- designing activities that focus attention on the collocations of particular lexical items (e.g. finding a number of words that might come after *high*);
- encouraging the use of dictionary research to check whether a collocation is typical or not;
- setting text gap-fill exercises;
- asking learners to guess meaning from clues in the context, rather than always relying on explanations or dictionaries;
- getting learners to predict likely meanings or lexical items before seeing or hearing a text (e.g. *This story is about two people arriving in a strange town at night. What words do you think might be in the story?*).

You'll find more ideas in Chapter 11.

Task 132: Finding collocations

Find one or more collocations for each of the following:

safety, blonde, feel, bad

C Relations between words

The meaning of words is often clearest when you can see them in relation to other words.

Task 133: Relationships between words

What is the relationship between the words within each group below?

1 *hot, cold*
2 *on, off*
3 *stroll, amble*
4 *drink, lemonade*
5 *flower, pot, spade, seeds, weedkiller*
6 *nation, national, international, internationalist*
7 *fair, fair, fair*
8 *fair, fare*

Commentary ■ ■ ■

1 *Hot* and *cold* are opposites or **antonyms**. Because we can vary their meaning with words such as *very* or *quite* (e.g. *very hot, quite hot*), they are known as **gradable antonyms**. *Hot* and *cold* could be represented diagrammatically as two points on a straight line representing a scale of temperatures. We could add other words at various points along the same scale, e.g. *freezing, warm, boiling*, etc.
2 Another type of opposite. In this case, we cannot grade the degree of oppositeness: a thing is normally either *on* or *off*. Lexical items such as these are known as **ungradable antonyms**.
3 These two words have a similar meaning; we could say they are **synonyms**. In fact, hardly any words have an exact synonym; the fact that two words exist usually means that there is some distinction between them.
4 One word includes the other. *Lemonade* is a type of *drink*. We can imagine this as a family-tree diagram, with *drink* as the 'parent' (**superordinate**) and *lemonade, whisky, water, milk*, etc. being the 'children' (**hyponyms**).
5 This group of words are all to do with the subject of *gardening* or *farming*.
6 If we take *nation* as the root word, it is possible to form the other words by adding **prefixes** (e.g. *inter-*) or **suffixes** (e.g. *-al* or *-ist*). These often change the grammar (noun, verb, adjective, etc.) of the word (usually through adding a suffix) and/or the meaning (by adding a prefix). Many of the effects are generalisable; for example, adding *-al* can make a noun into an adjective (e.g. *nation, national; music, musical*, etc.). (The study of such pieces and how they combine together is **morphology**.)

Relationships such as the ones in 1–6 are useful both in assisting an initial understanding of the meaning of new items and as a key to recording and remembering them. A group of related words is likely to be more memorable than a list of unrelated items. Diagrams, such as scales or trees, can provide a useful visual hook for memory. It may also be useful to analyse relationships such as 7 and 8 in order to help clarify confusions and problems:

7 Words can have more than one meaning, sometimes quite unconnected. Context and collocations are essential clues to deciding which meaning is intended (*fair hair, a fair trial, the county fair*).
8 Different words, with different spellings, can be pronounced the same. ■

5   Analysing concept: grammatical meaning

1   I'm playing tennis with Paul this evening.
2   I had the car repaired.
3   Helen used to smoke.

What do these sentences mean? How can I state the meanings as simply as I can, as clearly as I can and, if possible, using language that is itself less complex than the language I am trying to explain?

Do these criteria sound familiar? We are going deal with the meaning of grammar items in the same way that we looked at vocabulary in Section 3, by attempting to split sentences up into their component concepts.

Task 134: Analysing grammatical meaning

Here is sentence 2: *I had the car repaired.*

First of all, let's distinguish the grammar from the specific vocabulary used. At the moment, we are not primarily wanting to help students understand the meaning of *car* or *repaired*. Let's assume they know those for the moment. Rather, we want to help learners understand the grammatical concept, in this case the idea of *have something done*. We need a way of analysing concept that will be applicable even if the vocabulary items change.

Look at the sentences below and underline the ones that contain part of the essential meaning of the sentence I had the car repaired . Cross out those ones that you feel are wrong or do not apply.

1   I repaired the car.
2   I bought a car.
3   Someone repaired the car.
4   The car had an accident.
5   I used to have a car.
6   I didn't repair it myself.
7   I paid money for the repair.
8   I took my car to a garage.
9   I arranged for this to happen.
10   My car runs well now.

Commentary ■ ■ ■

Sentences 3 and 9 carry the essential meaning of *I had the car repaired*. Sentence 6 is also true and might help to make the meaning clear. We don't know if sentences 2, 4, 7, 8 and 10 are true. They may be, but the essential meaning of *I had my car repaired* does not tell us this information. Sentences 1 and 5 seem untrue. ■

The lexis changes but the concept remains

Consider some variations on *I had the car repaired*, keeping the grammar, but changing the vocabulary, e.g. *I had my hair cut, I had a new lock fitted, I had the swimming pool emptied.* The situations are all different, but the core meaning is always there. If we change the appropriate vocabulary words, in the concept sentences they still work:

Someone cut my hair; I didn't cut it myself; I arranged for this to happen.
Someone fitted a new lock; I didn't fit it myself; I arranged for this to happen.
Someone emptied the swimming pool; I didn't empty it myself; I arranged for this to happen.

Task 135: Creating statements that focus on concept

Focus on the meaning of the following sentences (and especially on the underlined words) by making two, three or four clear, simple statements.

1 She's been reading since she came home.
2 I'd rather have a beer.
3 Helen used to smoke.
4 I'm playing tennis with Paul this evening.

Commentary ■ ■ ■

Once you have decided on your sentences, it's simple enough to turn them into **concept questions**. These are basically the same as the statements, but in question form, with very simple answers – often no more than 'yes', 'no' or 'perhaps'. Again, they focus attention on the core meaning.

Consider the concept questions for *I had the car repaired*:
Did someone repair the car?   (yes)
Did I arrange for this to happen?   (yes)
Did I repair the car myself?   (no) ■

Task 136: Making concept questions

Turn your sentences for Task 135 into concept questions.

Commentary ■ ■ ■

1 *She's been reading since she came home.*
   Is she reading now?   (yes)
   When did she start reading?   (when she came home)
   Was she reading all the time?   (yes)
   Will she stop reading now?   (perhaps; I don't know)

2 *I'd rather have a beer.*
   Do I want a beer?   (yes)
   More than something else?   (yes)
   A lot more?   (probably not)
   Is it very important to me?   (no)

3 *Helen used to smoke.*
   Did Helen smoke?   (yes)
   On a number of occasions?   (yes)
   Regularly? Often?   (perhaps)
   Does she smoke now?   (no)

4 *I'm playing tennis with Paul this evening.*
   Will I play tennis with Paul this evening?   (yes)
   Have I already arranged this?   (yes) ■

Why analyse concept?

What are the reasons for being so clear about meaning? If you understand what the meaning is and can focus on it in simple and clear ways, then it is obviously more useful to the students than when you explain at length, fail to pinpoint the essential components of meaning and use complex language.

By asking concept questions, you can also establish whether students are clear about meaning. You could, of course, ask 'Do you understand?' every time you teach something, but whether the answer was 'yes' or 'no', it would actually tell us almost nothing (students say 'yes' for fear of seeming stupid, because they don't want to waste time, because they don't want to be asked any more questions, etc.).

Perhaps one other reason for doing this kind of analysis is also becoming clear. The grammatical name for the *I'm* + *-ing* structure in sentence 4 above is the present progressive. Yet, in the analysis of meaning, we discovered that the meaning is not really to do with the present – in fact, it's a sentence about the future (and, to some extent, about the past, when the tennis date was actually arranged). It's worth noting that the grammatical names of language items can actually get in the way of understanding the meaning. A student who believes that a present tense must talk about the present may need some convincing that it can also refer to the future! Similarly, a teacher who does not clearly separate the issues of form and meaning may confuse students. A focus on form is useful, but it will have considerably less use if there is no parallel focus on meaning.

6 Analysing communicative function

Why do people speak or write to each other? To show off their ability to make grammatically correct sentences? Obviously not. There is no point making perfectly formed sentences if we do not succeed in getting our point across. We speak or write because we have messages to communicate or there is something we hope to achieve. These purposes are the **communicative function** of what we say.

Task 137: Communicative purpose

If I say the following to you, what are the likely results?
1 'Could you pass the sugar?'
2 'Hey! Time to get up! Come on!'
3 'Can I help you?'
4 'Cheers!'
5 'A day return to Brighton, please.'

Commentary ■ ■ ■

1 You pass me the sugar.
2 You wake up, then get up (quite quickly).
3 You (a customer) see me (a shop assistant), reply and maybe give me a chance to sell you something.
4 We raise our glasses and drink.
5 You sell me a train ticket. ■

How we convey our meaning

It's worth noticing that we don't explicitly say 'I want to buy a day-return train ticket to Brighton, please.' The communicative function is not always directly stated or transparent. Its success is achieved because listeners are used to interpreting what such exchanges mean. We can clarify the purpose of many statements by adding back in the 'missing' verbs. For example:

2 I *request* you to pass the sugar to me.
3 I *alert* you with 'Hey' and *inform* you that it's time to get up! I *urge* you to hurry up with 'Come on!'.
4 I *offer* you help.
5 I *celebrate* our being together and *invite* you to start drinking.

In many cases, it's hard to decide exactly what the communicative function is unless we know the context and who is speaking.

Task 138: Analysing functional language

For each of the following, suggest one possible context and who might be speaking to who. What might be the speaker's purpose?

1 'Phew. It's cold in here.'
2 'The fish is very good today.'
3 'Well, actually I'm a bit busy at the moment.'

Commentary ■ ■ ■

Sentence	Possible context	Who?	Possible meaning
'Phew. It's cold in here.'	at home	husband to wife	I (politely) request you to close the door.
'The fish is very good today.'	in a restaurant	waiter to customers looking at menu	I recommend that you order the fish dish.
'Well, actually I'm a bit busy at the moment.'	in the office	business woman to colleague who has just asked a question	I suggest we could talk another time rather than now.

■

Contexts and meanings

Of course, many other contexts and meanings are often possible. It is worth working with your students to make sure they understand how language takes on different meanings depending on the context and how it is said, and that they get practice in making and interpreting language. We can use a grid such as that above to provide an interesting awareness-raising exercise by including only a part of the information and asking students to speculate on possible other elements.

Sentence	Possible context	Who?	Possible meaning
			Will you close the door, please?
'The fish is very good today.'		waiter to customers	
	in the office		Could we talk another time rather than now?

A fuller version of this task is given in Resource 17 in Appendix 2 at the back of the book.

Task 139: Making errors with function

What is the problem in these situations?

1 A foreign student staying as a guest with an English family says 'I want breakfast at seven o'clock. I want two sandwiches and a cup of chocolate.'
2 Student 2 stops someone in the street and asks 'What have you got on your watch?'

Commentary ■ ■ ■

Although each sentence is grammatically correct, each seems wrong in a different way. What is correct and suitable in one set of circumstances is partially or completely inappropriate in another. Example 1 might just be acceptable in a hotel, but as a guest in a family, it is plain rude.

We might ask a friend to 'Pass us that newspaper, will you?', but to a stranger in the dentist's waiting room, we are more likely to say 'Excuse me. Could you pass me that *Times*?' Knowing the grammar of the language backwards is often little help in forming expressions such as these; students need to discover what is appropriate in a particular situation. They also need to learn some complete fixed expressions. Thus, for example, in sentence 2 'Have you got the time on you?' or 'Can you tell me the time?' would be correct. ■

Functions and their exponents

Examples of language used to achieve a particular function are known as **exponents** of a function. Thus 'Have you got the time on you?' is an exponent of the function of 'asking for information'. Some exponents are fixed formulae that allow for little or no alteration: you can't really change any word in 'Have you got the time on you?' without losing the meaning. Other exponents have more generative possibilities: 'Could you tell me the way to the station?' is usable in a variety of situations by substituting different vocabulary for *station*.

For classroom purposes, teachers often think of communicative functions under general headings such as 'complaining', 'asking for information', 'sympathising', etc. and plan lessons to introduce students to sets of useful exponents which they can practise in activities such as role-plays and communication games.

Task 140: Functions and exponents

Match the functions below with the exponents on the right. There may be none, one or more than one exponent under each heading.

1 Giving instructions	a Put it in the bag.
2 Refusing	b Thanks, but I can't.
3 Apologising	c I don't think you're right.
4 Disagreeing	d Surely not!
	e Well, to my mind, the UN has the best chance.
	f I'm awfully sorry.
	g We regret any inconvenience caused.
	h I do apologise.
	i No. I won't.
	j Write the answer in your book.

Commentary ■ ■ ■

1 a, j
2 b, i
3 f, g, h
4 c, d, e ■

Task 141: Recognising functions

Here are some exponents. Name the function.

I wish I'd done it.
If only I hadn't gone there.
Why didn't I buy it when I had the chance?

Commentary ■ ■ ■

The function is 'expressing regret'. ■

Task 142: Stress and intonation in functional exponents

How important are stress and intonation to the correct use of the exponents in Tasks 140 and 141?

Commentary ■ ■ ■

Stress and intonation are very important. A change of stress and intonation (in relation to the specific context) can make an exponent change its function. For example, 'I'm awfully sorry' could be a genuine apology or a sarcastic expression of anger; 'It's midday' could be a reminder, information, a warning, an invitation, a demand to hurry up, etc. ■

Task 143: Filling in a function table

Try filling in the following version of the function table:

Sentence	Possible context	Who?	Possible meaning
'It's midday.'			Reminding him to phone.
'It's midday.'			Warning her to do it now.
'It's midday.'			Inviting him to have some food.
'It's midday.'			Hurry up!

Commentary ■ ■ ■

There are no right answers to this sort of task (though some answers seem less likely than others). Students often enjoy finding convincing but funny solutions. Everyday contexts are probably the most useful to explore, e.g. the first could be a girlfriend to boyfriend who has had a job interview and was told to call back at twelve o'clock to hear the results. Asking students to consider how to say this in an appropriate way (and to practise it) is very useful. ■

Working on appropriacy

A lot of work in the area of function is to do with common sense and common politeness – and most of all to do with an awareness of audience. This, of course, is partly cultural. We can help students become more aware of appropriacy by getting them to consider:

- Who are you talking/writing to? How well do you know them?
- How formal/informal is the relationship?
- Where are you? What unwritten rules or codes of conduct apply?

Some ideas for integrating functional work into a course:

- focusing on a functional area and studying a number of exponents;
- role-plays: considering what to say in particular relationships;
- listening: working out relationships between speakers;
- deciding how different situations make one sentence mean different things;
- building dialogues and picture-story conversations;
- acting out play scripts;
- writing letters to different people;
- altering written conversations to change the relationship.

Task 144: Relationships in functional exchanges

What is the relationship of the speakers in the following conversation? Keeping as much of the original meaning as possible, change the dialogue to make it sound like a natural exchange between (a) two close friends; (b) parent and young child.

A: I'm sorry to interrupt, but I was wondering if you wanted to break for lunch yet?
B: I'm afraid I'm still rather busy. But thank you very much for asking.
A: Perhaps I'll see you in the restaurant later.
B: Yes. That would be nice.

Chapter 11 *Lexis*

1 What is lexis?

Teacher attitudes to vocabulary have changed a lot over recent years. The use of the word *lexis* (rather than the more familiar *vocabulary*) reflects a fundamental shift in understanding, attitude and approach. The increasing availability of corpora (large computerised databases of analysable real conversations and other text), and dictionaries, grammar books and other resources based on them have revealed many surprising features of language that had been previously unrealised. An influential book, *The Lexical Approach* by Michael Lewis published in 1993, had a significant impact on the profession in raising awareness of the importance of lexis and of the weaknesses of much classroom vocabulary work.

So what is lexis? Is it more than just a fancy word for vocabulary? How does lexis relate to grammar? I'll give some definitions on the next page, but first it may be useful to see why there is a need for these different words.

Task 145: Lexis compared with grammar

Which of the following items would you consider appropriate for inclusion in a lexis/vocabulary lesson (as opposed to, for example, a grammar lesson)?

computer, water, stock market, go off, pass the exam, swim against the tide, it's up to you

Commentary ■ ■ ■

When teaching, should we consider every set of letters that is bordered by spaces as a separate entity? Or does it make more sense to take some combinations of words as a single grouping, a single meaning, a single **lexical item**?

Computer and *water* are familiar one-word vocabulary items, but what about *stock market*? These two words are regularly found together with a fixed meaning; this surely counts as a single item of vocabulary (it has its own entry in the dictionary). How useful would it be to only teach *stock* and *market* separately and hope that the learners will somehow find a way of combining them to make a new meaning? *Stock market* is an example of a single lexical item, in this case with two words rather than one.

One possible meaning of *go off* is *explode* (as in *The bomb went off*). Here (in contrast to *stock market*), the meaning is not guessable, even if a student knows the meaning of both *go* and *off* on their own. This two-word lexical item quite clearly has an individual identity that is more than the sum of its parts – and it also has variant forms (*go off, going off, went off*, etc.). In class, we need to deal with *go off* as a piece of vocabulary in its own right.

In *swim against the tide*, the four words have a specific, definable meaning (perhaps in another language it could be said in a single word). It is listed in dictionaries (sometimes classed as an **idiom**). Do we need to teach this as a fixed chunk of language? It seems to be a four-word lexical item – a single unit of meaning that requires four words to be expressed. If we change any one of the words, we lose the familiar chunk – *swim along the tide* or *dive against the tide* don't seem to work in the same way. Similar chunks are *jump on the band-wagon, kick the bucket, paint the town red, put two and two together, have both feet on the ground,* etc.

Pass the exam doesn't have quite the same kind of separate identity. *The exam* and *pass* seem more separable, i.e. we can think of lots of alternative words that could equally well go in front of *exam*. All the same, it's clear that *pass* very often goes together with *exam* (as do *fail, take, enter* and a few other words). These are all common **collocations** with *exam*, i.e. words that typically go together with that word. These are not fixed lexical items, but probable, common collocations.

A more difficult problem is provided by expressions such as *It's up to you*. Is this a single lexical item, or is it a sentence that a speaker (knowing the rules of grammar) constructs afresh every time he needs it? Consider some other examples: *It's all the same to me, What on earth ..., minding my own business, funny you should say that, Sorry I'm late, wouldn't you rather ..., it'll do,* etc. These items would probably not be found in most dictionaries, but, all the same, they do seem to have an element of being fixed items, in the same way that individual words do. It is now generally believed that native speakers do not construct expressions of this type word by word, but rather extract ready-made **chunks** of language from an internal store and then put them together with other language items in order to express complete meanings. ■

Lexis, vocabulary and grammar: a summary

- **Vocabulary** typically refers mainly to single words (e.g. *dog, green, wash*) and sometimes to very tightly linked two- or three-word combinations (e.g. *stock market, compact disc, sky blue, go off*).
- The concept of **lexis** is bigger. It refers to our 'internal database' of words and complete 'ready-made' fixed/semi-fixed/typical combinations of words that we can recall and use quite quickly without having to construct new phrases and sentences word by word from scratch using our knowledge of grammar. Lexis includes:
  a) traditional single-word vocabulary items;
  b) common 'going-together patterns' of words (e.g. *blonde hair, traffic jam*). These frequent combinations are known as **collocations**;
  c) longer combinations of words that are typically used together as if they were a single item (e.g. *someone you can talk to, on-the-spot decisions, I'd rather not say*). These longer combinations (which a few years ago would probably not have been considered as anything remotely related to vocabulary) are commonly referred to as **chunks** or sometimes as **multiword items**. (Categories b and c are both classed as **lexical items**.)
- **Grammar** refers to the generalisable patterns of the language and to our ability to construct new phrases and sentences out of word combinations and grammatical features (verb endings, etc.) to express a precise (and probably unique) meaning.

We could argue that *collocations* and *chunks* occupy an intermediate zone between *vocabulary* and *grammar* (see Figure 11.1).

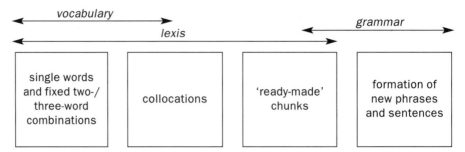

Figure 11.1   Vocabulary, lexis and grammar

Having said all that, most teachers still use the terms *vocabulary* and *lexis* fairly interchangeably. Similarly, as the term *lexical item* is quite a mouthful, staff-room chat tends to avoid it, referring instead to *words, collocations* and *chunks*. The word *word* is a useful shorthand for all three, and I shall occasionally use it as such in the rest of this book.

2   Lexis in the classroom

Lexis is a powerful carrier of meaning. Beginners often manage to communicate in English by using the accumulative effect of individual words. A student who says 'Yesterday. Go disco. And friends. Dancing' will almost certainly get much of his message over despite completely avoiding grammar; the meaning is conveyed by the lexis alone. A good knowledge of grammar, on the other hand, is not such a powerful tool. 'I wonder if you could lend me your ...' means little without a word to fill the gap, whereas the gapped word – *calculator* – on its own could possibly communicate the desired message: 'Calculator?'

A learner, recognising the communicative power of lexis, might reasonably aim to acquire a working knowledge of a large number of words: 'The more words I have, the more precisely I can express the exact meanings I want to'. But (as many of us will recall from our own studies of other languages) getting to be on familiar terms with lexis is quite difficult. The long lists of words and their translations in our exercise books somehow always seem to defy memory, and even when we can recall the word we want, it doesn't always seem to fit comfortably into our own sentences.

Perhaps the translation approach is part of the problem. Lexical items live within their own languages, and though a dictionary translation can give an introduction to the meaning of a word, it can never really let us into the secrets of how that word exists within its language. Instead, we are left with questions:

- What lexical items have a similar meaning to this one? How do they differ in meaning?
- Is this lexical item part of a family or group of related lexical items? What are the other members? How do they relate to each other?
- What other lexical items typically keep company with this one (often coming before or after it in a sentence)?
- Is the lexical item normally used as part of a fixed phrase?
- What other lexical items can be formed by adding or taking away bits?
- What are the situations and contexts where this lexical item is typically found or not found?

Many teachers find that a useful first step towards answering such questions is to encourage (and train students in) the use of English–English dictionaries rather than translation dictionaries. Such dictionaries usually offer sentences exemplifying typical usage, notes on common sentence patterns, pronunciation, relationships with other lexical items, etc. Learner training in the effective use of dictionaries gives students a valuable skill that they can use in and out of the classroom (see Chapter 14, Section 5).

You need to find other systematic ways of helping learners with lexis. Random explanations and examples off the top of your head in the middle of a lesson may solve unexpected problems on the spot, but lexical items dealt with in this way are unlikely to become a long-term part of the learner's own store of English. In contrast, a systematic approach might devote lesson time to helping learners at each of the following stages of learning lexis:

When the learners …
- meet new lexical items and understand their meaning(s), the ways they are used and the other lexical items they often come together with;
- practise using the lexical items;
- find ways that help them memorise the lexical items;
- recall and use the lexical items appropriately.

An important consideration for planning lexis work is the distinction between **productive** and **receptive** lexis. We all understand many more lexical items than we actually use in everyday situations; for example, in this section, you have seen the words *defy, conveyed, acquire* and *systematic*, yet it is unlikely that you have actually used any of these in the past few weeks. Our receptive lexis is the set of lexical items that we recognise and understand, but tend not to use ourselves in everyday speech.

At beginner level, most new lexical items learned by students have obvious immediate practical uses; they quickly become part of the learners' everyday English – their productive lexis. You can help this by giving students opportunities to practise new lexical items in spoken communication. Good pronunciation might be encouraged – getting the sounds and the stress right.

However, as students learn more and more lexical items, they will find that many items seem less immediately useful and are perhaps only occasionally met with in the context of reading or listening material. There may seem less point in getting students to practise such lexical items. Work on pronunciation can still be useful, but is more likely to be analytical (e.g. 'Which is the stressed syllable?') rather than as part of communication practice.

The role of lexis in the classroom

Five initial conclusions:
1. Lexis is important and needs to be dealt with systematically in its own right; it is not simply an add-on to grammar or skills lessons.
2. Our job does not finish as soon as students have first met some new lexis; we need to help them practise, learn, store, recall and use the items.
3. Training in the use of English–English dictionaries provides students with a vital tool for self-study.

4 We need to distinguish between lexis for productive use and for receptive recognition, and adapt our classroom work appropriately.

5 As we saw in the previous section, we need to deal not only with single-word lexical items, but also with longer, multiword items.

3 Lexis and skills work

A great deal of lexis work in class occurs in relation to reading and listening tasks. There are definite advantages in this, most importantly because learners meet the language in realistic contexts and see how the items fit into the meaning and style of a whole text.

The text that immediately surrounds a lexical item is referred to as **co-text**. Co-text provides important exposure for learners to samples of language being used. This suggests why texts are often more useful for teaching lexis than lessons that focus on lexis as separated, stand-alone items without such surrounding language.

When using reading or listening texts, a focus on lexis may occur before, while or after the students read or listen.

Pre-teaching lexis

The teacher may select some activities specifically designed to revise, teach and practise lexis before moving on to work on the text or recording. The lexis selected for teaching is likely to be that most needed for completion of whatever listening or reading tasks are to be set. Although this is usually called **pre-teaching**, remember that this work may be helping students to recall items they already know as much as introducing new items. The main aim is to help ensure that the following activity will work (because there will be fewer stumbling blocks of unknown lexical items). This work may, of course, also teach or revise some lexis that may be useful in its own right.

Task 146: Lexis and listening work

The following audioscript is for a recording that will be used with an Elementary class. The students have recently been working on ways of describing position (*next to, behind, beside*, etc.). Their task when listening will be to look at a picture (Figure 11.2) and note the mistakes.

Read the audioscript and underline three or four lexical items that you might pre-teach. What other items do you think students will need (or want) to understand?

Audioscript

Well, he's made a few mistakes, hasn't he? This place selling snacks – that should be a souvenir shop, shouldn't it? So, change that name from 'Snacks' to 'Gifts'. Yes, it'll be selling postcards and toys and things. And why is the phone box over by the lake? I'm going to sack that artist when I see him again! He's absolutely incompetent. He gets twice my salary and can't do a basic sketch. I mean, we wanted the phone next to the shop, didn't we, not over there by the lake. Yes, on the right of the shop, by that street lamp. And I think there should be a letter box there as well, on the wall of the shop would be fine. And there aren't enough trees – we could do with a lot more trees – beside the lake, along the edge of the water. Yes, that looks better.

Figure 11.2   Amusement park

Commentary ■ ■ ■

The following lexical items are useful to do the task: *snacks, souvenir shop, gifts, phone box, street lamp, letter box, trees, edge.*

Note that *sack, artist, absolutely, incompetent, twice, salary, basic* and *sketch,* although probably unknown to the students, are not necessary in order to complete the task, and therefore do not need to be pre-taught or otherwise focused on. It is likely that you would not deal with them at all, unless a student specifically asked about them. ■

Here are some common pre-teaching tasks of the kind you frequently find in coursebooks.

- Match the words with the pictures.
- Check the meaning of these words in the dictionary.
- Match the words with the definitions.
- Brainstorm words on a set topic (i.e. collect as many as you can).
- Divide these words into two groups (e.g. food words and hobby words).
- Label the items in a picture with the right names.
- Complete gapped sentences with words from a list.
- Discuss a topic (that will feature in the text).
- Say which words (from a list) you expect to be in a text about …

In addition to these ideas, you may want to do some teacher-led presentation or clarification. You could use ideas from *Presenting lexis* (page 234), for example offering students definitions or illustrations of words and eliciting the items from learners.

Using short anecdotes for pre-teaching

One difficulty you may find when planning pre-teaching is that you have quite a random collection of words, and it may be hard to organise the teaching into a coherent shape. One strategy teachers often use is to concoct a short story (perhaps a personal anecdote) that includes each of the separate items. The story can be designed to help make the meanings of the items clear and memorable. It may be similar to the text that students are going to read or listen to, but it shouldn't be so close that it diffuses later interest in working with that text. When the story has been prepared, you can:

- tell it, miming or showing flash cards or board drawings, etc. to illustrate meanings as you go;
- tell it, explaining or translating meanings as you go;
- tell it, asking comprehension questions and concept questions as words come up in the story;
- tell it, asking comprehension questions and concept questions afterwards;
- tell it, pretending to forget the words as you tell the story. Elicit the words from students;
- tell the whole story once with the lexis included, then retell it and 'forget' the items (as above).

Note that pre-teaching is not compulsory! It may sometimes interfere with or undermine the aims of your reading or listening work. For example, if one of the aims of a reading task is that learners read quickly and do not get worried about lexical items they don't know, you may upset this by dealing with some of this potentially unknown lexis before they even start the task.

Task 147: Planning a story including specific lexis

Work out a short story you could tell to help students at Elementary level understand the meaning of the following lexical items: *bridge, basket, goldfish, library, map, photographer.*

Dealing with lexis during and after reading or listening work

During listening or reading work

While students are mainly working on reading or listening skills, you are less likely to spend time on lexis, as this might clash with the reading, listening or other aims. During such stages, you are likely only to:

- deal with an item when a student specifically asks about it;
- give brief, to-the-point explanations or translations, rather than detailed presentations;
- offer help quietly to the one or two students who ask, rather than to the whole class;
- sometimes refuse help and tell students to do their best without knowing some items.

After the first phase of listening or reading work

Once the learners have become comfortable with the text, you can focus attention on lexical items in the text and how they are used. Here are some things that you could ask:

- Can you guess the meaning of this word from the meaning of the text around it?
- Find some words in the text that mean …
- Find some words in the text connected with the subject of …
- In line X, what does … mean?
- Find words and sort them into three separate groups under these headings: …
- Why does the writer use the word … here?
- Find words in the text that match this list of synonyms.
- What words come before/after the word … . What other words collocate with this word?
- Can you remember any other phrases you know with this word in them?
- Can you find any multiword items (i.e. groups of words that go together/chunks)?
- What's the opposite of this word?
- How many different words does the writer use to describe the …?

Lexis work after the main stages of reading or listening work

Coursebooks frequently offer follow-up tasks and exercises that focus on the use of lexis in the text and encourage learners to try using the items themselves. These are often similar to the practice activities we'll look at in Section 5 of this chapter.

Lesson procedures

Here is a brief lesson procedure for a reading and speaking lesson including lexis work at Elementary level for a multinational group of young adults who have recently travelled to the UK.

1 **Pre-teach lexis**
   Use board pictures to draw an airport. Elicit the following items (and clarify those they don't know): *plane, check-in, take off, delayed, passenger, customs, first aid, bureau de change*. Practise pronunciation. Focus on getting the stress correct. Make sure students get oral practice.

2 **Written practice of lexis**
   Give each student a handout showing photos of an airport, with a list of lexical items around the edges. Students match the lexical items to objects in the picture by drawing lines.

3 **Oral practice of lexis**
   Put students in pairs. Ask them to think about the last time they used an airport and describe to each other the procedure from arrival to the moment they took off. What did they like or not like about it?

4 **Reading to find specific information**
   Use a Heathrow Airport information leaflet for a fast-reading exercise. Students have to find the answers to ten questions as quickly as possible, e.g. *What time does the bureau de change close?* (The questions should involve using the lexis taught in Stage 1.)

5 **Further lexis work**

When they've finished, ask questions to focus them on *Arrivals, Departures, Duty Free, Immigration, Baggage Claim*, plus any useful lexical items the students ask about.

6 **Communicative activity (an opportunity to use lexis learned)**

Role-play in small groups: one student in each group is at the Information desk; the other students have various problems and come to get advice.

Task 148: Planning a procedure for a lexical lesson

Prepare a similar procedure for a lesson focused around lexis to do with the countryside.

Task 149: Selecting an order for a skills and lexis lesson

Here is a procedure of a reading, speaking and lexis lesson for Advanced students. Put the stages in a likely working order.

a Set the task: read the article and find two arguments for banning all cars and two against.

b Simulation: a formal meeting of the two opposing sides is held at the United Nations.

c Elicit/teach lexis that students have seen in the text: *scaremongering, pressure group, target, manifesto.*

d Show picture of the Earth. The globe has a cartoon face and is sweating and mopping its brow. Elicit what it means (*global warming*) and find out student opinions.

e Elicit/teach *ozone layer, iceberg, extinct, exhaust fumes, ultra-violet.*

f Divide students into two opposing groups and have them use the article to help prepare a detailed argument either for or against. Help with lexis problems while they are working.

g Students read the article and do the task. Discuss the answers together.

Commentary ■ ■ ■

A possible order would be: d, e, a, g, c, f, b. ■

You can find more about focusing on language when working on reading or listening texts in Chapter 12.

4 Presenting lexis

You may sometimes want to offer a short, teacher-led focus on the meaning, form and use of lexical items. This may be to clarify a single item, perhaps when a problem comes up unexpectedly in the middle of a lesson, though more often you will group items together and teach a small set at the same time. It is usually most useful when the lexical items presented are connected in some way, for example:

• words connected with the same location or event (e.g. shop words, wedding words);

• words that have the same grammar and similar use (e.g. adjectives to describe people, movement verbs);

• words that can be used to achieve success in a specific task (e.g. persuading a foreign friend to visit your town).

Task 150: Grouping lexical items for teaching

Think of one or two other ways to group lexical items for teaching.

Presentation techniques for lexis

If you just want to quickly convey the meaning of one or more lexical items, there are a number of ways you could do that. The most common technique probably involves a presentation-practice route:

- Present: you first offer some cues, pictures or information about the target items and elicit the words from students or model them yourself;
- Practice: you then get the students to practise, e.g. by repeating items, using them in short dialogues, etc.

These techniques are similar to those used in the present-practice section on grammar (see Chapter 12, Section 4).

Alternatively, there are many other ways to convey meaning. For each lexical item in the following random list, I've suggested a different way that you could help students begin to learn the meaning.

gloves	Mime putting them on.
disgusting	Mime (e.g. smelling old food) and make a facial expression.
swimming	Translate it.
café	Draw a quick sketch on the board or show a flashcard or picture in a book.
often	Draw a line. Mark *never* at one end and *always* at the other. Mark points along it: *usually*, *rarely*, etc.
chase	Get two or three students to act it out.
frightened	Tell a personal anecdote.
crossroads	Build a model with Cuisenaire rods or toy construction bricks.
window sill	Point to the object.
exploitation	Explain the meaning (with examples).
hope	Read out the dictionary definition.
put up with	Tell a short story that includes it.
stapler	Bring one into class to show them.
put your foot down	Act out a short conversation.
contact lens	Students who know explain to those who don't.
reduction	Draw a diagram or graph.

Some of these ideas used on their own might seem more time-consuming than is worthwhile for a single word. However, they may be valid if they are **generative**, i.e. if they also allow you to introduce other items using the same technique, context or illustration. For example, the idea given above for *crossroads* involves using Cuisenaire rods to make a little road scene, which presumably would take a minute or so to set up and introduce. That might arguably be long-winded, but becomes more usable if, having set up the scene, you can then also easily teach *traffic lights*, *zebra crossing*, *signpost*, *traffic* using the same situational context.

Bear in mind that, whatever you do, the stand-alone words are not much use on their own. For example, *disgusting* as a single word has some use but is limited.

But if students know that they can smell food and say 'Ooh! That's disgusting!' and 'That café was absolutely disgusting!', it starts to become a really usable item. So, if you present lexical items, remember not just to teach isolated items, but to make sure that learners get to hear and use them in realistic sentences.

Task 151: Teaching ideas for lexis

a Add a new teaching idea to the list above.

b Continue the list with teaching ideas for the following words: *Wednesday, tunnel, chilly, overtake, vodka.*

A simple lexis-presentation activity at Beginner or Elementary level might involve using techniques such as these to introduce students to a short list of new lexical items. This input (i.e. teaching) of new lexis would probably be followed by a practice activity in which students could find ways to use the words that they had just met or revised (see the next section).

However, even if you have used these techniques in class, you can't really say that the students have learned the new item. The first meeting with a lexical item (in class or elsewhere) is only one step. Coming to really learn the scope and limits of a lexical item is a long and gradual process; a lexical item learned initially at Beginner level (for example, *book*) can go on revealing more and more of itself even up to Advanced level (*to do something by the book, bookworm, bookish, little black book, to throw the book at at someone, to book someone,* etc.). The list of teaching ideas for *swimming* can be extended to include some ways of studying this lexical item beyond a first meeting, for example:

- draw a circle with the word *swimming* in the centre. Add lines leading from this word to a variety of collocations or phrases: *~ pool, ~ lesson, ~ trunks, Shall we go ~,* etc. These items could be elicited from students, searched for in dictionaries, found in texts, etc.;
- use *swimming* as starting point and collect a number of connected lexical items, e.g. *water polo, diving board, deep end, crawl,* etc.;
- collect grammatical variations on *swimming,* e.g. *swim, swam, swum, swimmer, swimmers.*

The teaching ideas in this section are mainly to do with showing, illustrating or demonstrating the meaning. This is possible for many words (particularly tangible, visible objects or simple verbs), but problematic for more complex meanings (e.g. *superficial, revelation, avert*). In such cases, learners are likely to need to see or hear words in specific contexts in reading texts or listening materials.

5 Lexical practice activities and games

After students have seen and heard a new lexical item for the first time, they will need opportunities to become more familiar with it, to practise recognising, manipulating and using it. Many simple lexical practice activities are based around the following ideas:

- discussions, communicative activities and role-play requiring use of the lexical items;
- making use of the lexis in written tasks.

There are many published exercises on lexis. These include:

- matching pictures to lexical items;
- matching parts of lexical items to other parts, e.g. beginnings and endings;
- matching lexical items to others, e.g. collocations, synonyms, opposites, sets of related words, etc.;
- using prefixes and suffixes to build new lexical items from given words;
- classifying items into lists;
- using given lexical items to complete a specific task;
- filling in crosswords, grids or diagrams;
- filling in gaps in sentences;
- memory games.

Many such tasks seem to be designed for students working on their own, but can easily be used in class.

Task 152: Using lexical practice exercises in class

This is a practice exercise from a lexis book for Beginner/ Elementary students. How could you use it in a class of students?

From *Word Games with English 1*, Howard-Williams and Herd (Heinemann, 1986)

Commentary ■ ■ ■

There are many options. For example:

- You could ask each student to do the exercise on his/her own.
- Students could work together in pairs or small groups to find the answers (possibly comparing with other pairs later).
- The whole class could decide on answers together.
- You could make teams and the exercise could be run as a competition, giving questions in turns to the separate teams and awarding points for right answers.

You could also use this exercise as source material for a series of activities, perhaps getting students to:

* match word groups with the pictures;
* look up any lexical items they don't know in their dictionaries;
* explain new lexical items to other students;
* do the exercise in pairs;
* check and compare answers as a whole class;
* in groups, write their own questions in the same style;
* use the new questions as a quiz between teams. ■

This kind of practice is mainly focused on reading and writing and on using the lexical items individually and away from any context. The students are learning **about** the lexical items rather than actually using them. In lexis work, you also need to provide chances for students to get oral and/or written practice in **using** the lexical items.

Task 153: Lexical items in a practice task

Here are two exercises from a higher-level lexis book. List ten or more items of lexis that students will practise when they do these exercises.

Practice

1 **Write or discuss the answers to these questions.**
  1 How much do you know about each of the planets in our system?
  2 How far do you think man will get in space discovery in the next hundred years?
  3 Do we really need to know what other planets and systems are like?

2 **You are an astronaut reporting back to Earth from outer space. Describe what you can see as you float through space.**

From *Wordbuilder* by Guy Wellman (Heinemann, 1989)

Commentary ■ ■ ■

Some possible lexis: *planet, solar system, Earth, Mars, Jupiter, Saturn, etc., Sun, star, galaxy, UFO, comet, spaceship, satellite, moon, rocket, alien, black hole, rings, asteroids, speed of light, ET*, etc. ■

Many practice activities combine giving the students a list of lexical items and setting them a task to do with those lexical items. The practice activity in Task 153, for example, is preceded in the book by an activity that focuses the students clearly on a large number of useful lexical items.

Task 154: Designing a task for specific lexical items

Look at the picture and lexical items on the next page. Design a task that will give students written or oral practice in using a number of these lexical items: *cash register, shop assistant, trolley, credit card, expensive, thief, purse, change, shopping bag, receipt, customer, pay, paid, shopping* (noun).

HOUSEHOLD GOODS

NO ENTRY

Commentary ■ ■ ■

Here are four ideas:

1 You were at the shops yesterday and you lost your purse. You think another person took it. Look at the picture and think about your story. The other student in your pair is a policewoman. Tell her exactly what happened.

2 Do you like shopping? What are some of the problems? Perhaps this picture will give you some ideas. Write five or six sentences about what you like and dislike. When you are ready, compare with other students.

3 Get into groups of three. Look at this picture. In your group, one student is this man, one student is the shop assistant, and one student is this woman. First of all, think about what they are discussing. Are they arguing? Why? Then stand up and practise the conversation.

4 Write a strong letter of complaint to the manager of this shop about a terrible incident that happened to you yesterday. ■

6 Remembering lexical items

There is no point in studying new lexical items if they are not remembered. Many students record newly learned lexical items in long lists in their files or exercise books. In many cases, these lists are disorganised and are often never looked at again after they have been written. If we can train students to record their new lexis in a more useful manner, we can do a lot to help their progress.

Task 155: Student word lists

Here is part of a word list from an Intermediate-level Xanadusian student's exercise book. Find some reasons why it is not as useful as it might be.

Word	Translations
express	atcito
opt out	organo kotor nganinot
	megumba stron
	(ff skulo, firmo)
star	galactio
interview	tuo baire medjurma
shun	bacawao ina terusco
kinsman	megrobaro
foyer	auditorio pri mecxt
piss	kchir
pottery	oborosto
o'er	tubea
hotchpotch	senico kotor emio ina tulmulenco
semi-conductor	semikonductto
prosecuted	epallis na magistralo

Commentary ■ ■ ■

Some reasons:

- The items on the list seem to have no connection with each other. They appear to be a random list (possibly written down in order of appearance in a text).
- There are no other words that might be useful in situations where one needs to use one of these words (e.g. *foyer: dress circle, stalls, stage, aisle,* etc.).
- How are they pronounced? Where is the stress (e.g. *prosecuted*)?
- There are no examples of the words in use, in sentences.
- Are the words usable as nouns, adjectives, verbs, etc. (e.g. *interview*)?
- How many different meanings does each word have (e.g. *star*)?
- What other words are connected in form to any of these words (e.g. *interviewer, interviewee, interview room*)?
- There is nothing to help the students remember the lexical items.
- Where might one typically come across these lexical items (e.g. *Trespassers will be prosecuted, We prosecute all shoplifters*)?
- Who uses them?
- Some of the lexical items are very specialised and would only be used in very specific contexts; not necessarily very useful to learn for active use (e.g. *opt out*).
- Some words may be archaic or literary, not used in contemporary speech. There is no indication of this restriction. (e.g. *o'er, kinsman*).
- What collocations are common (e.g. *job interview*)?
- There are not always direct translations; perhaps a complex cultural idea is being conveyed that four or five words cannot really explain (e.g. *opt out*).
- No indication or warning of taboos (e.g. *piss*). ■

Alternative ways of recording lexis

The action of noting down a list of lexical items is no guarantee that remembering will take place. Remembering involves four things:

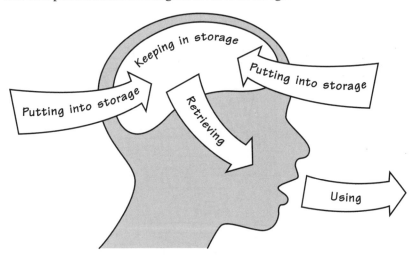

Figure 11.3   The four things involved in remembering

Figure 11.4 shows an alternative lexical item list that should provide more information than the one in Task 155. Fill it in for two or three English lexical items of your choice. (Decide yourself how you want to interpret the column titles; the last column is intended for the student to think of some 'bright idea' to help them remember the word – something it sounds like, a sketch or whatever.) A full, photocopiable version of this is given in Resource 18 in Appendix 2.

Lexical item	Pronunciation	Translation	Grammar	Collocations	Example	Idea
motorcycle	/'məʊtəsaɪkəl/	*pikipiki*	*noun*	*ride a ~,* *get on my ~,* *~ maintenance,* *~ race,* *~ courier*	*She's just bought a 600cc Suzuki motorcycle.*	

Figure 11.4   Alternative lexical item list

Encouraging students to keep a useful lexical item list is one way to ensure that the teaching of lexis has a value after the lesson is over. It is also possible to integrate the teaching and the storing of lexis in a more direct way by introducing the lexis into the lesson in a way that enables the students to record not only the word but also the way in which they learned the word.

One way involves grouping words so that a set is learned together. This is often more effective than studying unrelated individual words. For example, you could present a set of words connected with kitchens by using a picture of a kitchen (Figure 11.5); the students each have a copy of the picture and write the words on it as they learn them.

Figure 11.5   Kitchen vocabulary

A similar idea is to build a **word web** (or memory map or mind map, as it is sometimes called) where connections in meaning or use between different words are visually indicated in the structure of the diagram (Figure 11.6). Obviously a completed word web could be presented to the students, but it is probably more useful for the students themselves to think through the connections and to decide where each new word fits on the plan; thus the learning of new words and the recording of them are part of the same activity.

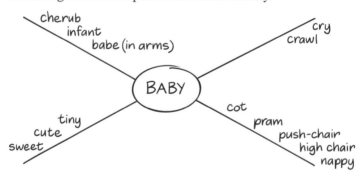

Figure 11.6   Word web

Task 156: Recording words in student notebooks

Figure 11.7 (pages 243–4) shows four examples of sets of words recorded in students' notebooks, using a number of different ideas. In each case, they represent the end result of a lesson procedure used in class. Read the brief lesson descriptions written by students – (a) to (d) (see page 244) – and match each one to a diagram. Try the tasks yourself.

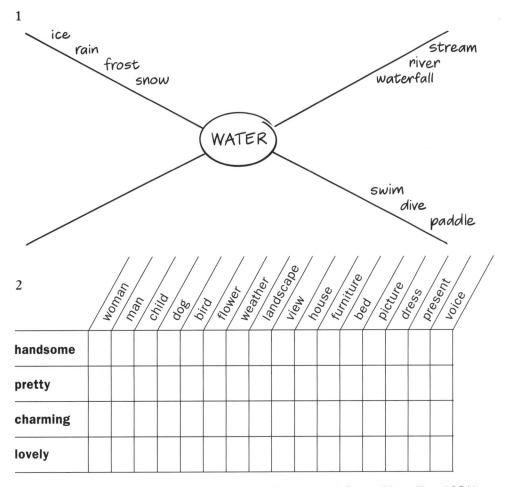

1

ice
rain
frost
snow

stream
river
waterfall

WATER

swim
dive
paddle

2

	woman	man	child	dog	bird	flower	weather	landscape	view	house	furniture	bed	picture	dress	present	voice
handsome																
pretty																
charming																
lovely																

From *The Words You Need*, Rudzka, Channell, Putseys and Ostyn (Macmillan 1981)

3

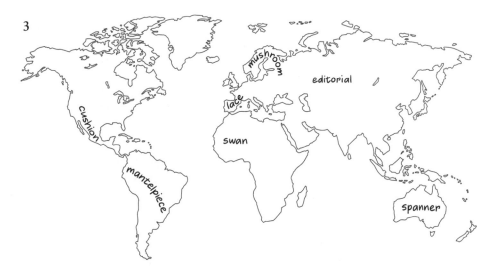

cushion
mantelpiece
lace
swan
mushroom
editorial
spanner

Figure 11.7   Ways of recording words

4

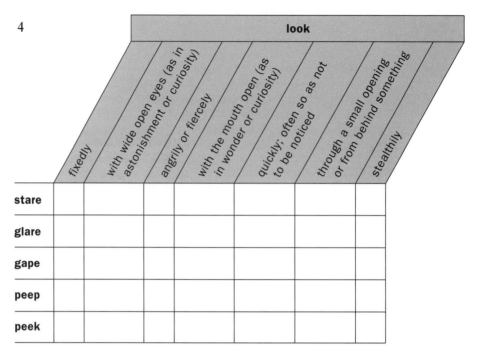

	fixedly	with wide open eyes (as in astonishment or curiosity)	angrily or fiercely	with the mouth open (as in wonder or curiosity)	quickly; often so as not to be noticed	through a small opening or from behind something	stealthily
stare							
glare							
gape							
peep							
peek							

From *The Words You Need*, Rudzka, Channell, Putseys and Ostyn (Macmillan 1981)

Figure 11.7   Ways of recording words (continued)

a   The teacher asked us to consider each word in turn, and we discussed the fine differences in meaning between them and tried to come to some agreement. We didn't always agree, but I think the discussion itself was very useful, as I became more aware about how subtle and precise meaning can be. I especially liked it when I realised that the teacher wasn't always entirely certain herself about what made one word different from another.

b   The teacher wrote one word on the board and then added a few examples, then she gave the pens to us and we had to add other words. If we made a mistake, got the spelling wrong or put a word in the wrong place, then she didn't correct us. She didn't need to, because usually one of the other students noticed it was wrong and we discussed it and then changed it. At the end, when we'd filled the board, the teacher pointed out three words that were still problems. Then we copied it all down into our notebooks. We used the words in our next activity making a story about a hike in the countryside.

c   We had to find our own way to remember some new words. As we learned each new word, we had to write it down in an appropriate place, finding a strong reason for putting it there. The teacher said we should try to make a mental link or association with that part of the picture; for example, one of the words was *spanner*, so I wrote it here and tried to imagine an Australian beach with a surfer coming in on a spanner instead of a surfboard. It sounds a bit crazy, but I haven't forgotten the word!

d   We worked in pairs trying to decide which words typically went together with other words, and which combinations were impossible. Our teacher told us that this 'going together' is called **collocation**.

Word page: Collocations and chunks

This page is for recording lexical items that typically go together in patterns with a single key word. The learner writes the key word in the centre box and then uses the columns before and after the box to write in phrases, sentences, chunks, etc. For example:

There was a terrible		jam round the ring road.
		lights
	traffic	warden
The		is really heavy today.
What's holding up the		?

Lexical item page: Topic webs

Learners write a topic in the centre box and then add some useful sub-headings in the other boxes. Then they collect and group words under these sub-headings, connecting each new word by a line to the appropriate box. Thus, for example, the centre word might be *station*, some sub-headings could be *places, timetable, people, things to buy*, etc. Lexical items within these categories might include: places – *platform, booking office, waiting room, ticket window*, etc.; timetable – *departure, delayed, ten minutes late*, etc.; people – *guard, ticket inspector, clerk, driver*, etc.; things to buy – *A single to X, please, A return to X, please, A day return to X, please*, etc. (see Figure 11.8). This way of recording lexical items may reflect more accurately the way that we store lexical item networks in our brains – and may therefore be more useful for students than the traditional lists.

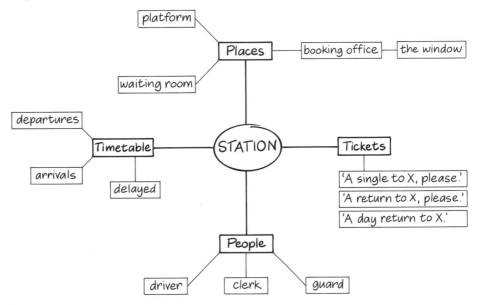

Figure 11.8   Topic web

Lexical item page: Lexical item collector

This page can be used to record lexical items and then collect and relate items, classified as different grammatical types. For example, if the student has found *happy,* they could then go on to find and record *happiness* and *happily.*

Noun (thing)	Noun (person)	Adjective	Verb (present – past – past participle)	Adverb	Phrases
happiness	–	happy	–	happily	Happy birthday! I'm not happy.

There's no need to fill in all columns. Different lexical items will let you to fill in different columns.

Noun (thing)	Noun (person)	Adjective	Verb (present – past – past participle)	Adverb	Phrases
report	reporter	reported	report – reported – reported		

7 Knowing a lexical item

Task 157: 'I know this word already'

You're in the middle of teaching some 'new' words in a lexis lesson when one of your students politely interrupts and says that he knows all these words already. What do you think he means by 'knowing a word'?

Commentary ■ ■ ■

He probably means that he has seen it before and knows a meaning for it. Quite a few students seem content with this; lexis learning involves matching a meaning in their language with an English word. But this definition of 'knowing a word' is fairly limited. Does he know more than this basic meaning? Can he actually use the word appropriately to do things in a variety of contexts? ■

Many teachers assume that the real work of teaching lexis is introducing students to the meanings of new lexical items, and perhaps to the spelling and the pronunciation. In fact, much of the difficulty of lexis isn't to do with learning endless new words, it's learning how to successfully use words one already knows, i.e. learning how 'old' words are used in 'new' ways. For example, the word *table* might conceivably be first met on Day 1 of a beginner's course. But it's unlikely to be fully explored and used, even as the student reaches advanced levels. From the basic 'core' meaning of table (a piece of furniture), we find there are various other meanings that grow out of that: the food spread on it to make a meal, the guests you meet at the meal, to table a motion, a table of data, a games surface, football league lists, part of a musical instrument, to postpone, etc. It also features in many chunks and idioms, e.g. *Do you have a free table?, a round-table discussion, to set the table, to be under the table* (= drunk), etc. To learn your way round all these takes time and requires exposure to a lot of samples of language in use.

What are some things you can know about a lexical item?

You can know ...	Notes
how it's spelled	
the number of syllables	
phonemes	The sounds that make up the word
which syllables are stressed	Short words usually have one main stress; longer words may have a number of secondary stresses, too.
which stresses are stronger or weaker	
what part(s) of speech it is	
grammatically related forms	e.g. the past-tense form of a verb
the basic, 'core' meaning	e.g. table = piece of furniture with a flat surface and legs
other meanings	
the 'semantic space' it occupies	Where the meaning of one word ends and another begins; for example, *fence/wall/ hedge*
metaphorical meanings	e.g. the uses of 'water' words to talk about business: *drowning in debt, cash flow,* etc.
connotation	The associations and 'feelings' that seem to attach to words quite apart from their literal, 'dictionary' meaning, e.g. *junkie* sounds more disapproving than *drug user*.
appropriacy for certain social situations, contexts, etc.	e.g. It may not be appropriate to call a job interviewer *mate*.
restrictions on meaning	Things that the item cannot be used for
immediate collocates	Words that typically go with the word
collocational field	The range of words that an item collocates with
colligation	The grammatical position in a sentence that the word typically takes, and the grammatical patterns that typically go with this item.
common chunks, phrases, idioms it appears in	→

translation(s)	words often do not have a precise correlation
false friends	Words which in translation suggest a wrong meaning, e.g. in Hungarian *kastély* looks similar to the English *castle*, but in fact means *palace*.
true friends	Words which mean almost precisely the same in the other language.
lexical families	Other words related to the word by its topic, e.g. *saucepan, frying pan, can opener, ladle, food mixer,* etc.
lexical sets	Many words are related to other words that cover a wider or smaller range of meaning, e.g. *sweater* is included within *clothes*. Similarly *sweater* itself includes *polo-neck sweater*.
synonyms	Words that mean the same or nearly the same.
homonyms	Words that have the same spelling but have different meanings.
homophones	Words that are pronounced the same but have a different meaning.
opposites (antonyms)	
suffixes that can be added to the word	e.g. *possess – possession*
prefixes that can be added to the word	e.g. *flow – overflow*
the visual image people typically have for this word	
personal feelings about this word	
mnemonics (things help you remember the word)	

Now this, of course, is a massive list. There is no way that an initial classroom meeting with a lexical item could deal with more than two or three of these. Naturally, therefore, initial teaching tends to prioritise on core meaning, spelling and pronunciation. However, problems arise when classroom work continually focuses on introducing more and more new items in this way – and doesn't explore in more depth. By Intermediate level, most students will have met a large percentage of the most useful English lexical items. It's arguable that by this point in a learner's progress, it becomes more important to explore uses of lexical items they already know than to learn new things, i.e. what is new is not the words themselves but the new combinations and patterns they are used in. This suggests that, rather than following a traditional teaching model such as 'teach new lexis, then practise it, then later on recycle it', we might do better to plan lessons that allow students to constantly meet the same items in use in different texts, recordings, conversations, etc. and notice them in new combinations with different surroundings with different uses, and then have repeated opportunities to try using the items themselves. The initial 'teaching' is of relatively little importance. Items need to be encountered again and again: many encounters, many associations. Seeing real examples of language being used is often more important than hearing 'cold' definitions.

How can we do this? How can we worry less about the 'input' of lexis and spend more time on going deeper with language, looking at how words are used, noticing patterns, encouraging students to notice more in the texts they see, encouraging long-term recognition and recall and getting our students to use the language themselves? Here are some ideas:

Record lexical items in useful ways

We have already looked at alternatives to the traditional 'word + translation' list and discussed encouraging learners to keep word pages that let them collect collocations, pronunciation, idioms, etc. Encourage them to use these. Help learners by giving out blank formats (e.g. word lists, collocation grids, etc.) and teaching them how to use them.

Revisit lexical item pages

Traditionally, word lists were written in class then never looked at again. Encourage students to revisit their word collections and keep amending and adding new examples, collocations, etc. (This is a good reason to tell students to make sure they leave blank spaces when they first record items.) Keep referring back to and making use of these pages in class, for homework, etc. Train students how to use them. Integrate their use into your lesson.

Collect lexical items

When students read a text or listen to a recording, encourage them to notice interesting items and 'collect' them on their word pages. You can provide specific 'collecting' tasks that focus away from the typical search for 'new' items, e.g. 'Find three words in the text that you already know but seem to be used in a different way'.

Sort and classify items

Get students to read specific texts to collect and classify items together on single word pages (e.g. from a cooking article: 'things found in the kitchen'; from a holiday story: 'travel words'; from a love letter: 'happy words'; from a job advertisement: 'adjectives describing people'; etc.).

Chunk and collocation spotting

Teachers sometimes ask 'Are there any words you don't understand?' after students have read a text.

But this may be a problematic question, as students could read a text and believe that they understand all the lexical items, but miss the fact that they have not registered that familiar words may be being used in new ways and combinations.

This leads us to a variation on the third idea: collecting items from a text but with a focus on longer pieces of text. For example, you could ask students to:

- find pairs of words that seem to go together: e.g. in the sentence *He had very good communication skills*, students may not know that *communication skills* is a common collocation (or that *good communication skills* is also very common);
- find phrases of three or more words long that seem to be a frequently used 'fixed' chunk: e.g. *It's well worth avoiding Guildford city centre if you possibly can* contains *It's well worth avoiding* and *if you possibly can* (and probably *Guildford city centre* is also a chunk, but one in which you can substitute different town names in the first position);
- underline ten nouns (or words used as nouns) and then search out which verb is used in connection with each one: e.g. in the sentence *Although the potatoes were rather old, we boiled them along with the carrots*, the noun *potatoes* is connected to the verb *boiled*.

'Chunk spotting' is a great classroom (or homework) learning activity. It often astonishes students and teachers to realise how much of authentic texts are made out of these 'pre-fabricated' pieces of language.

Redesign your pages

Encourage learners to sometimes reorganise, reclassify and redesign some of their word pages, writing them up nicely (maybe with coloured pens? sketches? diagrams?), perhaps changing format, e.g. a list into a mind map, labels on a picture, etc. The act of mentally sorting and rearranging will be a helpful learning activity.

When an error comes up, review a range of collocations

In class, a student says 'I made the exam last week'. Rather than just swiftly giving the correct verb, have a look at a number of useful 'exam' collocations and chunks: *took the exam, failed the exam, passed the exam, exam questions, exam results*, etc.

Record real language

Students often try to record 'pure' versions of language, e.g. separating connected items or writing verbs in the infinitive form. But *to have someone's cake and eat it* is much less useful than with the raw, original sample of text *You can't have your cake and eat it*. Many phrases and sentences only exist in a single form; there's no point in trying to generalise universal models out of them.

Challenge students to upgrade language

Students and teachers are often satisfied with getting language only approximately right. This is fine in activities mainly intended to promote greater fluency in speech, but at other times it's worth challenging students to improve. Point out to students that as well as making errors, they get language 'approximately' right, i.e. it communicates, but isn't the best way of saying something. For example, if a student says 'The food has a not interesting taste', then the meaning is clear, but the student doesn't know the best food collocations (*dull, bland*) to express her meaning. Help students by not enthusiastically celebrating inadequate language; give feedback that helps force learners to take their language up a grade.

Give collocations rather than definitions

When a student wants to know what the difference is between *late* and *delayed*, it's often hard to give a clear distinction of meaning. But there are clearly certain collocations and chunks that one is more likely to fit into than the other. When you want to make a sentence, knowing the typical collocations – and learning them, phrasebook-like – is probably going to be of more use than trying to select between two very similar meanings.

There are many games and activities specifically aiming to work on collocational understanding. Here are three of my favourites.

Quick choices

Choose two or three nouns, e.g. *food, cooking* and *meal*, that have a number of (possibly confusable) collocations. In this case, the list might include *baby, fast, slow, health, dog, home, evening, delicious, light, balanced, three-course, French, vegetarian, frozen, cat*. Tell the students that you will read out the list item by item and they must indicate which of the two (or three) words is the best collocate, or if the item goes with more than one word. Decide on how students will indicate their choices. You could go for quiet ways, e.g. students write their answers in a list; noisy ways, e.g. students call out their choice of words; physical ways, e.g. students point at the words written on wall notices; action ways, e.g. designate different parts of the room for different words and students run to the right part of the room (or between parts).

Guess the collocation

Divide the class into three or more teams. In each team, students are given a common word (e.g. *town*) and have to prepare a list of five common collocations (e.g. *planning, hall, home, market, centre, new*, etc.). Each team has a different starter word. When everyone is ready, students read their lists out one item at a time and the other teams try to guess the original word. If the word is guessed immediately on the first clue, both teams (list-makers and word-guessers) get ten points; for each extra word, the points go down by one. This scoring scheme encourages list-makers to find the most likely and distinctive collocations.

Chunk watching

Students work in groups of three, two of whom face each other. The teacher gives them a topic to talk about and they simply chat naturally for a few minutes. The third person sits out of their line of sight and takes no part in the conversation, but listens carefully and takes notes of as many 'chunks' as she can catch. At the end of the time, the listener shows her list to the speakers and they go through and discuss the items.

Chapter 12 **Grammar**

1   **What is grammar?**

For many years, 'learning the grammar' has assumed a central role in students' expectations about what learning a language involves. Nowadays, however, there are many different views about what learners need to learn and how best to go about teaching it.

Here are some key questions concerning teaching grammar:

- What is grammar?
- How do people learn grammar?
- How can I analyse form, meaning and use for teaching purposes?
- What are possible component parts of a grammar lesson?
- How can I provide relevant input for learners?
- How can I help learners notice, understand and memorise language?
- How can I help learners practise using language?

But before we decide how we can teach grammar, perhaps our first issue should be to work out exactly what exactly we mean by 'grammar'.

Task 158: Defining grammar

When thinking about teaching the grammar of a foreign language, which of these definitions of 'grammar' seems most appropriate?

- Rules about sentence formation, tenses, verb patterns, etc. in a reference book
- The moment-by-moment structuring of what we say as it is being spoken
- Exercises (fill in the gap, multiple choice, etc.) about tenses, etc.
- Our internal 'database' as to what are possible or impossible sentences

Commentary ■ ■ ■

I think all of these are arguably valid descriptions of something 'grammar like'. ■

When thinking of 'grammar', many people probably first picture a book full of explanations and rules that tell them which verbs have what endings, how to use adverbs, how to make a superlative, etc. That's certainly one kind of grammar, but it's not really what we are talking about when we say that we are 'teaching grammar'. Let's try a different starting point.

Imagine my friend Leona starts saying 'Yesterday afternoon I ...'. What's the next word going to be? Can you predict possible words that might come next? Maybe you think she's going to describe an action or something she did (so the next word might be *went* or *saw* or *broke* or *met*, etc.). Or maybe you imagine her describing something that didn't happen (so her next word might be *didn't* or *couldn't*, etc.).

How were you able to make such predictions? You could do it because you had a sort of mental list of possible patterns of English. You were able to look, even without thinking about it, at this internal collection of information and know what sort of words were possible and, also, what kinds of words were not possible. For example, you are probably quite sure that Leona didn't say 'Yesterday afternoon I green ...'. Similarly, she probably didn't say 'Yesterday afternoon I meet ...'. In grammatical terms, we might say that the next word could be a verb (e.g. *saw*) or an auxiliary verb (e.g. *didn't*). We could also say that the next word wouldn't normally be an adjective (e.g. *green*). We also expect that, whatever the word is, it will be in a form that follows certain other guidelines; for example, if we are talking about the past (*yesterday*), then the verb form will normally be in a past tense.

This, of course, is the kind of information you'll find systematically arranged in a grammar reference book, or maybe in a simplified form in a book for learners. And it's the sort of thing that grammar exercises practise and test . However, instead of being a dry record of facts and rules, the information in your head is a living resource that allows you to communicate and be understood. For this reason, learning rules in a grammar book by heart is probably not 'learning grammar'. Similarly reciting grammar rules by heart may not be 'understanding grammar'. Even doing tests and exercises may not necessarily be 'learning grammar'. There is actually no hard evidence that any of these things lead to people being able to use grammar accurately and fluently in speech. These things are only useful if there is some way that students can transfer this studied knowledge into a living ability to use the language. The information is not in itself of much use. In real life, people rarely come up to you and say 'Please tell me about conditionals'.

Scott Thornbury, in his book *Uncovering Grammar*, has suggested that we could open up our concept of 'grammar' if we start thinking of it as not just a noun (i.e. the information), but as a verb as well (i.e. the active skill of using language). It's probably this 'verby' kind of grammar that we most need to help our learners work with in class.

But, how can our students 'grammar' better? How do people get to that point where they are able to use language competently, fluently and accurately? Is studying and memorising rules a helpful waystage on the route to that goal? Are practice activities helpful? What role does teacher explanation and active 'teaching' have? And do we need to teach grammar at all?

We will look at these questions in some detail, but first I'd like to set out a brief overview of the conclusions you'll get if you read through all the following sections.

It seems likely that learners have to do a number of things to be able to start making any new grammar item part of their own personal stock of language.

They probably need to have **exposure** to the language; they need to **notice** and **understand** items being used; they need to **try using** language themselves in 'safe' practice ways and in more demanding contexts; they need to **remember** the things they have learnt.

The table on the next page expands on this description. If you look back at the diagram (Figure 6.1 on page 112) showing a hypothesis about how people learn, you can probably draw some connections between the table and that diagram.

To learn a language item learners need to:	It follows that, in class, you probably need to:
• **be exposed** to a lot of language while reading/listening.	• include lots of reading and listening activities. These should include realistic texts a little above the apparent current language level of learners so that learners are exposed to a lot of comprehensible new language (see Chapter 8).
• **notice** specific items when they are being used, in texts (e.g. in stories, in conversations, etc.).	• provide texts, exercises and techniques that help learners notice specific items. Texts specifically written for learners (e.g. containing multiple examples of a target item) may be particularly useful (see Section 3 of this chapter).
• **understand** the form, meaning and use of an item. **Form** refers to how the pieces fit together, the endings, etc. **Use** refers to the typical situations, conversations, contexts in which it might be used.	• be informed about form, meaning and use of language (see Chapter 10, Sections 2 and 4); • focus learners' attention on form, meaning and use by means of exercises, explanations, drills, games, questions, etc. (see Section 3 of this chapter).
• **try things out** in a safe environment with limited other linguistic demands. • **have opportunities** to practise new language, to 'get their mouths around' new items.	• give many opportunities to practise things in activities that call only for restricted language when they speak and write, with encouragement and feedback (see Section 2 of this chapter).
• **use the new language when speaking and writing** to communicate in different contexts.	• offer speaking and writing tasks that allow learners to make use of all the language they know (see Chapters 7 and 9).
• **remember** items.	• pay attention to how learners record items; • return to items again and again with revision tasks.

2   Restricted output: drills, exercises, dialogues and games

Language practice activities are arguably the most important part of any grammar lesson. Although teachers often spend a lot of time on 'input' stages – for example, in giving explanations – **the real learning experience is when learners try to use the language themselves**.

In order to give students intensive oral or written practice of specific language points, you can use activities carefully designed to restrict the language needed and require the use of the target items. Restricted output activities are defined by their focus on (a) limited options for use of language; (b) limited options for communication; (c) a focus on accuracy. Typical restricted activities are oral drills, written exercises, elicited dialogues, and grammar practice activities/games.

Drills

Drills provide intensive oral practice of selected sentences, giving the learners a chance to practise 'getting their mouths around' the language without worrying too much about meaning. The basic drill involves simple repetition:

TEACHER:	He's going to open the door.
STUDENTS:	He's going to open the door.
TEACHER:	He's going to drive the car.
STUDENTS:	He's going to drive the car.

Task 159: 'Drills are so old-fashioned'

You are planning a lesson that includes some drills. Your colleague spots you in the staff room and says 'Drills? Surely you don't still do those! They're so old-fashioned, and they've proved they don't work.' Is it worth arguing back? What would you say?

Commentary ■ ■ ■

Many teachers consider drills old-fashioned and never use them. I think they are wrong and they are depriving their learners of some important chances to learn. The next section outlines some possible reasons for drills. ■

Why drill?

Drills are often associated with the largely discredited behaviourist philosophy which suggests that we can be trained into automatic responses to stimuli through repetition or restricted response drills. However, I don't think we need to throw drills out with the behaviourist bathwater. We can still argue that our brains need to 'automatise' tasks without having to buy the entire 'stimulus-response' philosophy. It seems reasonably clear from day-to-day experience that we become better at doing certain things through practice – I can feel this myself when trying to learn to say a difficult sentence in a foreign language. I may need to 'rehearse' it slowly and carefully many times before I eventually start to get the sounds nearly right and in the right order. Only after a lot of this 'cutting a groove' in my brain's record can I start to get 'up to speed' with the new item. Eventually, it is so easy for me to say it that I hardly notice I'm saying it and I can stop worrying about it. But my own private 'drilling to myself' has helped.

Drilling is important for 'getting your tongue around it' problems. They can also help with other things, for example on issues to do with selecting the right form quickly (again, something that improves with familiarity).

For many years, some writers encouraged teachers not to offer students any speaking tasks that did not involve an element of 'genuine communication'. Recently, there has been a reassertion of the value of experimenting and playing with language even where the language doesn't represent realistic communication.

So don't worry too much about colleagues or methodology books who tell you not to bother with drills! Certainly there is some danger that students repeating are just making noises with little idea what they are saying, but of all activities in the classroom, the oral drill is the one which can be most productively demanding on accuracy.

When the students speak, you are probably listening carefully. You will use error awareness and correction techniques. You will give clear indications about what needs to be done in order to say the sentences better. You will encourage students to try a number of times to say the sentences with better pronunciation, with the words in the right order, etc. You will keep the level of challenge very high. When teachers are 'kind' and make drills easy ('That's good!' 'Not quite, but great!' 'Perfect!' 'Fantastic!' 'Wonderful!'), the exercise quickly becomes boring; it is the difficulty and the sense of achievement that make drills worth doing. Give precise, honest feedback rather than gushing praise. If the whole aim of a drill is to improve accuracy, it seems to make sense to aim for a very high standard. There is little point in doing a drill if the teacher and students are prepared to accept sloppy or half-good production. Honest feedback is vital.

Task 160: Variations on drills

What variations could enliven the basic drill technique (while still keeping the drill as no more than simple repetition)?

Commentary ■ ■ ■

The following section lists some possible variations. Note that even the apparently silly ones (like doing it with flat intonation) serve to raise awareness of the importance of intonation – sometimes messages are easier to take in when the example is exaggerated! ■

Factors that can vary a drill

Who speaks?
- Whole-group speaking ('choral') / Individual students practise
- Round the class / Random selection of individuals
- Male / Female
- This half / That half of the room
- As / Bs
- Pairs: alternate words
- Students lead drill (rather than teacher)

How do they speak?

- Normal volume/whispered/loud/shout/sing/mouth silently
- Normal speed/fast/slow
- Normal intonation/flat intonation/exaggerated intonation
- Change the stress
- With an American/Australian/Liverpool accent

Task 161: Moving beyond repetition drills

What variations can be given beyond simply repeating what the teacher says?

Commentary ■ ■ ■

Three ideas – substitution, transformation and true sentences – are explained in the following sections. ■

Substitution drills

Repetition, though useful for allowing full concentration on pronunciation, can be a little mindless. The following drill demands a little more thought:

TEACHER: He's going to drive the car.
STUDENTS: He's going to drive the car.
TEACHER: bus
STUDENTS: He's going to drive the bus.
TEACHER: taxi (etc.)

Not much more thought, admittedly! But it's not difficult to make it harder:

TEACHER: He's going to eat the cake.
STUDENTS: He's going to eat the cake.
TEACHER: coffee
STUDENTS: He's going to drink the coffee.
TEACHER: film
STUDENTS: He's going to watch the film. (etc.)

These drills are based on the principle of substitution. In the two examples above, the noun is being substituted by another – but it could be any word. And to make it really demanding, it could vary sentence by sentence:

TEACHER: He's going to eat the cake.
STUDENTS: He's going to eat the cake.
TEACHER: coffee
STUDENTS: He's going to drink the coffee.
TEACHER: Mary
STUDENTS: Mary's going to drink the coffee.
TEACHER: make
STUDENTS: Mary's going to make the coffee.
TEACHER: beds
STUDENTS: Mary's going to make the beds. (etc.)

Transformation drills

A completely different kind of drill is based on the students making their own sentence based on a model and information given by you. These are transformation drills, i.e. the student transforms a sentence of one kind into another form:

TEACHER: He's opening the cake tin.
STUDENTS: He's going to eat the cake.
TEACHER: He's standing beside the swimming pool.
STUDENTS: He's going to swim.
TEACHER: Susan's going into the post office.
STUDENTS: She's going to buy a stamp.
TEACHER: The students are waiting at the bus stop. (etc.)

True sentences

The most useful drill may be one where the student is giving real information in their answers – in other words, there is communication as well as language practice:

TEACHER: What are you going to do after school?
STUDENTS: I'm going to play football.
TEACHER: And tonight?
STUDENTS: I'm going to watch TV.
TEACHER: Are you going to watch the film?
STUDENTS: No, I'm not. I'm going to watch the concert.

Task 162: Designing a drill

Devise a drill to work on practising *Wh-* questions about the past (e.g. *Where did he go? What did they do? When did Mary arrive?* etc.).

Figure 12.1 summarises a range of drill types. Pick the options you like.

Variations on a drill

1 Repeat the grammar item on its own.
2 Repeat the grammar item in a phrase/sentence.
3 Repeat the intonation pattern (as hummed music, no words).
4 Repeat the grammar item with exaggerated attention to intonation.
5 Repeat only the stressed syllables in a sentence ('get the rhythm'), then later 'put back' the missing syllables.
6 Repeat a sentence, building it up bit by bit, starting with the first word(s)/syllable(s).
7 Repeat by 'backchaining' (i.e. build up the sentence bit by bit, starting at the end rather than the beginning).
8 You give opening of sentence, students complete it.
9 You give part of sentence, students complete it
10 You introduce sentence by repetition, then say new word that must be substituted within it.
11 You introduce sentence by repetition. Students must respond with a follow-on 'reply'.

---

12 You introduce sentence by repetition, then give an instruction for transformation of sentence (e.g. 'Change to the past perfect').

13 You say sentence with errors (e.g. words in wrong order), students put it right.

14 You say/show cues (e.g. some key words, pictures) and students construct a complete sentence.

15 You ask real questions about students' lives. Students respond with true sentences, all using the same grammatical item.

16 You invent or read a short text (one or two sentences), then ask questions about it, all using the same grammatical item.

Variations on the variations

All the above can be further varied by doing them …

1 as a whole class ('choral')
2 as a half/quarter of a class
3 as an individual in front of the whole class
4 as individuals around the class ('passing the baton')
5 as an open pair (everyone else can hear) next to each other
6 as an open pair across the room
7 as two halves of the class speaking to each other as if they were a pair (e.g. male/female; this side/that side)
8 as closed groups
9 as closed pairs (i.e. privately, simultaneously)
10 loudly
11 quietly
12 whispering
13 shouting
14 singing
15 slowly
16 fast
17 with exaggerated intonation
18 with flat intonation
19 with a specific accent
20 with exaggerated rhythm
21 with intonation for specific moods
22 walking around (separately)
23 mingling
24 changing places
25 taking on the teacher's role (once any individual drill is established)

Figure 12.1　　Range of drill types

A few possible feedback strategies (see Chapter 14, Section 1 for more about giving feedback on errors):

1 Tell students the correction ('reformulation')
2 'Hold' the error
3 Indicate/ask for self-correction
4 Indicate/ask for peer correction
5 The 'chain'
6 Facial expression
7 Movement
8 Echo: intonation indicates error
9 Echo: up to the error
10 Finger correction
11 Ask a question
12 Write/say clue or hint

Finally:

- keep the atmosphere humorous; keep the language focus serious;
- personalise some elements;
- jazz it up with mime, pictures, board cues, silly postures, etc.;
- don't worry too much about whether it is a 'meaningful' or 'communicative' drill;
- do worry about whether what you're drilling is a realistic piece of real-world language;
- don't drill possible but improbable English;
- keep the challenge high;
- make sure students get the practice, not you!

Written exercises

Written exercises are a common and useful way of giving students concentrated practice of language items. How can they be less of a chore and more of an enjoyable challenge?

Task 163: Analysing a textbook language exercise

Here is a textbook exercise. What area of language is it working on?

(1) _____ computer is certainly (2) _____ great invention, one of (3) _____ wonders of (4) _____ modern world. But late on (5) _____ cold Friday afternoon, towards (6) _____ end of (7) _____ miserable December, I'm beginning to wish that I'd never bought one. All I want to do is write (8) _____ letter to (9) _____ Aunt Diana. But (10) _____ machine seems to have (11) _____ different idea altogether. After (12) _____ two hours' work, all I have to show are (13) _____ torn piece of paper filled with (14) _____ inky, black smudges and (15) _____ computer screen that happily tells me 'There is (16) _____ error. Please restart.' Give me (17) _____ pen and (18) _____ pad of (19) _____ paper! If this is (20) _____ modern world, I'll vote for (21) _____ Stone Age!

Commentary ■ ■ ■

The exercise is designed to help students become more familiar with the use of articles in English (*the*, *a* and *an* or 'no article'). ■

Task 164: Different ways of using a printed exercise

The above exercise could obviously be done by students individually in class or at home. What other ways of using this material can you think of?

Commentary ■ ■ ■

Some ideas:
- Do it as individuals, then compare and discuss answers with neighbours.
- Work in pairs.
- Work in small groups.
- Work in teams – make a competition out of it.
- Do it together on the board – teacher-led.
- Do it together on the board – student-led.
- Hand out an jumbled list of answers to match to the questions.
- Do it orally in a language laboratory.
- Dictate the sentences, leaving spaces where the missing words are.
- Do it at great speed (give them, say, three minutes to do the whole exercise). Then shuffle papers and give to small groups to discuss and mark.
- Cut up the sentences and give one to each student; negotiate arrangement and answers.
- Hand out the exercise with your answers already written in, some right, some wrong. The students must correct your work.
- Make a game out of it, e.g. 'Auction': divide class into teams; allocate a certain amount of 'money' to each team. The aim is to use this money to 'buy' correct words to fill the gaps. Give students time to read through the exercise, then, starting with Gap 1, proceed to 'auction' pieces of paper with *the, an* and *a* on them. The teams must buy the word they need to complete the gap. The team that buys the correct word gets a 'money' prize. Anyone else loses the cash they spent on the wrong word. Keep a record of how much they have 'spent' on the board through the game; the winner is the team with the most money at the end. ■

Task 165: Making a printed exercise more game-like

Devise a variation on the following written exercise to make it more game-like.

Choose the correct verb form for each sentence:

1 I want *to see / see / seeing* the film.
2 I'd like *to have / have / having* a coffee.
3 I may *to go / go / going* to London.
4 I enjoy *to watch / watch / watching* TV
5 I must *to go / go / going* home now
6 I can *to play / play / playing* the guitar
7 I suggest *to have / we have / have* a rest

Commentary ■ ■ ■

This exercise is working on the difference between *-ing* forms and infinitives and helping students to sort out which ones go with which verbs.

By writing sentence halves on small squares of paper (or blank cards), we could, for example, turn an exercise like the one above into a game of 'Snap'. You deal out all the cards, which the students keep face down, not looking at them. The students (as individuals or in teams) take it in turns to play a card into one of two card piles (beginnings or endings). They must call 'Snap!' when the beginning and ending make a correct sentence. If they call 'Snap!' at the wrong time, they (or their team) must pick up both piles of discarded cards.

■

Elicited dialogues

These are short dialogues (four to ten lines) which contain a number of examples of specific items to be practised. Using a dialogue places these items in a typical or useful context, integrating practice of newer grammar with practice of items previously studied, social English expressions and pronunciation. The students will get many chances to repeat the dialogues in class and thus increase their familiarity with these items. They are often an amusing and enjoyable way to enable oral practice of language. The procedure is as follows:

Before the class

Write a short dialogue. Perhaps you have recently taught *It's too* + adjective + *to* + verb (e.g. *It's too hot to drink*). You can now make a short dialogue, set in a specific situation, that includes a few examples of this language item. For example:

Lazy boyfriend on sofa; girlfriend in doorway.

GIRL: Could you help me, Mike?
BOY: What do you want?
GIRL: Bring me that suitcase, please.
BOY: Oh, I'm too tired!
GIRL: It's too heavy for me to carry.
BOY: (*trying and failing*) And it's too heavy for me, too! What's in it?
GIRL: Your birthday present!

In class

1 Use board pictures (or some other way) to establish the context and the characters very clearly.
2 By using mime, gestures, questions or picture cues, try to elicit from the students each line of the dialogue you have prepared. The aim is to get **them** to produce as much of it as possible.
3 When the students say sentences in response to the eliciting, you need to select a suitable one, correcting it if necessary.
4 You must now establish this line of dialogue (i.e. every student in the class needs to be able to say it and remember it). This will probably be done through

choral and individual drilling and correction; the students are given lots of chances to repeat it, with you helping them to say it fluently and accurately with the best possible pronunciation (especially intonation!). You can help the students remember the dialogue by drawing up simple cue pictures on the board (e.g. a hand trying to pick up the suitcase).★

5 Steps 2, 3 and 4 are repeated for each line.

6 There are also frequent repetitions of the whole dialogue to date (in pairs, perhaps, or by dividing the room into two halves).

★ It's tempting to make Stage 4 easier by writing up the words on the board and reading it out from there. If you do this, the students won't need to think very much. The fun and challenge of the activity is in trying to recall previous words!

Follow-on activities

When the dialogue is complete, follow-on activities could include writing it out, acting it out, continuing it, etc.

Grammar-practice activities and games

Grammar-practice activities are designed to focus on the use of particular items of grammar. The design of the material is such that the students have few opportunities for avoiding working with the target language. Here are some examples:

Split sentences

Write out some sentences using the first conditional for warnings (e.g. *If you touch the dog, it'll bite you!*) and then cut each sentence in half. Hand out these pieces to the students, who have to read out their half and find the matching half amongst the other students.

If you eat that,	you'll be sick.
If you touch the dog,	it'll bite you.
If you steal my boyfriend,	I'll never speak to you again.
If you go out now,	you'll get soaked.
If you don't leave,	I'll call the police.
If you don't book a ticket,	you'll be lucky to get a seat.

Grammar quiz

Run a quiz for two teams. Write a verb infinitive on the board; the first team to put the past participle correctly on the board wins a point. It's not too hard to find variations to make a simple quiz like this more interesting. For example:

- use a noughts and crosses (tic-tac-toe) grid to score on – the team must get three symbols in a row;
- get students to prepare the questions themselves for the other team to answer;
- add in special rules of your own to allow penalties, 'jokers', bonus points, etc.

Memory test

Prepare copies of three pictures showing people doing various things. For example, shopping in a department store; dancing in a nightclub; having a picnic by the river. In class, this material is used as a 'memory test' to work on the present progressive tense (*is/am/are* + *-ing*). Show the first picture to the students for a length of time, and then hide it. Then read out some true/false questions about the picture (e.g. for Figure 12.2, 'The cat is walking past the litter bin', 'The policeman is talking to the shop assistant', etc.). In teams, the students discuss them, then give their answers and are awarded points. At the end, the teams are given a different picture and prepare their own list of ten questions to ask the other team.

Figure 12.2   Memory test

Picture dictation

The material for 'Memory test' above could be used as a picture dictation (you or a student describes the picture while other students, who haven't seen it, try to draw it from the instructions).

Miming an action

Students in turn are given a card with an action on it, which they must mime well enough for the other students to guess. For example, a student mimes swimming and the other students say 'You're swimming in the sea' (present progressive). Depending on your introduction, this could be used to practise a variety of tenses, e.g. 'Show us what you did yesterday'/'You swam in the sea'; 'Show us what you were doing at midday yesterday'/'You were swimming in the sea'. The mimes could also refer to future time. An interesting idea to practise *going to* would be for the student to mime what she would do **before** the actual action, e.g. mime walking down to the beach, putting on swimming costume, getting ready to dive: 'You're going to swim'.

The game works beautifully with adverbs. Prepare two sets of cards: one set with actions, one with adverbs. The students take one card from each pile. They tell the class what the action is, but not what the adverb is. They then do the action in the manner of the adverb. The others, of course, have to guess what the adverb is.

Growing stories

Story-building activities are excellent for work on the past simple. Here are two examples:

1 Start a story by saying one sentence in the past simple tense. The students continue the story by adding one sentence each.
2 Hand out a large set of different magazine photos, which the students, in small groups, look at. Then hand out a pre-written selection of verbs (e.g. *decided, wished, exploded*, etc.). The students match the verbs to pictures of their choice, and then invent a complete sentence including the verb. When a group of students has ten picture/verb matches, they attempt to invent the other details of a complete story, which they prepare orally and tell the rest of the class.

Questionnaires

Turn your current grammar items into a questionnaire. Get students to survey each other. It's usually better if your questionnaire does not contain fully written-out questions. Give them the 'bones' of the questions so that they need to think and make the sentences themselves (e.g. *Where | go | tonight?*). Otherwise it will be you who has had the most challenging language work, and all the students have had to do is read out your work! Even better, get them to write the questionnaire!

Board games

A board game such as the one in Resources 19 and 20 (see Appendix 2) could be used.

3 Clarification

You have reached a point in your lesson where you want the learners really to focus in on a piece of grammar, to see it, think about it and understand it, to become much clearer on its form, meaning and use. This is what many teachers refer to as **clarification** or **presentation**. However, these are quite broad headings; there is a significant difference between a presentation in which I give you a lecture for 60 minutes and one where I nudge and help you towards discovering much of the same information for yourself via a process of questioning and looking at suggested reference material. We could differentiate three general categories within the broad heading of 'clarification':

1 Teacher explanation
2 Guided discovery
3 Self-directed discovery

We can perhaps see these as falling on a continuum (see Figure 12.3):

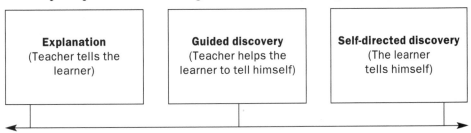

Figure 12.3   Three categories of clarification

Task 166: Grammar clarification activities

Classify the following grammar-clarification activities by placing them on the diagram in Figure 12.3. Are they mainly (E) explanation, (G) guided discovery or (S) self-directed discovery?

1 You write some sentences (all using the past perfect) on the board, but with the words mixed up, then hand the board pen to the students and leave the room.
2 You tell a story about your weekend. Every time you use a verb in the past simple, you repeat it and write it on the board. At the end, you write 'past simple' on the board and explains that you used all these verbs in the past because the story happened last Saturday.
3 You lecture about the construction of conditional sentences.
4 You create a board situation, clarify a specific meaning and then elicit appropriate sentences from the students or models them yourself.
5 You hand out a list of twenty *if* sentences. You ask students to work together, discuss and find out what the 'rules' are.
6 Students discuss interpretation of timelines on the board and try to make example sentences for them. You intervene when answers seem elusive and at one point explain the difference between two tenses.
7 Students decide they want to learn about reported speech. They go to the library or learning centre and find out more.

Commentary ■ ■ ■

Different people will, of course, interpret these short descriptions differently. I'm sure your positioning is not exactly the same as mine, but is the ordering from left to right the same?

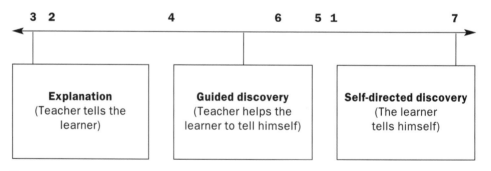

■

1 Self-directed discovery

In this book, we will spend only a little time looking at the right-hand side of the diagram. This is what learners do when studying on their own without a teacher – or in a class where the teacher's role is primarily to 'facilitate' the learner's own self-direction. It is the least commonly found in classrooms. Where you want a class to work mainly in this way, it is essential that learners understand and agree with the working method. You need to ensure that the learners have sufficient information and experience to be able to work out their own rules and explanations, and perhaps work out their own goals and learning strategies as well. The obvious danger here is that you will abdicate your real responsibilities.

2 Explanation

Task 167: Teacher explanations

Most teachers want, at some point, to give their class explanations about language points. Which of the following guidelines seem appropriate to you?

When explaining language …
1 talk at length;
2 talk fast;
3 use language more complicated than the point you are explaining;
4 bring in as many other language issues as possible;
5 don't give examples;
6 don't ask questions;
7 don't use any diagrams or visual aids;
8 assume that the class is following your points – don't waste time checking;
9 always explain every difficulty before students encounter the problem themselves.

Commentary ■ ■ ■

My personal list of guidelines for giving helpful explanations would (you've guessed!) be the opposite of that list – especially 'Keep it short'. ■

Giving helpful explanations

Two minutes of focused explanation can be really helpful; twenty minutes of the same is likely to get students confused, bored and embarrassed. The problem is that it is not necessarily a very involving teaching method; it is easy for a learner to switch off or misunderstand. It can appear successful because there is often an illusion of a large amount of work being covered, but the fact that the teacher has expounded on a particular topic does not mean that the item has been understood or internalised. Remember that they are foreign-language learners, not science undergraduates; lecture is not generally an appropriate style. Explanation will be better as a small component of lessons rather than the driving force. Having said that, a good explanation can often be the clearest and most efficient way to teach something.

The best way to avoid over-long, unhelpful explanations is to prepare them carefully when lesson planning. Decide what information will be necessary to state explicitly. Plan a simple, clear way to convey this information. Plan the use of timelines, substitution tables, annotated examples, diagrams, etc. that might make the information easier to take in.

Point 9 in Task 167 is really a matter of personal choice; teachers often hope to pre-empt learner problems by pointing difficulties out in detail before they arise. Sadly, many learners don't appear to be helped by this! Explanations given **before** learners really know what is being discussed often seem to make no difference. I find that I generally tend to let learners try using language first and give the explanation that clarifies the issue only when they hit problems.

3 Guided discovery

An alternative to giving explanations would be to create activities that allow learners to generate their own discoveries and explanations. Tasks at just the right level will draw attention to interesting language issues. Teacher questions (and use of other techniques) will 'nudge' the learners towards key points. In this way, long explanations can be avoided and learners take a more active role in their own progress.

Your role in guided discovery is to (a) select appropriate tasks; (b) offer appropriate instructions, help, feedback, explanations, etc.; (c) manage and structure the lesson so that all learners are involved and engaged, and draw the most possible from the activity. The key technique is to ask good questions, ones that encourage the learners to notice language and think about it. These questions may be oral (i.e. asked live in class) or they might be on a worksheet that leads learners in a structured way to make conclusions. This kind of guidance is sometimes referred to as 'Socratic questioning', i.e. leading people to discover things that they didn't know they knew via a process of structured questions.

You can:

- ask questions that focus on the meaning (concept questions);
- ask questions that focus on the context (context questions);
- ask questions that focus on the form;
- offer appropriate examples for analysis and discussion;
- ask learners to analyse sentences from texts;
- ask learners to reflect on language they have used;
- ask learners to analyse errors;
- ask learners to hypothesise rules;
- ask learners to undertake research;
- set problems and puzzles concerning the language item;
- offer tools to help clarify meaning, e.g. timelines, substitution tables (but perhaps encouraging the students to use them to solve the problems);
- encourage thorough working out of difficulties;
- guide their process of discovery so that it stays on fruitful lines;
- encourage different students to add their ideas;
- help them to stay focused if they get sidetracked;
- raise their awareness as to what they have learned.

Guided discovery is demanding on both you and the learner, and although it may look artless to a casual observer, it isn't enough to throw a task at the learners, let them do it and then move on. Guided discovery requires imagination and flexibility. Your job here is not simply to pass over a body of information, but rather to create the conditions in which that information can be learned. This seems to be a particularly fruitful way to work in the language classroom.

Task 168: Guided-discovery questions

Study the following brief transcript from a lesson involving guided-discovery techniques and decide what questions the teacher might have asked at the point marked *.

The Elementary students read a text that reviews and compares different dictionaries. The teacher first ensured that learners had a good sense of the general meaning of the text and is now focusing on the use of comparatives (which learners have worked on before) and superlatives (which learners haven't explicitly studied before).

TEACHER: How many dictionaries are mentioned in the article?
STUDENT 1:   Five.
TEACHER: OK. Look at this diagram. What does it show?

STUDENT 2:   How big.
TEACHER: Yes – how big or small the dictionaries are. Where can you put the different dictionaries on this diagram?

The teacher offers chalk/pen to student to add to the diagram; various learners come up and write the names of dictionaries on the diagram, placing them to reflect the writer's comments. As items are added, the teacher asks questions about their decisions, such as *

The teacher then works in a similar manner with diagrams showing *light— heavy, cheap—expensive*, etc.

Commentary ■ ■ ■

The teacher would be likely to ask questions that:
- encourage learners to reflect on and articulate reasons for their choices;
- encourage learners to return to the text and find textual evidence that supports their choice;
- draw learners' attention to the specific language used in the text that leads to this meaning;
- focus on how the language item is formed;
- build on earlier questions and answers to construct a growing picture of the language item;
- ensure that all learners are grasping the issues and not just the faster ones.

Questions might include:
- Why did you put that book in that position on the diagram?
- What does the writer say about that book?
- What were the writer's exact words?
- So, what does *biggest* mean?
- How do you pronounce this word?
- Do *bigger* and *biggest* mean the same?
- What's the difference in meaning between *bigger* and *biggest*?
- Do you know the name for this piece of grammar?
- How do you make a superlative?

Where a question is one that learners do not know the answer to, you can briefly offer the answer yourself. In this way, teacher explanations are only made when they are seen to be relevant and necessary. Later questions can be used to check if learners have grasped this input. ■

Guided discovery: examples of typical comments, instructions and questions

The following list shows various ideas and examples of guided-discovery questions from different lessons.

Questions about form

What word goes in this space?
How many words are there in the sentence?
How do you spell that?
Is that a verb?
What comes after the verb?
What's the name of this tense?

Questions about function

Do they know each other?
Is this formal or informal?
Where do you think they are speaking?
Is this polite?
Why does he say that?
How does he feel?

Problems and puzzles

Put these words in the right order.
Put the missing grammar back in these sentences.
Fill in the spaces.
How many sentences can you make from these words?
Change this into the past simple tense.
Write this sentence again, with exactly the same meaning, but only using seven words.
Rewrite the sentence using this word.
Put the words in the right list under the right heading.

Reflecting on use

Write down some of the sentences you used.
Write down some of the sentences you heard.
Why did you use that tense?
What was the answer?
What was the idea you wanted to express?
Where was the problem?
Which of those two sentences is correct?

Hypothesising rules

Is this possible?
What will the ending be in this example?
Is there a rule?
Why is that incorrect?
Can you think of another word that could go here?
Why is that word not possible in this sentence?'

Sentence analysis

Mark all the prepositions.
Mark the main stress in the sentence.
How many auxiliary verbs are there?
Cross out any unnecessary words.
What would happen if we moved this word to the beginning?
Does the phoneme /ə/ occur in the sentence?

Discussion about language

Which sentence do you prefer?
Why do you like this?
What's difficult for you here?
What might help you remember this?
What mistakes are you likely to make with this?
Is this the same in your language?

Contexts and situations

This is Paul. Where does he work?
Tell me what he does every day.
Jo's got a full diary. What's she doing tonight?
Look at this picture. What's going to happen?
If I throw this pen at the picture on the wall, what'll happen?

4   Present and practise

When you overhear other teachers in the staff room, you'll realise that many think of work in grammar lessons under just two categories: **presentation** and **practice**. The terms have quite wide definitions, and this does sometimes cause confusion between teachers who are actually talking about different things with the same name (or the same thing with different names!).

'Presentation' usually refers to ways of introducing supposedly 'new' language to learners, and typically involves exposure to language (usually in restricted form) alongside other language information via teacher explanation, elicitation and guided discovery. Thus the term 'presentation' tends to refer to a centre-left area of the diagram we saw in the last section:

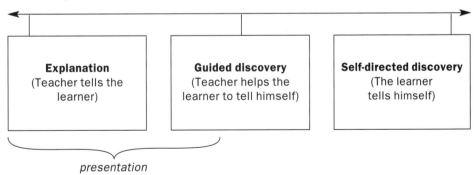

'Practice' involves the stages in which learners get to try using the language themselves (this may be integrated into the presentation stages).

How does this 'present–practise' cycle relate to the image of learning we looked at earlier in the book (see Chapter 6)?

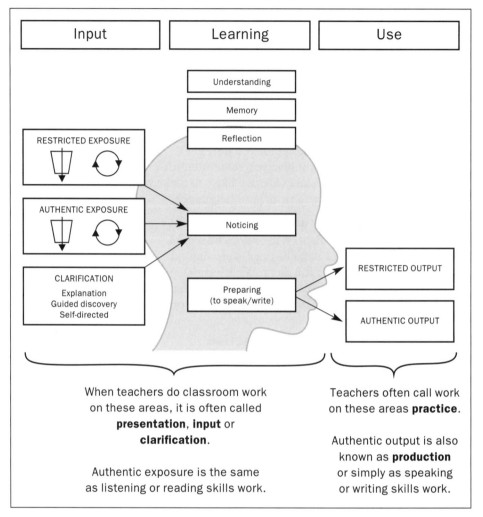

Input	Learning	Use

Understanding

Memory

Reflection

RESTRICTED EXPOSURE

AUTHENTIC EXPOSURE

Noticing

CLARIFICATION
Explanation
Guided discovery
Self-directed

Preparing
(to speak/write)

RESTRICTED OUTPUT

AUTHENTIC OUTPUT

When teachers do classroom work on these areas, it is often called **presentation**, **input** or **clarification**.

Authentic exposure is the same as listening or reading skills work.

Teachers often call work on these areas **practice**.

Authentic output is also known as **production** or simply as speaking or writing skills work.

If we want to plan a well-focused grammar lesson, we need to decide:

- which of these areas we want to spend time on;
- how long we want to give to each one;
- what the best sequence is to have them in.

If there is one basic teaching sequence used around the world with classes of all types it must be 'present then practise'. In other words, the teacher first presents/introduces/explains/clarifies/inputs the language point that the lesson is aiming to work on, and then, when it seems to be reasonably understood, moves on to give learners a chance to practise using the language themselves. Many 'present-practise' lessons are structured as shown at the top of the next page.

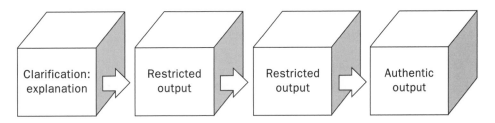

1 **Lead-in:** The teacher shows pictures connected to the lesson topic/context and elicits ideas from students.
2 **Teacher clarification:** The teacher gives/elicits examples of the language and explains/elicits information about them from students.
3 **Restricted output:** The students work on oral practice of examples of these items.
4 **Restricted output:** The students do a written exercise to practise these items.
5 **Authentic output:** The students are given the opportunity to use these items, along with the other language they know, in communicative activities.

At Stage 2, the teacher may use any of the clarification ideas (e.g. explanation) outlined in Section 3 of this chapter.

Many 'present–practise' lessons make use of restricted textual material (e.g. printed in the coursebook or recorded on the coursebook cassette/CD) to provide examples of the target language items being used in context. The lesson structure might then look like this:

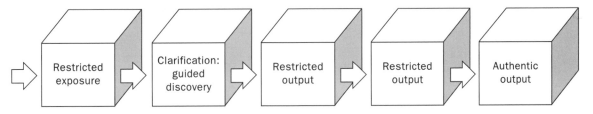

1 **Lead-in:** The teacher shows pictures connected to the lesson topic/context and elicits ideas from learners.
2 **Restricted exposure:** Learners read/listen to a text and get a general understanding of it (maybe via a sequence of tasks and feedback).
3 **Teacher clarification:** The teacher uses the text to give/elicit examples and explain/elicit information about the item of language
4 **Restricted output:** The students work on oral practice of examples of these items.
5 **Restricted output:** The students do a written exercise to practise these items.
6 **Authentic output:** The students are given the opportunity to use these items, along with the other language they know, in communicative activities.

This plan is expanded in more detail in the full-page plan in Figure 12.4.

Using a restricted reading or listening text to improve reading skills and focus on language

Basic principle

You need to tackle core comprehension issues before you can move on to a language focus.

- Stages 1 to 10 are primarily a reading-skills lesson (i.e. the main aim is to improve reading ability).
- Stages 1 to 14 make a lesson that uses reading to focus on grammar or lexis. If your main aim is to teach some lexis or grammar, you will probably do stages 1 to 10 more quickly and in less depth (but you must ensure you do enough comprehension work so that students will understand the material you are working with).

One possible sequence of stages

Lead-in
 1   Introduce topic, discuss pictures, connect to personal situation etc

Restricted exposure
 2   Pre-teach any lexis that you think is necessary or will get in the way if not known.
 3   Pre-reading/pre-listening tasks (e.g. predict story from headlines or from picture).

 4   Feedback.
 5   Simple introductory reading/listening tasks to 'get students into the text'.

 6   Feedback.
 7   More detailed reading/listening tasks.

 8   Feedback.
 9   More difficult reading/listening tasks.

 10   Feedback.

Clarification
 11   Draw attention to specific issues connected to target language area, especially meaning and form (by asking questions about specific parts of the text, focusing on specific lines/ideas, etc.).

Restricted output
 12   Do small practice exercises drawing on material from text. Use the text/recording where possible to check answers.
 13   Summarise what has been learned (as grammar rules, substitution tables, definitions, etc.) if not already done. Record in notebooks, etc.

Authentic output
 14   Extend to other work that offers more chances to use the language (communicative activities, etc.).

Figure 12.4   Full 'present–practise' plan

Of course, many 'present–practise' lessons are more complex than the ones we have looked at so far. In many cases, the stages will not necessarily be clear and distinct. Your use of examples, your explanations and some practice elements may all be integrated, e.g. a cycle of examples, explanations and learner drills all being offered within a few minutes.

Situational presentation

A interesting example of presentation is the popular **situational** presentation, in which language is introduced via a context that the teacher has created (using board drawings, for example). Here is a description of a teacher using a situational presentation to teach *used to*.

Establish the context

1 The teacher draws a picture of a country house and a rich man (holding dollar bills). She asks the students to tell her about him and his life (e.g. 'He's rich', 'He lives in a big house', etc.).
2 She adds more pictures one by one (e.g. champagne, a Rolls Royce, a four-poster bed, a swimming pool) and elicits more statements about his life (e.g. 'He drives a Rolls Royce'). She checks that all students are clear about this context.

Establish the meaning of the target item

3 She adds a picture of an 'interviewer' to the context and establishes that the old man is being interviewed about his past life.

4 She draws a picture of his thoughts about the past (e.g. a 'thought bubble' with a bicycle inside it). She invites the students to make a sentence about this. She taps the board to explicitly link the Rolls Royce (now) and the bicycle (past). She asks concept questions, e.g. 'What's this?' (a bike) 'Does he ride a bike now?' (no) 'Did he ride one in the past?' (yes) 'But not now?' (no) 'Does he ride a bike now?' (no). She has now introduced and focused on the target meaning of *used to* without actually using the target language. Note that the meaning comes first, before the students meet the target form – the students understand the concept being dealt with, and, hopefully, feel the need for a piece of language to express it, before the teacher introduces the target language itself.

Introduce and practise the target language

5 When the 'bike' concept is clear, she asks if students can say the sentence he said to the interviewer, i.e. that has the meaning of 'I rode a bike in the past, but not now'. If a student produces a reasonable sentence, she works with that; if not, she models it herself (e.g. 'He used to ride a bike').

6 She gets students to repeat this round the class (a drill) and corrects any problems, especially taking care that she doesn't only notice incorrect words and word order, but also notices unnatural pronunciation.

Generate more sentences from the context

7 She adds more pictures to the 'interview' (e.g. bottle of water). She elicits further sentences using the target structure (e.g. 'He used to drink water', 'He used to sleep in the street', 'He used to be poor', etc.).

Recording in notebooks

8 She recaps sentences made so far and invites the class to help her construct a substitution table which they can then copy into their notebooks.

Moving on to practice stages

9 Now that the class has met a number of examples of the target language and has had a chance to repeat these sentences, she moves them onto practice activities.

Figure 12.5 gives step-by-step guidelines for giving a classic situational presentation.

Analysis of the language
1 Select the grammar items you wish to teach.
2 Decide how the language is typically used:
   • list situations, contexts;
   • list functions;
   • list typical exchanges.
3 Select one realistic natural target sentence with potential for pattern generalisation.
4 Do a language analysis of:
   • the form (including substitution table);
   • the meaning with concept questions;
   • the pronunciation;
   • typical student problems.
5 Write a main language-learning aim for the lesson (What items do you want learners to take away and be better able to use after the lesson?).

Planning the presentation
6 Choose a realistic, natural, generative context that you could use to teach the item.
7 Decide what previously studied lexis/grammar is needed to elicit/tell this context.
8 Write out exactly the story/dialogue of your situation.
9 Decide how you will get precisely to the point where the target meaning you want arises.
10 Decide when/how you will focus on the target meaning with concept questions.
11 Decide when/how you will elicit/model the form.
12 Write out other sentences generated from the context and initial target sentence.

---

13 Plan how learners will get oral practice within the presentation stage.
14 Decide how students will see the written form.

Stages following initial presentation
15 Decide how students will get restricted oral practice in a follow-on stage.
16 Write out prompts for drills.
17 Decide how students will get more communicative oral practice.
18 Decide how students will get written practice.
19 Write out the procedure as a series of logical steps/stages.
20 Go for it!

Figure 12.5   Twenty steps to a classic situational presentation (planning a grammar lesson using a situational context)

Task 169: Balancing presentation and practice

What should be the balance of practice to presentation?

If your aim is to spend an hour helping learners get better at using a particular piece of grammar (for example, *too* + adjective + *to* + verb – *too heavy to lift*, etc.), which of these two lesson structures seems, in your opinion, likely to be more useful to the learners?

0   **60**

Lead-in	Presentation	Practice

0   **60**

Lead-in	Presentation	Practice

Commentary ■ ■ ■

Many teachers spend most class time on presentation because they see this as the most important thing they can do to help their learners with grammar. They see a language teacher's job as primarily supplying information. Are they right?

I'd say 'no'. For me, a language teacher's job is primarily to push, encourage and help learners to try using the language themselves. In fact, you don't need very much information before you can try using language yourself, and once you start trying to use it, you can get feedback, correction and help on how to do it better. The primary learning experience is doing the thing yourself, not listening to someone else telling you about how to do it. So, I'd argue that students in many classes do not need long explanations or detailed information. What they tend to need more are challenging opportunities to try using the language items themselves.

Thinking about grammar teaching as primarily 'practice' rather than 'presentation' can help to solve a number of problems that teachers feel they face in class, not least the situation where students say 'We have studied this before' or 'We know this already'. ■

Many students think they 'know' certain items; what they actually mean is that information about these items has been presented to them, but the chances are high that, when pushed to use that item, they will make errors. A major problem with many grammar lessons is that they provide too much 'information' and not enough 'expectation' of quality student production. This is not to say that learners don't need the information – they almost certainly need some (and they need it clearly) – but they don't need all of it every time they have a lesson on a certain grammar item. They don't need to always be starting again at Step 1. What makes the lesson challenging is not the level of theoretical knowledge the lesson deals in, but what you ask students to try and do. It's the difference between **up-here knowledge** in the head and **knowledge-in-use**, in other words:

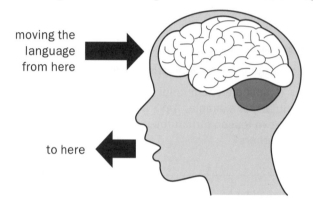

Thus, in theory, it is possible to have a really challenging involving lesson on, say, the present perfect simple, at Advanced level. This is not because you will add more and more complex information, but because you would expect more in terms of quality of student output.

5   Other ways to grammar

The lessons in the previous section were all based on the 'present–practise' structure. But let's look again at some possible 'building brick' components of a lesson (see Chapter 6) so that we can consider alternative lesson shapes.

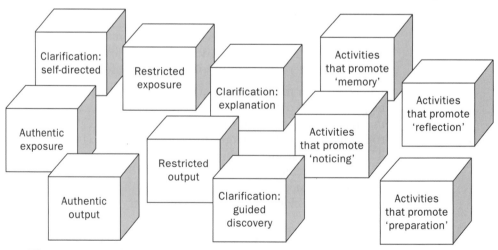

Figure 12.6   Alternative building blocks

If we select and then sequence components that seem important to us, we can construct various significantly different lesson structures.

Test–Teach–Test

What would happen if we 'turned around' the 'present–practice' lesson, and put a practice stage first?

0			60
Lead-in	Practice (restricted output)	Clarification (guided discovery)	Practice (restricted output)

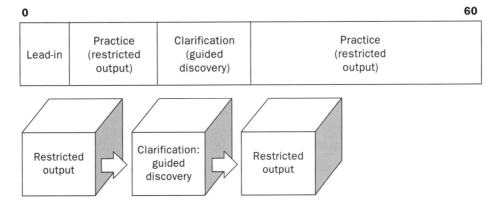

What's happening here? This suggests that we set the learners a task to do that requires them to use language and then, as a result of monitoring them while they work, we offer input, correction, explanation, etc. Here is an example lesson:

1 **Restricted output:** The students work in pairs. Both students are given a separate picture of the same hotel room (which they do not show to their partner). The pictures are identical, except that five familiar objects (e.g. a chair, a bottle, etc.) are in picture A but not in picture B, and a different five objects are in picture B but not in picture A. Students have to describe where the objects are to each other, drawing items when they find out exactly where they are.

2 **Clarification: guided discovery:** When the activity has finished, the teacher asks the students to compare pictures and recall how they described the various locations. Pairs work together for a while, then some are invited to put their answers on the board. She asks the class to decide together which sentences are correct and which not. She encourages the class to discuss and agree together (using reference books if necessary); she directs the discussion so as to get the class thinking and working together, but only offers specific help with the language problems towards the end if problems remain that the class could not solve.

3 **Restricted output:** Learners do a task very similar to the original hotel task, but involving a different location.

It looks as if we are throwing learners in the deep end and finding out what they need to know by first testing what they can use, then teaching those things that revealed problems or were absent but needed, then letting learners try again to use the language (i.e. test–teach–test).

The example we have just looked at involved 'restricted' tasks. A test–teach–test lesson could also set learners a general speaking task without restriction of language; in this case, learners may reveal a much more unpredictable set of errors, problems, etc.

		0		60
Lead-in	Authentic output	Clarification: guided discovery	Authentic output	

This lesson type is much harder to fully plan in advance, as you do not necessarily know what specific language items might come up and require work, information, etc. For this reason, this is a lesson type that teachers tend not to try until they have gained a certain amount of experience and sufficient familiarity with the basics of English grammar and usage.

You may be wondering how either of these lesson structures might be possible. How can learners use language before it has been taught?

When I come to teach many of my students a 'new' grammatical item, I may be surprised to find that they 'half know' it already. With students studying for a period of time on any course that includes skills work (reading, listening, etc.), this effect is even more marked because students have been exposed to a large amount of language on recordings and in texts, and they have often become half-aware of many grammatical patterns. A common example is the present perfect tense: students have often heard and read many examples of this tense before it is actually focused on in class.

From this I can conclude that 'new' grammar is often not completely new for students and they may have met it many times before it is actually 'taught'. Teachers often talk about 'teaching' (or 'presenting') new grammar; what is meant is that it is the first time that they have focused in detail on a particular item in class. And, in fact, it is extremely hard to do such teaching if learners haven't had this kind of exposure. It's almost impossible to learn something the very first time you meet it, but if it has 'drip-fed' into your brain over a period of time, you have a reasonable starting point. For these reasons, giving students chances to be exposed to, or to attempt to use, language 'above' their apparent level of knowledge of grammar is extremely useful and greatly aids future work on grammar. It both celebrates what students can do and clarifies precisely what still needs to be worked on. Maybe we should call these approaches 'exposure–test–teach–test' rather than just 'test–teach–test' for they will only work if learners have been exposed to language.

Task 170: Appropriate teaching strategies for Beginners

Do you think it would be possible to use 'exposure–test–teach–test' approaches with low-level students, say with Beginners?

Commentary ■ ■ ■

There are few people in the world who know nothing of English. Even someone who has studied no English has probably picked up a number of 'international English' expressions and words (*duty free, no smoking, it's the real thing*, etc.). Many adult learners who call themselves beginners have, in fact, studied English at school for two or more years; most of this has been 'forgotten' or is hard to activate through lack of use or lack of confidence. These are the so-called 'false beginners'. By providing listening and reading work at an appropriate level, this stock of half-known language will quickly increase. Provided learners have sufficient exposure, it is certainly possible to use 'exposure–test–teach–test' approaches at low levels. ■

Total Physical Response (TPR)

TPR is, in fact, a whole methodology and has proved to be very successful, especially at low levels. Initially learners are given restricted exposure to a large number of instructions (e.g. 'Walk to the door', 'Pick up Jolanda's pen', etc.). Gestures and demonstrations quickly help learners to understand the meaning, and learners then do what they are asked to.

Lessons continue in this manner for a long time, with increasingly complex instructions and, later, other sentences. Learners are not required to use the language themselves until they want to and feel ready. Many teachers, while not necessarily adopting the whole methodology, retrieve many teaching techniques from it. If you'd like to try out a lesson, look at Resource 21 in Appendix 2 for some sample instructions.

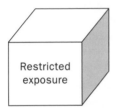

Task-Based Learning (TBL)

TBL is a general term for some more variations on the 'exposure–test–teach–test' lesson structure.

Lessons are centred round a task, i.e. the learners have to do a particular assignment (which will probably have a clear outcome). This task will usually be 'real world' rather than 'language focused' (e.g. 'Plan a birthday party' rather than 'Fill in the gaps in this exercise'). The lesson will often start with the task itself (maybe after some lead-in introducing the theme or topic) and may include other stages such as 'listening to a recording of competent language users doing the same task', 'Learners give a report back on how they did the task' and a 'Preparation of the report' stage.

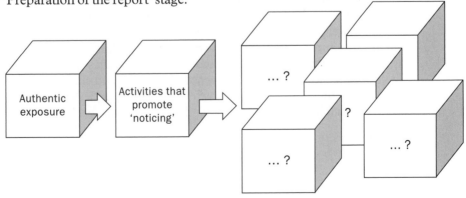

Text starts

In the section on 'present–practise', we saw how restricted texts could be used as a way of providing language exposure. You can do exactly the same with authentic texts, though you may need to take more care planning how you exploit them.

Because these texts have not been specifically designed for language students, they will have neither simplified, controlled language nor lots of specially placed examples of a specific target language item . As with the restricted texts, you will probably need to start out as if it were a normal task-based skills reading or listening lesson, following a sequence of tasks from general to specific so that learners get a reasonable understanding of the text (we could use the same route map as on page 274) before we focus on language points. Note that it's hard to do any useful language work unless the learners have a fair idea of their way around the text.

With an authentic text rather than a restricted one, there may be not be multiple examples of a particular grammatical point to study, and individual language items will probably not 'jump out' in the same way as with a restricted text. This suggests that an authentic text will often be more useful for drawing attention to a range of various language points in action rather than a single target point.

100% exposure

Someone going to live in a country who does not know the language and does not attend classes may learn by 'picking up' the language, i.e. they will receive lots of authentic exposure and will attempt authentic output in return (sometimes with helpful feedback from friends, shopkeepers, etc.). Some teachers believe that the best way to teach language formally may be to reproduce this approach as far as possible in class. A teacher who wanted to work in this way might therefore engage learners in lots of real activity and conversation (making coffee together, walking along the street and looking at shops, etc.) and hope that learners pick up language. Less strict interpretations would allow 'teaching' as well, to give feedback, explanations guidance, etc. A more structured variant would be based on a syllabus where the teacher had chosen a planned sequence of topics and tasks so that lessons had a clear sense of progress and challenge. Whether any of these can be termed 'grammar' lessons is arguable; they are more general 'language' classes.

Authentic exposure

Three more options

Of course, there are many variations on lesson structures, but not all are equally effective. Here are three examples of problematic lessons. Match the correct building block to the lesson descriptions.

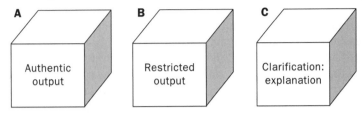

1 The teacher explained at length, and at random, a number of different grammar points until the bell rang.
2 A teacher on a lazy day didn't know what he was doing until he came into the room, opened the coursebook and said 'Do Exercise 1, 2, 3, etc.'.
3 An untrained teacher thought he was being lively and modern by doing a whole series of communicative activities one after the other.

Chapter 13 Phonology: the sound of English

1   Pronunciation ideas

Pronunciation can be an overlooked area of language teaching, partly because teachers themselves may feel more uncertain about it than about grammar or lexis, worried that they don't have enough technical knowledge to help students appropriately. However, when teachers take the risk, they are often surprised to find that it makes for very enjoyable and useful classroom work.

Anyway, no excuses. Here are some ideas that don't require that you or your students know phonemic symbols or any detailed background knowledge of phonology. Try these out and then, when you feel more confident, move on and study the other parts of this chapter.

Model new words in context

When you teach lexical items, give students a chance to hear you saying the item naturally spoken in the context of a typical short phrase or sentence. Take care to stress naturally (rather than as a 'perfect' sentence). Allow students to repeat the phrase and give them honest feedback if there seem to be problems. If necessary, remodel it and let students work out what they are doing differently

Modelling intonation

When you teach grammar, allow students to hear some typical examples of natural uses of the language. So, for example, when teaching present perfect progressive, don't just teach it as dry examples, but model a typical real-life sentence or two yourself with real feeling, such as 'I've been waiting here for two hours!'. A loud, angry sentence like this will be much more memorable than a written example. Get students to repeat it to each other – and don't let them get away with flat, dull intonation. Encourage them to say it with real feeling.

Recognise the feeling

Write up four or five short spoken phrases on the left of the board (e.g. 'Where are you going?' 'Yes, please.'). Write up a number of 'moods' on the right (e.g. 'angry', 'delighted', 'sarcastic'). Read out one of the phrases in one of the moods (adapting your intonation and stress to transmit a clear feeling). Ask students to compare ideas with each other and decide which was used. Later, learners can continue playing the game in small groups.

Use dialogues

When you work with printed dialogues, don't just read them silently, but get students to spend time thinking about how to say them. A useful task is to ask them to go through the text deciding and marking which syllables are stressed. After that, students can practise them, read them out and eventually perform them without scripts. The aim is to speak naturally – which is hard to do when you are reading from text, so it's important to include some textless work. Don't worry about students learning it word-perfectly; give feedback on whether they get the feeling right or not, rather than whether they get the grammar spot-on.

Chants

A 'chant' is a poem or dialogue particularly suitable for reciting aloud; it often involves strong rhythms, clear everyday conversation, often exaggerated feelings and a lot of repetition. Use published chants specially written for language students, or write your own. Aim to help students to learn them by heart so that they can say them confidently with suitable pronunciation. Teach them by modelling them line by line and asking students to repeat them. If you offer dull flat intonation yourself – or if students respond with dull flat intonation – there is little purpose in the activity. You might want to go for the enjoyment of exaggerating the feelings and volume!

In Resource 22 (Appendix 2), you'll find a sample short chant for two people (or two groups) practising *Wh-* questions. It provides opportunities to practise weak forms, elision and assimilation (if you want to).

Shadow reading

This means reading at the same time along with a competent reader. So, for example, you read a dialogue out loud, playing all parts, while the students follow the text and read aloud themselves. This is likely to be most useful if it is done more than once, so that students get a chance to improve; try short texts read a number of times rather than one long text read once. As an alternative, you could try using a recording.

Voice settings

One interesting approach to pronunciation may sound a little odd at first. It's based on the idea that, rather than work on all the small details of pronunciation (such as phonemes, stress patterns, etc.), it might be better to start with the larger holistic picture – the general 'settings' of the voice. If you think about a foreign language you have heard a number of times, you are probably able to quickly recall some distinctive impressions about how the language is spoken – the sorts of things that a comedian would pick on if they wanted to mimic a speaker of that language; for example, a distinctive mouth position with the lips pushed forward, a flat intonation with machine-gun delivery, a typical hunching of shoulders, frequently heard sounds, a generally high pitch, etc.

Do your students have such an image about British speakers of English? Or Australians? Or Canadians? One useful activity would be to (a) watch one or more native speakers on video; (b) discuss any noticeable speech features; (c) try speaking nonsense words using this 'voice setting' ('comedian' style); (d) practise reading a simple short dialogue in as 'native' a way as they can. (This will probably seem quite funny to your students, who will initially tend to do fairly bland copies, never quite believing that a voice setting may be so different or exaggerated compared with their own language; encourage them to risk looking and sounding really like a native speaker.)

2   Which pronunciation?

Before we go much further with pronunciation, there is one important question a teacher needs to consider, namely which pronunciation variety are you going to teach?

Task 171: RP

The abbreviation 'RP' refers to **received pronunciation**, a UK pronunciation variety, originally from south-east England, but sometimes regarded as a kind of standard educated British English pronunciation. UK-published coursebooks have mainly (but not exclusively) offered RP on their recordings.

When teaching pronunciation, do you want your students to aim to approach an RP accent themselves? Why? Why not?

Commentary ■ ■ ■

There used to be a fairly widespread (if unspoken) assumption in many teaching contexts that all students wanted and needed to learn to communicate in a way that sounded as close to a UK (or US or Australian) native speaker as possible. In fact, most learners are learning English to communicate with other non-mother-tongue speakers, using English as a **lingua franca** (a language used to communicate between speakers of different mother tongues), and many will rarely – if ever – meet or need to speak with an RP-speaking native speaker. In such cases, we could make a good argument that RP is not the most useful variety for students to learn, and it may actually hinder their communication, as many people may not be able to follow them if they use RP features such as elisions, weak forms and the lack of an /r/ sound in words like *car* or *hard*. Some of these issues are addressed in the section on World English in Chapter 6, Section 10. ■

Starting points for pronunciation

Whatever the political arguments, I think it is very hard to teach an accent that is not one you can naturally use yourself. So, for the moment, the work on pronunciation is this book is based on the following starting points:

- Students need to learn pronunciation that will allow them to be understood in the contexts where they are most likely to need to use the language.
- It is often appropriate and honest to (a) teach the pronunciation you speak yourself; (b) draw attention to local variations you are aware of; (c) highlight differences in accent that appear in course material.

The activities and examples on the next few pages are based on using RP as a basic pronunciation. This is mainly because this is what is found in the majority of current international coursebooks (and because it happens to be my own pronunciation variety). You need to consider how much the advice and sample materials may need to be adapted for your own teaching needs. As you read through the following sections, here are four questions to consider:

- Are the phonemes discussed in this book the same as the ones you use?
- Which other features discussed are **not** part of your own pronunciation?
- Is it appropriate for your students to practise recognising features such as weak forms and elision?
- Is it appropriate for your students to practise producing features such as weak forms and elision?

3 Sounds

Task 172: Phonemes

The phonemic chart in Figure 13.1 shows the individual sounds (phonemes) of the English language as spoken in a UK RP accent. Referring to a dictionary that uses the IPA (international phonetic alphabet), find out which phoneme is represented by the letters underlined in the following words. (Answers are on page 296.)

Vowels
schools
autonomy
participation
co-operation
valuing
trust
in
learners
respect
the*
good
teachers

Diphthongs
air
joy
hopeful
great
bright
pure
clear
sounds

Consonants
washing machine
yeast
potatoes
beans
knives
sink
herbs**
tomatoes
brotherliness
foresight
vision
bread
cheese
friendliness
sensitivity
jam
cake
eggs
empathy
fridge
food mixer
kettle
wisdom
compassion

* Be careful: how does this sound in a normally spoken sentence?
** UK pronunciation

iː	ɪ	ʊ	uː	ɪə	eɪ	
e	ə	ɜː	ɔː	ʊə	ɔɪ	əʊ
æ	ʌ	ɑː	ɒ	eə	aɪ	aʊ
p	b	t	d	tʃ	dʒ	k	g
f	v	θ	ð	s	z	ʃ	ʒ
m	n	ŋ	h	l	r	w	j

Figure 13.1   Phonemic chart

Students of most other foreign languages will find that, while a number of English phonemes are familiar, some will be distinctly different from ones they use. Particular problems arise when:

- English has two phonemes for a sound that seems, to an untrained ear, to be a single sound. A common example of this is the distinction between /ɪ/ and /iː/ (as in *hip* vs. *heap*), which sound the same to some students;
- English has a phoneme that does not exist in the students' own language.

In both cases, getting students to produce the sounds themselves can be difficult; it is necessary to raise their awareness of the fact that there is something to work on, and the first step is to get them to hear the difference. Receptive awareness comes before productive competence.

Simple variations on well-known games are helpful in familiarising students with phonemic symbols:

- **Phoneme bingo:** Hand out bingo cards with phonemes instead of numbers; call out sounds rather than numbers (Resource 23 in Appendix 2).
- **Anagrams:** Get students to work out anagrams of words using phonemes rather than normal alphabetic letters, e.g. /kbʊ/ (= *book*).
- **Category words:** Choose five or six categories – such as 'Food', 'Sports', 'Animals', 'Household objects', 'Clothing', etc. – which students should copy down. Students work in small teams. When you call out (and write up) a phoneme, the teams must attempt to find a word containing that phoneme for each category. So, for example, if the phoneme is /iː/, a team could choose *cheese, skiing, sheep, teapot* and *jeans*. The teams then compare words and points are awarded.

And here are some general ideas for working with phonemes:

- Integrate phonemic work into all your teaching of grammar and lexis. Always work on helping the students to achieve good pronunciation, and encourage them to make a record of the phonemic transcription as well as the spelling of new items.
- Observation of mechanics: let students watch how you and they make particular sounds.
- Ear-training: get students to listen to and distinguish words which have sounds that seem to them very similar (e.g. *hat* vs. *hut; thin* vs. *tin*; examples of this kind are known as **minimal pairs**).
- Tongue twisters, to work on particular sounds or to contrast sounds (e.g. *Three thin trees and three tall trees*).
- Transliteration: get students to write out a word or sentence in phonemic script. Jokes seem to work well.
- Train learners in using a dictionary to find pronunciation as well as spelling.
- Keep a phonemic chart on the wall of your classroom. Focus briefly on one phoneme each lesson.
- Tap out words on the chart and ask students to say the words.
- Use the chart for pointing out correct sounds when students pronounce something wrong.
- Try a phonemic crossword like the one in Task 173.

Task 173: Phonemic crossword

1		2		3		4
		5				
6				7		

Across

1 Past of 1 Down.
3 Some teachers do this too much!
5 Soldiers work for this organisation.
6 Past of 7 Across
7 '_____ here!'

Down

1 '_____ your time!'
2 No movement; still.
3 A clock makes this noise.
4 You use this to make your hair tidy.

For the answers, see page 297.

4   Word stress

Stress and its opposite – unstress – are very important aspects of English pronunciation. Getting the stress wrong can seriously damage your chances of being understood.

Words have their own stress pattern; for example, *water*, *cricket* and *justice* are stressed on the first syllable. A stressed syllable in a word is usually noticeable by being slightly louder, longer and higher in pitch than the syllables next to it.

Task 174: Stress and unstress

Unstressed syllables tend to be pronounced less loudly and with a more 'relaxed' manner; vowel sounds are typically 'weak'. Check this out: try saying the words *water* and *justice* with the stress on the wrong syllable. What happens to the previously stressed syllables?

Commentary ■ ■ ■

The unstressed syllables become weaker, i.e. shorter, spoken more quickly and with less well-defined (or even altered sounds), e.g. /wɒˈtɜː/, /dʒəsˈtiːs/. ■

Task 175: Marking stress

There are a variety of ways of marking stress in a written text. Which of the following do you personally find clearest?

for<u>ma</u>tion   'window   unhappy   impostor

magaZINE   ca⟨ssette⟩   **wat**erfall   de^light_ful

Task 176: Finding stressed syllables

Mark the stressed syllable in the following words using the method you chose in Task 175.

photograph   photographer   telescope   telescopic   chemical
computer   forest   dictionary   comfortable   reception

For the answers, see page 297.

Word stress is important because when it is wrong, words sound very strange or even incomprehensible. Would anyone understand you saying *sec<u>re</u>tary*? Sometimes wrong stress changes one word into another: *desert*–*des<u>sert</u>*.

Task 177: Sorting stress patterns

Put the words into the correct columns.

□ □ □	□ □ □

interview   computer   revision
innocent   completely   important
suitable   example   recorder
universe   opposite

For the answers, see page 297.

The kinds of tasks given in this section are also very useful for your students to work with. As with work on the sounds of English, awareness itself is an essential starting point, and it is worth devising tasks and activities that assist this.

5 Prominence

Although individual words have their own stress, stress is also an important feature of sentences, when it is known as **prominence** or, less accurately, **sentence stress**. Rather than considering sentences, we analyse utterances in terms of **tone units**, i.e. sections of speech with one main stress. The main stress is known as the **tonic syllable** (or **nucleus**); there may also be one or more **secondary stresses**. Changes in prominence make substantial differences to meaning.

Task 178: Intonation and meaning

In the following sentence, did the speaker go to Paris? (Warning! Think carefully!)

'I didn't go to Paris because of the food.'

Commentary ■ ■ ■

Based on the information we have, we can't say what the answer is. We need to hear the sentence spoken to know how many tone units are used. If the sentence is said as two tone units (i.e. almost as two separate statements) – 'I didn't go to Paris … … because of the <u>food</u>' – we learn that the speaker (a) didn't go to Paris; and (b) the reason was that the speaker had some problem with the food.

However, if the same text is said as a single tone unit – 'I didn't go to Paris because of the <u>food</u> …' – we understand that the speaker did go to Paris, but the reason for going was something other than the food. Practise saying both of these until you are happy that you can recognise the two separate versions. ■

Task 179: Stress and meaning

Mark possible positions for main and secondary stresses on the following sentence:

Caroline was going to leave for Africa on Tuesday.

For the answers, see page 297.

Stress typically marks out the content-carrying words in the sentence; thus it mostly affects nouns, verbs and adjectives. The content word that carries the main meaning of the sentence is usually the one you are going to stress.

Task 180: Effects of changing stress

Consider the effect that changing stress has on the meaning of a single sentence. Finish the explanatory notes in the same way as the first example.

1 Michael wanted to buy the red **shirt**.   (not the red jumper)
2 Michael wanted to **buy** the red shirt.   (not …
3 **Mich**ael wanted to buy the red shirt.   (not …
4 Michael wanted to buy the **red** shirt.   (not …
5 Michael **want**ed to buy the red shirt.   (but …

For the answers, see page 297.

We can demonstrate patterns of prominence either on the board or by using Cuisenaire rods or tapping, clapping, humming the rhythm, etc. By getting the students to work out the patterns themselves, we can help to make them more aware of the importance of stress. Poetry and songs are good for focusing on stress. Shadow reading (reading simultaneously with a recording, trying to keep up with the speed and follow the rhythm) is a useful language laboratory or classroom activity.

6   Connected speech

Weak forms

One important effect of prominence is to mark out a rhythm. There is also a dramatic effect on unstressed words in a sentence. Note, for example, the difference between the pronunciation of *for* when said on its own compared with how it appears in a normal sentence, e.g. *for* /fɔː/ vs. *What do you want for tea?* /fə/ or possibly just /f/.

Unstressed words tend to be pronounced quite fast, almost as if trying to cram themselves into the spaces between the beats of the rhythm (a common feature of student English is a failure to do this – giving each word in the sentence equal time in the rhythm). They also tend to be pronounced in a 'weak' manner; they typically have shorter vowel sounds: /ʊ/ rather than /uː/ and /ɪ/ rather /iː/, etc. This use of weak forms is one of the features of connected speech that makes listening comprehension more difficult for students. If you are expecting to hear *to* pronounced as /tuː/ or *was* pronounced as /wɒz/, then you are less likely to recognise the words when you hear /tə/ or /wəz/.

The schwa

The most common weak form vowel sound (and thus the most common sound in the English language) is /ə/. It is also the only sound to be given its own name – the **schwa**. If your learners are anything like mine, they will take a lot of convincing that words are really pronounced with schwa weak forms in natural English; they may feel that using 'full' vowel sounds must be 'correct' English.

Because the schwa is a short and unassertive sound, there is a danger that in focusing on it in classroom sentences, it might lose its naturally weak character. Here are some awareness-raising and practice ideas.

De-schwaed texts

Prepare a short text (three or four lines long). Wherever a schwa would be said in a word, insert a gap line instead of the vowel(s). Leave all other vowels as they are. In class, give out the text and explain what you have done. Learners must now go through the text and work out the missing written vowels. This will raise awareness about the many ways that the schwa sound can be spelt in English.

Stress and unstress

This would follow on well from the previous activity. Hand out a short text and ask learners to go through and mark every syllable that would probably be stressed, e.g. *When did you come to this college?* They then practise reading it to each other, but reading only the stressed syllables, e.g. 'When … come … coll … ?' This will obviously sound odd, but encourage them to really emphasise these syllables and find a sense of rhythm in saying them. The next task is to keep that stress and rhythm, but to insert the other syllables in the spaces between stresses without slowing down too much! This can help learners to get a sense of the important structuring and timing effect that stress has in English; it also encourages them to keep weak syllables weak.

Count the words

Record yourself saying between six and ten naturally pronounced sentences at a fast, natural speed, e.g. 'Are you going to give her that present for her birthday?' Record rather than read out in class, because you want to offer a consistent pronunciation when you replay it. Take special care not to overpronounce (i.e. not making weak syllables strong). Ask students to listen and count how many words are in each sentence. They will tend to miss the weak syllables. Replay a few times and encourage students to discuss and agree, maybe 'reconstructing' missing words by thinking about the surrounding language.

Learn a limerick

Poems are a good way to pull together some of these ideas. Teach a short poem line by line, modelling it and getting students to repeat it. Make sure rhythm and stress are accurate. When it's really well learned, hand out the text and ask students to mark it first with stresses, then with schwas. Here's a silly limerick that you might be able to make use of:

A curvaceous young phoneme called schwa
Said 'I never feel strong. It's bizarre!
I'm retiring and meek
And I always sound weak
But in frequency counts – I'm the star!'

Task 181: Marking schwas

At random, choose a sentence from anywhere in this book. Mark every schwa in it.

What do I actually say?

One important consideration in teaching is to make sure that, as a teacher, you offer realistic language samples to your students. So, for example, when you are presenting some grammatical point, it's necessary to think about how it's said, as well as about more familiar issues such as grammatical features.

Task 182: Transcribing pronunciation

Consider the following sentence: *What are you going to do about it?* Imagine that you want to say this sentence for your students to hear as an example sentence. Is the following transcription an appropriate model to offer?

/wɒt ɑː(r) juː ˈɡəʊɪŋ tuː duː əˈbaʊt ɪt/

Commentary ■ ■ ■

Well, if you looked up each word, one by one, in the dictionary, you might well come up with something like this. These are all possible pronunciations of the words if said clearly, distinctly and individually. Such forms are known as **citation forms**. But when words come together, something else happens. Connected speech is more than a string of the separate individual pronunciations. ■

Task 183: Connected speech

It's quite hard to catch oneself saying language naturally; as soon as you start observing, it changes how you say things! But all the same, try saying the same sentence as if it's in the middle of a conversation; maybe even say a few sentences before it. Speak at a natural speed and without any attempt to speak 'properly' (whatever that means). Can you detect any distinct differences between the transcription above and how you say it?

Commentary ■ ■ ■

In connected speech, the following things tend to happen:

- Unstressed syllables tend to have weak vowel sounds /ə/ or /ɪ/.
- Sounds get dropped (this is known as **elision**).
- Sounds get changed (this is known as **assimilation**).
- There may be additional sounds (**linking** or **intrusive** sounds) for bridging the space between words. ■

Analysing connected speech

In the sentence we have been looking at, I think I might say it naturally as:

/ˈwɒtʃə gənə ˈdʊwəbaʊdɪ/

Where has the /t/ in /ɪt/ gone? It has been lost (**elided**).
Where has the /t/ in /əˈbaʊt/ gone? It has changed (**assimilated**) into /d/.

This is a realistic, if relatively 'fluent', pronunciation of the sentence. It reflects the fact that my speech is British English. Your students probably need to be able to recognise and understand such sentences, even if you don't want them to produce language like this. In fact, it's worth remembering that one of the main problems learners have with listening to English is that they can't recognise pronunciations that are entirely different from what they are expecting. For example, if a student expects to hear /wɒt ɑː(r) juː/ but instead hears /ˈwɒtʃə/, they may well not register at all that it represents the same words. So a key point to remember is that it's vital to teach pronunciation – not just for the students' own speech production, but to help them listen better.

But what is a realistic language model to expect students to produce? The very 'fluent' model I use? The sentence based on 'citation' forms? This is a decision for the individual teacher, but I think it's reasonable to offer students something as close as possible to your own spoken pronunciation – the language you actually speak yourself. And in most cases, this will have at least some of the fluency features I've mentioned.

I can't see much point in getting students to repeat the citation-form versions of a sentence, though a surprisingly high number of teachers do, sometimes believing it to be a 'good', 'correct' or 'perfect' version of English. It's not. Even people who argue forcefully that they are 'certain' that they don't say /tə/ or /wəz/ or /ˈgənə/ almost certainly do say them. In many varieties of spoken English, it is normal to use weak forms, elision and assimilation, because it make sentences much easier to say.

As a teacher, you probably need to offer realistic (but not extreme) fluent samples:

/ˈwɒt ə jə gəʊɪŋ tə ˈduː əbaʊt ɪt/

This occupies a 'fluency place' on the continuum between the extremes of the unnatural-sounding citation form and the very rapid, reduced speech you might hear in some social contexts.

Citation form	/wɒt ɑː(r) juː ˈɡəʊɪŋ tuː duː əˈbaʊt ɪt/
Fluent	/ˈwɒt ə jə ɡəʊɪŋ tə ˈduː wəbaʊt ɪt/
	/ˈwɒtʃə ɡənə ˈduwəbaʊdɪ/
Very rapid	/ˈtʃə ɡə ˈdʊ baʊdɪ/

Task 184: Finding a linking sound

Find an example of a linking sound in the table above.

Commentary ■ ■ ■

The extra sound /w/ links the words *do* and *about*. ■

Task 185: Analysing connected speech

Practise analysing more sentences in this way, working out the citation forms and a continuum of fluency.

- Have you got your keys?
- She was very famous a year or two back.
- We won't play the tape to all of you.

Intonation

Intonation is sometimes referred to as the 'music' of the language, and we use it as a kind of oral equivalent of written punctuation. It is closely connected to prominence, for the main movement of intonation begins at the tonic syllable. This movement can be upwards (a **rise**), downwards (a **fall**), a rise with a fall (a **rise-fall**), a fall with a rise (a **fall-rise**) or flat. Intonation has a definite effect on meaning and also gives us information about the speaker's attitude.

It is hard to teach intonation systematically because, although there are some common patterns, there are few clear rules, and many people with an 'unmusical' ear find it hard to recognise or categorise intonation patterns. It is, however, so important that it is essential to include work on intonation in most courses. Many learners speak English with a flat intonation, which can sound boring, bored or uninterested. Using wrong intonation can also give offence.

Some ideas for working on intonation:

- Work with a function grid (Resource 17, Appendix 2).
- Get students to mark intonation patterns on dialogues. (How can you mark them? Arrows? Lines? Music? Write the words in a wiggly way to reflect the movement?)
- Get students to say the same single word (e.g. *hello*) with different intonation to convey completely different meanings.
- Use these differences to prepare and practise some one-word conversations, e.g.
  A: Cinema?
  B: No.
  A: Tomorrow?
  B: Maybe.
- Hum/whistle/sing the sentence without words before you say it.
- Indicate intonation with hand gestures, waves, etc.

- Exaggerate intonation (this can be very funny).
- Exaggerate lack of intonation.
- Encourage students to 'feel' the emotion as they speak. Emotions of anger, interest, surprise, boredom, etc. can naturally power the intonation.

Task 186: Intonation

Add the words *fall* or *rise* to the following guidelines:

1 *Wh-* questions (*Where, Who, What*, etc.) usually …
2 Questions that are answered *yes/no* usually …
3 Orders usually …

For the answers, see page 297.

Answers to tasks

Task 172 (page 287)

Correspondence is as follows:

/iː/	teachers		/p/	potatoes
/ɪ/	in		/b/	beans
/ʊ/	good		/t/	tomatoes
/uː/	schools		/d/	bread
/e/	respect		/k/	cake
/ə/	the		/g/	eggs
/ɜː/	learners		/tʃ/	cheese
/ɔː/	autonomy		/dʒ/	jam
/æ/	valuing		/f/	friendliness
/ʌ/	trust		/v/	sensitivity
/ɑː/	participation		/θ/	empathy
/ɒ/	co-operation		/ð/	brotherliness
			/s/	foresight
/ɪə/	clear		/z/	wisdom
/ʊə/	pure		/ʃ/	compassion
/eə/	air		/ʒ/	vision
/eɪ/	great		/h/	herbs
/ɔɪ/	joy		/m/	food mixer
/aɪ/	bright		/n/	knives
/əʊ/	hopeful		/ŋ/	sink
/aʊ/	sounds		/w/	washing machine
			/l/	kettle
			/r/	fridge
			/j/	yeast

Vowels

You'll have noticed that the words come together to make a complete sentence (*Teachers in good schools respect the learners' autonomy, valuing trust, participation, co-operation*). You may find a mnemonic of some kind helpful while you are learning the phonemes. Your students might also like this idea: you could write a simple story for them (e.g. *'Eat this good food,' said the bird* …) or, better still, get them to devise their own sentences. You could also attempt more 'poetic' versions, as with the diphthongs.

Diphthongs

These form three phrases: *clear pure air, great joy, bright hopeful sounds.*

Consonants

These fall into three sets:

1 Food: *potatoes, beans, tomatoes, bread, cake, eggs, cheese, jam*
2 Positive human characteristics: *friendliness, sensitivity, empathy, brotherliness, foresight, wisdom, compassion, vision*
3 Words associated with kitchens: *food mixer, knives, sink, herbs, kettle, fridge, washing machine, yeast*

Alternatively, devise sequences that make use of any current lexical items being studied.

Task 173 (page 289)

Across	Down
1 /tʊk/	1 /teɪk/
3 /tɔːk/	2 /kɑːm/
5 /ɑːmɪ/	3 /tɪk/
6 /keɪm/	4 /kəʊm/
7 /kʌm/	

Task 176 (page 290)

photograph pho**tog**rapher **tele**scope teles**cop**ic **chem**ical
com**pu**ter **for**est **dic**tionary **com**fortable recep**tion**

Task 177 (page 290)

□ ▢ □	▢ □ ▢
interview	computer
innocent	revision
suitable	completely
universe	important
opposite	example
	recorder

Task 179 (page 291)

The following pattern seems most likely (though other answers are possible).

<u>Ca</u>roline was <u>go</u>ing to leave for <u>A</u>frica on <u>Tues</u>day.

Task 180 (page 291)

2 not steal it/borrow it, etc.
3 not Fred/Jane/Susan, etc.
4 not the green one/blue one, etc.
5 but he didn't.

Task 186 (page 296)

1 fall   2 rise   3 fall

Chapter 14 Toolkit 2: focusing on language

1 Errors and correction

Task 187: Student errors

Which of these two sentences do you most agree with?

- Student errors are evidence that learning has not taken place.
- Student errors are evidence that learning is taking place.

Commentary ■ ■ ■

In most things, humans largely learn by trial and error, experimenting to see what works and what doesn't. It is the same with language learning

Student errors are evidence that progress is being made. Errors often show us that a student is experimenting with language, trying out ideas, taking risks, attempting to communicate, making progress. Analysing what errors have been made clarifies exactly which level the student has reached and helps set the syllabus for future language work. ■

In dealing with errors, teachers have looked for correction techniques that, rather than simply giving students the answer on a plate, help them to make their own corrections. This may raise their own awareness about the language they are using: 'What you tell me, I forget; what I discover for myself, I remember.'

Task 188: Different kinds of errors

Errors can be of many kinds. Match the errors in the following list with their descriptions.

Errors	Descriptions
1 Alice like this school.	a pronunciation (/ɪ/ vs. /iː/)
2 Where you did go yesterday?	b pronunciation (/ʃ/ vs. /tʃ/)
3 The sec<u>re</u>tary is in the office.	c pronunciation (word stress)
4 Give me one butterbread!	d grammar (wrong tense)
5 I eat shocolate every day.	e lexis (incorrect collocation)
6 After three years they made a divorce.	f grammar (verb-noun agreement)
7 I am here since Tuesday.	g grammar (word order)
8 I'm going to heat you.	h lexis (incorrect word) – and rude!

Commentary ■ ■ ■

Answers: 1 f 2 g 3 c 4 h 5 b 6 e 7 d 8 a ■

Sometimes language can be grammatically correct but completely inappropriate in the context in which it is used. Errors can also be made in intonation and rhythm; in fact, wrong intonation seems to cause more unintended offence to native speakers than almost any other kind of error.

Five teacher decisions have to be made when working with oral errors in class:

1 **What kind of error** has been made (grammatical? pronunciation? etc.).
2 **Whether to deal with it** (is it useful to correct it?).
3 **When to deal with it** (now? end of activity? later?).
4 **Who will correct** (teacher? student self-correction? other students?).
5 **Which technique** to use to indicate that an error has occurred or to enable correction.

Decisions 2, 3, 4 and 5 are discussed in detail below.

Task 189: Criteria for on-the-spot correction

Look back at decision 2 in the box above. What are your criteria for whether to give on-the-spot immediate correction or not?

Commentary ■ ■ ■

An important consideration here is the aim of the activity. Is it to improve learners' accurate use of English? If this is the case, then correction may be helpful. However, if the activity is aiming to encourage fluency, interruptions and corrections might get in the way of the work. ■

When to correct

There are other factors to take into account when deciding if a correction should be made: Will it help or hinder learning? Am I correcting something they don't know? (If so, there doesn't seem much point.) How will the student take the correction? What is my intention in correcting?

Decision 3 is about **when** to correct. The options include: immediately; after a few minutes; at the end of the activity; later in the lesson; at the end of the lesson; in the next lesson; later in the course; never. The distinction between accuracy and fluency aims is again important here (there's more on this in Chapter 7, Section 4) . If the objective is accuracy, then immediate correction is likely to be useful; if the aim is fluency, then lengthy, immediate correction that diverts from the flow of speaking is less appropriate. We either need to correct briefly and unobtrusively as we go (see *Scaffolding* below) or save any correction for after the activity has finished or later.

Main objective of speaking activity	When to correct
accuracy	focused immediate correction *or* later *or* not at all
fluency	later *or* brief, unobtrusive, immediate correction (**scaffolding**) *or* not at all

One strategy used by many teachers during fluency activities is to listen in discreetly and collect a list of overheard errors. Later on, you can use this list to provide sentences to discuss, to set an exercise, to plan the next lesson, etc.

For more on the correction of written work, see Chapter 9, Section 3.

Decision 4 concerns **who** corrects.

self-correction

student–student

teacher–student

small group

all class

coursebook/
reference books

Decision 5 concerns techniques to indicate that an error has been made or to give or invite correction. The following two steps can be used to encourage student self-correction or student–student correction:

1 Indicate that an error has been made. You may also indicate what kind of error it is, where in a sentence the error is, etc.
2 Invite correction or help the student towards a correction.

Task 190: Indicating that an error has been made

How could you indicate that an error has been made? How can you show what kind of error it is, where in a sentence it is, etc.?

Commentary ■ ■ ■

Some ideas for indicating/correcting errors:

• Tell students that there is an error (e.g. 'There's an error in that sentence').
• Use facial expression: surprise, frown, raised eyebrows, interest, etc.
• Use a gesture combined with a facial expression (e.g. worried look and hand outstretched to 'hold' the sentence – you won't let the class move on until they deal with the sentence you are 'holding').

- Use finger correction (hold on to the 'error' finger, e.g. the third word) (see page 321).
- Repeat sentence up to error (e.g. 'They looked for a ...?').
- Echo sentence with changed intonation or stress (e.g. 'You *go* to a disco yesterday?' or 'He wanted to eat a *kitchen*?'). Note that this is a use of echo with a clear purpose; it's rather different from the unaware echo described in *How to prevent learning* (see page 105).
- Ask a question (e.g. 'Was this last week?') (see pages 219–220).
- Ask a one-word question (e.g. 'Tense?' 'Past?').
- Draw a timeline on the board (see page 319).
- Draw spaces or boxes on the board to show the number of words in a sentence. Indicate which word is the problem, e.g. *He __ __ ? __ __* .
- Write the problem sentence on board for discussion.
- Exploit the humour in the error (e.g. Student 1: 'The doctor gave her a recipe.' Teacher: 'So she made a nice cake?' Student 1: 'Oh, not the right word?' Student 2: 'Prescription.') Be careful, though: this technique is often more amusing for the teacher than for the students!
- Use the phonemic chart to point at an incorrect phoneme (see page 287). ■

There is one important student–student correction technique worth looking at in detail, the 'chain'. If student A makes an error, elicit a correction from student B. If she also fails to get it right, then get another student to help her. This is where the chain comes in: C corrects B, and only when B has got the idea does B then correct A's error. A then gives the correct answer back to you. The effect of this is to involve many people in thinking about the problem and finding a solution; done effectively, the errors and their corrections can be passed around the class like a ball of string unwinding, tying together a network of enquiry and support.

There is one correction technique that I haven't really acknowledged yet: say the corrected sentence yourself. Sometimes this may be the quickest, most appropriate, most useful way of helping. I left it until last, because I suspect that it might be the one you thought of first and I wanted to show you a few other ideas!

Task 191: Responding to errors

Read the following examples of learner errors and decide on an efficient way of indicating what is wrong or correcting it.

1 *I am boring with this lesson!*
2 *I enjoy to swim.*
3 *He brokened the car.*
4 *I go to the party last Saturday.*
5 *Id like some informations about the plane times.*

Task 192: Observing errors

Use Observation Task 8 (Errors and correction) on page 390 next time you observe another teacher's lesson.

See ideas about timelines in Section 6 of this chapter.

2 Testing

Your director of studies or head teacher has asked you to prepare a test for your class. How do you go about this?

You could test:
- the students' progress over the course so far (a progress test);
- their general level of English, without reference to any course (a proficiency test).

Most internal school tests tend to be progress tests; most external ones (e.g. state or international exams) are usually proficiency tests.

You can test anything that has been studied; this usually means the four language systems and the four language skills. Remember your students' course has probably included not only reading and writing, grammar and lexis, but also speaking, listening, phonology and function. Somehow tests often seem to focus far more on the first four than the last four.

Traditional 'pen-and-paper' tests are usually made up of two types of questions:
- discrete item tasks (i.e. testing specific individual language points);
- integrative tasks (i.e. a number of items or skills tested in the same question).

These can be marked in two ways:
- objectively (i.e. there is a clear correct answer, and every marker would give the same marks to the same question);
- subjectively (i.e. the marking depends largely on the personal decision of the marker; different markers might give different marks for the same question).

Discrete items are likely to be marked objectively; integrative tests are more likely to be marked subjectively. Some questions may involve elements of both. Language systems are easier to test objectively; language skills tend to be tested subjectively.

Three criteria of a good test

- A good test will seem fair and appropriate to the students (and to anyone who needs to know the results, e.g. head teacher, other teachers, employers, parents, etc.).
- It will not be too troublesome to mark.
- It will provide clear results that serve the purpose for which it was set.

Task 193: A good test

Decide if the following examples fulfil the three criteria for a good test mentioned above.

1 It is the day when new students arrive at your school. When you chat to them, they seem to be very different in level. You give them a placement test to decide which level class they should go into. Everyone gets a mark between 63 and 67 out of 100.
2 You set a test for your class using material from the next three units of the book that they will be studying over the next month.
3 Your students have been studying a balanced course of skills and language improvement work for the last ten weeks. For the end-of-term test, you have asked each student to write you five essays. It is now midnight and you have the pile of essays in front of you.

Commentary ■ ■ ■

1 A test like this is virtually useless. A placement test needs to give a broad range of marks (e.g. between 10 and 90 out of 100) so that you can easily see who is stronger and who weaker.
2 Do your class know why they are doing the test? You may have a very good reason for doing it, but if they don't know what that is, then it's going to seem a very unfair trick to play on them to test them on work they haven't done. However, if they **are** informed, then setting a test in advance like this could be very useful as a diagnostic tool to help you plan the course and allow them and you to see what they already know and what they need to work on. It would probably also be a good idea to do exactly the same test again at the end of the next part of the course in order to see (and let them see) what improvement they have made.
3 Not really what you want to plough through late at night. It doesn't sound as if it fulfils the 'markability' criteria. Obviously there are going to be many occasions when it is essential to mark a great deal of written work, but there is no sense in creating unnecessary drudgery for yourself. The amount of writing hardly seems fair to students either. Finally, it doesn't serve its purpose if it's intended to check on their progress (how can you measure progress in speaking, listening and reading with a purely written exam?). ■

Task 194: Categorising test questions

Categorise the following questions. Are they discrete? Integrative? Will the marking be objective or subjective? (The answer may not always be clear cut!)

1 Talk about this picture with your teacher. (Students are given a picture of people doing various things.)

2 Choose the word or phrase which best completes each sentence.
John always ____ to the cinema on Saturday.
A go   B goes   C going   D gone

3 (In the language laboratory)
Voice on recording: 'Reply to these comments in a natural way.'
'Excuse me. Do you know where the nearest bus stop is?'
(ten-second pause)
'Would mind lending me your car, just for tonight?'
(ten-second pause)
'I've lost my watch. You don't have the time on you, do you?'
(ten-second pause)

4 Fill in the gaps.
a Have you _____ been to Moscow?
b How long have you _____ that new car?

5 You want to sell a new CD Walkman that you were given for Christmas (you already have one). Write a short notice to put on your school noticeboard. (Not more than 30 words.)

6 (In a private interview with an teacher)
Read this aloud:
'The advertisement states that the new design measures 20 m x 35 m. If you are interested in receiving more information, please contact Ms H. J. Jones of PORTILLO Warehouses, that's P-O-R-T-I-L-L-O Warehouses, on 071 489 2222, ext. 97.'

Commentary ■ ■ ■

Questions 2 and 4 seem to be clearly testing discrete items and to be suitable for objective marking, but even with simple examples such as question 4, the matter is not quite so clear-cut.

At first, it seems obvious that the answer to (a) is *ever* and the answer to (b) is *had*. But what about the student who writes *never* for (a) and *owned* for (b)? Both answers are perfectly good everyday English. Do we have to write a marking scheme for (b) that includes *driven, wanted, desired*, etc.? Or do we give a sample answer and leave it to the (subjective) discretion of the marker? Or do we give a mark only to the most obvious answer?

Another problem: what about the student who writes *been hoping to buy* for (b)? This is a problem with the instructions; although the small answer space allowed on the question paper implies 'one word', there is no instruction to that effect. Moral: make your instructions as complete and clear as possible.

The dividing line between subjective and objective is usually in the marking scheme. Question 6 could be marked by giving a subjective overall impression mark or it could be marked more objectively on discrete points
(e.g. pronunciation of *20 m x 35 m*: one mark for pronouncing numbers correctly, one mark for by; one mark for correct stress on advertisement; etc.). ■

Criteria rather than marks?

What's the aim of a progress test? Often it's to give encouragement that something is being done well or to point out areas where learners are not achieving as much as they could. With this kind of aim, giving 'marks' may not be the most effective way to assess, especially when skills (as opposed to language systems) are being tested.

An interesting alternative option is to base the tests around assessing if learners are 'successful' when compared against some 'can do' criteria statements (i.e. statements listing things 'I can do'), such as 'I can describe what's happening in a picture of town streets' or 'I can listen to directions and follow a route on a map' or 'I can check in at an airport'. These statements can reflect the syllabus of the course – and if the syllabus is itself stated in 'can do' terms, then students will have a very clear idea of what level of achievement they are aiming for.

A criteria-based assessment scheme could perhaps measure each 'can do' on a scale of four:
1 The candidate meets and surpasses the criteria.
2 The candidate meets all main aspects of the criteria.
3 The candidate meets the criteria in some respects, but with significant problems.
4 The candidate is unable to meet the criteria in any respect.

Some common discrete-item testing techniques

Gap-fill

* **Single sentence**
  Fill in the blanks. Use only one word in each space.
  I'd _____ go to the cafe than the pub.
  Answer: *rather*
  (If answers of more than one word are allowed, then other answers are possible; instructions need to be clear!)

* **Cloze**
  A cloze test is a gap-fill exercise using a longer text and with a consistent number of words between gaps (e.g. every ninth word). The word 'cloze' is often incorrectly used to describe any gap-filling task.

* **Multiple choice**
  Choose the word or phrase which best completes each sentence.
  If I went to Jakarta, _____ buy some jewellery.
  a I'll b I c I will d I'd
  Answer: *d*
  (Multiple choice is, of course, a very widely used testing technique and can be used for more than simple gap-filling tests.)

* **Using given words**
  Put one word from the list below in each gap.
  thought   switched   unlocked   arrived

  He (1) _____ home late that night. As he (2) _____ the front door, he (3) _____ he heard a noise in the sitting room. He tiptoed carefully into the room and (4) _____ on the light.

  Answers: *1 arrived   2 unlocked   3 thought   4 switched*

- **Using other clues** (e.g. pictures, anagrams, first letters, lines indicating how many letters in word, etc.)
  He looked through the _ _ _ _ _ _ and was amazed to see that she had finally come _ _ _ _ .

  (Students have pictures of a window and a house.)
  Answers: *window, home*

- Transformation of a given word
  He could produce no _____ evidence to support his argument. (photograph)
  Answer: *photographic*

Sentence transformation

- **Using given words**
  Starting with (or making use of) a given word or words; changing the form, but keeping the meaning
  He liked the theatre but hated the play.
  Although ...
  Answer: *Although he liked the theatre, he hated the play.*

- **Following a given instruction**
  Change this sentence so that it describes the past.
  She's looking closely at the sculpture, trying to decide if she likes it.
  Possible answer: *She looked closely at the sculpture, trying to decide if she liked it.*

Sentence construction and reconstruction

- **Rearranging words**
  brother / much / he's / than / his / taller
  Answer: *He's much taller than his brother.*

- **Using given words**
  Although / I / bad headache / go / concert
  Possible answer: *Although I have a bad headache, I'll still go to the concert.*

- **Finding and correcting mistakes**
  1 Cross out the incorrect word.
    When I will visit you, I'll see your new baby.
    Answer: *When I ~~will~~ visit you, I'll see your new baby.*
  2 Rewrite this sentence in correct English.
    I am enjoy swimming at the swimming pool of the sports centre.
    Possible answer: *I enjoy swimming in the sports centre swimming pool.*

- **Situational**
  You want to borrow some money from a colleague. What question would you ask?
  I wonder ____ borrow ____ ?
  Possible answer: *I wonder if I could borrow ten dollars?*

Two-option answers

- **True/false**
  Often used after a reading passage e.g. *Paul wanted to visit the castle.*
  True/False?)

- **Correct/incorrect**
  Write ✔ if the following sentence is in correct English. If it is incorrect put a ✗.
  They always play football on Sundays.
  Answer: ✔

- **Defined options**
  Jill is a fifteen-year-old schoolgirl. Mary is a one-year-old baby. Write J next to the things that belong to Jill. Write M next to the things that belong to Mary.
  (List of words: *teddy, Walkman, calculator, cot.*)

Matching (pictures, words, sentence pieces, labels, etc.)

- **Pictures and words**
  Write the correct word under each picture
  (sketches of transport)
  car bike ship motorbike van lorry caravan plane

- **Placing words in correct sets, lists, etc.**
  Put the following words in the correct list: *water, cheese, wine, lemonade, lunch, bread, butter, supper*

Food	Drinks	Meals
potatoes	milk	breakfast
rice	tea	dinner

- **Grammatical labelling**
  Mark each sentence a, b or c depending on the tense used.
  a = present perfect; b = past simple; c = present progressive
  1 He's just come back.
  2 I've never been to the Andes.
  3 When did you go there?
  4 I'm living in Vienna at the moment.
  Answers: *1 a   2 a   3 b   4 c*

- **Putting jigsaw pieces together**
  Which beginning goes with which ending?
  1 He planted   a the stones and weeds.
  2 She picked   b some beautiful red apples.
  3 She dug up   c the seeds in three separate rows.
  Probable answers: *1 c   2 b   3 a*
  Note that some other answers are linguistically possible (e.g. 3b), though they make less sense or seem more unlikely.

Task 195: Designing descrete and integrative questions

Design three discrete item questions and one integrative question to test your understanding of this section of the book.

Assessing speaking

Many teachers feel more comfortable with testing grammar or lexis with pen-and-paper tests than with testing skills. Speaking can seem a particular problem, as it is potentially demanding on teacher time, but if our students' work includes speaking, then it is also necessary to assess this. Here are some ideas:

Prepare criteria

Think of about ten kinds of speaking that students have worked on over the course and turn them into a criteria list (e.g. 'I can take part in a discussion and explain my point of view clearly and politely', 'I can tell a visitor to the company how to get to my office') then assess students against them.

Too many students!

A frequent problem for teachers is when there are so many learners in one class that it seems to make it unrealistic to assess speaking. However, with a list of criteria (such as those above), it becomes considerably more straightforward to assess even a large group. Explain to your class what you will be doing, then, the next three or four times you set speaking tasks (i.e. where learners work in pairs or groups), walk around class with a list of names, listening in to various groups and noting successes, keeping track of individual 'can dos'. Extend your assessment over a few lessons; keep listening and adjusting your evaluation over a variety of tasks.

Speaking tasks

What are possible speaking tasks for assessment? Well, almost anything you do in normal class work, e.g. narrating a picture story, role-plays, pairwork information-gap exchanges, discussions, etc. If you have a smaller class and enough time, then a 'three learners with one teacher' activity is a very good way to assess, i.e. setting a task that gets the three learners to interact together while you watch and evaluate.

Self-assessment

Although fear of bad marks can sometimes be motivating, it's surprising to find the amount of power that students feel when assessing themselves. It can be a real awareness-raising activity. Distribute a list of criteria and ask students to first write a short line comparing themselves against each criterion (in English or in their own language) – a reflective view rather than just a *yes* or *no*. Encourage 'guilt-free' honest reflection. After the writing stage, learners can meet up in small groups and talk through their thoughts, explaining why they wrote what they did.

3 Using the learners' first language

Activities that involve use of the learners' L1 (their first language) in the language classroom haven't had a terribly good press. Many teachers feel their training has discouraged them from using it at all in class. But this supposed prohibition was an over-strong reaction to some traditional teaching styles in which teachers used only L1 to explain and discuss language, and learners hardly got to hear or use any English. But there are many helpful ways of using L1 in class (even for teachers who don't know that language!). This section looks at uses of L1 in class and mediation skills. (If students are using L1 when you **really** want them to speak English, you might want to look back at Chapter 5, Section 10.)

Uses of L1 in class

A few ideas:

- When learners read an article or short story, sometimes ask them to summarise it orally in L1. This can reveal interesting insights about what learners have understood or misunderstood.
- When a new grammatical item is learned, encourage learners to think how they would say the same things in their own language. Don't just ask for a translation, but encourage learners to consider if there is a direct one-to-one correlation with their L1 and to notice differences between the two languages.
- When working on pronunciation, explicitly focus on contrasts between how a sound is formed in L1 and English. Get learners to work like laboratory scientists, trying out experiments to see if they can notice and characterise important differences.
- When watching a DVD film, the availability of switchable subtitles in L1 and English can be very helpful (see Chapter 16, Section 9).
- Compare three different L1 translations of the same English sentence (extracted from a longer text) and decide which is the best and why. (This will help students to understand that translation is not an exact science and that one language does not directly convert directly into another. Word-by-word translation isn't always possible and frequently misses the message. Frequently, context and style need to be seriously considered.)
- Compare layout and style between L1 and English conventions, e.g. for letters, formal notices, etc.
- If you feel that the best, most effective way to explain something is in L1, go for it! (But keep it for times it's needed, rather than as a matter of course.)
- A little teacher translation (in instructions or explanations) can bring things to light that would otherwise remain hidden. But exercise caution – use a little L1 when you have a clear purpose and then return to English. As the general main aim of your lessons is to get students using English, avoid the temptation to conduct the rest of the lesson in L1 just because it's easier! Learners need to hear your English; it's an important part of their exposure to the language.

Community Language Learning (CLL)

This interesting teaching methodology is drawn from a teaching method called Counselling Learning devised by Charles Curran. CLL aims to reduce anxiety and low confidence. It is particularly suitable for adult learners.

CLL is an unusual way of working in that it allows learners to express anything they want to in English – even at Beginner level. A CLL lesson allows learners to hold a genuine (if slow) conversation about things that they are interested in. A simple CLL lesson might go like this:

1 Learners sit in a circle, facing inwards. A calm atmosphere is created, maybe with L1 small talk, background music, etc. You prepare a tape recorder with recording facilities (i.e. a recordable Walkman or a larger tape recorder with separate microphone).

2 Stand **outside** the circle and explain what will happen. The learners are encouraged to have a conversation with each other in the circle.
3 When a learner wants to say something to someone else in the circle, she indicates to you; you go over and stand behind her.
4 The learner whispers what she wants to say to you using L1.
5 You translate this into English and whisper it back to the student using natural conversational pronunciation and intonation.
6 The student practises saying it to you; you help by, for example, repeating if asked to.
7 When the learner is ready, she indicates this. She (or you) switches on the tape recorder and says her sentence to the person in the class she wants to talk to (whilst also recording it).
8 When another learner wants to reply, they follow the same procedure (steps 3 to 7).
9 Slowly, a complete conversation in the target language is built up on the tape.
10 When the conversation has gone on long enough, take a break. The tape can now provide raw material for future work, e.g. learners can transcribe the text, study grammatical items in it, explore new lexis areas, etc.

Variation

CLL usually requires a bilingual teacher in order to do the two-way translation. With higher-level students (Pre-Intermediate and above), it is possible to use the technique using only English, i.e. the students say what they want to say in English (with errors and problems), and you 'upgrade' the language (i.e. say it in a normal, natural way).

Mediation

Many students find themselves in situations where they have to help a friend or colleague who doesn't speak the local language. This is **mediation**. It refers to the skills we use in real life when we have to help others to communicate by conveying a message from one party to another. For example, imagine that you are in a British railway station, waiting to buy a ticket. The person in front of you is a foreign visitor who is failing to communicate with the clerk – but you realise that you know his L1. You can now help as a mediator, translating the customer's messages to the clerk and vice versa.

Give students mediation practice tasks in class, for example:
• Help a friend who doesn't speak any English. He wants to send a letter to an English friend. Translate his letter for him.
• Help the conference-programme writer by providing summaries of the English text in your own language.

Even if you don't speak your learners' L1, there are many ways to practise this skill in class. Here are four interesting mediation games.

English whispers

Prepare about fifteen cards, each with a short everyday phrase (e.g. *Could you spare a moment, please?*). Ask seven students to stand in a line at the front of the class. Take the first card and give it to the student at one end of the line; he looks at the card and then whispers – once only – the message to student 2. No one else should hear the sentence. Student 2 now passes the message on in L1 to student 3, who must whisper it to student 4 in English – and so on, the message going from language to language, back and forth, down the line. When the message reaches the end of the line, the first and last student say their messages out loud so they can be compared. Often the confusions will be interesting and funny, and you can discuss if they are translation or listening errors. It may also be useful to hear what people said all along the line. When finished, play the game again with the next card and so on. Make new lines to give more students a chance to take part.

Diplomatic affairs

Students stand in groups of four: two 'ambassadors' and two 'interpreters'. One 'ambassador' only speaks and understands English; the other only understands L1. The 'interpreters' (one working for each ambassador) understand both languages.

The ambassadors now meet at a 'party' and must have a conversation with each other (about anything!). The ambassadors whisper their communication to their interpreter, and the interpreter must then communicate aloud (in translation) what their ambassador said to the other ambassador. (If you have a group of three, then only have one interpreter who does all the mediation.)

Diplomatic incident

Play the game as above, but each interpreter must completely mistranslate one communication. At the end, ambassadors should guess which messages came through wrongly.

Translation role-plays

Prepare a pack of cards with everyday situations on them, especially ones in which a foreign tourist needs to do something in an English-speaking country, e.g. 'Buying a ticket at the train station', 'Asking what time the film starts', 'Booking into a hotel', etc.

In groups of three, one student is a foreign tourist who doesn't speak English (and speaks only L1). The other people are the person they are talking to (e.g. a ticket seller who only speaks English) and their friend who speaks both languages. Each group picks one situation card from the pack. They read it together, decide exactly what the role-play will be, then do it. The friend translates in both directions to help the tourist and the native speaker communicate.

4 Cuisenaire rods

Cuisenaire rods are small coloured blocks of wood (or plastic). They come in different lengths, each of which is a multiple of the smallest rod. Each length is a different colour: 1 is white, 2 (twice as long as white) is red, 10 is orange, etc. (see Figure 14.1).

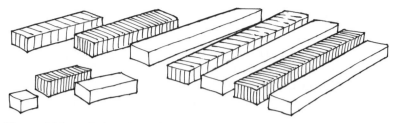

Figure 14.1   Cuisenaire rods

Originally used in primary maths teaching, Cuisenaire rods have now also come to be a very useful language-teaching aid. In this field, they first became widely known as a feature of Caleb Gattegno's 'Silent Way' approach in the 1970s. Although the Silent Way remains a strong influence (and a rich source of ideas for using the rods), their use has become widespread in many other classrooms worldwide. Sometimes, in some places, the rods seem to have acquired a semi-mystical status, and to carry your box of rods into class is almost like wearing a sort of badge of EFL eliteness. If you can get past that, then you may well find the rods are an excellent and very versatile classroom tool. There is no essential technique to learn; simply get hold of a box and set them free occasionally. Once you start thinking of possibilities, it's hard to stop. There isn't any 'right' methodology to use with them. Use them in any way that seems appropriate.

So what can you do with them? That's a little like asking 'What can I do with a blackboard?', for the rods are simply a visual aid in the same way that your board is. The difference lies in the fact that the rods are tangible; you can pick them up and move them around; a picture or an arrangement made with them can easily be altered many times; you can make a scene and later change it, etc.

Some starting points:
- The rods can be themselves (i.e. rods) or they can represent other things (e.g. trees, houses, people, syllables, diagrams, phonemes, words, intonation patterns, abstract ideas, money, graphs, etc.). Their lack of decorative detail is, in fact, a great help in enabling them to turn instantly into almost anything else.
- The 'magic' comes when people really start to 'see' the objects that the rods represent – suddenly they come 'alive', and you start to get whole little epic films, adventures, etc.
- The rods alone won't do the trick. You can use them as an unambiguous, tangible, visible point of reference, but you still need to find ways to extract language from them. You need to ask questions, elicit ideas, make sure people agree, etc.
- Rods help students to 'focus in' on meanings, ideas, stories, language items, etc. They seem to ask for more concentration and a narrowing of attention. For this reason, activities involving rods tend to be quieter and more focused rather than noisy and on a range of subjects.

If you're nervous of trying them, remember …
- you don't have to be incredibly imaginative to use them; the students have to do the imaginative work in order to 'see' what you say is there.
- they are great for teachers who think that they are 'bad drawers' – instead of drawing a hopelessly mixed-up car on the board or drawing a dog and students thinking that it's an elephant, you can just put one rod on the table and say 'This is a dog' (or a Lada, etc.).

I've heard a number of people worry that their students would find the rods childish. I have never found this a problem. I suspect that the slight hint of a childhood toy we see in the rods might actually be a positive factor, and in some way helps to set people a little freer from the 'adult' behaviour they feel is expected of them. The rods are only going to be childish if you do childish things with them! And of course, if you don't like them, don't use them. They're not compulsory.

If you do like them, my advice is – initially at least – don't 'plan' to use them; just try carrying a box into each class you teach with no specific intention of using them. At some point in a lesson, where a student asks a question about the meaning of a word, just think whether you could make a better picture with the rods than with the board – and try it out. Consider afterwards if it worked better or worse than the board might have done.

Some approaches and some examples

Focusing on grammar by restricting the lexis

By using only a single noun (*rod*), we can focus more clearly on the form or meaning of grammar, without distraction from other words. For example, if your lesson is on *Have you got?* with short answers, you and the students conceal rods in your hands. Then ask and answer around the class: 'Have you got a red rod?' 'No, I haven't./Yes, I have.'

The same exercise could be done without rods, using personal possessions, but confusion with the meaning and pronunciation of new or half-known items of lexis (e.g. *comb, chewing gum, calculator*) interferes with and often dominates the essentially grammatical aim of the activity.

This use of rods is not restricted to simple forms; it works equally well with sentences like *If I hadn't already given the red rod to Jo, I could've given it to you.*

Making meaning tangible and being precise about meaning

Imagine that some students are having problems with the meaning of some language. You and the students sit around a table and together attempt to create arrangements of the rods that show the meaning. Here is an example lesson sequence:

1 Place rods on one side of the table. Leave a working space in the middle of the table.
2 Introduce the rods to learners by explaining that the two areas are the 'bank' and the 'working area'.

working area

bank

3 Ask learners 'Show me X' (where X is a lexical item, a grammatical item, a phonological item or a functional exponent), for example:
'Show me *opposite*.'
'Show me *architect*.'
'Show me *He managed to start the car.*'
'Show me *ship* and *sheep*.'
'Show me *Would you like a coffee?*'

4 Learners come to the table and make a picture (taking rods from the bank and placing them in the working area). (Ensure that they leave a clear view for the other learners, i.e. not blocking the table). When their picture is ready, they should stand aside and say the original word or sentence clearly and naturally.

5 The other learners must decide together if the picture is accurate for the sentence. It should be as close as possible; encourage the learners to think about this – 'approximately' isn't good enough! Watch out for learners who want to jump up and immediately make alternative pictures; in this activity, you need to ensure that they agree on the existing picture first before they offer a new picture. (This may sound a little finicky, but it ensures that things are really thought about and you don't just get a chaotic stream of alternative ideas.)

6 If they agree that the picture is good, that's the end of that stage; you can move on. If they think it's not right for some reason, you can ask a new learner to try a new picture or adjust the existing one.

The tangibility of the rods helps you and the students to be extremely precise about meaning. The following detailed transcript is from a lesson on prepositions.

TEACHER: Show me *opposite*.
Student A places a red rod near a white rod.
STUDENT A: The red rod is opposite the white rod.
TEACHER: (*to class*) What do you think?
STUDENT B: It's not clear. It could mean 'near'.
TEACHER: Can anyone make it clearer?
Student C moves the red rod further away from the white rod.
TEACHER: Is that clearer?
STUDENT B: Not really. It must have a road or something.
Student D uses some long orange rods to make a road and other rods to make two square 'house' shapes, one on each side of the road.
STUDENT D: This is Maria's house. And this is Hiroko's house. Maria's house is opposite Hiroko's house, etc.

Clarifying structure

By dividing a word up into syllables or a sentence up into words, we can help clarify how they are constructed (or at least how many words/syllables there are). The rods are very helpful in making such structure visible and can help highlight problems with, for example, incorrect stress (Figure 14.2) or wrong word order (Figure 14.3). (In this use, they are similar to 'Fingers' – see Section 7 of this chapter.)

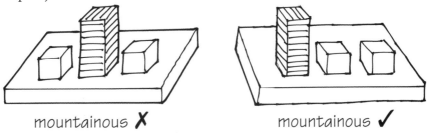

Figure 14.2   Incorrect word stress

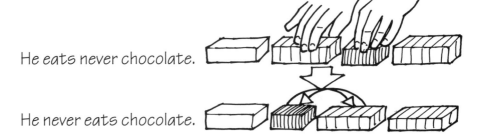

Figure 14.3   Wrong word order

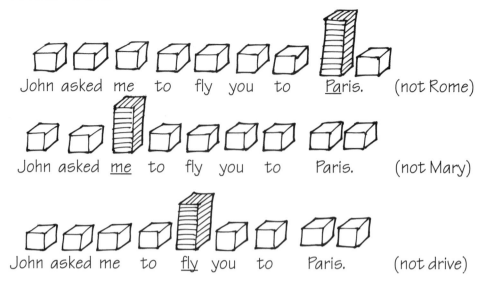

Figure 14.4   Effect of changing sentence stress

Contextualizing

Because the rods can move and quickly 'become' other things, it is possible to create remarkably absorbing little story situations, almost cinematic in scope and detail, despite the fact that the only actors are small blocks of wood (helped a bit by your own gestures and facial expressions). I quite often combine using the rods with storytelling to make a visual accompaniment to the tale.

The rods are also very effective for eliciting (e.g. for grammar work). They show the students what happens and provide the words. For example, when teaching the present simple tense, place a red rod on the table. Say 'This is Fred'. Add a green rod and show 'Fred' lying down on it (and make snoring noises if you like!). Ask 'What's this?' and elicit 'his bed'. Say 'Every day at six o'clock he …' and move 'Fred' to show him rising from the bed. Elicit 'gets up'. Continue in a similar way, adding rods and eliciting ideas, e.g. 'He has breakfast and then he catches a bus to work'.

Contextualizing is equally appropriate for lexis work. When combined with concept questions, it helps clarify meanings when two words are often confused. For example, *library* and *bookshop* are commonly mixed up. Here is a short lesson sequence to clarify them:

Tells and show a story of a woman (green rod) who wants to read a book. The book (white rod) is in a small building (made of various rods) where there is an assistant (green rod). She collects the book, takes it home reads it then returns it to the building. (Rods are great for these meanings that are best defined with some 'movement'.) Ask a range of concept questions – 'Did she read the book?' 'Did she take it home?' 'Did she give money to the assistant?' 'Why not?' 'What did she do when she had finished reading the book?' 'Did she keep it?' etc. – leading up to the question 'So what is the name of this place?' and confirm that it is a library. Having done this, you can contrast it with a second, very similar story, based on the concept of *bookshop*.

Task 196: Cuisenaire rod exercises

The best way to learn to use the rods is to play with them, to try out ideas and see if they work. Here are some exercises to start with.

1 Choose five or six words related to a particular location (e.g. 'kitchen' words, 'street' words, 'station' words, 'office' words) and build a complete rod picture that includes them.
2 How could you use rods to help you clarify or teach the meaning of some of the following words? *motorway, castle, discount, cricket, annually, reliable, south, engineer*
3 Make a short rod story to exemplify one use of *going to*.
4 Use rods to compare/contrast some of the following:
   *wages/salary; wood/forest/jungle; comfor*ta*ble/*com*fortable; steal/rob; must be/might be*

5 Dictionaries

Many students bring a pocket bilingual dictionary (or similar electronic version) to class. At lower levels, these can be very useful, offering a swift way of getting an idea of the meaning of some of the flood of new words they meet. They usually have significant limitations, though:

- It can be hard to work out which of a number of different translations is the correct one; little or no information is given to help you distinguish between entries.
- Grammatical information rarely tells you more than the part of speech.
- There are usually no examples of items being used in sentences.
- Important collocations are not mentioned.
- Pronunciation information, if given at all, tends to be idiosyncratic.

Thus, while helpful for simple receptive problems (e.g. a student in the street sees *chemist's* on a shop sign and can quickly find out what it means), they are less useful when faced with productive challenges (e.g. a German-speaking student wants to write the English for *Besuch* in a letter and finds *visit, call, attendance, visitor, visitors*, but has no 'fine-tuning' information with which to make an appropriate selection for her needs).

For such 'fine tuning', a monolingual (i.e. English–English) dictionary specifically designed for learners will offer significantly more relevant information. If learners can use it, they have a skill that allows them to work more independently. However, many students come to class with little idea how to use one well. You can actively help by including systematic training in dictionary use. Two key general skills to work on are:

- knowing alphabetical order;
- knowing phonemic script.

Beyond that, some important dictionary-using skills include:

- Using alphabetical order to quickly find a keyword entry.
- Checking whether your spelling of a word is correct.
- Using phonemic script to find which sounds are pronounced.
- Finding how many syllables a word has.
- Learning where a word is stressed.

- Interpreting definitions.
- Selecting the word that best expresses the meaning you want.
- Selecting between different meanings of the same word.
- Selecting the correct grammatical form of a word.
- Finding the plural of a word.
- Extrapolating from example sentences.
- Making use of collocations.
- Finding idiomatic expressions.

Rather than take up classroom time with random fillers and games, consider adding a regular thread of activities on dictionary use, say for seven minutes every two or three lessons. Below are some ideas for short dictionary tasks. Most of these follow the pattern of students using their current knowledge to predict an answer, then using the dictionary to confirm/correct this.

(Note: rather than repeat the same instruction endlessly, I'll use 📖 to mean … *then afterwards check in the dictionary.*)

- **Order:** Give students a list of words and ask them to put them in alphabetical order … 📖
- **Anagrams:** Give a list of anagrammed words. Students work out the probable answers … 📖
- **Guessing spelling:** Write out some words with missing letters. Ask students to recall or guess the missing letters … 📖
- **Which word?:** Give gapped sentences and a choice of two or more possible words (probably unknown to the learners) for each space. Students first guess the answers, then use their dictionaries to decide the best choices. This game is perhaps most useful and most difficult if the word choices are close in meaning and high in confusability.
- **Sounds to spelling:** Write up a number of phonemic transcriptions of words. Students have to find the correct spellings for each.
- **Same sounds:** Write up a list of words and a vowel phoneme (e.g. /æ/). Students have to guess which words contain this sound … 📖
- **Where's the stress?:** Write up words. Students predict which syllable has the main stress … 📖
- **Dictionary race:** Set a number of different challenges (such as the ideas above) that students need to work through quickly within a relatively tight time limit. They aim to work accurately and quickly. At the end, students compare with each other to see how they did.

Longer-term and less game-like work would actively encourage students to see their dictionaries as a resource when writing, speaking, reading and listening. Here are some suggestions:

- **Upgrading:** When students have written a draft of a story/article/letter, etc., go through and suggest three words that they could 'upgrade' (i.e. find a better way of saying) by using the dictionary. NB These are not 'mistakes' – they are things that could be said better.
- **Alongside reading:** With most texts, readers do not need to understand every word. So unless it is important for a specific purpose, encourage students not to look up each word one by one, but to first read the whole text and 'get the gist', then economically select those items that will really help their

understanding by checking them in a dictionary.

- **Explore:** Help learners to use dictionary entries to look around words they know already in order to enrich what they can do with apparently familiar items, e.g. by building word webs (see page 242) of collocations, connected items, grammatical forms, etc.

As well as dictionaries, thesauri (and thesaurus-like resources) are very useful when students are preparing their own texts.

6 Timelines

These are a tool for clarifying the 'time' of various verb tenses. A timeline attempts to make the flow of time visible, and thus enable learners to see more clearly exactly how one tense differs from another, or how a single tense can refer to different 'times'.

The starting point is a line representing time. On this line, we need to mark *now* – the precise present moment. From the left, time flows from the past towards *now*. To the right of this, time flows into the future.

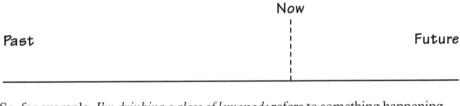

So, for example, *I'm drinking a glass of lemonade* refers to something happening now, that started just before now, and finishes just after now.

We can mark it:

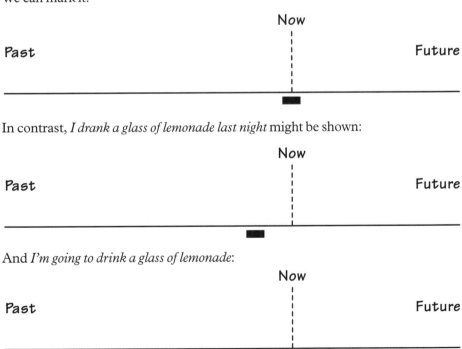

In contrast, *I drank a glass of lemonade last night* might be shown:

And *I'm going to drink a glass of lemonade*:

Unfortunately, the appealing clarity of diagrams like these may be an oversimplification. English verb forms tell us about more than just the time something happened. The timeline above shows a decision made before the present about something that will happen in the future. *I'm going to drink a glass of lemonade* suggests a decision to drink made **before now**, which we can show as:

It also includes a sense of the speaker speaking now and looking forward to the future:

Which time line is the most truthful? Which most helpful to learners? You'll have to decide for yourself.

Some tenses are quite difficult to diagrammatise: the present perfect progressive, for example:

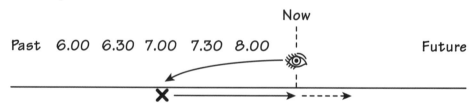

I've been waiting since 7.00.

The diagram shows that we are looking back into the past to the time the waiting started. It shows us that the waiting has continued up to now. It also shows that there is a possibility it could continue into the future.

We can also show the relationship between two or more different tenses:

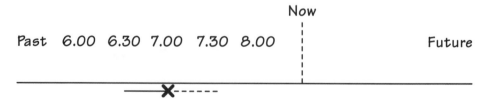

I was cooking supper when the cooker exploded.

One action (that might have continued) has been interrupted by another (simple past interrupted by past progressive).

Timelines are one way of making English grammar more accessible. But do remember that their meaning and use may not be transparently clear to everyone. Some learners may be as much confused or puzzled by them as enlightened. Use them to help clarify the meaning of tenses for yourself and then to help your learners. When you are asked for an explanation of the meaning of a verb tense, try putting a timeline on the board as a visual aid. Ask questions; invite ideas. Use timelines as a cue for elicitation (see Chapter 5, Section 9). Get students to draw timelines for themselves to help check understanding. Invite students to the board to work out timelines together. Adapt timelines and personalise them to suit your own approach (some people use colours; some draw little people all over them; etc.). As we have seen, there is not necessarily one right answer.

Timelines are one way of becoming clearer about meaning. For other useful ideas, see the sections on Concept and Concept questions (Chapter 10, Sections 3 and 4).

Task 197: Tenses and timelines

Using a grammar book to help you if you want, name the tenses and make timelines for:

1 I used to smoke cigars.
2 I live in Nairobi.
3 I'm living in Nairobi.
4 I was walking past the station.
5 I heard the explosion.
6 I was walking past the station when I heard the explosion.
7 Bob cooked lunch while they were sleeping.
8 While they were sleeping, Bob was cooking the lunch.
9 Have you been to Thailand?
10 He's just walked in the door.
11 I'd hidden the money before she came in.

See page 323 for sketches of answers.

7 A useful correction technique: fingers

This section introduces a simple but effective basic technique for clarifying the structure of sentences and for instant error correction, especially useful when you are working mainly on spoken English without immediate use of written models. For example, you're teaching *He went to Milan yesterday*, and one of your learners is confused about the word order.

Basic technique

- Put down any pens, paper, etc. you have and hold up one hand in front of you.
- Each finger represents one word. Use your other hand to indicate each word/ finger in turn as you say the sentence (or you elicit the sentence from the students).

- The learner gets a clear visual indication of the shape of the sentence.

(NB The word order for your students must read left to right, so from your position 'behind' your fingers, the sentence will appear to be right to left.)

Students may need a little 'training' before this technique shows its real simplicity and power. The first time you use 'finger sentences', make sure your students are clear that fingers represent words. Don't let them rush you; allow time to focus clearly on the individual words/fingers and clarify the problem they have. Once learners have seen the technique used three or four times, it soon becomes a valuable classroom tool.

Variations and ideas

A learner says a sentence wrongly. You get her to repeat the sentence while you indicate with your fingers each word as it is said. When the error is reached, indicate that this word is the problem by facial expression or a gesture. You can then clarify the error by means of more specific signs:

- These two words are in the wrong order (draw a small circle above the two appropriate fingers – see Figure 14.5).
- You don't need this word (fold down the finger corresponding to the extra word).
- There should be an extra word here (point to the gap between the appropriate fingers).
- Say it quickly (hold out spread fingers, and with the other hand close them together).
- Third syllable is wrong (use the joints of your finger to represent the syllables).
- Contraction (e.g. *I am > I'm*) (hold the appropriate fingers apart and then move them together).

Figure 14.5   Pinpointing the error: these two words are in the wrong order

Task 198: Using finger sentences

Practise this with a colleague facing you (or a mirror, if there are no volunteers around). Think of a nonsense sentence, e.g. *Pop tee tipple on ug*. Say the sentence quickly and get your colleague to repeat it. Then use the techniques above to get them to:

- improve their pronunciation of individual words and the whole sentence;
- learn a question form with two of the words in a different order.

Answers to Task 197 (page 321)

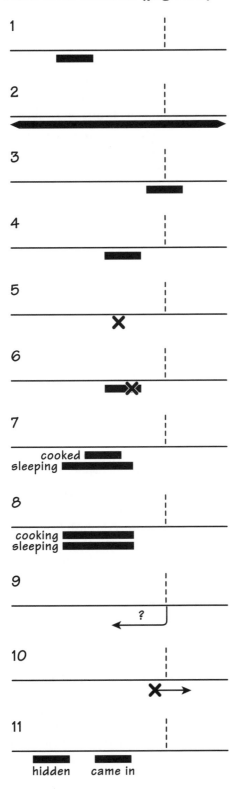

1

2

3

4

5

6

7

cooked

sleeping

8

cooking

sleeping

9

?

10

11

hidden   came in

Chapter 15 Teaching different classes

1 ESP and Business English

ESP stands for **English for Specific Purposes**. That may mean English for hotel receptionists, English for pharmaceutical salesmen or English for telephoning. It may also mean the rather wide title of 'Business English'.

In one sense, every individual student has his or her own 'specific purpose', even if it may seem a little vague in some cases – perhaps 'to improve my job prospects' or 'to make my holidays more interesting'. ESP contrasts with the rather mischievous acronym LENOR (Learning English for No Obvious Reason); it implies that we are going to take the client's needs and goals more seriously when planning the course, and rather than teach 'general English', we are going to tailor everything to his or her character and particular requirements.

But I don't know about nuclear fission and I have to teach a three-week ESP course for nuclear engineers!

Don't panic! You are an English teacher; no one expects you to know anything about nuclear power (other than what the person-in-the-street might know). You know about English; they know about the topic. Put the two together, and you have the potential for some exciting lessons. For one thing, there is a genuine information gap and thus a real reason for communication. The learners can speak and write about their field of work and do appropriate tasks that they need to perform in English. You can help them find ways to do this more effectively.

Thus ESP often means 'Go on teaching all the normal English you already teach in all the ways you know how to do already, but use lexis, examples, topics and contexts that are, as far as possible, relevant to the students and practise relevant specific skills'. If you don't have the appropriate texts/recordings/etc. to hand, then it may be possible to get your students to provide them.

A Needs analysis (see Chapter 4, Section 3) is a good – almost essential – starting point for ESP teaching. We can't really address a student's specific needs unless we are absolutely clear about what they are. A typical ESP Needs analysis might be a questionnaire that you and the client(s) talk through and fill in together. This might include an analysis of what the client uses English for, what their expectations are, what they need, what they want and what they don't have.

Task 199: Selecting activities for ESP

Here is a brief description of a student who is going to attend a one-week 'private' course (i.e. one-to-one). Name two or three classroom activities that would be useful for her.

Maria works as a member of the sales team for a company that sells video cameras around the world. She frequently speaks on the phone to clients and often receives complex orders by phone. She sometimes visits potential customers in different countries and makes presentations about the firm and its products. She also has social contact with many clients and needs to feel more confident about talking with them. Her English level is Pre-Intermediate and frequently causes problems in doing these things. Her pronunciation is particularly weak, and many words are incorrectly stressed.

Commentary ■ ■ ■

Some ideas:

- Maria listens to detailed information and makes notes on, for example, numbers and product names. This activity could be done over the phone if one is available to use.
- For homework, she prepares a ten-minute presentation on a work-related subject. In class, she makes her presentation and you give her oral feedback on the language she used. She could also be given a short written feedback form which notes grammar, lexis and pronunciation problems, together with a general comment about the success of the presentation. Later in the course, she could try the task again and see if she has improved.
- You prepare a worksheet listing many words she commonly uses in her work. She then attempts to mark the stress patterns on each word and to pronounce them correctly.
- You role-play meeting at a party and chat with her about topics of interest. ■

One point to bear in mind is that ESP courses are sometimes booked and paid for by people other than those who actually do them (e.g. a company training manager arranges for an executive to study on an intensive two-week course). Sometimes the needs/expectations of the two may be very different, and you may find it a hard act to balance.

Task 200: Activities for ESP needs

For each of the following specific skill requirements, find one activity that you could do in the classroom to practise it.

1 Travel agent: taking telephone bookings for flights
2 R&D manager: making presentation to large conference audience about new products
3 Marketing manager: sending short, clear fax messages to overseas representatives
4 Company director: meeting important clients on social occasions
5 Hotel receptionist: dealing with foreign holidaymakers

Commentary ■■■

The following activities are some possibilities:

1 Design an information-gap activity that involves one person knowing names, numbers, etc. that they have to communicate to the other person so that they can write it down.
  A Book flight to Athens on 13th Feb. in the morning, if possible.
  B Flights to Athens leave at 02:45, 09:05, 12:35, 17:55.
     Book flight for … on … at …
The activity could be done in pairs in class or between you and the student in a one-to-one lesson.

2 Find a detailed description of a product in a magazine. Give the article to the student to (a) read for homework; (b) discuss and study in class; (c) prepare a presentation to give to the other students and/or the teacher.

3 Set aside one section of the lesson in which to communicate only by writing. The students sit in separate parts of the room. Give each person a pile of blank 'fax' paper and get writing. The students only approach other people in order to deliver messages they have written. This activity works well simply on a personal 'letter-writing' level, but if each person involved also has some specific information to hand, or has some specific tasks to achieve (e.g. 'Find out who is offering the lowest price for a transport contract and agree a deal with them'), then the activity can be very demanding and useful.

4 Role-play an appropriate meeting and (either before or after) study the language that seemed most useful. Video the activity for more detailed analysis.

5 The receptionist 'real-plays' himself/herself while other students and/or you role-play a variety of typical or difficult guests. (Again, video recording would be useful.) (See role-play and real-play ideas in Chapter 7, Section 3.) ■

Task 201: Business English needs

List some areas of grammar or lexis and some skills that are likely to be important to a large number of 'business' ESP students. Some suggestions are given.

Grammar: present perfect progressive (*Figures have been improving for the last three months*), ...
Lexis: numbers, currencies, ...
Skills: talking about graphs, listening to financial news on radio, ...

2 Exam classes

Many teachers at some point need to teach a class preparing for an exam. This may be a national or school exam or it might be one of the British- or US-based international exams. This table shows the popular exams run by some exam boards and their approximate level.

Common European Framework	Cambridge ESOL	IELTS	TOEFL	
			Pen-and-paper test	Computer test
C2 Mastery	Proficiency (CPE)	7.5	633	267
		7.0	600+	250+
C1 Operational proficiency	Certificate of Advanced English (CAE)	6.0–6.5	540+	207+
B2 Vantage	First Certificate (FCE)	5.0–5.5	500+	170+
B1 Threshold	Preliminary English Test (PET)	4.0–4.5	350+	75+
A2 Waystage	Key English Test (KET)	3.0–3.5	250+	50–
		2.0–3.0		
A1 Breakthrough				

A popular American English exam is TOEFL, which is geared towards testing English level prior to entering an American university. IELTS is an exam from the UK and Australia which is widely recognised for academic and professional purposes. Of all the exams, it is Cambridge First Certificate which seems to have established itself as the most widely accepted basic qualification in English, and the exam is taken by a large number of students worldwide each year. Many students follow a preparation course before doing the exam. This section will concentrate on ways of planning for and teaching classes preparing for this or similar exams.

An examination preparation course should probably include:
- language work that is likely to be relevant to that needed in the exam;
- tasks and activities to raise general language awareness, ability and skills;
- specific practice on exam techniques (e.g. multiple-choice questions, writing essays, etc.);
- work on study skills (e.g. use of dictionaries and grammar books, ways of working with recordings at home, etc.).

Even if the exam is only concerned with reading and writing, there is still a strong case to be made for including a fair amount of speaking and listening work in the course, as the students' English is most likely to improve from balanced work on all skill areas as well as on grammar and lexis. It is also worth taking the time to help students learn some basic techniques for studying. A student who can understand the phonemic symbols in a dictionary, or who can take a tape home and use it efficiently, or who can make usable notes from the lessons, is likely to get more from the course than one who has not thought about these things. A basic skill that often needs some time assigned to it is how to organise your file/exercise book: do you just record page after page, day after day, or do you try to organise it into sections at the start of the course (e.g. lexis, grammar, pronunciation, etc.)?

A common problem with exam preparation courses arises when too much time is spent on exam technique and not enough on the other areas.

Teachers often feel pressure from students to do exam-practice work right from the start of a course, as if writing out countless mock tests will markedly improve their English. Clearly, students need to be very familiar with the form the exam takes, but doing practice tests alone will not in itself help the students to learn very much and can easily lead to 'burn-out'.

A more balanced approach for, say, a twelve-week course might be to give students a lot of general language work and study skills in weeks 1 and 2 to give them the foundations for working successfully through the course. As the course progresses, the study skills work could be reduced and much more specific work on typical language problems could be done. Work on examination technique would be introduced gradually and increasingly through the course and build up towards complete 'mock' tests in the week or two just before the exam.

It is often a good idea on exam preparation courses to be even more systematic than usual about what has been studied and to take care that items, once met, are recycled usefully. I have seen the following ideas used by a number of teachers on exam courses:

Posters

When new language is studied, the students (or you) make posters to help them remember it. As the course progresses, these slowly take over the room, acting as a very useful aide-memoire and a source of further work. I often find students browsing through these before class starts or in lunch breaks. Typical posters might be on phrasal verbs, tense problems, articles, present participle or infinitive?, etc.

Lexis box/file

Whereas posters are a good way of recording lexis, the sheer quantity of new words met on a course could soon fill the walls. An alternative is the 'lexis box'. At the end of each lesson (or day), the students review what they have learned that day, record any words worth recording on squares of paper (or card) and file them in the box or file. This record is a good source of material for you to exploit in future lessons (e.g. exercises and games recycling these words) and for students to look through.

Both of these ideas are, of course, also applicable to a wide variety of non-examination courses.

Finally, here are a few ideas to make practice of exam techniques a little more interesting. Many of these ideas also perform the essential task of raising awareness about how the tests are marked and the criteria the examiner will use.

- Students do exercises in pairs or small groups. (Possible rule: they **must** all agree on the same answer within each group.)
- Students mark each other's tests.
- 'Blitz' it: do an exercise at great speed (e.g. 10–20 per cent of the normal time allowance – no thinking time, just do it!) Keep the atmosphere light-hearted – it's not a serious test. Then let them go over it and consider their answers at leisure.
- A 'teacherless' lesson: give the students the chalk or board pens and let them discuss and work through an exam paper together on the board. Only look at (and mark) the board when they have completely finished. (This is also a good 'group-building' exercise, as it becomes a joint responsibility to get the best possible answers.)
- Students set tests in a particular style for each other (e.g. they take a text and rewrite it with gaps, they prepare multiple-choice questions on a text, etc.).
- Take some written information about the exam (e.g. from a prospectus or a marking scheme) and turn it into exercises in the style of typical exam questions.
- You do the exercise (including a mistake or two!) and the students correct it.

3 Teenage classes (age 13–16)

Task 202: Teenage classes compared with adult classes

List some ways in which the atmosphere and work in a class of teenage students might differ from a class of adults studying similar material.

Commentary ■ ■ ■

In teenage classes, the learners are discovering a range of new possibilities for themselves. They are discovering what impact they can have on the world and can be very motivated. The learners can bring a strong enthusiasm for topics they are interested in. and they can get very focused on specific things relevant to themselves. They often respond well to work that is clearly organised and takes their interest into account. But although teenage classes can be among the most interesting and exciting, they also have some reputation for being demanding on the teacher. Some of these are listed in the next section. ■

Why might teenage classes seem demanding on the teacher?

- It's a difficult period of life. Teenagers are often not sure about themselves and how they feel about things.
- Strong emotions of various kinds may be rising and falling. Sexual or romantic feelings may alter the workings of some techniques and activities.
- Teenagers have changing interests. They get bored quickly.
- Activities might be rejected or done without personal investment because the learners feel silly or embarrassed when doing them. Basic things like speaking English in activities may become issues.
- Motivation may appear to be low, especially if learners feel that they have been forced to attend something they don't want to.
- Teenagers can come across as outspoken. They may be more willing to state clearly what they think and stand up to a requirement they disagree with.
- Discipline can seem to be a problem. Teenagers seem particularly averse to things that they see as imposed on them.
- 'They say they're fed up,' 'They sit there and do nothing,' 'They try my patience,' etc.

I'm sure that some teachers could extend this list a good few more lines! So having said that, we can conclude that the teacher of a teenage class might need to have a few specific techniques to hand for dealing with teenage-related problems – and I'll suggest a few below. But before that, I'd like to offer a general proposal that might apply to all classes, whether adult, child and teenage.

Personal choice and investment

I have a suspicion that many of the problems that teachers notice in teenage classes – especially ones related to boredom, discipline, answering back, rudeness, etc. – reflect issues that also exist in adult classes. It's just that the adults are generally more restrained and do not state as openly what they think or want, and the teacher may remain unaware of the depth of feeling, disillusionment, lack of engagement or boredom. A lot of issues that surface as ill-discipline or rudeness may just reflect the fact that the learner is feeling powerless and out of touch with something that they are being required to do. There is very little chance of learners doing something with conviction or interest unless it is something that they have, at least in some degree, chosen to do. Which leads me to a general proposal that the more a learner feels that they have chosen what to do and how to do it and feels in control while working, the more they will be likely to feel engaged and to achieve something worthwhile from it.

When these things are absent or at a low level in any class, there are likely to be problems. With adults, we might get students not coming to lessons, remaining quiet and passive, writing negative feedback comments, complaining to school management and so on. With teenagers, we might get more instant, more tangible outcomes: refusals, complaints, rudeness, abdication, etc.

All of which suggests that key techniques for teenage classes might include:
* a willingness to listen and be flexible in response;
* following the class as much as leading;
* where appropriate and possible, sharing the responsibility for key decisions – topics, work methods, work rate, homework, tests, etc.;
* ways of getting useable feedback regularly through lessons and courses.

Teenagers also need a sense of security amid the sometimes bewildering world they are meeting, so your task would be to find a way of offering the more flexible, democratic, inclusive approaches suggested above while also providing an ordered, organised but unthreatening environment.

Some specific ideas for teenage classes

Virtually all of the ideas and activities in this book apply equally to teenage classes as much as to adults. Here are a few extra hints:

* Avoid anything that might be seen as childish to students. Many materials that adults would happily work with may be rejected by teens if they see them as unsuitable or patronising in any way.
* If whole-class work doesn't seem to be working, try avoiding it where possible. Instead, consider the possibility of work groups, i.e. small sections of the class that work independently on tasks that you agree with them.
* Experiment with a mixture of quiet, working-alone activities and activities that require active participation. Find out which individuals seem to respond better to these different kinds of work.
* Avoid too many activities that put embarrassed students in the spotlight.
* Select reading and listening materials from up-to-date sources that are relevant for learners, e.g. current magazines, websites, recently released films, hit songs, etc.
* Better still, ask learners to bring in materials they want to work with.
* Consider project work on topics entirely selected by the learners and involving research methods that they will find both interesting and challenging, e.g. preparing a report on a live topic that interests the students (see Chapter 16, Section 14).
* If your school, syllabus and exam requirements allow it – and your class is keen – consider the possibility of throwing out the whole coursebook and syllabus and working on one very large project with a definite outcome, e.g. staging a play or show in English or preparing a local magazine in English. (Again, I stress that this will not work if you impose the idea on students; there must be genuine investment from them.)
* Be truthful. Try not to be just a spokesperson for school or society. Say what you really think about things. Explain to learners why certain activities may (or may not) be valuable. Let them agree if they want to do them or not.
* Don't get bothered when challenged. Listen and don't feel undermined. Be prepared to back down if a strong argument is presented.

- Dare to ask important questions such as 'What could we do in English lessons that would really be interesting for you?'
- Rather than setting out with the assumption that discipline and difficulty will be the order of the day, start out with the intention of working with the learners and listening to them.
- If discipline becomes a problem, as far as possible ask the learners themselves to give advice as to what should be done. Where possible negotiate and agree codes of behaviour and penalties in advance of problems boiling up.

4   Large classes

Laura works in a state high school. She says 'I can't use groupwork and pairwork in my class because there are so many students and they can't move from their seats.'

In many countries, teachers find that the main constraint on creative teaching is the sheer size of their classes. Of course, 'large' is relative; it depends on what you are used to. If you are used to groups of eight students, then you might regard 25 as large. Some teachers regularly teach classes of 40 students, others 80. Some teachers work with 100 or more students at a time.

Some common resulting difficulties:
- Students can't move easily.
- You can't move easily.
- The seating arrangement seems to prevent a number of activities.
- There is limited eye contact from you to students.
- There is limited or no eye contact amongst students.
- You can't give attention equally to all students.
- Interaction tends to be restricted to those closest to the front.
- The seats at the back tend to attract people who want to do something other than learn English.
- People 'hide' away.
- There is often a very wide range of abilities.
- Discipline can be a problem.
- Lecturing seems to be the only workable lesson type.
- A lot of techniques outlined in this book seem impossible.

I hesitate to propose any easy solutions to such problems, mainly because I don't know about your specific situation and the particular constraints you have – though in teaching there are often interesting options available in response to any problem. Sometimes the constraining factor may be our own worry or doubts, or our fear of trying something different from what is normally done.

It's certainly worth checking how much any problem is an 'inside' or an 'outside' issue. Many things that teachers describe as 'outside' constraints (i.e. imposed by school or parental expectations or syllabus or government, etc.) may be also be partially 'inside' constraints, i.e. a personal decision not to do something. For example, 'They can't move from their seats' could really mean 'I choose not to get the students to move from their seats because I think it would be difficult, very noisy and I am frightened that there would be chaos in the room'. By simply blaming the school or government (or whoever), we sometimes avoid recognising that we do have some potential for affecting the situation.

Task 203: Large classes

It's always a bit dangerous offering quick answers when you don't know much about someone else's problem, but, all the same, see what suggestions you might offer if Laura came up to you with the problem outlined at the beginning of the section.

Commentary ■ ■ ■

Here are a few brainstormed ideas. Most will be unsuitable for specific situations, but something may suggest a possible answer that is workable:

- Rearrange the seating.
- Move to a different classroom.
- Get them to climb over the seats.
- Push the seats up against the wall.
- Get half the students to turn around and face the students behind them.
- Let them sit or stand on the desks.
- Go into the school hall for English lessons.
- Go outside on the grass.
- Don't worry about the noise.
- Warn other teachers in advance about potential noise.
- Ask other teachers what they do.
- Take the risk that getting them to move will be OK.
- Ask the students what they think about these ideas.
- Tell students the problem and get them to work out a solution.
- Negotiate a contract: quiet movement in exchange for more variety of activities.
- Divide the large group into smaller 'classes' within the class. ■

When looking for answers to a problem such as this, it may be too easy just to say 'Well, I'll try these ideas one day'. How about pushing yourself into action with a concise, written action plan – i.e. make a simple statement of what you intend to do – and perhaps a small 'try-out' of one idea in your next class. Choose modest steps. For example: 'Next lesson, I will try a short five-minute speaking activity where I will ask the students to turn around and work with the student in the row behind them' or 'I will talk with the deputy head teacher and find out if our class can use the school hall for the Tuesday afternoon class'.

Chapter 16 **Toolkit 3: tools, techniques, activities**

Here is a wide-ranging collection of ideas. Dip in here and try some out in class. (But also keep tinkering with them. Don't let any of them set like concrete.)

1 Flashcards

Flashcards is ELT jargon for pictures (or diagrams, words, etc.) that you can show to students, typically something you can hold up when standing in front of the whole class. They are also useful for handing out as part of various activities. Schools sometimes have their own library of flashcards, but many teachers build up their own stock. They are a very useful teaching aid, especially in your earlier years of teaching.

To start collecting, you need to approach the world with a 'flashcard' frame of mind! Whenever you look at a magazine, advertising leaflet, etc., keep your eyes open for suitable pictures. When the publication is ready to head for the bin, cut out the pictures you need. Generally, choose larger pictures that will be clearly visible even from the back of the classroom. You will find some subjects are very easy to find (cars, food products, perfumes, etc.) whereas others (people doing specific everyday tasks, faces expressing different moods, etc.) are harder. After a while, you'll need to start looking for specific things that fill in gaps in your set.

When you have a number of pictures, you'll have to find some way to organise them, maybe in folders sorted by topic. It may also be worth taking the extra time to make cards longer-lasting, by sticking them down on cardboard, keeping them in plastic pockets or even by laminating them.

What can you do with them? Here are a few typical uses:
- to quickly show the meaning of a lexical item, e.g. *to iron*;
- to illustrate presentations of language, for example by giving a visual image to an imaginary character e.g. 'This is Marilyn. Every day she gets up at six o'clock ...' etc.;
- to tell a story, providing occasional images to give students something tangible to look at and help their understanding, e.g. '... and then a large green lorry turned around the corner and drove towards them';
- as prompts to remind them of a specific grammar point or typical error, e.g. a flashcard with the word *past* on it to quickly remind students to make verbs in the past form;
- as seeds for student-based storytelling activities, e.g. handing out a small selection of pictures to groups of students and asking them to invent a story that incorporates all those images;
- as prompts for guessing games, definition games, description games, etc. For example, one person in a team has a picture of a person, which they describe. Then the other students are shown a pile of seven pictures (including the original one) and have to work out which picture was described.

2 Picture stories

Pictures and picture stories can be in a book or handout, drawn on the board or OHP, on flashcards or on posters. Traditionally they have been used a starting point for writing exercises, but they are also very useful for focusing on specific language points or as material for speaking and listening activities. Most picture stories seem inevitably to involve practice of the past simple and past progressive.

Look at this picture story.

We could approach this material in a variety of ways. I'd like to contrast two broadly different approaches: 'accuracy to fluency' and 'fluency to accuracy'.

Accuracy to fluency

This heading suggests that we start by looking at the language involved in the story and work on getting this understood and correct before we move on to work on telling the story. Thus we could follow this route:

1 Introduction of topic/subject;
2 Focus on interesting or essential lexis, grammar or function;
3 Look at the pictures and discuss; possibly more language focus;
4 Tell the story;
5 Writing exercise.

In the spaceship example, the lesson with a high-level class might be as follows:

1 Ask 'Do you believe in UFOs?' or 'Would you like to travel to another planet?' Students discuss.
2 Draw a blank UFO-shaped frame on the board, hand out board pens and invite students to fill the frame with words connected with space and space travel. Students are encouraged to discuss words, to check meaning, to look words up in dictionaries, and correct mistakes. Occasionally add words yourself. By the end of the activity, the board may look like Figure 16.1.

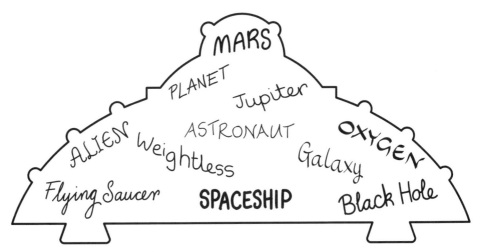

Figure 16.1   Space vocabulary

3 Reveal the first picture and encourage students to talk by asking questions such as 'What's he doing?' to focus on the picture and 'Why is he doing it?' to invite ideas about motive, intentions, feelings, etc. Specific language could be focused on (e.g. modal verbs for speculation – *he might be …, he could be …, he must be …*, etc.). When it seems appropriate, ask for predictions about what is in the next picture, and, after a little discussion, reveal picture 2 and start to work with that.
4 When students have had enough opportunities to talk through the story, put them into pairs and ask them to tell the complete story to each other.
5 Finally, still working in pairs, they write it out.

The focus on accurate use of language in stages 2 and 3 prepares students for an opportunity to use the language more fluently in the speaking activity (stage 4).

If writing is the main aim, it still makes sense to start with work such as this because such oral preparation ensures that students are more familiar with the grammar and lexis, and are thus better prepared for the inevitably tricky task of writing a good story.

Fluency to accuracy

An alternative lesson procedure could start with a fluency activity and only focus in on accurate use of language at a later stage. The lesson might have this shape:

1 Introduction of topic/subject;
2 Look at the pictures and discuss;
3 Tell the story;
4 Focus on interesting or essential lexis, grammar or function;
5 Tell the story more accurately;
6 Writing exercise.

Here is an example of a fluency activity that could be used as starting point for the lesson. (It is an information-gap activity that uses a 'jigsaw' technique, i.e. some of the students have information that others don't have; in order to piece together a complete description of what is happening, they need to communicate and work out how the separate pieces fit together.)

The students are put into groups of four. At stage 2, each student is handed one picture from the sequence, with the instruction 'Keep it secret! Don't show it to anyone else!' The task is for each group to work out what order the pictures go in without looking at each other's pictures. This can be done by intelligent questioning, good describing and a few leaps of imagination.

When they have achieved this task, in stage 3 students will probably find they are able to tell the story. At this point, you might choose to move on to later stages in which students do some accuracy work, as described above.

Variations

These basic recipes for picture-story lessons are easy to adapt or abandon. A little thought will reveal many ways of doing each of the stages differently, or not doing one of the stages at all, or doing them in a different order, or doing something completely different with the pictures. For example:

- Introducing the topic: set up a 'TV debate' on UFOs with role cards.
- Written work: instead of getting students to write out the whole story, give them a text that you have written earlier. Students have to decide on missing words and fill in blank spaces, or perhaps put jumbled-up sentences in the correct order.

Task 204: Planning work with a picture story

1 Decide what lexis is going to be essential or useful for students to know if they are to tell the story.

2 Decide on a grammatical item that you could focus on at some point(s) in the story.

3 Devise a communicative activity.

4 Devise a writing exercise that involves the whole class working on writing out a single text.

3 Storytelling

One of the messages that teaching supervisors and teacher-training courses tend to hammer home as much as possible is that teacher talking time (TTT) is a bad thing, and that it should be cut down. Well, just to prove that there really are no golden rules, here's a delightful classroom technique that involves virtually nothing but TTT.

Many teachers use stories as an interesting route into grammar lessons, but bear in mind that stories have a great deal of value in their own right. Just tell stories for pleasure; not stories and then comprehension exercises; not stories and then students retell; not stories and then write it up for homework. The aim here is the same as that of the tribal elder round the campfire or the mother reading to her children at bedtime or a group of friends in a bar telling anecdotes – to tell a story for the listener's pleasure. Storytelling is a useful short activity for the end of a lesson, perhaps, or mid-lesson to provide a change of mood.

Basic technique

1 Mentally prepare your story beforehand; internalise the mood, the smells, the look, the colours, the key events, any special words or expressions; make skeleton notes if you wish but (perhaps) don't write it out in too much detail (this tends to dull the edge).
2 Give a clear instruction along the lines of 'I'm going to tell you a story. Listen and see if you enjoy it. There will be no comprehension questions afterwards, no exercises.' This essential instruction sets your audience free; there is often a visible reduction in tension among the students: changes of posture, relaxing of facial expression, etc.
3 Tell your story (however you like but, if possible, don't read it – a 'told' story is often far more immediate and involving than a 'read' one).
4 When it's over, let them talk about it if they want to (discussion of feelings, interpretations, etc. should be a genuine reaction to what they have heard; don't break the promise you made before the story).
5 Leave it and go on to something else.

Can we justify this in the ELT classroom? What are the students getting from it?

This exercise is about real listening; not listening because I am going to hound you with questions afterwards or listening because you don't want to seem less alert than the other students, but listening because you want to. For that reason, it is all the more focused and involving. There is much academic speculation that students learn language best when they forget about studying the grammar and get totally involved in the content itself.

Good seeds for stories are: small incidents in your own life (maybe slightly dramatised); fairy tales and legends, especially rare or local ones (raid the second-hand bookshops for Chinese, Arab, African tales, etc.); ghost and mystery stories; single incidents from longer biographies and novels; versions of stories you read in the newspaper or magazine; soap operas or TV shows, etc.

As a starter, here is a set of story notes you could flesh out in the telling. It's a classic 'urban myth'.

> ### The view
>
> *My friend Misha worked in a hospital for elderly people.*
> *In one old, dark room - two very ill men - couldn't move.*
> *One - in bed beside window.*
> *Looked out - all day.*
> *Described everything he saw to friend in next bed: park - children playing - river -*
> *boats - young couples - sunshine, etc.*
> *Other patient loved these stories.*
> *One day man by window died.*
> *His friend very sad.*
> *Asked Misha if could have his bed.*
> *Misha asked why?*
> *'I've been in here for seven months. I'd love to see the world again.'*
> *'But,' said Misha, 'there's nothing outside this window. Just a solid brick wall.'*

4   Songs and music

Songs on recordings, video/DVD or perhaps played on a guitar in the classroom are often used as a 'filler' activity to change the mood or pace of a lesson. They sometimes tend to get relegated to the 'Friday afternoon' slot as a sort of reward for the week's hard work. Fine, but do be aware that songs can also be usefully integrated into the main flow of your course.

Many coursebooks nowadays include songs that specifically focus on grammatical or functional items; these may have been selected because of their content (e.g. *Tom's Diner* uses a lot of present progressive) or specially written and recorded for students of English. Of course, you can also select interesting authentic songs yourself, with the advantage, perhaps, that they are often more up-to-date.

Songs can be used in many of the same ways that you might use an ordinary speech recording. Interesting lyrics and clarity of vocals help to make a song into appropriate classroom material, and for this reason folk music or a solo singer-songwriter are often a better bet than a heavy-metal band.

Task 205: Using a pop song in class

Think of a specific pop song. How could you use this song in class with your students?

Commentary ■ ■ ■

The section below gives some basic ideas for using songs. ■

Ideas for using songs in class

*   **Reading or listening comprehension:** Use the song text as a normal reading or listening text with the bonus of hearing it sung afterwards (use the lesson ideas in Chapter 8, Sections 1 and 2).
*   **Listen and discuss:** Get students to listen to the whole song once or twice, or to a shorter section. Discuss what happened, reactions, interpretations, predictions, etc. Printed lyrics could be given out if you wish.

- **Gapped text:** Give students the lyrics with certain words blanked out. They have to listen carefully and fill in the missing words. This is, perhaps, the 'classic' way of using songs in class! It's so common that it's a bit of an ELT cliché. Vary the task usefully by, for example, using the gaps as a pre-listening exercise, with students predicting what the missing words are.
- **Song jumble:** Cut the lyrics up into separate lines. In small groups, students try to work out the original order. When ready, they listen and compare their guess with the actual song.
- **Sing along:** The aim is to learn the tune and to get the rhythm well enough to sing along with the original recording. This can be quite challenging and requires some careful preparation work on practising stress and rhythm (probably with spoken rather than sung sentences, perhaps using individual, mouthed and choral practice). And if you have access to a video machine with a karaoke recording, the possibilities are limitless!
- **Compose:** 'Here's the tune – now you write the lyrics.' (Again, an activity that is quite challenging on stress and rhythm.)
- **Matching pictures:** 'Here are twenty pictures connected with the song. Listen and put them in the order in which you hear them in the song.'
- **Action movements:** Listen to one line at a time. For each line, the students invent a mimed action, which they teach each other and then all perform. Regularly replay the song from the beginning for them to recall and do the relevant actions. After they have done one or two verses, hand out the complete lyrics; in small groups, the students find movements for the rest of the song. At the end, all come together to watch a performance of the different versions.
- **Dictation:** Dictate the chorus or the whole song. Compare with the recording.
- **Picture dictation:** Decide on a representative picture of something that happens in the song. Dictate the information about this picture, a line at a time, to the students who draw (not write) their interpretation. For example, 'The sun is shining in the sky, there are a lot of people in the street, there is a dark cloud overhead, it's just starting to rain,' etc. By the time you have finished, a lot of the essential lexis and phrases from the song will have been circulating, and the song should be not too difficult to follow.

Ideas for using music in class

Music on its own, especially classical, can also be useful in the classroom:
- to set the mood at the start of the lesson;
- to give you something to talk about with your students at the start of the lessons (especially useful with a class you don't know);
- as background music while students work on 'dull' exercises;
- as background music to set the scene while students do a particular task (e.g. 'space' music during a discussion on life on other planets; fast, exciting music during a competition);
- simply for pleasure or as a break between activities;
- to help students relax;
- for 'imaging': students close their eyes and visualise images from their own imagination or from your words or someone else's (this is a good way to personalise topics – 'Think back to a time when you ...');
- to close down, conclude, round off the lesson – to say goodbye with.

With any of these, you do, of course, need to remain sensitive to the wishes of your students; some may hate to have music on while they work, and it would hardly be advisable to impose it on them. As with most ideas in this book, the key is to ask your students and to take your cue from them.

One more thought: sharing music can be fun. Encourage learners to bring in their favourite recordings, tell you why they like them, share the lyrics, etc. It's a great starting point for discussion and study.

5 Getting to know a new class

Task 206: Aims for a first lesson with a new class

What would you hope to achieve in a first lesson with a new class where the adult learners are meeting each other and you for the first time?

Commentary ■ ■ ■

Some possible aims:

By the end of the lesson, you will have:
- spoken to everyone at least once;
- learned everyone's names;
- started to learn some personal information about them;
- started to learn something of their individual characters;
- started to feel a little more comfortable.

… and the learners will have:

- spoken to a number of other students in the class;
- learned some people's names and a little about them;
- taken part in a number of interesting and involving activities;
- started to find ways of working co-operatively with others;
- learned some information about the course;
- gained some insight into the methodology and working methods of the course;
- learned some English;
- used some English;
- heard and responded to people speaking English;
- started to feel more comfortable in their class. ■

'Getting to know you' activities

Activities that fulfil some of these aims are sometimes called 'getting to know you' (GTKY) activities or 'icebreakers' (an odd term, as it seems based on the assumption that any new course will automatically start with 'ice'). Here is an example of a short GTKY activity for students of Intermediate level or above:

Give the following instructions: 'Stand up. When I say "go", shake hands with every person in the room as quickly as you can. When you shake hands, have a short conversation – ask their name and where they come from. When you have finished, move quickly on to the next person until you have said "hello" to everyone.'

Task 207: Visualising a GTKY activity

Visualise the above activity happening. What does the room look like? What can you hear? What are the learners' faces like? How do they feel?

Commentary ■ ■ ■

Perhaps: A lot of people talking at once. A lot of movement. Learners a little nervous? Confused? Wondering whether they really want to be in this class? But also interested? Pleased to meet the others? A little less nervous to see that other learners are not so different from them? ■

Task 208: Adapting a GTKY activity

How might you adapt this basic activity idea to suit a class of school students (aged ten to twelve) who already know each other?

Commentary ■ ■ ■

One simple tactic would be to change the questions so that they ask about something they don't know the answer to (e.g. 'What did you do last Saturday?'). ■

Task 209: Following on from a GTKY activity

At the end of the adult learners' activity, when everyone is sitting down again, how could you continue the lesson, following on from what has just happened, in some useful way?

Commentary ■ ■ ■

Some possible continuations:
- As the students have just spoken to everybody in the room, see what they have managed to remember from the activity. For example, ask them to write down the names of every student they talked to (they are very unlikely to remember them all). They then compare their list with the person sitting next to them, trying to compile a complete list out of the two lists.
- Put anagrams of all the names up on the board. The students, working in pairs, have to unscramble as many as they can. The team with the most wins.
- Repeat the original activity, but this time slowly, adding the suggestion 'Have a longer conversation'.
- Repeat the original activity: the students must recall the name of the person whose hand they're shaking and say it to him or her.
- Repeat the original activity: ask the students to find out and remember a piece of personal information told them by each person they met. At the end, find out what is recalled and compare it with the truth.
- Repeat the activity. Maybe after a few goes they could start to introduce learners to each other. ■

Task 210: 'Find someone who ...'

Here is an icebreaker called *Find someone who ...* Read the handout shown in Figure 16.2 and predict what instructions you would find if you read notes about it in an accompanying teacher's book.

```
Find someone who ...
• has two sisters or two brothers.    _____
• has visited the capital city.        _____
• watched the TV news last night.      _____
• played tennis last month.            _____
• likes chocolate.                     _____
• has nice dreams.                     _____
• doesn't like football.               _____
• is wearing coloured socks.           _____
• would like to visit Mars.            _____
• never goes to discos.                _____
```

Figure 16.2   *Find someone who ...* handout

Commentary ■ ■ ■

The teacher's notes say 'Give one copy of the handout to each learner. Tell the learners that they must move around the room, asking other learners questions until they find someone who replies "yes" to a question. When they find a "yes", they must write that learner's name in the space after the question. After each "yes", the learners must change partners. The learners should try to complete the form by finding a name to go with every question.'

It's worth noting that learners don't just read aloud from the paper. They have to do some work turning the prompts into questions; for example, 'Find someone who likes chocolate' needs to become 'Do you like chocolate?' With a lower-level or less confident class, you might want to offer a little input here, maybe by writing up some examples on the board and discussing the changed grammar. You could also allow students some preparation time before the activity to make notes about what they could say. ■

Variations on *Find someone who ...*

Find someone who ... has achieved a sort of language-teaching 'classic activity' status! Variations on it are widely used in day 1 lessons, and I can't think of a coursebook that doesn't use it at some point. Here are a few different versions:

• Prepare the *Find someone who ...* handout with genuine personal information (e.g. '... who has done a bungee jump') that you have already found out about the students before the lesson (from previous teachers, application forms, chats with the students, etc.) so that you know that every statement relates directly to a specific person.
• Don't prepare a handout, but elicit the sentences from students in class. Tell them to take a blank piece of paper, write the *Find someone who ...* heading and then dictate a first example or two, after which get students to suggest other interesting ideas.

- A variation on the previous idea would be to get students to suggest people they would really like to find, e.g. someone who has a similar hobby or who likes the same music. Each student could write their own 'I'd like to find someone who …' list with maybe just three or four sentences.
- After your initial lessons, you can use *Find someone who …* to provide practice on specific language points, e.g. present perfect (… someone who has been/seen/done things).

More GTKY activities

Some popular GTKY activities involve the use of badges or labels. For example:
- Give students a sticky label or ask them to tear off a piece of paper (about 5 cm x 10 cm). Say 'In the top left-hand corner, draw your favourite food.'
- Wait while they do that, then add the other instructions:
  'In the bottom left-hand corner, write something you like to do in your free time.'
  'In the top right-hand corner, write the name of someone who is important to you.'
  'In the bottom left-hand corner, draw a picture of a dream you have for the future.'
- When everyone has finished, ask them to attach their 'badge' to their clothes (you could hand out sticky tape or paper clips) and then stand up and walk around the room. When they meet another person, they can talk about each other's badges, guessing what the pictures mean and chatting about their lives.
- You may want to arrange a signal (e.g. a bell) that means 'move on to a new partner' or you may prefer to allow conversations to last as long as students want to talk. It's probably a good idea to make sure everyone meets at least five or six others before you end the activity.
- You could vary the activity by asking different questions (e.g. 'Draw a sketch of what you did last weekend', 'Write your favourite number,' etc.).

Here are a few more ideas specifically aimed at helping people learn each other's names.

People bingo

Each student draws a large three-by-three grid (i.e. nine squares). Slowly read through all the names on the register (spelling difficult names). Students must randomly select nine of these names (of people they don't already know) to write into spaces on their grid. When everyone has a full grid, the students walk around the room, find their nine people, chat a little and make some notes about each person. Afterwards, play 'bingo' by calling out names randomly – students tick a name if they have it on their own grid. For each name, ask the class to indicate who the person is and tell you something about the person. When someone completes their grid with nine ticks, they win. (But you could always play it again!)

The small difference

On the board, draw a seating plan of the room and get the class to copy it. Each student round the room then says their name and everyone else writes it down in the correct place on their plan. Ask the class to study the names for two minutes, then put their plans away. Ask a volunteer to leave the room; while he/she is out, two other students change places. When the volunteer comes back, he/she must notice and name both students that have moved. Repeat the game a few times with different volunteers. After a few turns, make the game more difficult by changing two pairs at a time.

Anagrams

Put up a mixed-up spelling of your own first name on the board, e.g. I might put up 'Mij'. Now ask students to write an anagram of their own name. Collect these in and write them all up on the board. Every student now tries to write down all the original names. When they've finished, they can check by walking round the room, meeting people and finding out if they have written each person's name correctly.

Spy

Prepare a set of small cards, one for each student. On about half of the cards write 'True'; on the other half write 'False'. Distribute them; students must not let the others see their card. Students then stand up and mingle, meeting people and talking. When asked questions, anyone with a 'True' card must give true answers; anyone with a 'False' card must lie (except about their name), inventing false life stories. Afterwards, form small groups of between four and six people. Each group should try to work out who was 'true' and who was 'false', writing a list identifying all the suspected 'false' people. Finish up with a whole-class stage when the lists are read out and the truth is revealed. Groups get a point for each 'false' person correctly spotted, but lose one for anyone incorrectly identified. There is a set of photocopiable 'True/False' cards in Resource 24 (Appendix 2) at the back of the book.

Another option

This section has introduced a number of ideas for activities that may help a new class to get to know each other. Despite all this, you might feel you don't need any 'activity' at all. It's possible that the best way for people to get to know each other is simply by meeting and talking, without specially prepared games or activities. I find that in classes with more than a basic level of English, I increasingly prefer not to use 'icebreakers' at all, choosing instead to start simply with conversation and introductions. If you would like to do this in a slightly more 'organised' way, you could try this:

Ask students to work in a pair with someone they don't know. Explain that they should chat for ten minutes about anything they want to – life, interests, hopes, etc. – dividing the time about equally between them. Each student should make a few notes about his/her partner – basic information and any particularly interesting or unusual things. At the end of the ten minutes, ask three pairs to meet up together in sixes. In each group, students introduce their partner to the others, saying a few interesting facts about them. The others can ask questions if they want to. (In a small class, you could skip the group stage and have students introduce their partners to the whole class.)

Join in

GTKY activities are not just for the students' benefit! You may feel just as many concerns when meeting a new class. GTKY activities can help you feel more comfortable yourself. Take the chance to join in the games and activities rather than just watching them all from the sidelines; it helps a lot.

6 Fillers

Most teachers find they need a small collection of 'fillers', i.e. things to do when they've run out of other material, perhaps because the main activity went much faster than expected and (even having stretched it) there is still a seven-minute gap at the end of the lesson before the bell rings.

Fillers are also useful at the start of a lesson as a warmer (particularly when you are waiting for some latecomers) or mid-lesson as a way of changing the pace, or of breaking up similar activities. Fillers may be quite separate from the surrounding lesson or they might connect in some way. They are often useful as a chance to recycle lexis from earlier lessons or as an opportunity to work on activities that have a 'group-building' aim rather than a purely language aim.

I suggest you aim to get together a list of your own favourite fillers (and prepare any necessary material); file these in a handy place – at the front of a course file, for example – so that in an emergency, you can quickly look at the list and be reminded of the likely choices.

Here are a few much-used fillers:

Revision dictation

Divide the class into teams. Choose between five and fifteen sentences (or words) from the lesson. Dictate the words, challenging the teams to write down the sentences/words with correct spelling. Allow them time for arguing and agreeing. At the end, go through the whole list. Give points for completely correct answers.

'Yes' and 'no' questions

Quick story puzzles often go down well. Describe a slightly cryptic basic situation or problem (perhaps an incident from your own life); the learners have to question you further, discuss and find a solution that explains the story. You can only answer 'yes' or 'no' to any questions asked. For example: 'A stranger crawled all over my sitting room today.' (Answer: 'I'd dropped a contact lens; the TV repair man helped me find it.') There are some famous examples; this seems to be the favourite:

'Feargal McDonald lived on the twentieth floor of a block of flats and every morning took the lift down to the ground floor and caught the bus into town. When he came home, he took the lift to the seventh floor and then climbed the stairs all the way to the twentieth floor. Why?' (Answer: 'He was a schoolboy and couldn't reach the lift control buttons higher than floor 7.')

And I like this one: 'A man is pushing a car on a road. When he gets to the hotel, he will lose all his money. What's happening?' (Answer: 'It's a game of Monopoly.')

The hotel receptionist game

Prepare a list of likely (and unlikely) sentences that a guest would say to a hotel receptionist (e.g. 'What time is breakfast?' 'Where's the restaurant?' 'My TV has exploded', 'I've lost my wallet'). Hand one of these sentences to a student who must mime it well enough for the class to guess the original sentence. It could be a team game with points; it could use other situations such as airport, theatre, family at dinner, etc.

Kim's game

Prepare a tray with about 25 to 30 small objects on it (e.g. pencil, cassette, paperback, comb, etc.). Show it to the students for two minutes, then cover it (or remove the tray from sight). The students must make a list (as individuals or in teams) of all the objects they can remember. The winner is the one who gets most. (Could be done with a list of words on the board or with flashcards, if you can't get enough objects.)

Ordering

Instruct students to stand in line according to their birth month and date (i.e. Jan. 1 stands on the left, Dec. 31 on the right). They will need to discuss and rearrange themselves a little. Once they have got the idea of organising themselves in this way, you can try some other instructions: for example, by alphabetical order of first name; by first letter of your favourite hobby; by distance lived from school (furthest to closest); by how much you like sport (most to least), etc.

Students provide the fillers

You need to set this one up beforehand! Ask students working in pairs to prepare their own five-minute filler (a game, a physical exercise, a recording of a song to listen to, a story, etc.) and to keep them somewhere safe. Every time you need a filler, invite one of the pairs to introduce and run their activity.

'Change places' games

One specific set of useful games falls into the category of 'change places' games. These are ways to get students to work with different people without specifically saying 'OK, now all stand up and find a new partner to work with' (along with the subsequent groans and mumblings). 'Paintbox' below is one idea.

Paintbox

Assign one of three or four colours to each student in the class, e.g. green, red, blue, orange. Arrange the seating in a circle so that there is one less seat than the students present. The leftover student stands in the middle. He must call out a colour, e.g. 'Green'. At this, all 'green' students must stand up and find another seat for themselves. They cannot sit down in the same seat that they have just left. The student in the middle is also using this opportunity to find a vacant seat for himself. Whoever is left without a seat at the end continues the game by calling out a new colour. She also has the option of calling 'Paintbox', in which case everyone must move and find a new seat! Lots of movement and happy chaos. Watch out that it doesn't get too rough; the game should be played with cat-like stealth rather than rugby tackles!

This popular movement game has many names and variations – I've heard it called 'Fruit salad' and 'The wind blows'. It's easy to see how it can be adapted: the lexis area could be changed to offer practice in many different areas, e.g. fruit, grammatical terms, clothes, etc. You could also personalise it: 'All people wearing white socks change places', 'All people who arrived late to this lesson change places', etc.

Task 211: Adapting games for classroom use

Recall a game you have played outside the classroom. What adaptations or variations would you need in order to make it into a classroom activity?

7   Lexical games

Many well-known word games can be used in the classroom as fillers or as integrated practice activities. Perhaps the most popular one is 'Hangman' (although I prefer variations where something a little less gruesome happens!), but many other word games are possible. Here are some I have found useful. In every case, the rules are very adaptable and I encourage you to decide on whatever variations might work best with your class.

Back to the board

Divide the class into two teams. One team sends one member to the front, who then sits facing the class, with his back to the board. Thus everyone except this student can see what you write on the board. Write a word on the board (probably one recently studied or met); the team of the student sitting at the front must define the word or give examples of its use without saying the actual word itself. As soon as he guesses the word, write another word up and so on until a time limit (perhaps two minutes) is reached, at which point the teams change over. Clever players use all manner of techniques to convey the word: rhyme, collocations, synonyms, etc. A great game for revising and consolidating earlier lexis work.

Category list

Do an example first: slowly read out a list of ten items; the teams must guess what the title of the list is, i.e. what the connection between the items is. They start with ten points and lose one for every wrong guess. If they get it right, they score a point for each remaining (unread) item. Once the example has been understood, give them some time to work in their teams and prepare their own similar lists, which they then challenge the other team with. This game is usable, with varying degrees of difficulty, from Beginner to Advanced.

Low-level examples: *sink, spoon, cooker, frying pan, fridge,* etc. (kitchen words)

High-level examples: *a Beatles CD, a wedding ring, file paper, a doughnut,* etc. (things with holes).

Fictionary (or Call my bluff)

The students, working in teams, are given a list of five words; for each word, they must look up and copy out the correct dictionary definition and also invent and write out two completely false definitions. When they are ready, the teams come together and challenge each other by reading out a word and all three definitions. The other team(s) must guess which is the correct definition.

Word seeds

Dictate a list of about twenty words which the students all write down. Their task then is to work in small groups and orally prepare a story that uses all the words, exactly in the form dictated (i.e. if *see* was dictated, that is the word they must use, not *saw* or *seeing*) and in exactly the order they originally came in. Finally, each group tells its story; it's fascinating to watch what very different results can grow from the same seeds. This could also be done as a writing task.

Word dominoes

Prepare a set of cards, or pieces of paper, each with a different picture on. After the first picture has been placed, the game is continued by the next player putting another picture next to it and justifying the placing by explaining a connection of some sort that links the two words. This may be as tenuous or peculiar as you, or the other students, wish to allow, but the idea is certainly to encourage creative links. You may need to ban some links (like 'They have the same first letter') if they get overused. The game continues like dominoes until one player has used up all his/her pictures.

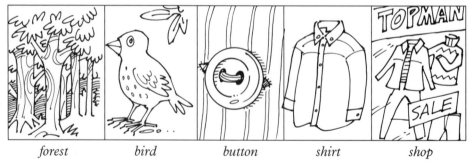

| *forest* | *bird* | *button* | *shirt* | *shop* |

(There are *birds* in the *forest*; *button* and *bird* start with B; *shirts* have *buttons*; *shirt* and *shop* begin with *sh*, etc.)

Word thieves

Choose a fairly long reading passage on a particular topic, e.g. cars. Explain that the students must attempt to steal words from you. You will read the passage aloud once only and they must try to catch and write down every word they hear that fits the topic of 'cars'. Their aim is to catch as many words as they can in this lexical area. Score and check it as you wish; it's probably useful to allow individuals to compare what they heard against other lists and to end up with them looking at the whole text.

I went into town

This is a useful game for revising lexis and is especially good for considering countable and uncountable nouns. In this example, 'food' has been specified as the lexis area. The first student says 'I went into town and I bought an apple'. The next student must repeat the sentence and add a second item beginning with the next letter of the alphabet, e.g. 'I went into town and I bought an apple and a banana'. The third then says 'I went into town and I bought an apple, a banana and some carrots', etc. Make the rest of the rules up yourself!

Word jumbles (or Word clouds or Word pools)

Take a number of words that the class has met over the previous lesson or two and write them up on the board with their letters mixed up. The students try to decipher them. (Possibly the words could then be formed into a sentence?)

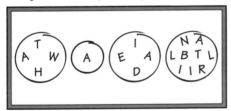

Instant crossword

Ask the class to look back over words that they have studied in the last two or three days. Get them to shout out two to you that have at least one letter in common; write them clearly on the board, interlocking, as in a crossword puzzle.

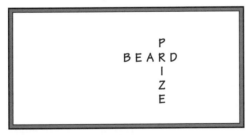

This could now continue as a competitive team game (teams take it in turns to add a new word to the grid) or as a class effort, trying to make the grid as big as possible. The students could take over the writing once the rules have been established.

It might help to divide the board up into squares beforehand, though the game works well enough without, so long as the writing is clear.

Don't finish a word

The class is divided into two teams. Each team takes it in turn to call out a letter, which is written on the board. They also say whether their letter goes in front of or behind the letters already on the board. Thus the chain of letters on the board grows longer turn by turn. If (a) a team thinks the previous team has finished a complete word; or (b) a team thinks the previous team could not possibly make a word from the letters now on the board, then they 'challenge' (i.e. you must always have a word in mind when you place a new letter). A correct challenge wins the round.

Example 1

TEAM 1: B
TEAM 2: BA
TEAM 1: BAC (Thinking of back)
TEAM 2: OBAC
TEAM 1: Challenge! (They think Team 2 is bluffing and cannot possibly make a word from these letters.)
TEAM 2: Tobacco. (They win the round.)

Example 2

TEAM 2: N
TEAM 1: AN
TEAM 2: Challenge! (They win – *an* is a complete word.)

Biting your tail

Choose a topic, maybe one you have recently been working on (e.g. 'Houses'). One student starts off by saying a word (e.g. *kitchen*). The next student must say a new word that starts with the last letter of the previous word. If he fails or if the word is challenged (i.e. not on the topic or wrong first letter), then he is out. No word can be repeated once it has been used.

Keep going faster and faster till you are all out or bored or the bell rings. Make up any other rules as you wish.

Example: Topic – Food and drink

water > rice > egg > grape > er ... er ...
No word, the student is out. The game restarts with a new word.
Next student: *lemon > nut > tomato > orange > er ... elephant*
The class now discusses/argues about whether an elephant is acceptable as 'food', etc.

8 TV, DVD and video

This is the obvious way of using visual equipment: sit students in front of the TV. Switch it on. Let them watch the programme through. This is the classic 'lazy' teacher's lesson. It works fine, and most teachers who have access to the equipment will have done this at some time. But there must be more to video than this! By simply playing around with this basic scenario a little, we can create some excellent lessons.

There are a lot of good video courses published, with accompanying materials. Some of these focus on helping students listen and understand better; some aim to teach grammar or function. An increasing number of recordings are integrated with coursebooks and have a wide range of aims and activities. However, you can do a great deal with things you record yourself – TV news, advertisements, pop songs, etc. – even if the language used is not English (though do check copyright). In this section, I'll refer to 'video' for most ideas which apply to video tapes and DVD – but there are some specific DVD ideas later on.

When I use video in class, whether my own off-air material or published recordings, I try to keep hold of a few basic guidelines. These may sound simple, but they often make the difference between a slick video lesson and technomuddle:

- Keep it short.
- Exploit the material.
- Switch the TV off when the students don't need to look at it (a fuzzy, buzzing machine is very distracting).
- If possible, find your place before the lesson (otherwise you end up with 'Just a minute, I think it's just after this bit, oh perhaps it's ...').
- Don't only use video to extract language for study. Video can be a great starting point for communicative activities, too, for writing or for introducing discussion topic areas.

Video is simply another classroom tool; it doesn't do the teaching for you. It's not too hard to extract 30 to 60 minutes' work out of a three-minute recording, and that may be a lot more use than putting a one-hour recording on and just letting it run all the way through while the students quietly nod off.

Task 212: Video in class

In order to exploit video recordings, we need to consider what there is to exploit. Think about these basic questions.

1 What has video got that my classroom/blackboard/textbook/tape recorder hasn't got?
2 What about DVD?

Commentary ■ ■ ■

A video has:
- sound;
- moving pictures (The pictures give context to the sounds we hear. We can see facial expressions, eye contact, physical relationships, background, etc.);
- a 'rewind' button: we can replay these images again and again;
- a 'pause' button: we can freeze-frame images, stopping the action at any point;
- a volume control; we can turn the sound off, or make it quiet or very loud;

If we also have a video camera, there are even more possibilities (for making programmes, recording students speaking in activities, etc.).

In addition to these, DVD technology adds a few more possibilities:
- You can accurately jump to a specific moment.
- You can replay small sections with precision.
- You can have subtitles in English – or any included language – on screen.

- There is a much clearer fast-play or fast-rewind facility, allowing you to watch the images while you wind.
- You can also pause a single image more clearly.
- Many discs have isolated sound cues and music available (i.e. for use without watching the film).
- DVD discs (e.g. of feature films) often have bonus supplementary materials which are an excellent source for student research, 'jigsaw viewing' (see below), short complete programmes, etc. 'Deleted scenes' and 'out-takes' can provide interesting discussion matter. ■

Using video and DVD in class

We can divide video playback activities into three general categories:
1 Preview: what you do before you watch a section of recording;
2 Viewing: what you do while you watch;
3 Follow-up: what you do after watching.

Any one lesson might include a number of these as different sections of the recording are used, e.g. preview first section; view first section; preview second section; view second section; follow-up first and second sections; preview third section; etc. Each section might be minutes long or could be only a few seconds.

Preview activities

Here are four typical preview activities:
- A language focus on lexis, function or grammar that will come up on the recording;
- Students predict what will happen from some given information or pictures;
- Students discuss a topic that leads into or is connected with the subject on the recording;
- Students study a worksheet that they will use when watching the recording.

The whole of the previous lesson (or week) could itself be a sort of preview task leading up to the recording. For example, if a particular function is being studied, the students might already have spent a lesson or two working with it and now view the recording to expand their knowledge of it.

Viewing activities

As with audio recordings, it usually helps to set clear viewing tasks and to follow similar procedures to those outlined in Chapter 8 on listening. The task–audio–feedback circle still works well as a basic procedure for video. Tasks might be in the form of oral instructions or in the form of a worksheet, or they might be a natural follow-on from the preview activities. You may want to play the recording through many times with harder tasks.

Tasks can be listening, looking or interpreting; for example, 'Why are they so keen to get into the museum after it's closed?' or 'What seven things does the man do after leaving the gondola?' or 'How does the shop assistant feel? What will they do next?' The tasks can focus specifically on function, grammar, lexis or pronunciation; for example, 'How many ways do the couple ask for help?' 'Which of the following verbs does he use?' 'What is on the shelf?' 'Is she being polite or rude?' The answers to many of these questions will involve active interpretation of the visual as well as the audio messages. Focusing on gestures, facial expressions, body language, etc. is especially useful when studying functional language.

Follow-up activities

There are many activities that you can do after viewing; here are just a few ideas.

* Discussion, interpretation, personalisation (e.g. 'What would you have done?' or 'Has this ever happened to you?');
* Study of new language;
* Role-play the scene (or its continuation);
* Inspiration for other work: 'What did the newspaper/*Hello* magazine say the next day? Design the front page';
* Write a letter from one character to another;
* Plan what they should do next.

Other ideas

Those are the basics. Now, if you're feeling keen, here's a mixed bag of ideas to liven up the lessons. (Don't try all of these in one go, But do try one or two of them sometime!)

* Don't let students mentally switch off; make them think; challenge them. Cover up the screen and ask questions: 'Listen to the words/music – what's the picture?' 'What are they describing?' 'Where are they?' Then, look at the images and compare.
* In pairs, the above idea becomes an instant communicative activity: 'Tell your partner what you think was happening'. It could lead to drawing and comparison of pictures.
* Switch off the sound: 'What are they saying?' Advertisements work beautifully: in pairs, imagine and write the script. And then the two students 'lip-synch' it: 'Come up to the TV; sit on either side of it and while I play the (silent) recording again you speak the words'. (Hilarious – try it!)
* Use the pause button to freeze images: 'What happens next?' (Talk about it; write the story, etc.) Then (later) watch and compare.
* Divide the class in two, on separate sides of the room. Only one half can see the screen. Have the sound turned off. Half (A) watches for one minute. Then (as a group or in pairs) tells the other half (B) what happened. Then swap over and repeat. This is great with short, silent comedy sketches. For a very noisy variation, everyone in A tells a pre-chosen partner in B what is happening while it is happening, i.e. live commentary. The quiet variation: A watches and mimes to B what is happening; at the end, B must tell the story to A. All of these sound quite silly (and they are), but there's loads of excellent and challenging speaking and listening practice.
* With a camera: make your own news/entertainment/documentary/advertisements, etc.
* Film students doing something else and play back later for focus on pronunciation, grammar, effective communication, error analysis, etc.

Task 213: Activities for video

Recall a specific TV advertisement that you know well. Devise separate activities to use in class to give students (a) speaking practice using past verb forms; (b) practice in writing formal letters; (c) a role-play that does more than simply getting them to re-enact the ad.

Task 214: Exploiting a TV weather forecast

Find several ways to exploit a TV weather forecast in your class.

The DVD advantage

Most of the ideas above apply equally to DVD and video. Here are a few DVD-specific suggestions.

- Play through a section of an unknown film at 8x or 16x speed. Ask students to watch and try to work out what is happening. When finished, groups can compare and argue. Maybe the class as a whole could then try to reach a consensus, after which everyone can watch the film at normal speed and check.
- Watch a one- or two-minute clip a number of times with the sound down and English subtitles. Ask students to first copy these subtitles. Replay it often enough for them to do this. When all have the text (and have checked it), ask them to work in pairs to decide what the subtitles would be in their own language. When they have finished writing and have compared (and acted out their versions?), they can, of course, watch the DVD with subtitles in their language and see how close they got.
- Choose a one- or two-minute clip no one is familiar with, perhaps of a very visually dramatic or humorous moment. Cover up the top three-quarters of the screen. Switch on English subtitles. Play the clip. Ask learners to sketch what they think is happening on screen. When finished, they compare, and at the end get to see what is really on screen.

The final frame

I know quite a few teachers who never use video, even though their school has one available. It's true the machines (not to mention their cables) are often a real headache to set up and use, but it's still worth persevering. I've found that if you (a) take a little time before the lesson to set it all up; and (b) go in expecting the worst, the machines usually give in and let you have a useful and exciting lesson. It will all go wrong sometimes; the secret is simply not to panic when it does. The real key to a successful video lesson is always to have an emergency non-video lesson up your sleeve.

9   Computers and the Internet

Many teachers nowadays have access to computers and the Internet, whether in a separate 'Computer lab' or perhaps with single machines in the students' normal classroom. Reactions to this high-tech equipment vary a lot amongst teachers, and the popularity of CALL (Computer Assisted Language Learning) seems to go in waves over the years. Sometimes it is 'the future of language teaching' and at other times a fairly expensive white elephant. I suspect that it's really somewhere in between. There is obviously a great deal of value in computers for home study, self-access and distance learning. In terms of classroom work, computers have many of the same advantages and disadvantages as video recordings. You need to make sure you exploit the materials rather than just plonk students down in front of the screen and expect the programs to do all the work.

An obvious initial problem may be to do with your own computer literacy. However, you don't need to know very much in order to be capable of providing some useful lessons. There are various commercial programs designed for language learners, popular as self-access activities for students working on their own, but which also work well as class activities. They often involve flexible variations on standard pen-and-paper exercises and activities – fill in the gaps, match the words to pictures, choose the best answer, etc. Teachers have increasingly found ways to also exploit computers in classroom time; even if you don't have any special programs, there are still useful things to do with just a computer and standard office-user software.

Here are a few general thoughts about using computers with students:
- Teachers often think in terms of a 'computer lesson'. That's fine, but also consider planning lessons that involve short periods of computer usage, e.g. ten minutes writing a text as a follow-on from a previous classroom activity, then printing it out for others to read.
- Up to three or four students can often share a single terminal, with one typing and the others suggesting ideas, reading and checking, etc. With more students than this, it may become hard to maintain engagement and motivation levels.
- If you have only a single machine in your classroom, think of lesson ideas that allow learners to work on different things at different times so that each pair/group gets to work for a short time at the machine.
- Computer-based reference materials are very useful. A good thesaurus, dictionary and encyclopaedia are great classroom resources, allowing students to quickly check things during lesson time.

Word processors

- **Writing texts:** This idea may seem too obvious, but it's worth noting that the single best use of a computer is probably just to work on writing, in the same way that people in the world outside the classroom work on it. So, for example, when students have a text to produce, let them work on it using the computer. Three or four students could work on a single console and co-operate in preparing a final text. The standard editing options (i.e. cut, copy, paste, replace, etc.) can help make correction and re-drafting less traumatic. Encourage students to spell-check, use the built-in thesaurus, experiment with different layouts, fonts, paragraphing, etc.
- **Marking students' work:** Ask students to submit homework, etc. on e-mail attachment or computer disk. Mark it using a notes-adding or comment option so that students can go back and review their work and prepare a new draft. (NB Make sure you specify the format in which they supply their documents so that their work is legible on your machine and vice versa.)
- **Mark the teacher:** Prepare a text yourself. Include spelling and grammar errors. Get students to work together to look at the text and correct it.
- **Simple gap-fills:** Write a text – but with spaces. Students discuss and fill in the gaps.

- **Edit source texts:** Provide a number of source texts (e.g. short pieces with relevant information or opinions) and set students a task that requires them to copy, paste and then edit to make a short text answering a specific question. For example, set the task of writing a decision (with reasons) about where to hold a professional conference. Provide source texts, such as short descriptions of two possible towns and hotels, the needs of delegates, the chairman's suggestion, feedback from last year's conference, etc.

Presentation software

Although less familiar than word processors, computer presentation programs (e.g. Microsoft PowerPoint) are a good way of storing and showing images and text in unusual ways, a sort of high-tech slide show. Here are two teaching ideas based on using such a program to flash images or text only briefly to students; both ideas are suitable for classrooms with only a single computer.

- **Flash pictures:** Flash pictures for one second each. Students meet up afterwards, recall them and make up a story including them.
- **Flash lexis:** Do the same, but instead of pictures, show recently studied words (maybe all from one lexical area, e.g. kitchen words). Students try to recall them.

The Internet

Many Internet-based lessons will involve research to find information for some specific purpose. For this reason, it is important that students are able to efficiently use search engines and directories. Beyond that, the web can be used for many purposes including:

- live text communication with other online users (e.g. 'Messenger' programs);
- live audio (and/or webcam) chat with other users (e.g. 'Net meeting');
- delayed-response text communication (e.g. e-mails, message boards, forums, contributions to websites, etc.);
- reading web-based text (newspapers, magazines, articles, catalogues, entertainment, etc.);
- downloading or using web-based content (e.g. language exercises, films, music, etc.);
- designing their own web pages and websites.

Here are a few ideas for activities involving the web:

Reading and research
- 'You have ten minutes to answer these three general knowledge questions.'
- Integrate use of web research into ongoing classroom projects.
- Follow up topics met in the coursebook with 'find an interesting article we can read about this subject'.
- Ask students to find some exercises on specific language points.
- Get the class to agree on certain sites of relevance to them which will be monitored on a regular basis (e.g. an upcoming film, developments in space travel, etc.).
- Join specific interest groups focused on areas relevant to students.

Communication

- Arrange live on-line messenger-chats with students in other towns/countries.
- Organise e-mail pairings between students in different locations.
- Send e-cards to people.
- Add comments to user forums at club sites of interest to students.
- Send messages with suggestions, feedback, offers, complaints, etc. to companies, manufacturers, government, webmasters, fan clubs, etc.

Tasks and projects

- Find real writing projects online, from simple things like registering for websites to taking part in surveys, making contributions to collections of stories or opinions.
- Get students to design and start up their own website on a topic of interest. (This is becoming increasingly easy with some free locations having simple site-editors built in.) Nowadays it's easy to get a page with just a few lines of text up and running; there's no need to have multiple pages. They do not need to be dense with flashy graphics and buttons.

10 Dictation

Traditional dictation – where you read a text aloud and the learners must write it down accurately – is often quite unpopular with learners. It can feel like an unfair test. Could we make it more enjoyable and useful? Maybe the key question is: Who does what? Usually the teacher makes all the decisions about a dictation. How about turning the tables? Let the learners choose the text. Or let them decide how many times it should be read. Or who should read it. In fact, could the learners choose everything and then dictate to the teacher? Here are a few ideas:

Keywords dictation

Find an interesting short story and underline fifteen to twenty of the most important words in it (e.g. key nouns and verbs). Dictate these words to the class, but don't tell them the original story. They now must make a new story that uses those words, in exactly the original order and the original form you dictated. At the end, the class can swap stories, reading or telling them. You could also tell them the original if you wanted.

Collocation dictation

Prepare a list of between ten and twenty useful two-word collocations (i.e. words that naturally go together like *traffic jam*). For the dictation, read out one word from each collocation (e.g. *traffic*). Learners must not write this word (check that they don't cheat!), but instead write a collocation – a word that goes with it (e.g. a learner might write *light* or *policeman* or *heavy* to go with *traffic*). When you have read the whole list, put the learners into small groups. They can compare their answers, see if they can remember the original collocating words and decide if all their collocations are good or not.

Wall dictation

Choose a short printed text. Divide the class into 'readers' and 'writers'. Pair each reader with a writer; writers sit down, readers stand. Stick the text up on a wall far away from the writers so that they cannot possibly read it. (If you have a large class, you'll need to place more than one copy of the text in different places.) Each reader walks to the text, reads and memorises part of it and then goes back to their writer to dictate it. The writer writes it down, asking any relevant questions about words, spellings, punctuation, etc. Whenever necessary the reader goes back and reads more and returns for more dictation. The pair is aiming to write the most accurate text they can. It's a race, and students tend to get quite competitive about it. You may need to set some rules, such as 'Walk – no running', 'No shouting across the room'. Students swap roles about half way through. (By the way, the popular staff-room name for this activity is 'Running dictation'!)

Variation: Use one text, but cut it into separate sentences. Write a letter (A, B, C, etc.) randomly next to each sentence. Place these cut-up texts around the room in different locations so that students have to read all of them, one by one. When pairs have all the pieces written down, they should work together to work out the correct order for a complete coherent text.

The 'bad cold' dictation

Explain that you have a bad cold today (sneeze or cough a bit to prove it!). Tell the class that you're going to do a normal dictation, but if you have to sneeze or cough (and they can't hear a word), they should write any good word that fits the space. For example, you might dictate 'Last Thursday, Maria decided to have some [cough] for breakfast.' The learners could write the sentence with a word like *eggs* or *cornflakes* or *whisky* instead of the cough.

The wild dictation

Dictate a numbered list of descriptions of words, like this: 'No. 1 – the name of a male pop star; No. 2 – an adjective describing some food; No. 3 – a verb of movement, No. 4 – a kind of animal,' etc. The learners should write down answers to these prompts, e.g. *Robbie Williams, salty, swim, kitten,* etc. When the lists are finished, dictate a short story you have prepared, but with appropriate gaps (into which the learners will write their own previously chosen words), e.g. 'A car drove up to the zoo and stopped suddenly and No. 1 got out. He looked really No. 2 as he started to No. 3 towards the No. 4's cage', etc. You'll get some very funny stories. Don't forget to prepare both the story and the list of word descriptions before the lesson.

Dictogloss

For many teachers, this is a favourite technique. But note that it's one activity where it's important that students really understand the instructions before they start.

Choose a short text that is longer than the students could completely remember, e.g. about twenty words at Elementary level. The text could include an example of a grammatical item you are interested in. Tell the class that you will read a dictation at normal speaking speed and you will read it only once. Students probably won't believe this – so check that they do! Then check that students understand that they may find this difficult but must keep quiet and not distract others by complaining, sighing, etc.! Read the text at a normal pace, then give students about three minutes to write down everything they remember – words, phrases, etc. It's important that students get a good, quiet time to do this. They must not compare during this phase. When they have finished, invite students to compare with another, then later to come together as a class to see if they can reconstruct the entire text at the board. The aim is to get as close to the meaning of the original as possible. It is a very interesting task, which may feel impossible to students and teachers at the start, but which proves to be an excellent group-building activity.

Living tape recorder

Draw some tape recorder controls on the board (e.g. a symbol for a Play button, a Rewind button and a Stop button). Introduce yourself as a 'living tape recorder'. Get two students to stand near the board to control the 'tape recorder' while you read the dictation. Members of the class can call out to ask the 'controllers' to 'press' the buttons. You ignore anything said, but strictly obey any button presses. In this way, you will read the dictation, rewinding, replaying, rewinding, etc., until the students are happy that they all have the dictation. It's a bit chaotic at first, but it's great after that!

11 Sound-effects recordings

Sound-effects recordings are a useful teaching resource. These are recordings that have hardly any words on, but instead contain a sequence of noises such as crashes, bumps, bangs, whistles, screams, etc. Heard together, they may add up to a story. There are many commercial recordings of this type or you could make your own.

Making your own 'sound sequence' tape.

Plan a sequence of between seven and ten distinctly different easy-to-make sounds. Choose noises that will be loud and easy to record, for example, a set of plates being dropped, rather than a glove. Do some test recordings. If possible, use a recorder that doesn't set an automatic recording level, otherwise you will get very 'hissy' recordings when no one is speaking.

This is an example sound sequence:
1 Someone says 'Shhhh!'
2 Noisy footsteps.
3 Something breaking.
4 Someone moving with difficulty, grunting, etc.
5 Someone rapidly opening and closing a number of boxes, drawers, etc.
6 Someone saying 'Oh!'
7 Lots of things being dropped.
8 Someone running.
9 Someone saying an amused 'Ah-ha!'

Story-building

Learners listen to the sequence, then in pairs work out what they think the story is. They then compare with others and try to agree a consensus story. Groups tell their versions to the class.

What's wrong with my story?

Prepare – and tell – a story with parts that do not match the recording (e.g. characters use a motorbike rather than walking). Learners discuss and agree which noises do not fit with your story.

Pictures from noises

Bring a set of Cuisenaire rods or building bricks★ to class and distribute these around the class. After hearing the recording, groups use their rods or bricks to create a picture of a scene they imagine from the recording (e.g. walls with other pieces representing burglars breaking in). Afterwards, mix up people from different groups, keeping at least one of the original group with their 'picture'. New people to the group should look and ask questions to find out what the construction represents (and work out the story), e.g. 'Is this a person?' 'Is she climbing through a window?' etc. Members of the original group can only answer 'yes' or 'no'.

★ If you don't have rods or bricks, you could do the activity by asking learners to draw a sketch of the scene.

Verb hunting

Play the recording a few times. Learners find as many verbs as possible to explain what people are doing. (Of course, you could do exactly the same task with nouns, adjectives, adverbs …)

Wacky ideas

Ask learners to think of the wackiest, most amazing, most unlikely interpretation for the sound sequence.

Tense focus

Prepare a story yourself. In class, tell it like a football commentary, using present tenses, i.e. as if it is happening now; for example, 'The burglar is lifting up the window. He's climbing through it', using the recording to provide exciting sound effects at various points. Afterwards, ask the class to write down the story as a news item about the past.

12 Poetry

Why poetry? Because it stimulates, wakes us up to see things in new ways, hear things in new ways, think of things in new ways. Language teaching can be a bit dull if we constantly look at linguistic points using only predictable textbook examples. It may be very helpful to teach 'I went to the shop yesterday and I bought some bread' or 'Jack was having a bath when the telephone rang', but it doesn't stir my heart. I'm not moved by it. I'm sure I'll forget it. But then again, linguists point out that the language used in 'real communication' is also frightfully dull to study. It's bland, repetitive, completely forgettable. To remember something, we need to be surprised by an odd idea or use of words. It's how children learn many things in their first language.

Many teachers don't feel confident using poetry because they are not confident about reading it or writing it themselves. They may say 'I'm not creative', imagining that creativity is something that one must wait for. But of course you have to start writing to find out what you want to write about, how you can say what you have to say. Creativity arises out of the act of writing. You start with nothing. The difficulty of writing forces the new ideas to the surface.

Here are some ideas for using poems in class:

Reading poems

- Choose a poem with some interesting and accessible metaphors. Before they see the poem, dictate to students the sentences that have similes or metaphors (e.g. 'My girlfriend's eyes are … ', 'The river moved slowly as a …'), but leave out the actual comparison itself. Ask students to brainstorm their own comparisons. They can then compare them with each other and finally with the ones used in the poem itself.
- Tell students the topic of the poem and let them brainstorm as many words as they can that might be in it.
- Alternatively, look at a list of words and decide which words might be in a poem about a certain subject.
- Before the lesson, write out a poem as if it were a newspaper article/mini story, etc.; students study and understand this (easier version) before they look at the poem.
- Do a picture dictation: describe the scene in the poem, item by item, and students draw a picture. At the end, they compare pictures and then read the poem, deciding who is closest to the original.

Writing poems

- **Finish it:** Provide a nearly complete poem with gapped parts to complete. (Could be great for slipping in a target grammar point!)
- **Form to poem:** Give or elicit specific aspects of a poetic form, e.g. a rhyme scheme (or actual rhymes), a precise rhythm, the precise number of syllables, etc. Students then make a poem following this exact pattern.
- **Alterations:** Give each student group a different published poem. The groups must copy out the text with a fixed number of altered words (e.g. 'Change five nouns and five verbs to something different'). When they see the copied text, the other teams must guess what is not from the original.
- **Found poems:** Students search for and find potential 'poems' within prose texts (or in signs, posters, etc.) by selecting phrases or blocks of normal text, copying them out and adding line breaks.
- **Cut-ups:** Students are given (or find for themselves) various lines from magazines, brochures, newspapers, etc. They order these to make a poem. (Low-risk activity – it's not the students' words, so they feel less threatened!)
- **Facts to metaphor:** Students write list of facts following your instructions (e.g. 'Write down how you came to school today'); then, when they've finished, they go back over their list adding a metaphor to each (e.g. 'I came by tram' > 'The tram is like a yellow snake').
- **Instant poetry:** This is a surprisingly simple activity that often produces outstanding results. Give a series of instructions that ask students to look, listen, notice what is around them and within them. Each instruction is given, followed by a longish pause to allow students to follow the instruction.

Afterwards, the students go back and 'poemify' it. This is an example set of instructions:

1 Look around you and notice the things you don't normally notice.

2 Look at one item in the room – furniture or object. Write one sentence describing this object. Don't try to be clever. Don't use imagination. Really look and write just what you see. Don't be poetic – you are not writing a poem yet. You are trying to look and write accurately what you can see.

3 Notice the light in the room – the shadows and patterns. Write one sentence about this.

4 Look at one other person. Don't just half-look at them, really study them. I give you permission to stare, as if you'd never seen a human before! Write one sentence about one person you see.

5 Write a sentence about what he/she's thinking.

6 Look at yourself in the same way. Your hands, your clothes, etc. Write one sentence about one thing you see.

7 Describe the view through the window in a few words.

8 Listen to the noises around and outside the room. Write one sentence about what you can hear.

9 How do you feel now? Really? Check it out. Write one sentence.

10 Write something about the future.

11 Now you have ten minutes. Look at what you have written. Change anything you want to. Put things in a different order. Cross things out. Think about how it sounds and looks. Your aim is to finish with a short poem (which could be shared between individuals or read out or put up on a poster, etc.).

13 Drama

Six types of drama activity are commonly found in English language teaching classrooms:

- **Role-play.** Students act out small scenes using their own ideas or from ideas and information on role cards (see Chapter 7, Section 3).
- **Simulation.** This is really a large-scale role-play. Role cards are normally used, and there is often other background information as well. The intention is to create a much more complete, complex 'world', say of a business company, television studio, government body, etc. (see Chapter 7).
- **Drama games.** Short games that usually involve movement and imagination.
- **Guided improvisation.** You improvise a scene and the students join in one by one in character, until the whole scene (or story) takes on a life of its own.
- **Acting play scripts.** Short written sketches or scenes are acted by the students.
- **Prepared improvised drama.** Students in small groups invent and rehearse a short scene or story that they then perform for the others.

All of these are good ways to get students using the language. By bringing the outside world into the classroom like this, we can provide a lot of useful practice that would otherwise be impossible in cafés, shops, banks, businesses, streets, parties, etc. There may also be a freeing from the constraints of culture and expected behaviour; this can be personally and linguistically very liberating. Curiously, it is sometimes the shyest students who are often most able to seize the potential.

Success or failure of drama activities depends crucially on your perceived attitude and that of the other students; without a certain degree of trust, acceptance and respect, the chances for useful work are greatly diminished.

Here are three short examples of drama games and a brief discussion of guided improvisation.

Interesting situations

Students call out any interesting or 'difficult' situation involving two people, and pairs act it out together; for example, a well-meaning hostess serving meat to a polite vegetarian. This technique could, in appropriate circumstances, be used to 'real-play' (i.e. act out and explore some of the students' own real-life problem situations).

Strange meetings

- Prepare three sets of cards (each set should have one card for each student):
  1 a set with character names (alive or dead, fictional or real), e.g. Mel Gibson, Einstein, Madonna;
  2 a set with locations (e.g. 'in the kitchen', 'on the bus');
  3 a set with unusual problems (e.g. 'You have lost your cow', 'You are desperate for a strong coffee').
- Hand out one card from each set to each student (so that every person has a person, place and problem) and then allow them a few minutes to work out their story (i.e. what explains the incident).
- Students then stand up and walk around the room, meeting each other and having short conversations (e.g. Britney Spears meeting Shakespeare; Nelson Mandela meeting Batman) where they try to explain their problem and get help and suggestions.
- When you tap on the table (or ring a bell, etc.), students must move on to a new meeting with another person. It's quite possible that bigger meetings will naturally start to form after a few turns as one character suggests another who might be able to help a particular problem.
- Afterwards, ask learners to recall interesting things they heard.

Making a picture

Call out a subject; the students must agree and make a frozen 'tableau' of that scene. For example, call out 'Airport'; the students take different positions. Some are check-in clerks, some become desks, some become planes taking off, some become tourists, until the whole room 'becomes' an airport. Now unfreeze the tableau and bring it to life for a short scene with improvised dialogue. Everyone can talk and play their part – even the desks and planes!

Guided improvisation

Select a scene – say, a winter landscape with a frozen lake. The idea is to turn the classroom into the scene, and then to let the story unfold in any way it can, by the group improvising together.

You might start by describing the scene and getting students to become people in the landscape, slowly building up a living, moving scene, or you might jump in the deep end by adopting a character yourself and encouraging others to join you in the improvisation as and when they are ready.

The skill of running this kind of complex improvisation is to find a balance between allowing a free-flowing, growing, alive improvisation and the necessity of keeping some control over it to ensure that it keeps momentum and avoids silliness or trite solutions. Most of your interventions to achieve this can be done subtly by saying something, in character, to some of the participants, rather than by stepping in and making grand announcements to everyone.

Some ideas for guided improvisations:
• the perfect school;
• a museum (or waxworks) at night;
• the beach;
• inside a plane;
• kitchen implements come alive;
• an amazing party;
• the secret life of the characters in your coursebook.

14 Projects

Lessons can sometimes feel a little separate and disconnected. Activities may have small, isolated outcomes and sometimes don't seem to offer much in the way of tangible progress or achievement. You can too easily get caught into thinking of lesson content purely on an isolated, lesson-to-lesson basis.

Projects are one useful way of providing an ongoing 'thread' to classroom work. They supply a longer term goal to focus on, and students can invest their energy in something that has a tangible outcome. They also offer a valuable chance for learners of mixed levels to work on something at their own current ability level. Projects are usually **task-oriented** rather than language-oriented; in other words, the learners focus on doing something practical rather than directly on studying language. They typically involve learners in decisions about precisely what is done and how to do it, as well as in collecting information, solving problems and presenting the final outcome as a written or performed presentation. The planning, decision-making, ideas-collecting, structuring, discussion, negotiation, problem-solving, etc. are all an integral part of the work. The language learning arises from learners having a reason to communicate authentically in English to achieve a specific goal. Projects often also have a strong group-building outcome.

Teachers often fear that a project will be troublesome to organise, especially as they may involve different groups of learners working on quite different things. This sounds like it may require a lot more teacher preparation. In fact, it rarely does, because projects quickly become very learner-centred, and learners generally require guidance and advice rather than to have work specially devised for them. The most demanding part of a project for a teacher is in the initial planning and then in the starting-off phase.

Most projects will work best if undertaken by small groups of three or four learners. Individuals could do one, but it can be isolating, and learners on their own tend to lose motivation and focus as time goes on. Working together provides mutual support and a wider range of ideas.

Projects will typically follow a flow plan something like this:

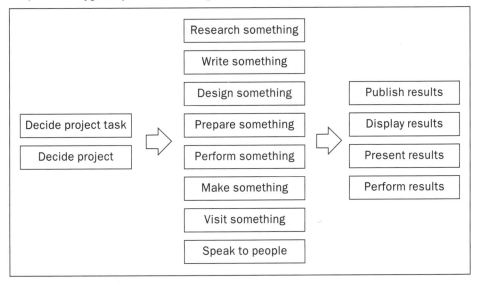

Organising a project: first decisions

In order to begin, you need to decide a few basic things:
- Will the project be a single class project, which smaller pairs and groups undertake some aspect of? Or will groups work on separate and unconnected projects?
- Will the project be one large task that you set and then learners work on, or will it be structured into a series of cumulative steps and stages?
- How much of lesson time will this take up? Will it supplant normal class work entirely? Or will it only take a proportion of each lesson – or of some lessons?
- How long will it last? Is this a three-lesson project or one that will last all term?

Ideas for specific projects
- Write a tourist guide for something in your local area. Use descriptions, photos, diagrams, maps, etc.
- Prepare a web page that gives people in other countries a picture of your everyday life.
- Keep a diary. Prepare a poster/booklet/presentation about 'Your life', including predictions for the future as well as details of your current life.
- Brainstorm/script/storyboard/rehearse/make a three-minute film. The class could all work in the same genre (e.g. horror film; romantic story; advertisement; news programme; etc.) or different ones.
- Put on a live performance of a comedy sketch or a full-length play.

- Invent a new country; draw the map; design the capital; Write the basic laws. Prepare a poster presentation introducing it to others.
- Research and look for ideas to help solve specific real local problems, e.g. lack of entertainment facilities, crime, environmental issues, shops, etc.
- Undertake some public research interviews to find and then analyse a range of people's opinions on certain topics, e.g. attitudes to fashion, taste in music, wishes for the locality, etc.
- In situations where you know your class well and are relatively sure that the learners can work successfully, you might want to approach more difficult, important or controversial topics such as bullying, politics, honesty, attitudes to HIV/Aids, peer pressure, prejudice, etc.

15 The pack of cards

When observing new teachers in class, I usually keep a note of issues we talk about after the lesson. I've noticed that many of the same comments and advice tend to come up again and again. Here, I've selected some of the most frequent or more interesting thoughts and presented them as a random list. Think of it as a pack of cards – if you're feeling bored or in need of a nudge to move you forward a little, try picking one of these 'cards' at random, think about it, check if it applies to you and see if you can make any use of the suggestions.

1 Don't correct good, natural sentences because you want them to use 'full sentences', e.g. in answer to 'Are you going to visit Greece next year?', 'No, I'm not' is actually a better answer than 'No, I'm not going to visit Greece next year'.

2 Getting students to repeat single words is less useful than real-world phrases, e.g. 'marry' is less useful than 'He's married' or 'She's going to get married'.

3 Don't just aim for students to 'understand'. Plan for students to be better able to **use** items.

4 Don't teach and teach. Teach and check. Check again! Check the quiet ones! (Try: Input 5% Checking 95%)

5 Don't over-rely on the stronger students. Don't assume everyone has got something because one has 'got it'. Don't say 'Excellent!', pouncing on the first answer, and rush on. Did all the learners agree? Find out! Throw language and answers around.

6 Teachers often worry that students 'are too good' and maybe 'know it all'! Don't let this get in your way or put you off. It can lead you to rush because you're a little embarrassed at the possibility of boring them.

7 Do you need to keep organising all the time? Do you typically take quite an over-active, motivating role? Can you leave it up to them a bit more?

8 You ask 'All agree?' (there is silence from students). You say 'OK ... and continue to the next item. Is it worth waiting until you get some real answers? Watch out for a tendency to 'fill all the silences'.

9 Be careful that games don't become more important than the language work itself. If you get too focused on who's first, winners, points, etc., it can obscure the real aim.

10 Check out different individual students. Don't rely on the general mumble from the room as a whole. Pick random victims, rather than 'round the circle'.

11 To stop one student dominating, name students to answer. Don't 'hear' the loud student when he shouts out over the top.

12 Try using 'traffic cop' gestures to control interaction. (e.g. 'Stop talking', 'You can speak'). Nominate students with hand gestures to show who's to speak. Postpone giving your 'rubber stamp' of teacher acknowledgement to students' answers. Let them discuss a little. Try the 'blank face' technique when students give a response (i.e. look around without immediately smiling and nodding). Once you 'rubber-stamp' an answer, all discussion is ended.

13 'Feedback after an activity with correction' is a key lesson stage, but tends to be underplanned. Exactly how will you get the answers and do the correction?

14 Is your plan just: (1) Students do lots of exercises; (2) You go through them validating correct answers. How can you get more variety into that?

15 When students ask a question or try to explain something to you, don't talk over them! Listen! Separate your talk from theirs (it's not a 'café chat').

16 Are you getting **real** feedback from the learners? More than just an 'it's all OK' or a bland pat on the back? Give yourself space to listen and find out how they are really doing.

17 Are you really finding out if they all know the items ... or is it just the first person to call out? One person gave an answer. What about the others? Are you steamrollering answers? One person half-catching something doesn't equal 'Everyone got it and there were no problems'.

18 It can be useful to 'disappear' sometimes. There are tasks you can just let them get on with. Your visible presence can be an interference.

19 Are students only telling you, the teacher? Does all communication goes through you? If you set up an activity well, they should often be able to do it on their own. Constant micro-management will drain the task of any pace or fun and you can end up doing the task more than students. Find ways to encourage them to tell each other more.

20 Don't start speaking into a general classroom hubbub. Get their attention first.

21 You can only **elicit** things they know/half-know. Otherwise you need to **input**. If you anticipate words will be 'new', plan to teach more than elicit.

22 Do you sometimes work with a stronger student to clarify a word's meaning ... but with relatively little evidence that others have got it?

23 When students ask 'Can I say …?' (i.e. they want to check with you if they have the right meaning for a word), try to avoid artificial encouragement like 'Maybe' or 'We could say that' if it's not true.

24 Do you tend to make eye contact mainly with the centre of the room? Could you spread it around more?

25 Remember that it's always much, much harder for students to listen than most teachers ever believe!

26 'Were there any words that you found difficult?' (Well, almost certainly yes! It's not a very useful question.)

27 Are you more concerned with collecting right answers than with helping students listen? Listening should not primarily be a 'test'; rather your aim is to help them get better at listening. (How can you do this?)

28 If you tell students what was on the recording, then you end up doing the difficult listening work, not them.

29 Does this classroom moment ring any bells: 'Did they meet the famous person?' All students say 'no'. You start rapidly nodding 'yes'. A student says 'yes'. You say 'So the answer's "yes" because on the recording she said …'

30 A centimetre of input; a metre of practice!

31 When teachers make requests like 'Can you say that for me?', I keep thinking 'Why "for me"?' To please the teacher? Whose benefit is the practice for? There are a lot of underlying assumptions in the language that teachers use, and it is sometimes worth challenging them by looking at everyday language use and seeing what lies behind it. If we believe that a teacher's job is to help students learn – and that learners are not doing things to please us, but from their own motivation – then maybe the reflection of attitudes in small 'inconsequential' phrases and little actions may be worth noting.

32 To get some things to really 'take off', you may need to send out a slightly more argumentative, playful or 'devil's advocate' tone.

33 Don't get stuck in 'large class teacher' mode all the time.

34 With mumbling students, be careful not to get locked into inaudible one-to-one loops. Walk further away rather than closer.

35 Don't keep apologising, telling them how hard, fast, tedious, etc. it was/will be. If you really want to raise this, ask for their ideas in a way that doesn't apologise.

36 Don't put embarrassed individuals in the spotlight to admit their failures! It can be excruciating.

37 Don't ask big questions like 'Did you understand anything on the recording?'

38 While students listen, sit still! Don't fuss around; it's distracting.

39 When listening, don't just automatically replay. Let them check if they could do the task.

40 If timing is a worry, try planning a lesson backwards, i.e. if you really want them to have time to do presentations at the end (and discuss them), plan your timing backwards from that and calculate back to the lesson start.

41 Be careful of interrupting too much once you have set students to do a task. Basic guideline is 'Set it up, then get out!' Consider when certain things need to be done and plan ahead.

42 Is your lesson a little on the easy side? Are you holding their hands a bit too much? Do you back off a little from really grabbing some bulls by the horns? Do you side-step to avoid the tricky, interesting, challenging bits of a lesson (maybe because it might put you on the spot)?

43 With grammar, the theoretical understanding is the smallest part of the problem. It's actually making use of that knowledge to make 'live' decisions when communicating that is difficult.

44 Are some of your lessons good but a little 'mechanical', as if you are doing the lesson 'to' the students more than working with them? Make sure that, in execution, you leave space for students to influence the flow (at least a little). How much are you really listening to them and altering the lesson in subtle ways to respond? The students need to inhabit more space than just giving one-word answers or repeating sentences.

45 Lots of oral practice!

46 Could you 'demand' better/louder/more natural-sounding student sentences?

47 Don't over-help. The learning is often in the struggle. Don't feel you have to 'save' them from every difficulty.

48 If the main aim of a task is 'reading', maybe one of the skills they are working on is understanding text even when they don't know every word. So maybe lexis work could come **after** the task rather than interrupting the reading? Let them struggle and try to 'read' first.

49 When you teach or check a word, make sure your definition is as precise as possible rather than just in the general area. If a student didn't understand the meaning of *crash*, would someone hitting their hand on the board help? Or could they equally totally misunderstand? If it's not precise, what is the purpose of the mime activity?

50 Don't let 'intro' stuff take too long. Work on 'getting to the meat' quicker.

51 Student writing on the board can be very hard to read. Don't avoid it, but remember that they may need encouragement to write more clearly if it's for 'public' reading.

52 If you want a 'learner-centred' lesson but your internal image of a 'teacher' is someone who sits at the front, talking, helping, questioning, etc., there may be a clash. If you ask the students to 'tell each other' but then still sit very visibly upfront looking at them, frequently interrupting, helping, guiding, questioning, etc., you'll probably get a largely silent room, waiting for your next response rather than a lively discussion.

Joker Hey! Slow down!

Chapter 17 **Learning teaching**

1 What is 'learning teaching'?

The title of this book suggests that there is a kind of teaching that is also a kind of learning – a 'learning teaching'. It's not just the students who do the learning, but you do as well. You teach and you learn – and the two things are intertwined. Outside and inside the class, you live and you learn.

It is not just something you do while you are on an initial training course or while you are a 'green', new teacher. Instead, it is how you could be throughout your teaching career. I'd go so far as to suggest that any teacher who has stopped learning themselves has probably also stopped being useful as a teacher.

One good way to keep learning about teaching is to never let your ideas 'set in concrete', to remain open to the possibility of being wrong – or to more interesting alternative ways of doing things, to always be questioning (and possibly changing) some of your ideas.

As you read this book – or any other ELT writing – collect any practical ideas and techniques you need, but also keep questioning and challenging the author's suggestions. Keep your mind working on discovering what you believe about how people learn and how best to enable that. In many ways, the questions are more important than the answers; knowing that something is not fixed and certain encourages a different, more exploratory way of working.

Task 215: A step towards being a 'learning teacher'

Be uncertain!

Commentary ■ ■ ■

Don't be too keen to rush to certainty about the best way of doing something. In fact, I'd argue that there's a lifetime of fruitful work in enjoying your uncertainty! If you ever start getting too sure of the answers, try having a rethink on one of the questions below to keep you alert!

- Do I really know how someone learns to use a new item of language?
- How exactly does my teaching make a positive difference?
- What do I do that gets in the way of my students' learning? ■

Teaching is very exciting and challenging in the first few months and years. But as it becomes more familiar and you grow in confidence, there is a danger that things may grow staler and less enjoyable.

Teacher development

Learning about teaching doesn't stop whenever your training courses finish. In fact, this is where your development as a teacher really begins. You could:

- read new ideas in magazines and try them out.
- write an article for a magazine (most articles in magazines for language teachers are by teachers like you).
- start a local newsletter.
- try a 'bold parabola' (see Chapter 6, Section 9).
- go to a conference or a seminar.
- go to a conference and give a talk about what you have been working on in class.
- learn about a completely different approach.
- discuss what you are doing with other teachers.
- make an agreement with a colleague to observe each other's lessons.
- find a way to get involved in some in-service teacher training.
- do a seminar for your colleagues.
- become a director of studies or a head teacher!
- start your own school!
- give private lessons.
- specialise (e.g. computers, business, self-access centres, video, music, exams, etc.).
- write a message for a website. Write a magazine article. Write a book.
- read this book again!

Some key ideas for moving forward are addressed in this chapter:
- Ask for someone to observe your lessons – or observe other teachers' classes (see Sections 2 and 3).
- Do some small-scale action research (see the end of Section 3).

Teacher development groups and associations

The quality of the progress you make in teaching (and how you feel about it) is partly to do with other people. If you work in a staff room where people are open and ready to discuss and exchange ideas (and materials), you have a huge bonus. Many teachers have found that membership of a local, regional or national teachers' group has tremendous benefits. So my main suggestion if you are feeling at all stuck would be to join (or start) a teacher development (TD) group.

Local TD group

Invite colleagues working in your school (or in the local area) to come together for a meeting. Tell them that this will (initially, at least) be without a fixed agenda beyond offering a chance for everyone to meet up and discuss any current issues, problems, developments, etc. Although it may be tempting to programme talks, events, etc., the most useful support may simply be the chance to meet up and share stories. A typical surprise is when teachers discover that they are not alone in how they feel, but that other teachers share many of their interests, worries, questions, etc. Once the group is under way, more ambitious schedules can be agreed upon. Be careful not to become side-tracked into being a one-issue group (e.g. to promote a political or administrative change that teachers see as important); make sure you keep the space for conversation as well.

Regional, National and International Teachers' Associations

These provide another brilliant line of support. Frequently such organisations prepare conferences, courses and newsletters. They are a great way of **networking**, i.e. meeting other teachers and keeping in touch. IATEFL (International Association of Teachers of EFL) is perhaps the largest such organisation, with important national groups in many countries, gigantic international and regional conferences, and extremely useful Special Interest Groups (SIGs) with their own newsletters. Remember, the people who run these are not distant bureaucrats, but teachers like you – and just about every organisation I have ever come across is delighted when teachers express an interest in helping run things. That's a great way of getting inspired, while doing something useful for yourself and others.

How can I change?

In order to grow, we need to remain open to the possibility of change. That may be difficult, for change is risky and potentially threatening. It can feel safer to stay fixed, unmoving. But this means, week by week, hour by hour, we grow stale and our lessons grow tired – recreations of old, dead lessons, rather than new, living ones.

Here are two interesting views on change from thousands of years apart. Both suggest that a keener awareness of the present is the key to changing.

Tao

The ancient Chinese philosophy of Tao sees everything in the universe as interdependent and constantly changing. We, like everything else, are part of this process. Change is natural. The best way to live is to remain open to the natural flow of change and move with it, i.e. going with the flow, rather than trying to swim upstream. We do our best when trying to act in accordance with nature, using minimal interventions rather than strong force.

Thus, in the Taoist view, we do not need to struggle to change ourselves. Rather, we need to be aware of the world around us and our place in it – and remain open to moving with the changes that take place and involve us. In other words: be here now, fully and alertly.

Krishnamurti

Krishnamurti (1895–1986) was an Indian thinker who had a most extraordinary life. Much of his philosophy is of direct relevance to people who work in education. The following passage is part of Krishnamurti's answer to a child who asked 'How can you change yourself?'

When people say 'I am changing from this to that', they think they are moving. They think they are changing. But in actual fact, they have not moved at all. What they have done is projected an idea of what they should be … But it is not a movement. They think it is change, but what is change is first to be aware of what actually 'is' and to live with it, and then one observes that the 'seeing' itself brings about change.

Krishnamurti on Education (**Krishnamurti Foundation, 1974**)

I find this very powerful guidance on a way to change. He is arguing against setting up distant goals and trying to reach them. If you are fully aware of the present and what 'is', he suggests, then that awareness, of itself, already produces change.

2 Observed lessons

Task 216: 'I'm going to observe you …'

A trainer (or head of department or director of studies) stops you in the corridor and says 'I'm going to come in and observe your lesson on Tuesday.'

- How do you feel?
- What would you like to know before she comes in?

Commentary ■ ■ ■

Observation is a common feature of teacher-training courses and is a part of in-service teacher support in many schools. It is worth clearly distinguishing five types of observation (although a single observation could incorporate more than one of these). ■

Five types of observation

Observation may be:

- **Training:** As part of a training programme to help trainers identify your current level of skills and your needs. Training observations are typically on 'someone else's agenda', i.e. you are being observed and assessed as part of a programme or syllabus to achieve a certain set of specified goals.
- **Developmental:** This contrasts with training, in that 'development' suggests your own agenda is paramount (rather than that of a course requirement or a trainer). In a developmental observation, you would typically specify yourself what would be most useful to have feedback on.
- **Assessment:** To assess you and your teaching against criteria of quality, acceptability, appropriacy, etc. An assessment may be part of a course (with grades, levels, points, etc.) or it may be an internal or external inspection, for example by a national association of school recognition.
- **Data collection:** Sometimes schools or teachers or others may want to objectively investigate some aspect of classroom life (such as 'comparing participation levels of male and female students' or 'varieties of teacher questions'). Often such observations will be based on making quantitative studies (i.e. how often, how much, etc.) of what goes on. Such observations are often by peers rather than by trainers or members of the school hierarchy.
- **Peer observation:** Peer observation is when a colleague comes in to watch your lesson (or part of a lesson). The aim is for both participants to learn something. You are not expecting your colleague to give you 'trainer-type' feedback, but there can probably be an exciting exchange of ideas, discussion about different ways of working, comparison of views, etc.

Formal observations

I'll say something more about peer observation in the next section. For this section, we'll now focus on 'formal' observations.

Many teachers respond to news of an upcoming formal observation with some degree of trepidation (or sheer terror). Whatever the stated purpose, it may feel like a 'test' of some sort – and there is always likely to be some degree of 'intrusion' when an extra person is sitting in your classroom. Students may respond differently (often more reticently), and it is often hard for you to do what you do naturally when, every time you blink, that guy in the corner scribbles a new comment. It can lead to a heightened degree of self-consciousness which, in the worst cases, can interfere with your natural skills and the success of the lesson.

Having said that, observation, done well, provides perhaps the most useful help a learning teacher can get. When we are teaching, it's very hard to take in coolly and objectively the whole panorama of what is happening around us in the classroom. We may naturally get locked into particular habits, ways of working, ways of speaking, avoidances, etc. that we are unable to notice, simply because it is we who do them. An observer can be an outside eye, someone who can tell us things. If we trust the person coming in, there is an opportunity to get insights from a different viewpoint, from someone who is not emotionally involved with the class, but who can notice things we can't and can tell us things we can't see, or half-see but have not fully taken on.

So, the trepidation on hearing of an observation is fully understandable (I still get it myself), but it is worth getting past that as soon as possible and looking for ways of maximising the learning possible from such help.

All kinds of observation can lead to useful learning. The chances of this are significantly less if there is no feedback discussion following the lesson (for example, in an inspection), though even then, the challenge of preparing and delivering a high-quality lesson may spur you to discover things about yourself and your students that you hadn't known before.

If an observation is to happen, both parties usually need to know and agree as many of the following things as possible:

* All the logistical details (when, where, how long);
* Information about the class (level, what the students are like, recent study, current issues, etc.);
* Information about the intended type of lesson (a 'by-the-book' lesson? a 'wing-it' lesson? an experiment? a 'driving test' (i.e. attempting to show off the best that the teacher can do)?) In other words, to what extent is the observer going to see a representative lesson?;
* The type of observation (training, developmental, assessment, data, peer);
* Who sets the agenda, i.e. who decides the specific aims of the observation. It could be (1) the observer; (2) the teacher being observed; or (3) some external source (e.g. a school code or a teacher-training course syllabus;
* Specific aims of the observation, i.e. what the observer will look out for and plan to make comments on afterwards (which will depend on who set the agenda);
* How you would like the observer to be ('invisible', participating in the lesson, taking lots of notes, videoing, etc.).

3   Studying your own teaching: feedback, reflection and action research

Teaching English can be very exciting, but at 3.30 on a Monday afternoon, with a whole term ahead of you, it can seem a lot of other things, too.

For the first two years or so in the profession, the demands of getting to grips with subject matter, technique, organisation, school politics, not to mention students, can be very stressful and tiring, and it may often feel as if you stand no chance at all of winning through. Ideals and enthusiasm that you started with may fade away as it becomes clear that you can't make every lesson perfect, that some students, some classes simply won't like what you do. And there are the days when you may have to struggle just to get through.

As time goes on, you will probably find that you have more experience to lean on, more tried-and-tested lessons in the bag to recycle endlessly. Then boredom and staleness are the dangers, once the challenge of becoming competent has faded. Twenty years of teaching experience can become no more than two years' experience repeated ten times over. Repeated venturing down well-travelled roads leads sooner or later to boredom, to fossilisation of routines, to increasing defensiveness and fear of change. The question becomes not 'How can I survive?' but 'How can I keep moving forward?' or 'How can I become the best teacher that I can be?' The more established and safer you are in your job, the harder it can become to take risks, to try something completely different.

The first important steps towards becoming a better teacher involve an increased awareness about what you do now and an openness to the possibility of change.

If you want to move forward, you have to be clear about what it is that you do now. Do you actually **know** what you are doing in class? Do you ever stop and examine your actions, your intentions, your motives, your attitudes? You keep planning for the next lesson, the next day, but to look back, to recall what happened, to reflect on it: this seems harder to do. What did happen in that class? What were you like as a teacher? Did you enable learning or prevent it? Why did you do the things you did? What were the other options, the ones that you didn't take?

We can teach and teach. Or we can teach and learn. This kind of teaching, a 'learning teaching', is a refusal to say 'I know it all. I can relax for the rest of my career.' Learning teaching is a desire to move forward, to keep learning from what happens. It involves feedback from others and from ourselves about what happened. It involves reflection on what happened, together with an excitement about trying a slightly different option next time. Learning teaching is an aware and active use of the experiential learning cycle in one's own life and work. Learning teaching is a belief that creativity, understanding, experience and character continue growing throughout one's life.

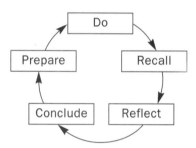

Getting feedback on teaching

Feedback from colleagues

Ask other teachers to come in and observe some of your lessons, and do an exchange observation with them, not to judge each other or score points but to learn from each other. The growth in trust and respect that comes from sharing ideas and skills in this way can really help all involved move forward, as well as having a markedly positive effect on the whole atmosphere of a school.

Even if a colleague cannot come in and observe a lesson, then you could still set aside some uninterrupted time (perhaps fifteen minutes or so) when he/she will sit and listen to you talk through your thoughts about the lesson. Your colleague could make a 'contract' with you that he or she will not offer suggestions or advice or help or opinions, but will simply listen and support you. This kind of helping is very simple to describe, but extremely powerful in action. It can be surprisingly beneficial to talk through one's own experience with another person who is really listening.

Feedback from you

When you have taught a lesson, it can be tempting to see it completely uncritically in broad shades of extremes either as a huge success or as a complete failure. Teachers sometimes find themselves diving from one extreme to the other in the space of a few minutes.

You may equally be tempted not to think about the lesson at all, to put it away in the back of your mind and forget it, or alternatively to brood over it, picking away at it for hours afterwards, regretting what happened and seeing every possible alternative way of doing things as an improvement on what actually happened.

The alternative (and more difficult option) is to try and take an objective, more balanced view of what happened: first to recall what happened, then to reflect on that and look for what was successful and for what could be improved. Whatever the lesson was like, there will have been good points in it and things that could be worked on. This is true for the most experienced teacher as much as for a beginner.

If you are taking an initial training course, then your tutors may be just as interested in encouraging your own self-awareness as in pointing out successes and problems themselves. They could spend the whole time praising what you did, or tearing your lesson into little pieces, but the only thing that is going to move you forward as a teacher is if you yourself become aware of what works and what doesn't.

'Hot and cold feedback' is one way of becoming more aware of what you are doing. It works like this:

Hot feedback

As soon as you sit down after teaching (and as soon as you have got your breath back!), write down a description of some of the things that happened and/or your first reactions and feelings about what happened. None of this needs to be more than a sentence or two; you may find that the simple act of trying to get your thoughts together in writing will help you to clarify exactly what it is that you are thinking. For example:

The oral practice seemed to work well. The students got really involved and didn't want to stop. I noticed that I was concentrating on students to my right; I rather left out the five sitting near the door. Checking the homework with the whole class was very dull. There must be a better way to go through all the answers.

Cold feedback

When the lesson has become a bit clearer in your head – maybe an hour or so later, or perhaps the next day (or, if the lesson was observed, after the observer has talked over the lesson with you) – add a few more sentences, remembering to look for the positive things as well as things that need work. For example:

What was successful: the lexical game – fast and fun – they practised a lot of words. I felt more confident in this lesson; I'm beginning to get used to the way this class works.

To work on: I could be clearer with instructions. They were definitely confused at the start of the game. I talked rather a lot. I noticed myself talking over some their answers when I got impatient – I'll try to watch for that in future. I don't think Joanna said anything all lesson. I must have a chat with her and find out if everything's OK. Perhaps I could ask questions direct to named individuals, rather than general questions to the whole class. That would stop the two strong ones always coming in first.

The 'feedback' sheet will now represent your views at two different stages of considering the lesson. You may well find that your reaction is rather different at these two points. Finding which view of these two is the most objective, realistic and supportive to yourself may improve your ability to analyse your own lessons in the future, and thus help your development as a teacher.

Your own approach to this kind of self-feedback will reflect your own style and your own perceptions, but if you find it hard to get going, try using the self-assessment model described below.

Lesson self-assessment

For each lesson you teach, choose one question from part A below, one from part B and one from part C. Write your answers. If possible, talk through your answers with another person who has agreed simply to listen (rather than take part in a conversation).

Roughly speaking, A focuses you on recalling what happened in the lesson. B focuses on reflecting on the lesson, particularly looking for what was successful. C focuses on drawing conclusions from the experience and finding ways to move forward in your future teaching.

A Recalling the lesson
1 List a number of things that you did during the lesson.
2 List a number of things that the students did during the lesson.
3 Note down any comments or feedback that a student gave you during the lesson.
4 Note any important personal interaction between you and a student during the lesson.
5 Summarise the main stages of the lesson as you remember it.
6 What was the balance of 'teacher doing things' compared with 'students doing things' in the lesson?
7 List some things that happened approximately as you planned them.
8 List some things that happened differently from your plan.
9 Recall one moment in the lesson when you had a clear decision to make between one option and another. What were the options you chose and rejected?

B Reflecting on the lesson
1 Note several things that you are proud of about the lesson.
2 What was the high point of the lesson for you? Why did it feel good?
3 Can you answer that same question from the students' point of view?
4 Name several specific points in the lesson where you feel the students were learning something.
5 At what points could you have been clearer?
6 Which part of the lesson involved the students most completely?
7 Where were the main challenges for the students?

8 Where was time not used efficiently?
9 At what point did you feel most awkward or uncomfortable?
10 Did you achieve what you wanted to achieve?
11 Did the students achieve what you hoped they would achieve?

C Drawing conclusions; making plans

1 If you taught the lesson again, what would you do the same?
2 If you taught the lesson again, what would you do differently?
3 What have you learned about your planning?
4 What have you learned about your teaching procedures and techniques?
5 What have you learned about your students?
6 What have you learned about yourself?
7 What have you learned about learning?
8 List some intentions or 'action plans' for your future teaching.
9 Write a brief description of yourself as a teacher seen from a student's viewpoint. What is it like to be taught by you?

Action research

Action research is a teacher's personal study of his/her own teaching or of the students' learning. It contrasts with a more common image of research as something done by academics in distant universities. Action research has the advantage that it can be very small scale. Anything you do in your work that is actively seeking to help you learn and progress is a kind of action research. A more systematic route (e.g. when you want to experiment with a new classroom technique) might follow the route shown in Figure 17.1.

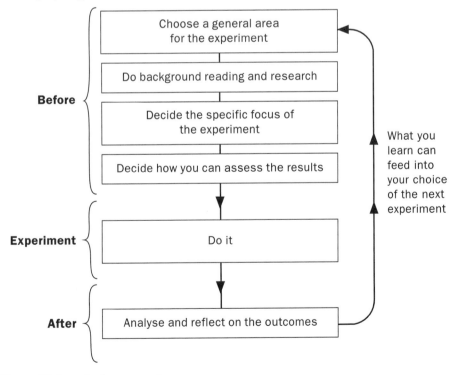

Figure 17.1   Action research

Task 217: Action research

Fiona is talking about her own small-scale action research. Match parts of her description to the diagram in Figure 17.1.

I began to worry that I was talking too much in class and that it was getting in the way of students' learning. I found a book on the school bookshelf with a very short mention of the Silent Way method that sounded interesting. I researched Silent Way on the Internet and found some sample lesson plans. I thought there was no way I could do a full Silent Way lesson, but I decided I could try something from one of the plans. I planned a normal lesson but with a ten-minute stage when I would try out a student activity where I would say very much less than usual. I decided to record the whole 50-minute lesson and listen back to it afterwards. When listening, I would make a rough assessment of how much I talked every three minutes. So I did the lesson, and the activity sort of worked, but the most interesting revelation was how much I talked in the other parts of the lesson – even more than I'd thought. This led me to design my next experiment in which I ...

4   A closing comment: language and people

As language teachers, we are privileged to work with a vital and fascinating subject matter. Language is the way we express our very being. It is the way we come to terms with the world. It is the way we make our understanding of life concrete. It is the way we make contact with other humans beings.

As a teacher, you will often find yourself tied up in the nitty-gritty atomistic side of language: the verb endings and the prepositions, the schwas and the falling intonation patterns. But try to keep hold of the 'whole' as well. Don't lose touch with the fact that people need language to communicate with other people. Remember this in class, and let it sound an occasional warning bell in your head. Don't only hear the mistakes and the verb tenses and the adverbs; try to hear the people using the language. Education is too important to be lost amid a constant focus on smaller problems.

At its widest, I think all education is an answer to a single basic question: 'What are humans for?' Clearly everyone has their own different, individual answers, or will be searching to find them. As teachers, our major contribution to life and to education is to help others find their own way towards their own solutions within their own lives.

As a teacher, you are also a learner – learning about language, methodology, people, yourself, life ... I suspect that the moment you stop learning, you also stop being involved in education. So, rather than being a teacher, be a learner. There's no need to role-play someone with all the answers; be honest with yourself and actively find ways to learn alongside your students.

In this book, I have tried to deal with methodology not as a series of rules and truths that already and permanently exist, but as options available to us all, to use or not to use as we wish. *Learning Teaching* is about our personal search for our own answers, rather than merely re-enacting other people's solutions. In looking for ways to move forward as a teacher, you will also find ways to grow as a person.

Good luck. I hope you enjoy it all.

Appendix 1 **Observation Tasks**

1 **Classroom snapshot**
2 **What helps people learn?**
3 **Teachers and learners**
4 **Classroom interaction**
5 **Options and decisions**
6 **How can a teacher influence the learning environment?**
7 **The learners**
8 **Errors and correction**
9 **Thoughts and questions**
10 **Stolen goods**

This appendix is a collection of lesson observation tasks. I include them because I strongly believe that observation of other teachers (or of other trainees on a course) is an excellent way of helping oneself to become more aware of options and possibilities.

Doing tasks like these can help an observer to focus more clearly on what is happening in a lesson. They may provide useful information or insights for personal reflection or for a post-lesson discussion. This does not imply that 'evaluation' or 'criticism' is required. Observation and discussion are learning tools for the observer and the teacher. In the right environment, where both people are respectful and supportive of each other, and where there is a clear agreement to be honest, then a post-lesson discussion can be invaluable as a way of moving forward.

Using the tasks

You could:
- observe a more experienced teacher's lesson;
- observe a colleague's lesson;
- agree to observe each other's lessons;
- observe a trainee teacher's lesson;
- ask someone to observe your own lesson;
- ask a colleague to teach your class and watch how your students work with a different teacher;
- think back to a lesson you have already seen;
- think back to a lesson you have already taught.

You could:
- discuss the lesson before it happens;
- discuss it afterwards;
- not discuss it at all;
- fill in the task during the lesson;
- not fill in the task, but use it to focus your thoughts;
- give the filled-in task to the teacher;
- keep the filled-in task for yourself;
- discuss the filled-in task.

You could, of course, also:
- invent your own task;
- agree a new task with the teacher.

OBSERVATION TASK 1   Classroom snapshot

Ask permission to go into a colleague's class for just five minutes. Your aim is to gain a 'snapshot' image of what is happening. Persuade the teacher not to prepare any special activity for this time.

For the first questions, aim to describe factually as far as you can (rather than interpreting or finding positive or negative aspects). Add your more subjective impression in answering the last question.

1   Describe how the learners are seated/standing in the room.

2   Describe generally what is happening (e.g. 'A tape is being played and learners are writing answers to printed questions').

3   Who is talking? Who is doing any other things?

4   Describe (a) the atmosphere; and (b) levels of engagement in the room.

OBSERVATION TASK 2   What helps people learn?

What is there about the classroom, the activities, the teacher and the learners that helps to create conditions for effective learning? What things do you observe that seem to play a part in preventing learning?

The classroom

Make notes on seating, sight lines, space, air, warmth, light, whiteboard, equipment, etc.

The activities

Make notes on the kind of activities used, the nature of student involvement, balance of students doing things and teacher doing things, etc.

The teacher

What personal qualities does the teacher have (i.e. not teaching techniques)? What kind of rapport does this teacher have? What is the personal psychological atmosphere generated by this teacher? What is it like to be a student in this classroom?

The learners

How motivated are the learners? Why? To what extent are they taking an active part in their own learning? To what extent are they expecting the teacher to do the work for them?

OBSERVATION TASK 3   Teachers and learners

For each line, decide if the statement on the left or right fits best as a description (or somewhere in the middle). You could use the chart to:

- think back to a language lessons you can recall from your past;
- use the chart as an observation task the next time you go into a class to watch someone else teaching;
- review your own teaching style, perhaps in a specific lesson.

The teacher			
The teacher smiles.			The teacher doesn't smile.
The teacher is unnaturally loud or quiet.			The teacher speaks at a natural, conversational volume.
The teacher behaves and interacts as he/she might outside the classroom.			The teacher behaves and interacts in a distinctively 'teacherly' way.
The teacher talks a lot.			The teacher talks very little.
Task instructions are clear.			Task instructions are not clear.
The teacher asks mainly open questions.			The teacher asks mainly questions with expected/fixed answers.
The teacher seems impatient.			The teacher is patient.
Information is conveyed clearly and is understandable by learners.			Information is conveyed unclearly or is not understood by learners.
Teacher doesn't seek or take note of learner feedback through the lesson.			Teacher seeks and takes note of learner feedback through the lesson.
Teacher adjusts the lesson content in response to learners.			Teacher doesn't adjust the lesson content in response to learners.
The teacher is working at his/her own pace.			The teacher is working at the pace of the learners.
Comments			

The learners			
Learners are generally engaged.			Learners are generally not engaged.
Learners are largely passive.			Learner take an active role in lesson.
Learners are mainly obeying instructions.			Learners are largely autonomous.
Participation levels are roughly balanced			Some learners dominate.
Comments			

OBSERVATION TASK 4   Classroom interaction

Who talks? Who do they talk to? Who gets left out? By recording information objectively over a short period of time, it may be possible to notice some factors that make an important contribution to the working environment.

Task 1: Who speaks?

Draw a rough sketch map of the classroom, marking each seating position and the place where the teacher is standing or sitting.

Choose a two-minute period near the start of the lesson and simply put a mark (e.g. a tick or a line) next to each person who says something. Repeat this task at one or two other points in the lesson.

Here is a map I made during one teacher's class:

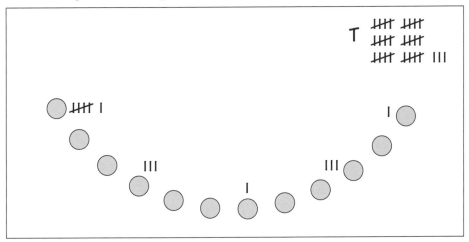

Task 2: Interaction patterns

Draw a similar map of the classroom. Choose a two-minute period during a whole-class speaking stage of the lesson. Add arrows to the diagram to indicate who is speaking to whom (similar to the diagrams in Chapter 5, Section 2 on pages 85–6).

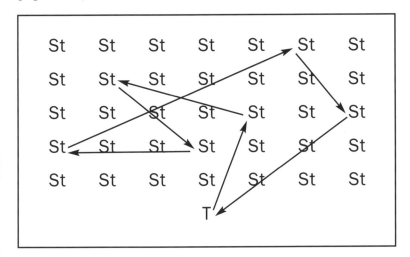

OBSERVATION TASK 5   Options and decisions

The term 'classroom management' refers to the moment-by-moment decisions made and actions taken by the teacher in class, e.g. writing on the board, giving instructions, organising the class into pairs, etc. For every decision made, there will have been other options that the teacher did not choose.

For each of the following headings:

1 note one example of a classroom situation in the lesson you are observing. What does the teacher do?
2 note one or two other options that the teacher had at that point in the lesson, but did not choose.

Example: Dealing with unexpected problems

Situation: A student arrived twelve minutes late for the lesson.

Action: Teacher said 'hello' politely. (The student then sat down quietly and found out what was going on from his neighbour.)

Other options: Teacher could have asked why the student was late. Teacher could have pointed out the time to the student.

```
Student participation in lesson
Situation:
Action:
Other options:


Grouping of students; arrangement of seating
Situation:
Action:
Other options:


Setting up activities; instructions
Situation:
Action:
Other options:


Board; classroom equipment; visual aids
Situation:
Action:
Other options:


Dealing with unexpected problems
Situation:
Action:
Other options:


Teacher's role and participation
Situation:
Action:
Other options:


Other notes about the lesson:
```

OBSERVATION TASK 6   How can a teacher influence the learning environment?

The table lists some ways a teacher can influence the environment in which students learn. Choose a few of these headings (four or five is probably enough). Observe and make detailed notes about what the teacher does/doesn't do to help learning. Where possible, note specific concrete examples of techniques, e.g. what precisely does the teacher do to help create a warm classroom atmosphere?

Aspects of the learning environment	The teacher's role
Classroom atmosphere	The teacher can help establish and maintain an appropriate, warm, focused working atmosphere.
Organisation	The teacher can take an active role in organising how time, space, materials, etc. are used.
Encouragement and support; promoting participation	The teacher can provide positive, realistic support and encouragement to take an active role.
Promoting guided discovery	The teacher can elicit answers, construct questions, offer partial examples, encourage hypotheses, etc. that lead the students to work out answers for themselves.
Presenting content information	The teacher can explain, lecture, answer questions, etc. on areas of the learning content.
Provision of samples of language	Instructions, comments, questions, stories, etc. in the target language provide language exposure for the learners.
Materials and tasks	The teacher can propose, suggest or select what work is done in class and the texts and other materials used.
Monitoring	The teacher can monitor what is happening in class.
Informative feedback	The teacher can offer objective information that may help the learning process; for example, information about errors made, information about how language is formed or used, information about how a task was performed, suggestions for future work, etc. The teacher can notice and help to draw attention to progress made, problems encountered, etc.
Habit of learning	As part of a regular timed lesson, the teacher can help provide a sense of form, regularity and concreteness to an otherwise more formless learning process.
Selecting, packaging and grading	The teacher can plan that new material is met and worked with in ways that students may find more manageable than if they had to deal with the entire language in one go.
Structuring and sequencing	The teacher can suggest or help select what to study and how to organise the programme of learning and the shape of individual lessons. →

Authority	The teacher can use her authority where appropriate, e.g. to make decisions, to close activities or discussions, to require certain actions from individuals, etc.
Raising awareness	The teacher can ask questions, give information or do other things that help learners to notice areas they may otherwise not have been aware of. These may be to do with the subject being studied or about other things, for example, about themselves and their way of learning, their relationships with other students or their behaviour.
Guidance and direction	The teacher can use her knowledge and experience where appropriate to counsel, guide and direct individuals.
Learner training	The teacher can raise learners' awareness about their own process of learning and can suggest ways they could become more efficient and effective learners.
Democracy and personal responsibility	The teacher can help ensure that all students are equally respected and their views and working styles equally valued and catered for. The teacher can make efforts to allow students to stay at the centre of their own learning and not resign ownership to the teacher or other members of the class.
Natural motivation	The teacher can work to allow natural motivation to flower – and especially take care not to get in its way or otherwise prevent it!

Areas chosen	The teacher's role – comments

OBSERVATION TASK 7   The learners

This task may help you to see a lesson from a student's point of view.

As you arrive in the classroom, choose (privately!) one student to focus on in your observation. Watch this student throughout the lesson and make notes under the headings below.

A Choose a random two-minute period. Write a narrative description of what he/she is doing.

B Choose a random two-minute period. Write a narrative description of what you imagine he/she is thinking/feeling.

C Towards the end of the lesson, write the student's own description of what has happened in the lesson. Have you enjoyed it? Have you learned something? What helped you? What would you have preferred? What worried you, annoyed you, hindered you? How are you feeling?

OBSERVATION TASK 8   Errors and correction

Note down some student errors. Categorise each error (e.g. wrong tense, wrong phoneme, meaning unclear, etc.). Describe in detail what happened.

Error: *I am agree.*

Type of error: unnecessary word

Indication/correction: The teacher held up three fingers (to represent the three words of the sentence) and then 'picked out' and 'threw away' the middle finger. The student looked puzzled, then said the sentence again without the middle word. The teacher acknowledged this correct sentence with a smile and said 'Good'. The student seemed to not quite believe that this was now a correct sentence. He repeated 'I agree'.

Error: *Give me that pen.*

Type of error: rude

Indication/correction: not commented on or dealt with

Some considerations:

- Did anyone notice that there was an error? Who?
- Did the teacher do anything?
- Did the student do anything?
- Did the other students do anything? Who?

- Did anyone indicate that there was an error? Who?
- Did anyone correct the error? Who?
- How was it corrected?

Error:

Type of error:

Indication/correction:

Error:

Type of error:

Indication/correction:

Error:

Type of error:

Indication/correction:

OBSERVATION TASK 9   **Thoughts and questions**

This form may help you recall what happened in a lesson and remind you of your own thoughts at the time. This may be especially useful for post-lesson discussions with the teacher you watched.

For each box, note down a specific thing that you observed in the lesson and then record your own thoughts or questions or suggestions.

During the lesson:

I noticed:

and I wondered:

I noticed:

and I wondered:

I noticed:

and I wanted to ask you:

OBSERVATION TASK 10   Stolen goods

Note several things that you would like to 'steal' from the teacher and the lesson in order to make them part of your own teaching, i.e. personal qualities, teaching skills and techniques, activities, classroom atmosphere. Finally, choose something you feel you would like to give this teacher in return for your many thefts.

Stolen item 1

Description of item:
I stole this because:

Stolen item 2

Description of item:
I stole this because:

Stolen item 3

Description of item:
I stole this because:

Stolen item 4

Description of item:
I stole this because:

Stolen item 5

Description of item:
I stole this because:

Gift

I'd like to give you:
I think you'd like this because:

Appendix 2 **Resource Materials**

See more
information in:

No.	Photocopiable resource	Summary of instructions	Chapter	Section	Page
1	Pairwork information exchange: Beach picture	Resources 1–3 are all are 'spot the difference' activities for pairs. One student has picture A; their partner has B. They don't show each other the pictures. By discussion, they try to discover fifteen differences. A full worked lesson example for Resources 1–3 is in Chapter 3, Section 3.	3	3	52–53
2	Pairwork information exchange: Office scene		3	3	55
3	Pairwork information exchange: European holiday		3	3	55
4	Pairwork grammar exercise: What happened?	Picture description and comparison task. In pairs, students describe the scene in their picture to their partner and listen to their description. Together, they try to work out what actually happened.	3	3	55
5	Pairwork information exchange: What shall we do tomorrow?	Planning and discussion task. Students have different information about some events in their area (some have Set A, some Set B). They discuss and decide what to do tomorrow.	3	3	55
6	Small-group discussion: Board game	Students play a board game. They discuss topics on cards as they go round the board.	3	4	56
7	Topic cards for board game		3	4	56
8	Grammar game: What's happening?	Pairs write sentences to describe their picture, then swap descriptions with another pair. The new pair tries to reconstruct the picture from the description.	3	5	58–60
9	Questionnaire for learners: Individual learning prefernces	A form for students to fill in, to get them thinking and to provide data for you.	4	1	66
10	Needs analysis cards: Set 1	Cards that students can discuss, sort and select to raise issues about learning.	4	3	71
11	Needs analysis cards: Set 2		4	3	71
12	Needs analysis questionnaire	A form for students to fill in.	4	3	71
13	Blank lesson plan	You could use one of these formats when writing your own lesson plans.	6	4,5	118
14	Blank lesson plan (short version)		6	4,5	118

15	Group planning task: Lost in the forest	A discussion task. You tell a short, exciting 'We were travelling on a bus through the jungle ...' story and then explain that the bus broke down miles from nowhere. Students must decide how best to escape from the forest using the map and information.	7	2	153
16	Worksheet for recorded radio/ TV news headlines	A worksheet with a sequence of tasks for using when students listen to recordings of the news headlines.	8	4	181
17	Functional worksheet	See Chapter 10, Section 6 (Analysing communicative function) for a detailed description of this task. Choose a set of cards (Set 1 or Set 2) and give a copy to each student. Use the first row as a worked example. Students then meet up in pairs to discuss and fill in some possible answers for the blanks. When they have finished, they can join with another pair to listen to and discuss their answers. Hopefully there will be a few laughs at this stage! You can use the other set of cards to do the task again on another day.	10	6	223
18	Learner's word list	A photocopiable blank word list for students to use.	11	6	241
19	Board game: The block of flats (present simple)	Play the game in small groups like snakes and ladders, using die and counters. The aim is to go from the front door to the penthouse flat. Go up or down in the lifts when you land on a lift square (NB squares 4 and 22 don't go up!) When a player land on a sentence, he/she must decide if it is correct English or not before anyone else says what they think. When the player has decided, the others say if they agree or not. If they agree, the player remains there. If not, they go back to the square they came from. Don't help or judge during the game! Students should note any uncertainty or disagreement for the end of the game. Win by getting to the penthouse.	12	2	265

20	Board game: The block of flats (blank for teacher's own use)	The sample game above practises the present simple. Easily adapt this for any grammar point of your choice by writing in sentences on the blank game board.	12	2	265
21	Script sheet for Total Physical Response/drama lesson	You read out the script slowly, line by line. Students don't speak but must do the actions. If there are comprehension problems, show them an action. Don't explain anything. If problems continue, repeat small sequences of lines a few times. Stage 1 is easy, for lower levels. Start with stage 1 and go on to stages 2 and 3 for a more exciting story!	12	5	281
22	Chant	The idea of using a chant is described in Chapter 16. You could model the chant and get students to repeat or follow a procedure such as that for an elicited dialogue.	13	1	285
23	Cards for 'Phoneme bingo'	Each student gets one card with four phonemes. Call out phonemes one by one. All students must write down each phoneme as it is called (so that you can check and find problems later). If a student has the phoneme on their card, they cross it off. When someone gets all four phonemes, they get a point and a new card. Variation: call out short words. Students can cross phonemes off if it is in the word.	13	3	288
24	True/False cards	Before students have to tell stories to each other, hand them a true/false card (which they do not show anyone else). When they have told their story, others must guess if it was true or false. NB This idea can be integrated with many other speaking activities.	16	5	344

RESOURCE 2   Pairwork information exchange: Office scene

RESOURCE 4   Pairwork grammar exercise: What happened?

A

B

Set A

Have you ever wanted to make a film?

Special one-day workshop for beginners by local film director.

You'll learn many essential skills:
- picking the right subject
- making a storyboard
- selecting your shots
- getting the sound right
- editing

Limited places – apply early. Cost: £150

Medieval Days
and early music exhibition

Medieval marketplace – Roast meats and traditional ales – Archery display – Life in Middle Ages – Demonstrations of traditional crafts – Battles and attacks
Meet some of the area's finest musicians and instrument makers

Adults £10.50 Child £7.80 OAP £7.80 Family (2+2) £20.00

Robbie Williams
TRIBUTE CONCERT

Great live show!
All the hits you love!
Performed by Angels,
the no.1 Robbie tribute band

Special guests:
Calico School of Dance

Sports Stadium 7.00 p.m.
Entrance £10.00
Fireworks at 10.00 p.m.

All-day mackerel fishing trip

Experience the real life of a sea fisherman!
£20 per person. Rod and bait hire £5
BEGINNERS WELCOME.
We leave at 7 a.m. from the harbour arm.
You can also come for the ride if you don't want to fish!

Ghost walk

Find out what really lives in the spooky corners of the old town. Your costumed guide will tell you tales of dark deeds while you explore the ancient streets. And there will be some terrifying surprises along the way!

Meet at 7.30 outside the Blue Dolphin pub – rain or shine! No need to book. Pay your guide £2.50

Set B

CAR BOOT SALE

Come along and spend a great time browsing through over 200 stalls filled with treasures, antiques, collectables and junk.

Boot sale opens at 8.00 a.m.
Entrance for customers 50p, children free.

Hot and cold food available.
Ice cream. Free parking. Toilets.

If you want to sell:
Cars: £6 Vans £8.
(Arrive between 6 a.m. and 7 a.m.)

Port Vittoria Zoo

The greatest little zoo for a hundred miles!
Get face to face with the meerkats!
Check out the penguins underwater.
Test your jumping ability against the monkeys!
Huge adventure playground.
Miniature train service round the whole park.
Full catering facilities – fast-food and family restaurants.
All-day ticket Adults £17 Children £15

'Ave you ever been 'orseracing?

A great day out – and not expensive.

Full day's racing card – 8 races.
Come and watch from the luxury of our terrace restaurant and bar – or have a bet! Who knows?
Today could be your lucky day!
Entrance £6.60
Children welcome – £2.00

EXTREME!!!

The story of dangerous sports

An exciting special exhibition at the Museum of History and Culture.
Learn about the origin and history of sports such as bungee-jumping, BASE jumping, free-diving, speed-skiing and many others.

Find out the current records. Watch demonstrations by experts. Try your skills on our special Virtual Reality simulators.

Entrance free. Open 10.00–5.00 Simulators £2.00 per go. Demonstrations at 11.00, 1.00 and 3.30.

Fancy a Day in France?

One-day coach trip to France. You can explore the town, have a great lunch in a top-class restaurant or shop till you drop in the famous hypermarkets – lots of bargains.
Coach leaves 6.50 a.m. – return 10.20 p.m.
ONLY £22.50 per person.
NB You must have a valid passport.

? = Take a card. Read it out. Ask the group to discuss. Everyone who speaks gets 1 point.

TALK = Take a card. Read it out. Say your own opinion about it for at least 30 seconds. You get 3 points. Everyone else can then join in a short discussion.

BONUS = 1 point (when you go past)

PHOTOCOPIABLE

RESOURCE 7   Topic cards for board games

General issues: Intermediate and above

Hunting is a historic and exciting sport.	Globalisation makes people freer – they can buy what they want and live the life they wish.
Watching TV is a complete waste of time.	It's important to follow fashion.
Boxing should be banned.	It's disgraceful to ban smoking in pubs or restaurants; we should have the right to choose.
We should teach our children to eat healthily.	Eating meat is murder.
Our whole attitude to drugs is confused.	We are all town people nowadays; the country is for multinational food companies.
The rich countries have a duty to help the poor ones.	Aids is the most important problem of today's world.
It's natural that some people in the world should be a million times wealthier than other people.	Books are dead. Long live the e-book.
The Internet is more dangerous than useful.	Western society is obsessed with sex.
We drive and fly everywhere. We need to learn to walk again.	Dieting is a waste of time.
Love makes the world go round.	Men don't iron. Men won't iron.
The whole world has been influenced by Hollywood values.	Travel is a great educator.
Capital punishment must be banned.	You start learning as soon as you leave school.

PHOTOCOPIABLE

RESOURCE 9   Questionnaire for learners: Individual learning preferences

You could use this as a questionnaire to give your students – or maybe as a
source of questions for a class discussion or in an oral interview.

I like ...	often	some-times	just a little	never
• working in pairs.				
• working in small groups.				
• whole-class discussions.				
• whole-class teacher explanations.				
• when the teacher asks the whole class questions.				
• when the teacher asks me individual questions.				
• when the teacher asks me to repeat language.				
• to see things (pictures, words written down, etc.).				
• to hear things (examples of language, recordings, etc.).				
• to touch and hold things (e.g. models, pictures, etc.).				
• the class to move very fast.				
• doing exercises on my own.				
• doing exercises with other students' help and ideas.				
• listening to the teacher telling stories, etc.				
• speaking without a lot of correction.				
• most work to come from the coursebook.				
• the teacher to adapt coursebook material.				
• when the teacher explains every new point.				
• when the teacher helps us to work things out ourselves.				
• language games.				
• having lots of chances to use the language myself.				
• homework.				

RESOURCE 10   Needs analysis cards: Set 1

Preparation

Photocopy and cut out one set of cards for each group of three students. Remove any cards that you don't want students to consider. There are actually two packs: the first pack is of 'general lesson content'; the second pack is of 'classroom activities'. Use the blank cards to add new things you feel should be included.

Instructions

1 Each group starts with their cards face down. Players reveal the cards one by one. Students should discuss whether the item on the card is important for them or not and compare its importance with other cards revealed. Gradually, they must agree a set of cards that the three agree are the most important for them.

2 Bring groups together. Each group shows the cards they have selected and explain why. At the end, bring the class together. Compare the results and see if you can reach a whole-class consensus.

Pack 1

Speaking	Reading	Writing
Listening	Pronunciation	Grammar
Vocabulary	Social English	Exam techniques
Ways to study better	Special English for … ?	Business English

Pack 2

Tests	Groupwork	Pairwork
Discussions	Role-plays	Coursebook
Projects	Video	Homework
Drama	Games	Songs
Dictionary work	Drills	Exercises
Tape recordings	Correction of mistakes	Revision lessons
Computers		

RESOURCE 11   Needs analysis cards: Set 2

Preparation

Here is a second set of cards, this time with pictures, but usable in a similar way to the first set (see Resource 10). In this case, students must discuss why they will/might need English in the future. Alternatively, these can be used in an interview, say during a Placement test.

RESOURCE 12   Needs analysis questionnaire

Instructions

Photocopy one sheet for each student. Explain carefully the purpose of the forms and allow enough time for students to think and fill them in. Before collecting them in, you might want to allow students to compare ideas with each other.

Needs analysis

1 What is the most important reason that you need English for (now or in the future)?

For travel, study, business meetings, an exam, reading literature, friendship, emigration, relationship, to study something, general interest, attending conferences, etc.?

2 Write five things you would like to be able to do better in English (e.g. write a letter to a friend).

a _____   d _____

b _____   e _____

c _____

3 Which of the following things do you want or need to study more of? Mark the box in the correct places to show your opinion and then add a comment to explain why you chose that answer.

	I need to study more of this	I don't mind	I don't want much of this	Comment
Reading				
Writing				
Speaking				
Listening				
Grammar				
Vocabulary/ phrases				
Pronunciation				
Social English				
Business English				

4 What do you find enjoyable, boring, easy and difficult when studying language?

a I enjoy it when ...

b I get bored when ...

c I find the following things quite easy:

d I find the following things quite difficult:

RESOURCE 13   Blank lesson plan

Teacher's name		Lesson start time
Observer's name		Length of lesson
Class name		Observation start time
Room	Date	Length of observation

Observation agenda (observer)	
Observation agenda (teacher)	
Teaching point (i.e. what you will be working on: language items/language skills)	
Target language items	
Main lesson aims (i.e. what you hope the learners will achieve/be able to do better after your lesson)	
Evidence (i.e. how will you know that this has been achieved?)	
Personal goals (i.e. what you are trying to improve in your own skills as a teacher)	
Class profile	
Timetable fit	
Assumptions (about what the students know/can do)	
Predicted problems	
Context (to use in teaching)	
Materials used	

RESOURCE 14   Blank lesson plan (shorter version)

Teacher's name	
Observer's name	
Class name/Room	
Date/Lesson start time	
Observation start time	
Length of lesson/Length of observation	
Main lesson aims (i.e. what you hope the students will achieve/be able to do better after your lesson)	
Personal goals (i.e. what you are trying to improve in your own skills as a teacher)	
Timetable fit	
Assumptions (about what the students know/can do)	
Predicted problems	
Materials used	

© Jim Scrivener and Macmillan Publishers Limited, 2005. This page may be photocopied for use in class.

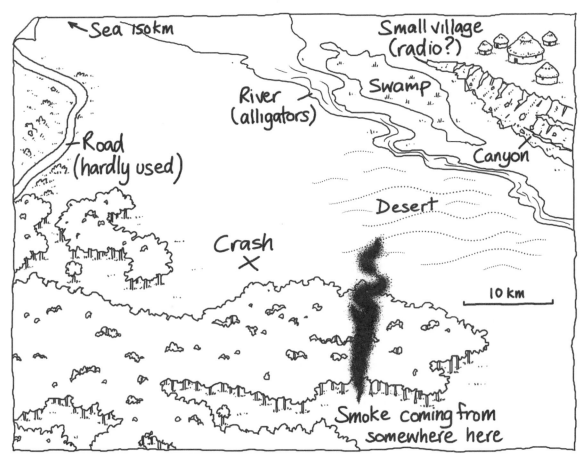

Sea 150km

Small village (radio?)

River (alligators)

Swamp

Road (hardly used)

Canyon

Desert

Crash X

10 km

Smoke coming from somewhere here

Notes
9 p.m. moonlit night
We've crashed!
3 badly hurt – Jo serious – needs urgent help! 2 of us ok.
What to do?
Wait till daylight? (Jo might die)
Find who's lit the fire. (friendly?)
Head for the road, river or village? How long will
it take? – only food and water for 1 day!

RESOURCE 16 Worksheet for recorded radio/TV news headlines

Today's News

Pre-listening: prediction
Which people or places do you expect to hear mentioned in today's news?

Listening: Task 1
Which of the people or places you predicted do you hear mentioned?

_____

Listening: Task 2
How many headlines are there?

_____

Listening: Task 3
What are the key words in the first headline?

_____

Listening: Task 4
What is the story about?

_____

Listening: Task 5
Write out the text of the first headline.

_____

_____

_____

Listening: Task 6
Mark the stressed words in the headline – first by predicting, then by checking with the recording.

Repeat Tasks 3 to 6 for each headline.

Further tasks
- What do you think will be in the full story that this headline is about?
- Which headline was most interesting for you? Why?
- Which story would you like to read more about on the Internet/in a newspaper article?
- We can discuss one story – which one shall we talk about?

RESOURCE 17   Functional worksheet

Set 1

Sentence	Possible context	Who's talking?	Talking to who?	Possible meaning
'It's raining.'	hotel lobby	tourist	husband	Maybe we should go to an indoor museum and not to the market.
'That's the third time.'				
	in a hot TV studio.			
'Oh, no. You're a policeman!'				
	standing underneath a large bridge			
		exhausted chef	restaurant manager	
				I can't hear.

Set 2

Sentence	Possible context	Who's talking?	Talking to who?	Possible meaning
'It's raining.'	hotel lobby	tourist	husband	Maybe we should go to an indoor museum and not to the market.
		flight attendant	pilot	
	in a gym			
				Give me the money quickly.
'Keep your head down.'				
				The tigers have escaped.
		a window cleaner	a person inside the building	

Lexical item	Pronunciation	Translation	Grammar	Collocations	Example	Idea
motorcycle	/'məʊtəsaɪkəl/	pikipiki	noun	ride a ~, get on my ~, ~ maintenance, ~ race, ~ courier	She's just bought a 600cc Suzuki motorcycle.	

31 My brother he's a doctor.	**32**	**33** Are you agree?	**34** **35**
30 The TV in our hotel room isn't work.	**29** You live here, don't you?	**28** What you do want for your birthay?	**27** Does the video recorder works? **26**
21 What do you at the weekend?	**22**	**23** I think this is delicious.	**24** I eat not meat. **25**
20	**19** Do you like chocolate?	**18** I usually walking to school.	**17** **16**
11 What do you do?	**12** Elise and her husband eats lunch at 12.00.	**13** I am work here.	**14** I get up at 7.30. **15**
10	**9** Go you to the shops?	**8** I don't smoke. Do you?	**7** **6**
START **1**	**2** Does he likes this song?	**3** Why do you want to go?	**4** **5** I usually reads a book on the train.

Board game: The block of flats (blank)

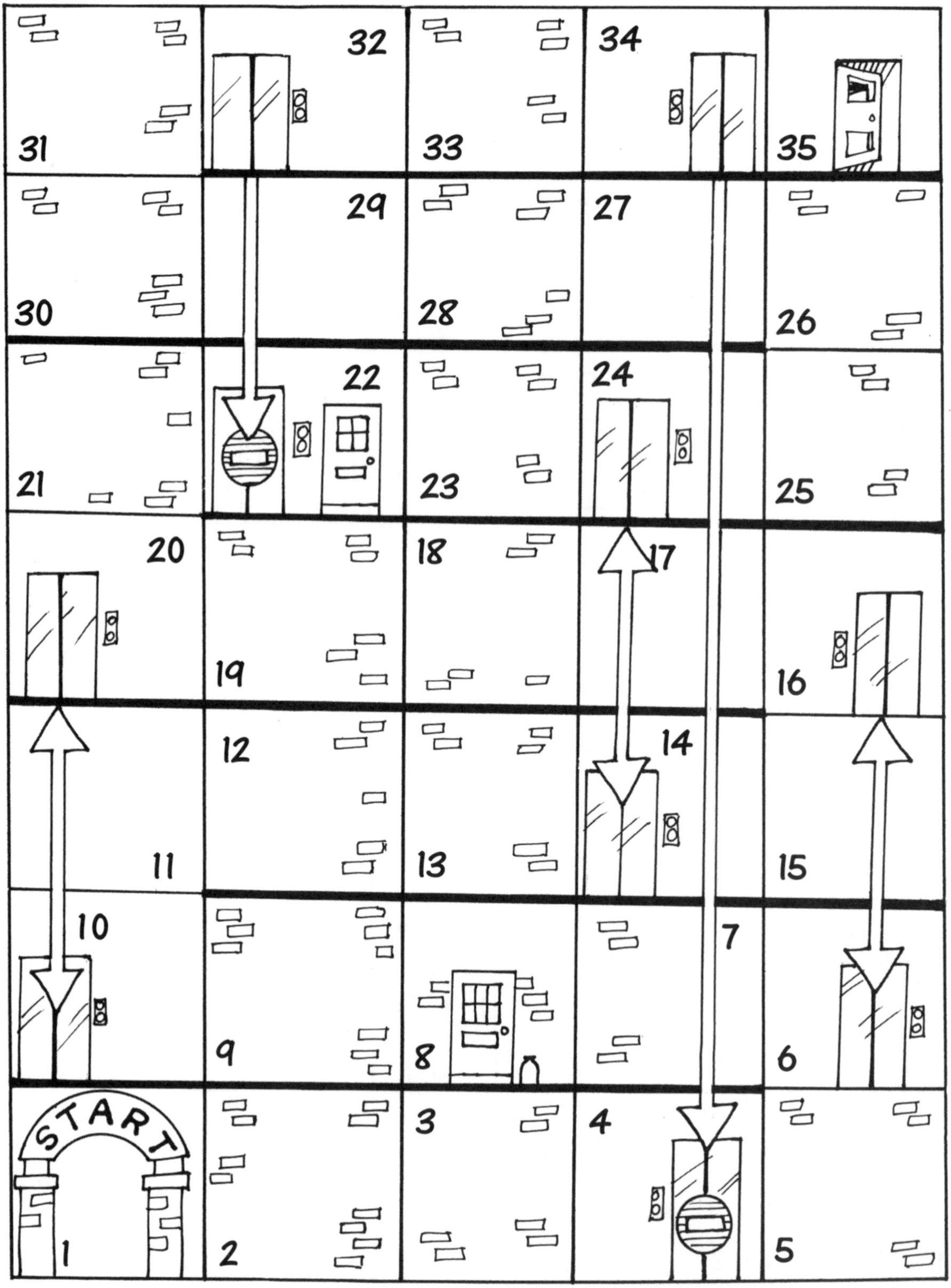

RESOURCE 21   Script sheet for Total Physical Response/drama lesson

Stage 1

- Wake up in the morning.
- Get up.
- Stretch.
- Put on your clothes.
- Walk slowly to the bathroom.
- Brush your teeth.
- Walk to the kitchen.
- Make some coffee.
- Look for bread.
- Complain – there isn't any!
- Find an apple.
- Bite the apple – mmm!
- Put on your coat.
- Finish the apple.
- Throw the core into the waste bin.
- Ah – you missed!
- Open the front door.
- Go out.
- Close the door.

Stage 2

- Walk down the street.
- It's raining.
- It's windy.
- Walk to the sea.
- Look out over the sea.
- It's raining.
- It's windy.
- Find your boat on the beach.
- Walk to your boat.
- Push your boat into the water – it's heavy!
- Quick, jump into your boat.
- It's raining.
- It's windy.
- The boat's rocking.
- Ooh – you feel a bit sick!
- The storm's getting worse
- The boat rocks to the left!
- The boat rocks to the right!
- Be careful – here's a big wave!
- Oh no! The wave knocks you into the water.
- Swim – try to get back to the boat.
- Watch the boat move away!
- Look around – you are on your own!
- Swim!

- Swim. You're getting tired.
- It's getting dark.
- You're cold.
- You're frightened.
- You can see a light! Hurray!
- Swim for the light.
- Walk onto the dry land.
- Run around and shout – you're saved!
- Lie down and sleep!

Stage 3

- Wake up.
- Try to remember where you are.
- Look around – it's a beach.
- Remember the boat – and the swimming!
- Look more carefully – there's a small village.
- Walk towards the village.
- Creep quietly into the village.
- Push open a door.
- Peep inside.
- Tiptoe over to the kitchen.
- Notice the food.
- Feel very hungry.
- Take a piece of cheese – mmm!
- Hear someone come in the door.
- Decide whether to hide.
- Too late!
- Cover your ears – they're screaming.
- Run – they're chasing you!
- Try to explain who you are.
- Stop running.
- It's OK – they believe you.
- Shake hands.
- Sit down.
- Have a drink.
- Have a meal.
- Relax.
- Go out.
- Get in a car.
- Someone is driving you home.
- Hurray! You are safe back home.
- Undress.
- Get into bed.
- Fall asleep.
- Dream about the sea.

Where did you put it?
> I can't quite remember.

Where did you put it?
> I really don't know.

Where did you put it?
> I think it's … perhaps it's …

Where did you put it?
> I really don't know.

I need it. I need it.
It's very important.
I can't live without it.
Please find it right now

> I'm sorry. I'm sorry.
> I think that I lost it.
> I'm ever so sorry.
> I lost it. I know.

> But listen. I'll buy you
> a new one tomorrow.
> I'm ever so sorry.
> It must be my fault.

You really are stupid …
Oh, hang on a minute …
It's here in my pocket.
Bye! Thanks for your help!

iː	tʃ		ʊ	θ		ʃ	ɔː
b	ʌ		f	ɔɪ		eə	ð

aː	r		ɪ	j		eə	l
h	æ		s	ə		m	ʌ

e	ŋ		ɔː	z		ɪə	d
ʒ	aʊ		ð	uː		b	iː

ð	ɜː		h	ə		ʊə	ŋ
uː	k		ʊə	ʃ		dʒ	iː

ɔɪ	θ		ʒ	æ		v	ɪə
k	ɜː		əʊ	ŋ		ɔɪ	θ

ʒ	aʊ		aɪ	dʒ		eɪ	ʃ
eɪ	tʃ		ʃ	ʌ		b	ʊ

True	True	False	False
False	False	True	False
True	False	True	False
True	True	False	True
True	True	False	False
False	False	True	False
True	False	True	False
True	True	False	True
False	True	True	False
True	False	True	False

© Jim Scrivener and Macmillan Publishers Limited, 2005. This page may be photocopied for use in class.

Some key terminology

accuracy/fluency — You often need to decide on whether to focus on one or the other. There are times in classroom work where a focus on getting language correct is more useful than a focus on fluency and vice versa.

activity — Something that students do. A single task, exercise or game, etc.

aims — Things that you hope will be achieved during a lesson.

authentic exposure — Exposure to language when it is being used fairly naturally.

authentic output — Students speaking or writing using the full range of language at their disposal. The language used has not been restricted in any way (e.g. not by your instructions, by the coursebook writer, etc.).

backchaining — A technique for helping students say a difficult sentence by breaking it down into smaller parts and practising saying those pieces, slowly building up again to the complete sentence; for example: 'n't you?' 'aren't you?' 'thirty, aren't you?' 'You're thirty, aren't you?'

the chain — An error-correction technique that involves students passing corrections to each other across the classroom.

citation form — The way that a word is pronounced if you say it on its own. This is often different from the typical in-sentence pronunciation in fluent connected speech.

clarification — A part of a lesson in which students become clearer about language system items, especially concerning how they are formed, what they mean, how they are pronounced and how they are used.

classroom management — The moment-by-moment decisions and actions concerning organisation of the classroom and activities, e.g. seating and grouping arrangements, starting and stopping activities, dealing with unexpected problems, etc.

cloze procedure — A gap-fill exercise with regularly spaced gaps (e.g. every seventh word). A **modified cloze** has gaps for selected items of grammar or lexis.

CLL — Community Language Learning: a method that employs use of L1 and L2 to allow students to communicate real messages to each other.

CLT — Communicative Language Teaching: a broad description of current language teaching in which the need to use language in successful communication is seen as more important than having a purely theoretical knowledge of how language works.

collocation — The going-together relationships of words with other words, e.g. *clothes* collocates with *put on, fashionable, well-fitting,* etc. but not normally with *put off, handsome, well-dressed.*

communicative activity — An activity that has communication as its main aim (as opposed to practice of particular language items). A communication activity will normally involve an 'information gap'.

concept questions — Questions that focus on the meaning of a language item.

concordance	A list of words from a text (or texts), sometimes showing the ways they are used (i.e. sentences that they appear in).
connected speech	Fluent speech in which words are not pronounced separately. A number of recognisable pronunciation changes occur, including weak forms and elision.
context	Language items do not exist independently. They might be found in a text, a piece of classroom conversation, a tape recording, etc. These are the **contexts**. To help clarify the meaning or use of an item, we can also create imaginary contexts or example 'situations', perhaps using board pictures, in order to provide a context for a language item and give the students an illustration of a way that it would typically be used.
corpus	An analysable computer database of real language use, drawn from a range of texts.
co-text	The language that you can find before and after a language item.
Cuisenaire rods	Small coloured rods of wood or plastic.
diphthong	A phoneme containing two vowel sounds, one gliding into the second.
Dogme	An approach to teaching that aims to minimise use of technology, teaching aids and other excesses and instead emphasise the importance of the learner–teacher relationship and interaction.
drill	A common restricted production activity, involving students in repetition or very controlled oral practice.
echo	Repetition of what a student has just said. This may be 'aware' echo, with a purpose (e.g. indicating that an error has been made), or 'unaware' echo (e.g. you are feeling the need to fill silences).
eliciting	A much-used technique for involving students more in lessons. Eliciting involves drawing language from the students (rather than giving it to them).
elision	The loss of some sounds in connected speech. For example, in *Good morning* sometimes the /d/ sound is completely lost and the greeting sounds more like *G'morning*.
exponent	An item that is an example of a particular function. For example, 'Could you make me a cup of tea, please?' is an exponent of the function of 'making polite requests'.
extensive reading/ listening	Reading or listening to longer pieces of text without pausing and worrying too much about details, usually for pleasure.
false beginner	Someone who has studied the language before, but appears to have forgotten most of it. Progress can be fast, as the 'lost' language may return relatively quickly. A true beginner, by contrast, has none of this deep-stored knowledge, and progress will likely be much slower.
false friend	A word that reminds you of one in your own language and misleads you into guessing that it has the same or a similar meaning in the new language (e.g. *ropa* in Spanish means *clothes* not *rope*).
fluency	Speaking naturally without worrying too much about being 100% correct.

function	The purpose for which language is used in particular situations.
getting-to-know-you activities	Activities to help students and teacher get to know each other at the beginning of a course (sometimes called *ice-breakers*).
groupwork	Students working together with a number of other students (rather than in pairs or as a whole class).
information gap	One person knows something that the other doesn't. Such gaps of information between people give us a need and desire to communicate with each other.
intensive reading/ listening	Careful and detailed reading of (or listening to) sections of text or speech.
intonation	The musical patterns of speech.
intrusive sounds	Extra sounds that appear in fluent, connected speech to help link two words, e.g. when saying *sea air*, speakers might add a /j/ sound between the words.
jigsaw reading/listening	A jigsaw activity involves different groups of students (or individuals) reading or listening to different content. When they come back together they can report back and compare what they have learnt.
key words	The most important content-carrying words in a text. From a whole article, we might be able to pick out a small number of key words that represent the main subject matter and message.
language skills	Teachers commonly talk about four language skills: listening, speaking, reading, writing. Listening and reading are 'receptive' skills; speaking and writing are 'productive' skills.
language systems	Teachers commonly refer to the following as language systems: grammar, lexis (vocabulary), phonology, function, discourse.
lexical item	A word or a number of words that could be considered to be a single item of vocabulary, e.g. *house, first-aid kit, solar system, put up with*.
lexical set	A set of words that are connected in some way (e.g. items found on a farm; words starting with *head*; words that describe human qualities, etc.).
lexis	Vocabulary.
metalanguage	The language used to describe language items (e.g. present simple tense) or used in class to give instructions, get things done, explain things, etc. Metalanguage usually needs to be clear and concise and avoid complexity.
monitoring	When the students are working on an activity where you do not have an active role, you can keep an active eye over what is going on, perhaps with a view to checking that instructions are being followed, being ready to help if needed, collecting a list of language used for use later in the lesson, etc.
Needs analysis	Ways of finding out (e.g. using questionnaires, interviews, etc.) what students need (or want) to study on a language course.

observation task	A specific task to be done while an observer is watching a teacher in class.
pairwork	Students working with one other student. This may be to discuss something, to check answers, to do a communicative activity, etc.
phoneme	The basic unit of sound from which we build up words and sentences. For example, the word *caught* has six letters but only three phonemes: /k/, /ɔː/ and /t/.
phonology	The study of phonemes, intonation, word stress, sentence stress, rhythm and aspects of connected speech.
PPP	Presentation, Practice, Production: an approach to grammar lessons based on the idea of giving (presenting) small items of language to students, providing them with opportunities to use it in controlled ways (practice) and finally integrating it with other known language in order to communicate (production).
practice	Giving the students chances to use the language being studied.
presentation	The 'giving' or 'input' of (probably new) language to students.
prominence	The main syllables emphasised in a tone group.
ranking task	A task in which students must put things into an order, usually by discussing, e.g. 'List in order the five most important things to consider when choosing a new flat'.
rapport	The quality of relationship within the classroom.
real-play	A variety of **role-play** in which students play themselves in familiar contexts, perhaps to help study and resolve problems they have had in these situations.
restricted exposure	Students read or listen to texts specifically designed to draw attention to language points. The language available for the students to hear or read has in some way been restricted (e.g. a coursebook text containing multiple examples of *used to*).
restricted output	Speaking or writing when students use less than the full quantity of language they know. Practice that uses language in ways that are controlled or deliberately simplified (maybe by an instruction or by the nature of a particular task) in a way that makes the load on the students less demanding.
role-play	Students take on a character or make use of given information or ideas in order to get speaking practice.
RP	Received Pronunciation: a UK pronunciation variety, originally from south-east England, but sometimes seen as a kind of standard educated pronunciation. UK-published coursebooks mainly offer RP on their recordings.
scanning	Reading with the aim of finding out items of specific information.
schwa	The phoneme /ə/. (The only phoneme with a name!)
skimming	Reading, usually done quickly, with the aim of understanding the general meaning or 'gist' of a piece of text.

stage	One distinct part of a lesson, usually a single activity. Stages may link together to help make a complete lesson.
structure	= Form.
STT	Student Talking Time: the amount of time that students get to talk within the lesson.
substitution tables	A way of writing out grammar information as patterns that can be allow for generation of further sentences.
syllabus	A list of course contents.
task	Something students are asked to do. Many tasks are in the form of questions requiring answers, but a task may require students to do things like draw a picture, choose an object from the table, etc. A stricter definition of *task* would restrict the term to activities that replicate 'real world' ones.
TBL	Task-Based Learning: classroom work centred around the doing of tasks more than, say, the presentation and practice of selected items of language.
TTT	Teacher Talking Time: the amount of time you talk within the lesson.
weak form	Vowel sounds in unstressed syllables tend to have a weak pronunciation. Compare *for* when you say it on its own (strong form) and when it comes in the middle of a sentence, e.g. *I came back for my books.* The vowel sound has changed from /ɔː/ to /ə/ (the **schwa**, the most common weak form vowel).
word stress	The emphasised syllable(s) in a word.
work plan	Also **timetable**. The plan of work showing lessons as units and identifying what goes on in each one.
world Englishes	The many varieties of English used in different places around the world.

Abbreviations

ELT = English Language Teaching and **ESOL** = English for Speakers of Other Languages (or **English as a Second or Other Language**) are both general umbrella terms that include:

- **EFL = English as a Foreign Language**
  English for learners who come from a country where English is not spoken as a mother tongue.

- **ESL = English as a Second Language**
  English for learners who come from a country where English is spoken.

- **EIL = English as an International Language**
  English for learners who need to communicate with a range of people from different countries.

- **ESP = English for Specific Purposes**
  English for people who have clear language requirements and needs. ESP includes:

    - **EAP = English for Academic Purposes**
      English for learners who need to read texts, attend lectures, write exams, etc.

    - **EPP = English for Professional Purposes**
      English for learners who need English for work-related reasons.

      EPP includes:

      EFB = English for Business
      English for learners who need to use English in business environments.

Bibliography and references

There are hundreds of EFL books around. This is a short list of just a few books you might find helpful, inspiring, time-saving or life-saving during your first years of teaching.

Working with people

Houston, G. *The Red Book of Groups* (1990), The Rochester Foundation
Rogers, C. and Frelberg, H. J. *Freedom to Learn* (1994), Prentice Hall

The English language

Close, R. A. *A Teachers' Grammar* (1992), Language Teaching Publications
Lewis, M. *The English Verb: an Exploration of Structure and Meaning* (1986), Language Teaching Publications
Parrott, M. *Grammar for English Language Teachers* (2000), CUP
Sinclar, J. (ed.) *Collins COBUILD English Grammar* (1990), Collins Cobuild
Swan, M. *Practical English Usage* second edition (1995), OUP
Thornbury, S. *About Language: Tasks for Teachers of English* (1997), CUP

Speaking

Frank, C., Rinvolucri, M. and Berer, M. *Challenge to Think* (1982), OUP
Klippel, F. *Keep Talking* (1984), CUP
Ur, P. *Discussions that Work* (1981), CUP

Listening

Underwood, M. *Teaching Listening* (1989), Longman

Reading

Grellet, F. *Developing Reading Skills* (1981), CUP
Nuttall, C. *Teaching Reading Skills in a Foreign Language* new edition (2005), Macmillan Education
Wallace, C. *Reading* (1992), OUP

Writing

Hedge, T. *Writing* (1988), OUP
White, R. and Ardt, V. *Process Writing* (1991), Longman

Activities

Davis, P. and Rinvolucri, M. *Dictation: New Methods, New Possibilities* (1988), CUP
Morgan, J. and Rinvolucri, M. *Once Upon a Time: Using Stories in the Language Classroom* (1983), CUP

Grammar

Aitken, R. *Teaching Tenses* (2002), ELB
Batstone, R. *Grammar* (1994), OUP
Davis, P. and Rinvolucri, M. *More Grammar Games: Cognitive, Affective and Movement Activities for EFL Students* (1995), CUP

Hall, N. and Shepheard, J. *The Anti-Grammar Grammar Book* (1991), Longman
Rinvolucri, M. *Grammar Games* (1985), CUP
Scrivener, J. *Teaching Grammar* (2003), OUP
Thornbury, S. *Uncovering Grammar* new edition (2005), Macmillan Education
Ur, P. *Grammar Practice Activities* (1988), CUP

Lexis

Gairns, R. and Redman, S. *Working with Words* (1986), CUP
McCarthy, M. *Vocabulary* (1992), OUP
Morgan, J. and Rinvolucri, M. *Vocabulary: Resource Book for Teachers* (2004), OUP

Pronunciation

Bowen, T. and Marks, J. *The Pronunciation Book* (1992), Longman
Hancock, M. *Pronunciation Games* (1995), CUP
Underhill, A. *Sound Foundations* new edition with CD (2005), Macmillan Education

Other topics

Cook, G. *Discourse* (1989), OUP
Harmer, J. *Practice of English Language Teaching* (2001), Longman
Krashen, S. *Principles and Practice in Second Language Acquisition* (1981), Prentice-Hall
Swan, M. and Smith, B. *Learner English: A Teacher's Guide to Interference and Other Problems* (2001), CUP
Wilberg, P. *One to One* (1987), LTP/Heinle
Wright, A. *1000+ Pictures for Teachers to Copy* (1995), Longman ELT

Useful websites

http://www.onestopenglish.com/
http://www.hltmag.co.uk/
http://www.developingteachers.com/
http://www.bbc.co.uk/worldservice/learningenglish/
http://www.etprofessional.com/
http://www.iatefl.org/

Index

Macmillan Education
Between Towns Road, Oxford OX4 3PP, UK
A division of Macmillan Publishers Limited
Companies and representatives throughout the world

ISBN 978-1-4050-1399-4

First edition published 1994
This edition published 2005

Series design by Mike Brain
Page layout by Anthony Godber
Cover design by Andrew Oliver
Cover photo © Yann Arthus-Bertrand/CORBIS

Illustrated by Kathy Baxendale, Jim Eldridge,
Martin Sanders, Val Saunders, Ian West

Author's acknowledgement
Although books have been important through my career,
most of my learning about teaching has come from actually
teaching, talking with people, attending seminars,
conferences and courses and watching others teach.

The following friends, colleagues, teachers and trainers have
been a considerable help and influence over the years, and I
am very grateful to them:
Adrian Underhill, Allan Bramall, Steve Oakes, Vic Richardson.

The description of 'Three kinds of teacher' is drawn from
Adrian's article *Process in Humanistic Education* published in
English Language Teaching Journal 43/4, 1989.

The views on lexis and language teaching in general have
been very influenced by the work of Michael Lewis and
Jimmie Hill, especially:
Michael Lewis, *The Lexical Approach* (1993), Language
Teaching Publications
Michael Lewis, *Implementing the Lexical Approach* (1997),
Language Teaching Publications
Michael Lewis (ed.) *Teaching Collocation* (2000), Language
Teaching Publications

Books, articles, seminars and passing comments by the
following have been important in jolting my thinking at
various key moments:
Roger Hunt, Martin Parrott, Mario Rinvolucri, Scott
Thornbury

A considerable influence from people I have never met:
Earl Stevick: for his wide-ranging writing and clarity on
humanism and humanistic approaches. The idea of having
'options' originally comes from him.
Carl Rogers: cause of perhaps the single most important shift
in my thinking about what teaching and learning were.
John Heron: for the insights of six-category analysis and on
the importance of listening.
Donald Freeman: who made me think about the influence my
own teachers had on me.

This book is for Noémi.

The author and publishers would like to thank the following
for permission to reproduce their material:

Pearson Education Ltd for extracts from *Cutting Edge
Pre-Intermediate* by Jane Comyns-Carr, Sarah Cunningham
and Peter Moor (Pearson Education, 2001), copyright
Pearson Education 2001 and extracts from *Market Leader
Intermediate* by David Falvey, Simon Kent and David Cotton
(Pearson Education, 2000), copyright Pearson Education
2000; Philip Kerr for extracts from *Straight Forward Pre-
Intermediate Student Book* (Macmillan Education, 2005),
copyright © Macmillan Education 2005; HarperCollins
Publishers Limited for extracts from *Collins English
Dictionary* (HarperCollins Publishers Limited, 2004),
copyright © HarperCollins Publishers Limited 2004,
Bank of English® is a registered trademark of HarperCollins;
Krishnamurti Foundation Trust Limited for extracts from
'On violence' taken from *Krishnamurti on Education*
(Krishnamurti Foundation, 1974), copyright Krishnamurti
Foundation, 1974.

Printed in Malaysia

2009 2008 2007
10 9 8 7 6 5